Interrogations, Confessions, and Entrapment

Perspectives in
Law & Psychology

Sponsored by the American Psychology-Law Society / Division 41 of the American Psychological Association

Series Editor: Ronald Roesch, *Simon Fraser University, Burnaby, British Columbia, Canada*

Editorial Board: Jane Goodman-Delahunty, Thomas Grisso, Stephen D. Hart, Marsha Liss, Edward P. Mulvey, James R. P. Ogloff, Norman G. Poythress, Jr., Don Read, Regina Schuller, and Patricia Zapf

Interrogations, Confessions, and Entrapment

Edited by

G. Daniel Lassiter

Ohio University
Athens, Ohio

KLUWER ACADEMIC/PLENUM PUBLISHERS
NEW YORK/BOSTON/DORDRECHT/LONDON/MOSCOW

ISBN 0-306-48470-6

© 2004 by Kluwer Academic / Plenum Publishers, New York
233 Spring Street, New York, New York 10013

http://www.kluweronline.com

10 9 8 7 6 5 4 3 2 1

A C.I.P. record for this book is available from the Library of Congress.

To my dear ones, Kim and Emma

Contributors

RAY BULL • School of Psychology, University of Leicester, 106 New Walk, Leicester LE1 7EA, United Kingdom.

JULIE CHEN • Department of Psychiatry, Division of Child and Adolescent Psychiatry, Stanford University School of Medicine, Stanford, California 94305-5719.

BETH A. COLGAN • Perkins Coie LLP, 1201 Third Avenue, Suite 4800, Seattle, Washington 98101-3099.

STEVEN A. DRIZIN • Northwestern University, School of Law, Chicago, Illinois 60611.

VANESSA A. EDKINS • Department of Psychology, University of Kansas, Lawrence, Kansas 66045.

CAROLINE EVERINGTON • Richard W. Riley College of Education, Winthrop University, Rock Hill, South Carolina 29732.

SOLOMON M. FULERO • Department of Psychology, Sinclair College, Dayton, Ohio 45402.

ANDREW L. GEERS • Department of Psychology, University of Toledo, Toledo, Ohio 43606-3390.

SUAL M. KASSIN • Department of Psychology, Bronfman Science Center, Williams College, Williamstown, Massachusettes 01267.

GEORGE R. KLARE • Department of Psychology, Ohio University, Athens, Ohio 45701-2979.

G. DANIEL LASSITER • Department of Psychology, Ohio University, Athens, Ohio 45701-2979.

RICHARD A. LEO • Department of Criminology, Law and Society, University of California—Irvine, Irvine, California 92697-7080.

ELIZABETH F. LOFTUS • Department of Psychology and Social Behavior, University of California—Irvine, Irvine, California 92697-7080.

CHRISTIAN A. MEISSNER • Department of Psychology, Florida International University, University Park, Miami, Florida 33199.

BECKY MILNE • Institute of Criminal Justice Studies, University of Portsmouth, Portsmouth, P01 2DY, United Kingdom

JENNIFER J. RATCLIFF • Department of Psychology, Ohio University, Athens, Ohio 45701-2979.

ALLISON D. REDLICH • Policy Research Associates, Inc., 345 Delaware Ave., Delmar, New York 12054.

MELISSA SILVERMAN • Department of Psychiatry, Division of Child and Adolescent Psychiatry, Stanford University School of Medicine, Stanford, California 94305-5719.

HANS STEINER • Department of Psychiatry, Division of Child and Adolescent Psychiatry, Stanford University School of Medicine, Stanford, California 94305-5719.

SHANNON WHEATMAN • Federal Judicial Center, Thurgood Marshall Federal Judiciary Building, Washington, DC 20002.

ELIZABETH C. WIGGINS • Federal Judicial Center, Thurgood Marshall Federal Judiciary Building, Washington, DC 20002.

LAWRENCE S. WRIGHTSMAN • Department of Psychology, University of Kansas, Lawrence, Kansas 66045.

Foreword

I wish I had read Daniel Lassiter's fine collection of chapters before I had consulted on the case of Texas Tech University professor Thomas Butler, a well-respected researcher of bubonic plague. Dr. Butler's troubles began in January, 2003, when he reported missing from his University laboratory 30 vials of *yersinia pestis*, the bacteria that causes plague. He thought they might have been stolen (see Piller, 2003 for more details). Scores of investigators spent days scouring the area in search of the missing vials, amid fears that terrorists would get their hands on the vials and spread disease into the community. Dr. Butler was intensively interrogated, on one occasion for 12 hours until 3 o'clock in the morning. Although ill, exhausted, unfed, and under substantial stress, he was allowed precious little sleep before the interrogation resumed. Under enormous pressure, which included telling Dr. Butler that he had essentially flunked a polygraph test, he changed his story to one that would comport with the government's suggestion that he had accidentally destroyed the vials. Although Dr. Butler had no recollection of any accidental destruction, he was encouraged to think hard about it, and eventually to make a written statement. Dr. Butler relented and in his statement he "confessed" to the destruction. "I made a misjudgment by not telling (the supervisor) that the plague bacteria had been accidentally destroyed earlier rather than erroneously first found missing" Butler said. He was given a second polygraph to prove to him that his "confession" was "truthful." Conveniently for the government, the confession ended the investigation, and the community could rest free that the dangerous plague was not in sinister hands. Shortly thereafter, Dr. Butler was arrested and charged, among other counts, with lying for having originally said that the vials went missing and denying knowledge of their whereabouts.

In my interview with Dr. Butler, I learned that in his weakened state he came to believe that he had perhaps accidentally destroyed the vials, but he never developed a "recollection" of the destructions, one that had any sensory detail associated with it. From the messy state of his laboratory, one

could easily imagine things being misplaced. Even still, accidental destruction would have been a tricky thing to accomplish given the layout. Butler
was able to generate some hypotheses about how accidental destruction
might have happened, but even after all that coercion he never came to
"remember" that it had. Later, as he came to appreciate what had been done
to him, he realized that he really had no idea what happened to the missing vials. He would later tell the press that he had been tricked and deceived
by government investigators into falsely confessing to the destruction of
vials because they wanted desperately to conclude the investigation and
reassure the public that there was no danger.

Eventually Dr. Butler was indicted, not only for lying, but also for
improperly transporting plague cultures, and later for embezzling funds,
tax violations and other charges. Before being gagged, one of Butler's lawyers
called the new charges an attempt to buttress a weak criminal case by pil-
ing on excess charges. The case garnered national attention, including an
effort by members of the National Academies of Sciences to intervene with
a warning about witch hunts.

In early December, 2003, a Texas jury returned a split verdict. It acquitted Dr. Butler of smuggling plague samples and lying to the U.S. Federal
Bureau of Investigation (FBI) about them but convicted him of a number
of the "add-on" charges (Miller, 2003).

Assuming that Dr. Butler's "confession" about destroying the vials
was false, why did he do it? A reasonable argument is that it was the coercive influence of the interrogation. It is just this kind of coercive influence,
claim volume editor Daniel Lassiter and his co-author Jennifer Ratcliff in
their introductory chapter, that ties together the three "topics" that title this
volume: interrogations, confessions, and entrapment. The scholars who
have contributed to this volume greatly expand our understanding of the
extant literature in this area, and explore how such knowledge can guide
changes in the legal system.

The last decade has revealed a growing number of post-conviction
exonerations based on new DNA testing. These wrongful convictions have
been studied, and we now know a fair amount about their causes. Although
faulty eyewitness memory appears to play a role in the large majority of
cases, we also now know that coerced or false confessions can play a significant role in leading to a wrongful conviction. Faulty eyewitnesses, faulty
confessions—the two are related in some ways. In the case of a faulty
eyewitness, it is often true that suggestive post-event information has led
someone to claim to have *seen* something that wasn't seen (e.g., the defendant at the crime scene, or Mr. Jones pulling the knife first rather than
Mr. Smith). In the case of faulty confessions, it is occasionally true that suggestive interrogation has led someone to claim to have *done* something that
he didn't do. The form of psychological coercion required to elicit a false

confession might be greater than the forms required to distort eyewitness memory, but many of the ingredients will be the same. Eyewitnesses are sometimes exposed to the opinions of others, or questioned in leading and suggestive ways. These tactics can get them to "remember" seeing things that didn't happen, or happened differently. Crime suspects often are subjected to more—as revealed in many of the chapters in this volume. These include "minimization" tactics, by which interrogators make the behavior seem normal and provide moral justification for it and "leniency" tactics, in which suspects are led to infer that leniency will follow from a confession. They also include the presentation of false evidence. In the case of Dr. Butler, the interrogation involved feeding him false information, while in a vulnerable state, and encouraging him to imagine how the to-be-confessed-to act might have happened. Moreover, he was led to believe that he and the world would be better off if he "confessed."

The techniques to which Dr. Butler was subjected may not be the worst that our citizens have endured. As George Klare so eloquently reveals (Chapter 2), things were a lot worse for the prisoners of war captured during World War II. Nonetheless, the modern techniques are psychologically powerful and have been perfected in the United States over many decades, as Richard Leo shows us (Chapter 3).

Experimentally, studying eyewitness testimony and how it can go awry has been quite a bit easier for psychological scientists than studying false confessions. This is undoubtedly why there have been thousands of published studies in the eyewitness arena, but only a handful in the false confession area. The widely cited study by Kassin and Kiechel (1996) involved a clever attempt to induce people to falsely confess to damaging a computer by pressing the wrong key. High rates of false confessions were obtained when subjects had been engaged in a fast-paced task, and when a confederate claimed to have seen the subject commit the "criminal" act. The procedure was criticized because the "destroyed computer" act was not associated with any genuine negative consequences, so a research group from the Netherlands (Horselenberg, Merckelbach, & Josephs, 2003) replicated the study with a few procedural changes. The major one was adding a financial incentive; if subjects confessed they would lose money. Even though it was costly, the large majority of participants were willing to sign a false confession.

These "destroyed computer" studies have been criticized for not being particularly emotional for subjects. I once coincidentally met a subject from the original Kassin/Kiechel study. Years after her participation she recounted how mortified she felt by the belief that she had ruined an important experiment and computer of a beloved professor at her college. Nonetheless, the "destroyed computer" studies are steps removed from the kinds of crimes to which some actual suspects have falsely confessed.

Scientists in this area are busy trying to create innovative paradigms that close that obvious gap, and there seems little doubt but we will see significant advances in the near future.

There are so many incredibly important issues that the scholars contributing to this volume are exploring. Here's just a sample.

—Who is particularly susceptible to falsely confessing or being entrapped? Tales from the juvenile confession front (Drizin & Colgan) should make us especially wary when dealing with younger individuals. We know from the work of Allison Redlich and her collaborators that children and adolescents may be especially susceptible. In one study using the "destroyed computer" paradigm, younger subjects (12–13-year olds) were more likely to confess than older ones (15–16 years or young adults). If the coercive tactics worked on an educated, well-respected 61-year-old scientist like Dr. Butler, imagine what they might do to an adolescent.

Similarly, imagine what they might do to one who is mentally impaired. Mental retardation can make individuals less able to understand their rights and more susceptible to suggestive questioning, as Sol Fulero and Caroline Everington point out.

—What exactly are the effects of these techniques on the truly innocent? In the case of Dr. Butler, he came to believe that he had accidentally destroyed the vials, but never developed an explicit recollection of having done so. In other cases, the false belief is the first step in the process, but some false confessors later go on to develop rather explicit recollections, including details that they pick up from the interrogation and from other sources.

If coercive techniques can make the innocent falsely confess, it seems almost certain that they can also make the guilty confess. This might not seem like much of a problem. After all, we like the idea of the bad guys being caught. But can the coercive tactics go further? Can they make someone *commit* a crime who would not ordinarily do so? Here is where the subject of "entrapment" joins the other two topics that make up the title of this volume. Edkins and Wrightsman worry that some individuals will be led into criminal activity by overzealous investigators bent on catching criminals. Should we allow this, and under what conditions?

—How can coercion be minimized during interrogation? What other reforms in the criminal justice system are called for as a result of this knowledge? Videotaping is a word that comes up repeatedly, but other ideas are offered here that constitute a radical departure from current norms. Excellent practical strategies for implementing reform can be found in many of the remaining chapters.

Lassiter's volume is badly needed. It should take readers a long way toward a goal that we share, namely that our system would develop and use techniques that draw confessions from those who are guilty, but not from those who are innocent. If reforms had been in place prior to the inter-rogation of Dr. Butler, would his fate have been different? One might be tempted to say that the system worked for Butler since a jury acquitted him of the lying charge related to his "false confession." But did that confession lead investigators to add on charges to secure some conviction? Did the jury compromise by acquitting Butler on some charges and convicting on others? We may never know, but surely the process would be cleaner and trustworthier if suspects weren't feeling "tricked and deceived" by investigators employed by our government.

And just where are those 30 missing vials?

ELIZABETH F. LOFTUS

REFERENCES

Horselenberg, R., Merckelbach, H, & Josephs, S. (2003). Individual differences and false confessions. *Psychology, Crime & Law, 9*, 1–8.

Kassin, S. M., & Kiechel, K. L. (1996). The social psychology of false confessions. *Psychological Science, 7*, 125–128.

Miller, D. (2003, December 2). Thomas Butler convicted. Retrieved December 31, 2003, from http://www.the-scientist.com.

Piller, C. (2003, October 28). A trying time for science. *Los Angeles Times.* pp. A1, A18.

Contents

CHAPTER 4: "You're Guilty, So Just Confess!" Cognitive and
Behavioral Confirmation Biases in the Interrogation Room ....

Christian A. Meissner and Saul M. Kassin

CHAPTER 5: The Police Interrogation of Children and
Adolescents..

Allison D. Redlich, Melissa Silverman, Julie Chen, and Hans Steiner

CHAPTER 6: Tales From the Juvenile Confession Front: A Guide to
How Standard Police Interrogation Tactics Can Produce Coerced
and False Confessions from Juvenile Suspects ....

Steven A. Drizin and Beth A. Colgan

CHAPTER 12: So What's a Concerned Psychologist to Do?
Translating the Research on Interrogations, Confessions,
and Entrapment into Policy 265

Elizabeth C. Wiggins and Shannon R. Wheatman

Exposing Coercive Influences in the Criminal Justice System

An Agenda for Legal Psychology in the Twenty-First Century

G. DANIEL LASSITER AND JENNIFER J. RATCLIFF

The inquisition held by police before trial is the outstanding feature of American criminal justice, though no statute recognizes its existence.

ERNEST J. HOPKINS (1931)

Police interrogators may now hurl "jolting questions" where once they swung telephone books, may now "play on the emotions" where once they resorted to physical violence, but [the above quotation] is no less true today than it was thirty years ago . . .

YALE KAMISAR (1965)

Around the beginning of the 1970s, social and behavioral scientists began conducting systematic research on issues related to the accuracy of eyewitnesses in recounting details observed during the commission of a crime. Twenty-five years later, more than 2,000 scientific articles in psychology demonstrated that eyewitness accounts were susceptible to a variety of influences that could potentially render them unreliable (Cutler & Penrod,

G. DANIEL LASSITER • Department of Psychology, Ohio University, Athens, Ohio 45701-2979 (lassiter@ohio.edu). JENNIFER J. RATCLIFF • Department of Psychology, Ohio University, Athens, Ohio 45701-2979.

1995). For example, Loftus (1979) showed that eyewitness memory was malleable and could be readily altered by information encountered *after* the initial event. Work by Lindsay and Wells (1985) established that the manner in which police lineups were conducted greatly impacted the number of mistaken identifications made by eyewitnesses. The weight of three decades of such research, in combination with other factors, has recently prompted the legal system to take action in an attempt to prevent erroneous eyewitness testimony from influencing trial outcomes (Wells et al., 2000). Specifically, the United States Department of Justice, with the input of psychological researchers, has translated the scientific literature on eyewitness reports into a first ever set of national guidelines for the collection and preservation of eyewitness evidence (Technical Working Group for Eyewitness Evidence, 1999).

As we enter a new century, additional aspects of the criminal justice system have become as controversial as eyewitness identification was 30 years ago. Police interrogations, confessions, and entrapment, which are linked together by the fact that they can all involve some degree of coercive influence, are beginning to receive close scrutiny in the legal community and beyond. Behavioral and legal researchers interested in these topics are in the early stages of producing important data that eventually will have policy ramifications, as was the case with eyewitness identification. In this volume, many of the significant scholars contributing to our growing understanding of the psychology of interrogations, confessions, and entrapment present chapters that review and analyze the extant literature in this area as well as discuss how this knowledge can be used to help bring about needed changes in the legal system. It is hoped that this volume will serve as a clarion call for further investigation directed at both exposing the variety of ways in which coercive influences can adversely affect criminal justice and generating research-based solutions for minimizing such effects.

THE NEW (AND HIDDEN) FACE OF COERCION IN MODERN CRIMINAL JUSTICE PRACTICES

Roget's Thesaurus lists several synonyms for the verb *coerce: browbeat, bulldoze, concuss, dragoon, menace, pressurize, shotgun, strong-arm,* and *terrorize* to name a few. Although coercion of the type denoted by the foregoing list of words once flourished in our system of criminal justice, it is virtually nonexistent today. During their heyday, torture and other "third-degree" tactics were quite successful in producing self-incriminating behavior that was sufficient to convict an alleged criminal; however, such physical intimidation was considered by society at large to be morally abhorrent, and, more critically, did not reliably yield the truth. It was believed that the abolishment of the third degree would essentially eliminate wrongful convictions linked to false confessions and other forms of untrustworthy self-incriminating behavior.

Unfortunately, this has not been the case. Due in large part to several post-conviction, DNA-exoneration cases that have occurred over the last decade, we now know that coerced or false confessions are a contributing factor in a significant number of undeniably wrongful convictions. According to records kept by the Innocence Project (n.d.), "37 of the [first] 123 [post-conviction] DNA exonerations in the United States involved homicides. In two thirds of those cases, false confessions or incriminating statements were used to obtain the conviction." Similarly, Warden (2003), Executive Director for the Center on Wrongful Convictions, reported that of 42 wrongful murder convictions documented in Illinois since 1970, nearly 60% "rested in whole or part on false confessions." Leo and Drizin (2003) have compiled a list of 98 proven false confessions in cases that were dismissed prior to going to trial.

Even though physical force has all but vanished as a common tool of the police interrogator, it can only be concluded from these disturbing statistics that a new, psychologically oriented coercion—perhaps more insidious because it is often not recognized as such—has emerged in the interrogation room. In the chapters that follow, many questions will be posed, and at least in some instances, partial answers will be provided. For example, what are the various forms of psychological coercion? When and to whom is it applied? What effect does it have on the truly innocent suspect? To what extent is this modern-day version of coercion detected by trial fact finders? What are some ways in which such coercion can be minimized during interrogations or in other contexts in which law enforcement is seeking to obtain self-incriminating evidence from suspected criminals?

PSYCHOLOGICAL COERCION AND ITS ROLE IN AMERICAN JURISPRUDENCE: SCHOLARLY PREDECESSORS

Before previewing the remaining chapters in this volume, we would like to acknowledge a few individuals who were among the first to bring attention to how psychology was a critical factor in modern interrogations and confessions. Yale Kamisar, a distinguished law professor whom we quoted at the outset, first wrote about police interrogations and confessions in the early 1960s. His careful analyses alerted us to many issues about interrogations and confessions that the contributors of this volume are still investigating today. Moreover, his writings were most influential in persuading the United States Supreme Court of the inherently coercive nature of police interrogations (*Miranda v. Arizona*, 1966). Another prominent law professor, Welsh White, provided some of the earliest observational data with regard to what actually transpires behind the closed doors of the interrogation room, and he along with Kamisar continues to be a strong advocate for protecting the rights of individuals subjected to custodial interrogations.

Philip Zimbardo, an internationally known social psychologist, was one of the earliest behavioral scientists to direct the psychological community to the theoretical and practical importance of the phenomena of police-elicited confessions. As stated by Zimbardo (1971):

> How can the court formulate criteria to assess "psychological coercion," "voluntariness of a confession," "ability to resist pressure" and similar concepts without reference to psychology? Central in the definition of these concepts is a knowledge of personality, behavior deviations, performance under stress and deprivation, the effect of social demand characteristics, research on persuasability and attitude change, and many other areas of psychology. (p. 493)

Around the same time, another influential social psychologist, Daryl Bem (1966), published a report suggesting how even subtle, seemingly non-coercive manipulations in the context of an interrogation can lead to distortions in an individual's ability to clearly differentiate what is true from what is false. Bem (1967) believed "strongly that we must learn, and quickly before it is too late, how to cope with the more subtle forms of control over human behavior which do not involve [explicit] force or coercion" (p. 25).

Finally, Saul Kassin and Lawrence Wrightsman, who each co-author a chapter in this volume, are largely responsible for the growth in psychological research on interrogations and confessions that has occurred over the last 20 years. Their 1985 chapter entitled *Confession Evidence* was especially influential, as it introduced their now widely used typology of false confessions as well as effectively set much of the American research agenda in the area for the next two decades.

INTERROGATIONS, CONFESSIONS, AND ENTRAPMENT: CURRENT STATE OF KNOWLEDGE

The work described in the following chapters represents the advances in our understanding of the role of psychological factors in inducing potentially unreliable self-incriminating behavior that have been achieved since the contributions of the aforementioned individuals. The scholarly backgrounds of the authors are impressively diverse, and the methods employed in their research are equally heterogeneous (e.g., experimental, observational, case studies, and first-hand accounts). Importantly, however, there is resounding agreement among the authors that the problem of subtle but nonetheless coercive influences in the legal system is real and that steps to deal with it should be taken immediately.

The two chapters following this introduction focus on interrogations as they were conducted in the early to middle twentieth century. In Chapter 2, George Klare, a cognitive psychologist, provides an autobiographical account of his World War II experiences as a prisoner of the Luftwaffe (German air force) during which time he was subjected to various forms of military and political interrogation. This first-person description of what it is like to be interrogated graphically conveys the confusion and disorientation that can arise from psychologically oriented questioning techniques. It is interesting to note that some of the guileful attempts at eliciting information from prisoners of war described by Klare are disturbingly close to those practiced today in American police stations on a daily basis. In Chapter 3, Richard Leo, a criminologist and social psychologist, writes a detailed history of third-degree interrogations, and describes how the virtual elimination of such interrogations led to the development of today's psychologically oriented interrogations. Leo points out that although there is the appearance of a "scientific" basis for various tactics and techniques used by police interrogators to extract the truth from detained suspects, the reality is that none of these "tools of the trade" has been subjected to credible scientific validation. This chapter, along with Klare's, sets the stage for everything that follows and thus provides an essential backdrop to modern interrogation approaches.

In Chapter 4, two social psychologists, Christian Meissner and Saul Kassin, describe how confirmation biases can put truly innocent suspects at risk. They show that a presumption of guilt influences the way police conduct interrogations, leading them to adopt a questioning style that is confrontational and highly aggressive. This approach, in turn, causes innocent suspects to behave in ways that appear to confirm the initial presumption of guilt. Such "guilty" behavior further intensifies the pressure exerted by the interrogator, thereby increasing the risk of eliciting a coerced false confession. Meissner and Kassin discuss possible mechanisms underlying such confirmation biases and suggest ways of neutralizing their influence in the interrogation room.

The next three chapters focus on populations that are particularly at risk during police interrogations. In Chapter 5, Allison Redlich, a developmental psychologist, and her colleagues write on the special vulnerability of children and adolescents to the coercive (albeit currently legal) interrogation techniques that are employed by police. The authors review the relevant research and conclude that further empirical investigation of child and adolescent suspects is sorely needed to help improve the methods police use to question youths. Two legal professionals, Steven Drizin and Beth

Colgan, present five detailed case narratives in Chapter 6 that dramatically illustrate how young people exposed to standard interrogation tactics can be induced into providing false confessions. Based on their careful analyses of these cases, the authors suggest several reforms which they believe will better protect children during police interrogations and minimize the risk of obtaining false confessions. The final chapter in this section, written by social/clinical psychologist and attorney Solomon Fulero and special educator Caroline Everington, reviews the literature indicating that mental retardation often impairs the ability of individuals to comprehend their Miranda rights as well as makes them more susceptible to suggestive questioning. Implications for policy and practice in the criminal justice system are discussed.

In Chapter 8, two British psychologists, Ray Bull and Becky Milne, provide an overview of attempts being made in the United Kingdom to persuade/train police officers to move away from trying to get denying suspects to confess and instead focus their efforts on gathering relevant and accurate information. They describe ongoing changes in police policy, training, and practice that are designed to transform "interrogations" into more effective "investigative interviews." Results of preliminary research assessing whether these initiatives have had a salutary impact on interviewing officers' beliefs and performance are presented.

In Chapter 9, two social psychologists, the volume editor and Andrew Geers review the literature on problems that arise when triers of fact attempt to assess the reliability of confessions. Although it is assumed by the highest court in the land that jurors can readily distinguish voluntary from involuntary confessions, research shows that this is, in fact, not the case. Recent work demonstrating that the manner in which confession evidence is presented to trial decision makers can potentially bias the evaluation of such evidence is also summarized. Based on these findings, recommendations are made regarding how best to capture and later present what transpires during interrogations so as to avoid the possibility of unreliable confessions exerting any influence on trial verdicts.

Chapter 10, by Vanessa Edkins and American Psychology-Law Society Distinguished Contribution Awardee Lawrence Wrightsman, addresses the following question: "In their zeal to catch criminals, do the police go overboard and sometimes encourage criminal activity in order to stifle it?" The authors review what research there is on this issue of entrapment as well as present the findings of their own recent studies that provide new insights about entrapment, which like interrogations, often involves the employment of demonstrably coercive tactics. Edkins and Wrightsman conclude "that if law enforcement officials feel the use of entrapment is necessary in a certain situation, or regarding a certain individual, they should be required to provide sufficient evidence—akin to a warrant—before the targeting begins."

Chapter 11, the second chapter written by Solomon Fulero, focuses on how scholars and practitioners can serve as effective expert witnesses to educate judges and jurors regarding what is currently known about how systematic psychological coercion can lead innocent individuals to falsely incriminate themselves when in police custody. Fulero notes that the case law is becoming increasingly clear on the parameters of acceptability for expert testimony in confession cases. Courts appear to be receptive to "testimony about the phenomenon of false confessions, social psychological testimony about the police interrogation procedures that are commonly used, clinical psychological testimony about personality or clinical factors that might be linked to confessions, and even specific clinical testimony about a particular defendant, but not testimony that purports to determine if a particular confession is true or false."

In the twelfth and final chapter, Senior Research Associate Elizabeth Wiggins and Research Associate Shannon Wheatman of the Federal Judicial Center begin by gleaning from the preceding chapters the fundamental findings about interrogations, confessions, and entrapment that ought to be reflected in police investigative policies and that ought to affect how confessions and other investigative information are used at trial. They then suggest how these findings might be translated into policy, in part by drawing parallels to how other psychological findings (e.g., those about lineups) have or have not been integrated into policy. The role of individual psychologists, professional organizations, and policy-makers themselves are discussed, with a focus on practical strategies for promoting and implementing reform.

REFERENCES

Bem, D. J. (1966). Inducing belief in false confessions. *Journal of Personality and Social Psychology, 3,* 707–710.

Bem, D. J. (1967, June). When saying is believing. *Psychology Today, 1,* 21–25.

Cutler, B. L., & Penrod, S. D. (1995). *Mistaken identification: The eyewitness, psychology, and the law.* New York: Cambridge University Press.

Innocence Project. (n.d.). Featured issues: False confessions. In *Case profiles.* Retrieved January 15, 2003, from http://www.innocenceproject.org/case/index.php

Kassin, S. M., & Wrightsman, L. S. (1985). Confession evidence. In S. Kassin & L. Wrightsman (Eds.), *The psychology of evidence and trial procedure* (pp. 67–94). Beverly Hills, CA: Sage.

Leo, R. A., & Drizin, S. (2003). *Proven false confessions cases.* Retrieved August 15, 2003 from http://www.innocenceproject.org/docs/Master_List_False_Confessions.html

Lindsay, R. C. L., & Wells, G. L. (1985). Improving eyewitness identification from lineups: Simultaneous versus sequential lineup presentations. *Journal of Applied Psychology, 70,* 556–564.

Loftus, E. F. (1979). *Eyewitness testimony.* Cambridge, MA: Harvard University Press.

Miranda v. Arizona, 384 U.S. 436 (1966).

Technical Working Group for Eyewitness Evidence. (1999). *Eyewitness evidence: A guide for law enforcement* [Booklet]. Washington, DC: United States Department of Justice, Office of Justice Programs.

Warden, R. (2003). *The role of false confessions in Illinois wrongful convictions since 1970.* Retrieved August 15, 2003 from http://www.law.northwestern.edu/depts/clinic/wrongful/FalseConfessions.htm

Wells, G. L., Malpass, R. S., Lindsay, R. C. L., Fisher, R. P., Turtle, J. W., & Fulero, S. (2000). From the lab to the police station: A successful application of eyewitness research. *American Psychologist, 55,* 581–598.

Zimbardo, P. G. (1971). Coercion and compliance: The psychology of police confessions. In R. Perruci & M. Pilisuk (Eds.), *The triple revolution emerging* (pp. 492–508). Boston: Little, Brown.

2

Questions

GEORGE R. KLARE

During World War II, I served as a navigator on United States Army Air Force B-17 aircraft "Flying Fortresses" during bombing raids on German military targets. At that time, I was a 22-year-old second lieutenant and a member of the 100th Bombardment Group (Heavy) stationed in Thorpe Abbotts, England. My aircraft was shot down during an attack on a synthetic oil plant near Hamburg on December 31, 1944 and I parachuted into Wesermünde County, Germany and became a prisoner of war (POW). After capture I underwent an interval of solitary confinement and three interrogations during early January, 1945, which included a Red Cross interview (interrogation), a military interrogation, and a political interrogation. All took place at Auswertestelle West, usually referred to as Dulag Luft, the Luftwaffe (German Air Force) Interrogation Center at Oberursel, Germany.

I have often thought about these experiences and wondered not only about the questions asked of me but also about others that were not asked but that occurred to me then and since. To relate these questions, I will present the most significant points in the interrogations and solitary confinement as I recall them, with explanatory information based on my notes made shortly afterward during World War II in a subsequent prison camp, Stalag Luft I in Barth, Germany.

[*In addition, I will present relevant information discovered since World War II based on books and articles, and on national archival materials I have uncovered. I will also refer frequently to an extensive web site devoted to the World War II experiences of POWs, where other relevant material can readily be accessed <http://www.merkki.com/kriegies.htm>; for convenient reference in the text, this*

GEORGE R. KLARE • Distinguished Professor Emeritus of Psychology, Department of Psychology, Ohio University, Athens, Ohio 45701 (klare@ohio.edu).

*site will simply be referred to as Merkki (nd). All such additional information will
be bracketed and in italics as shown here. I have chosen this method rather than
the more traditional footnotes because, in my view, this material deserves equal
emphasis for an understanding of my experiences. One who wishes to read only
the story itself as I believe it occurred, however, can easily skip this material.]*

As a psychologist, I am well aware of how fallible recollections can
be and the way they can become distorted over time. This is especially true
for details, and for the influence of subsequent reading upon memories.
But I am also aware of evidence showing how strong significant memories can be when emotionally loaded, which is certainly true of the recollections appearing here. With these caveats in mind, and based upon the
references listed, I have attempted to present the background and the questions I was asked as well as my own questions. This material is then followed by a summary section with possible answers where they appear relevant and plausible.

RED CROSS INTERVIEW (INTERROGATION)

German soldiers captured all nine members of our B-17 crew and brought
us together in a local jail. We were especially happy to discover that everyone had survived since we did not know until then whether all had made
successful parachute jumps from our burning aircraft before it exploded. We
were surprised to be together, moreover, since we found we had landed a
considerable distance apart and different soldiers had taken us prisoner.

*[I have been able to locate microfiche copies of the Missing Air Crew Reports
Nos. 11365–11367 (1945) from Dulag Luft for our crew in the files at the National
Archives. All crew members were reported as taken prisoner by various members
of the Wesermünde County Guards except the radio operator; he was captured
by members of Flak Battery Spaden.]*

I was threatened with death as a spy in a jail cell on the first night of
my capture. The threat resulted in only a sleepless night, but made me wonder whether it was because of my knowledge of German. I had said a few
words in German to two boys who had rushed up to me just after my parachute landing. They had a German police dog, and I was afraid they would
sic the dog on me if I did not seem friendly. They kept the dog in check,
but may well have reported to the two soldiers who soon captured me that
I spoke German to them.

One of the soldiers, conversing in German with the other, said I should
be taken into the nearby woods and shot as a "terrorflieger," but the other
dissuaded him, saying that I had no "pistole." I remembered with thanks
that the officials at the base in England had taken back our pistols recently,
saying that they would be useless landing in fortress Germany as opposed

to landing in an occupied country earlier. Carrying a gun, they said, might well increase the likelihood of being shot when captured.

After marching and being moved by military truck, we were loaded into the compartment of an old German railway car on the way to an uncertain destination. It was a harrowing trip that included surviving a bombing by American B-17s in the city of Fulda where we were being held prisoner temporarily. We had also gotten out of a burning freight station that the bombers had hit, luckily just before it collapsed.

Our guard was an English-speaking Luftwaffe captain who was injured and apparently no longer on flying status. He had ordered us to unload packages from the station, many of them, ironically, undelivered Christmas presents. He then took us from the station through an angry mob that must have assumed we were the bombers rather than the bombed. Though armed only with a pistol, he managed to hold off the mob and get us on our way again. Why he had risked his life to protect ours was one of the many questions to come, and we were grateful to the captain for this reprieve.

The date was January 3, 1945, a date I remembered especially well because we had survived the three life-threatening situations on that day alone. I had already felt many times that my chance of living through the war was poor at best, but now began to feel hopeful that I had at least a chance. By then we were told we were on our way to the dreaded Luftwaffe Interrogation Center, Dulag Luft, so it would have been the time to try to escape. Possible escape was always at the back of our minds and discussed briefly during transit, since we were accompanied by only the one guard. However, during the bitter winter weather and without adequate food, water, and maps, we knew that success was virtually impossible. Besides, we owed our lives to the one guard we had. We would have to await possible opportunities for escape later.

We received no food the first day of capture, but on the next, January 1, we were given two small boiled potatoes for the day. We would have eaten turkey and trimmings at our base in England had we gotten back, since we had seen the preparations before leaving, but were grateful for any food by that time. We received two pieces of German black bread January 2 for the train trip. We had not received water all day, which made eating and swallowing the hard, crusty bread difficult. Consequently I left a piece on the luggage rack on the train car, which I came to regret. We could scoop up and eat some snow from the ground in periods of marching but—bitter and tasting of dirt and cinders along the tracks—it was a poor substitute for water.

Because our experiences to then had been so dangerous and life-threatening, I almost looked forward to reaching the safety of a camp. I felt survival might be more likely there, but the first view of the Center, Dulag Luft, on January 3 was not reassuring. Arrival time was in the dark of night, and the gate and barbed-wire fence around it were lighted by searchlights that emphasized the high enclosure. When the gate closed behind me I could not help wondering if and when it might ever swing open for me. Since I had already been threatened earlier, would grilling and further threats along that line be likely?

[*A photograph of the main entrance gate of Dulag Luft as it was during World War II is presented in The Interrogators section of Merkki (nd). First seeing the gate again in the picture many years later made it seem as real as having been there again. Perhaps my emotional feeling from that time was still strong enough to spark my recall.*]

Guards first herded the nine of us into a small room where we conversed in whispers, reminding each other that what we said would probably be recorded. I recall that the togglier on our crew worried that he would be punished as the person in our aircraft who dropped the bombs. He begged us not to divulge his role as the bomb-dropper, so that when interrogated he could say he was only a gunner.

[*We had no bombardier on our crew; the togglier was a gunner who simply flipped a switch when he saw the lead bombardier in a formation drop his bombs. He had reason for concern, however, since bugging of rooms was common according to Hanns Scharff, the former interrogator, as reported in Toliver (1978). One building in Dulag Luft was, in fact, devoted to the microphone monitoring of rooms in the Center. Also, the fact that the Missing Air Crew Reports came from Dulag Luft indicates that the composition of our crew was already known at that time.*]

Crew members were taken individually from the room. I was taken to a solitary cell, and assumed that is what happened to the others also. My cell seemed about 10 feet long and 5 feet wide (11 x 5 1/2 meters) when I paced it off, and had a ceiling that I took to be about 10 feet (5 meters) high. It had a straw-tick mattress on a wooden frame with crossed wires beneath for support, a dirty blanket, and a stool.

The wooden walls and ceiling were painted off-white, with a window of opaque glass, an electric heater, and a sign saying "Any destruction of this property will be severely punished under the Geneva Convention" at one end. A door at the other end had a tiny peephole at eye level. The heater as well as a naked bulb hanging from the ceiling were controlled from outside.

The door could not be opened from the inside but a red handle nearby said to "Turn handle for guard." This was the way to indicate I wished to go to the latrine located near the end of a long row of cells. I soon discovered that such a request was seldom quickly fulfilled and never when another prisoner was anywhere in sight. The delay and the inability to see any friendly faces and converse seemed clearly to be part of the softening-up treatment before interrogation. I remember the trip to the latrine with gratitude whenever it was finally permitted and which, from the odor in the cell, was at one time or another apparently not granted soon enough for previous occupants.

[*Various dimensions have been given for the cells. For example, the Cuddon report (1952) provides the figures 9'9"x 6' x 9'2," Dulag Luft (1944) gives 12' x 5' x 8,' and Foy (1981) lists 13' x 6'6" x10.' I believe the Cuddon dimensions (approximately 10 1/2 x 6 1/2 x 10 meters) to be most accurate because of the official nature of the report and therefore of the cell measurement. The report also provides details of cell construction, electrical heating, lighting, and other data.*

It may be, of course, that the cells differed in size, although anything other than slight variation seems unlikely from the diagrams I have seen. I have not been able to locate a photo of one of the cells, but two sketches appear in Merkki (nd). They, as well as the Cuddon report, confirm the details I have recalled except for the presence of the sign.]

I had been strip-searched soon after being taken prisoner and now again. A list was made in my presence of all such personal possessions as my billfold, watch, cigarettes, money, etc., as well as my escape kit, when they were taken. My heated flying suit and my flying boots were now also taken, presumably to discourage escape attempts. More significant at the time, the loss of boots made for continuous cold feet and thus lowered morale.

[*I discovered lists of personal items taken from several former POWs in the files at the Washington National Records Center. I was able to find one for Shelton Brannen, who later happened to be in my room at the permanent camp, Stalag Luft One. The list includes: wristlets; water bag; escape package; pipe; three handkerchiefs; two combs; pocket knife; mechanical pencil; wrist watch; compass; one Camel cigarette in package; and two metal hangers. Both the amount carried by this downed flyer and the detailed record amazed me. Though I did not find my own list, I know from my later notes that I lost 81 cents in American coins, 2.07 in Icelandic kroner, and 6 British pounds.*]

During what was left of that first night in the solitary cell I was able to sleep off some of my fatigue. Even the uncomfortably thin mattress, the odor in the poorly ventilated room, and my anxiety could not keep me awake. The next morning I had my first interrogation, an interview with the purpose of my filling out a Red Cross form. It was conducted, as I recall, by a Luftwaffe non-commissioned officer referred to as a receptionist. He was probably a sergeant (Feldwebel der Luftwaffe), not a professional interrogator (Sonderführer).

I was told that the information would be needed to notify the Red Cross that I was a prisoner so that relatives could be informed that I was no longer called "missing in action." I was eager that such information be passed along, but had been prepared at the base in England to give only name, rank, and military serial number since that was enough for the Red Cross authorities in Switzerland. I also knew that no more was required by the Geneva Convention and that US authorities emphatically insisted that no more be given.

I was handed a sheet, and once I had given name, rank, and number handed it back to the receptionist. It also asked for additional personal information as well as military details such as my bomb group, mission, etc. The receptionist appeared upset at this, and said the additional information was needed because without it the Red Cross could not properly notify my next of kin. Also, he said it would help to demonstrate that I was not a spy. When I responded that name, rank, and number were all that were required of prisoners under the Geneva Convention, he called me uncooperative and reiterated that I would regret this failure to fill it out since proper information could not be sent to the Red Cross. He again urged me to complete the form, and also said failure could mean a long stay in solitary confinement as well as poor treatment. I still refused to provide further information. It was an unpleasant welcome to the Center, and I had no way of knowing whether he was speaking the truth.

[*Merkki (nd) presents a typical Red Cross form, as does Cuddon (1952). In addition, Merkki refers to the existence of a number of such forms as does Foy (1981), some asking as many as 50 questions. The first four questions typically include the information a prisoner is obligated to provide, i.e., name, rank, and military serial number, but the next group usually requests added personal information. A subsequent group usually requests military information of the sort that the US Air Force particularly did not wish to have given out. Merkki also says that despite complaints from the Protecting Power about German use of this kind of phony Red Cross form to elicit such information, the German staff's preoccupation with it "bordered on obsession." Flammer (1972) not only reports that the Germans continued to use the forms throughout the war, but primarily as a "psychological test" of how prisoners would react to later interrogation. Foy (1981) also says that the receptionists made a "psychological assessment" of POWs to aid the interrogators who would question them later.*]

SOLITARY CONFINEMENT

After the Red Cross interview, I began a stay in solitary confinement prior to interrogation. I could hear noise from the hall when someone was either put in or taken from the cells on either side of me and wondered whether they were some of my crew. I never found out, however, since the guards were careful not to let me see or talk to any other prisoners. The endless days soon became broken mostly by the series of meals and trips to the latrine. I hoped to get some reading and/or writing material, but my requests were turned down. This seemed clearly a part of the softening-up process before interrogation, as were the inadequate meals and too long waits for access to the latrine.

Three times a day two armed guards probably of private rank (*Gefreiter der Luftwaffe* and/or *Soldat der Luftwaffe*) opened the door and served the meals. They announced their presence with calls of "Kaffee" or "Wasser" and "Brot" or "Suppe." The announcements would have been unnecessary after the first day or so, since the diet was so nearly uniform. Breakfast typically consisted of a cup of ersatz coffee and two half-slices of German black bread, with a thin, almost invisible coating of margarine on one and jam on the other. I soon found that the only way to get a taste of the margarine and the jam was to move each coating to a corner of the bread with my tongue and save it for my last bite. The taste was not all that great, but it was an improvement over the bread alone. Lunch consisted of watery soup with some kind of vegetable greens in it, possibly from parsnip, rutabaga, or turnip tops. I can remember, at least, that their unpalatability suggested to me they could have been swept off the floor of some kitchen. Supper was again bread and water, but without the margarine or jam. I can also remember, however, that although the foods could hardly be called tasty, all began to improve in taste as the days wore on, and I looked forward eagerly to the meals.

[*As might be expected under such conditions, thoughts about food became a dominant topic in daydreams as well as night dreams. Many examples of such dreams can be found among the stories reported in Freeman (1991a), my own among them (pp. 136–137).*]

Which leads to one of my unforgettable experiences. My left ankle was swollen and was bothering me a great deal, so I tried to ask a guard for medical attention, even just a pain killer. His satiric response was that I would get a long rest for my ankle while there. This not only irritated me but meant no relief from the pain, which disturbed my nights as well as my days.

My predicament led me to try a new tack: one day, I refused food at each meal. I could tell this bothered the guards, who urged me to eat by almost trying to push the food off on me. They may not have faced this kind of crisis before since the POW diet caused growing hunger. My refusal might well have created a problem for them, especially if it continued for a long period. They as well as I knew it would not have taken very long to reach a lethargic state, considering my lack of food since being shot down. Unfortunately for my wish to get medical help, I could only hold out for one complete day; the second day I ravenously ate the food offered me at each meal. This added to my discomfiture, since I had demonstrated weakness by not holding out longer and thus failing to get medical attention.

[*My notes written later in Stalag Luft One indicate that I had landed backward on my left leg and ankle at the end of my parachute jump. I recall trying to twist the risers on the chute as I came down, so I would face forward on landing as I had been trained to do, but the wind was too strong to be able to manage that. Consequently, I had what could have been a fractured ankle and badly bruised knee. Whatever the specific injuries, they were made worse by the marching I did on the way to Dulag Luft and the lack of any medical treatment. When forced to march I moved more slowly than desired, and my notes indicate that I was roughed up once—knocked down—by a guard because of my slow movement.*]

After supper, the lone light which had been turned on to facilitate serving the meal was turned off. Since this was January in northern Germany, no light came in through the opaque glass window much of the day, so the darkness was complete. It was difficult after the first day or so to sleep the usual length of time, so many unpleasant hours were spent in total darkness. To add to the discomfort, the radiator in the cell was turned on only for sporadic periods during the day and night. My guess is that it was on for about two hours and off for about four hours during the night.

[*Most references to the temperature of the solitary cells at Dulag Luft do not comment on the cold; perhaps the conditions might not have been so bad at the time if it were not for the unusually cold winter of 1945. Unbearable heat gets more attention in descriptions of life in the cells. During the hot summer months the radiators were, on more than one occasion, said to be turned to their hottest setting to make cells especially uncomfortable. One prisoner recounts it had grown so hot that he lay on the floor of his cell and tried to breathe under the door. In fact, this incident was one of those that led to the war crimes trials of the commanding officers reported in Cuddon (1952).*]

I recall waking up shivering and unable to return to sleep on various occasions during the long nights. The lone, thin blanket in the cell offered little warmth and comfort. My hands as well as my feet were cold most of the time, but they were coldest during the night. This contributed as much to my physical discomfort as any other single aspect of solitary confinement. The unpleasantness of my cell seemed clearly designed to make me willing to talk when interrogated.

[*Toliver (1978, pp. 354–5) provides the following information from the British Air Ministry's Weekly Intelligence Summary No. 305 concerning treatment of POWs in Dulag Luft. "The wooden cells were described as grimy and badly ventilated, were always evil smelling, and the fittings were of the most primitive order. There seems little doubt that the living conditions were expressly designed to lower morale and to produce mental depression of the most acute kind."*]

Since social interaction with other prisoners as well as reading and writing materials were prohibited, I tried various other activities to pass the time. During the day I was able to stay more or less mentally active in several ways to avoid the depression I felt was ready to set in. I tried the obvious things at first and continued them during my entire stay in solitary: pray and recite poetry. I ran through all the Bible verses and the poetry I could recall, and wished I could recall more.

I became familiar once again with the Lord's Prayer and the 23rd Psalm, "The Lord is my Shepherd. . . ." I doubted that the Lord was really my Shepherd on many occasions, but religious thoughts did serve as both a source of comfort and a diversion. Besides, I gave thanks to have so far avoided three outcomes most of my friends and I feared in combat (in decreasing order of importance): cowardice in front of others, debilitating injury, and death. I remembered several persons who had refused to fly because of the dangers from enemy fighters, flak and collisions; they were more pitied than envied, and usually given menial military tasks of some kind. The fear of suffering incapacitating injury, or becoming a vegetable, was also greater than fear of death.

I recall praying particularly for two things: first, courage to face whatever might come next; I did not want to disavow the United States during interrogation or disgrace myself. Second, comfort for my mother, stepfather and stepsister when they got the news I did not return from the mission on December 31. Being an only child because of my father's death when I was two weeks old, I knew the news would be especially hard for my mother to endure, harder than imprisonment for me. I wished there was some way to tell her I was still alive.

[*Interestingly enough, I was afforded an unusual way to get word to my mother once I was in Stalag Luft One later. As the end of the war grew nearer, the German military used various strategies they apparently hoped might get them as favorable treatment as possible when the war was over. One of these was an offer to send prisoners' short-wave messages to next of kin in the United States. Some of my friends in the camp felt this plan would never be carried out, that it might just be some sort of ploy, or might even be a trick of some kind. Any wording that might be critical of the Germans, they felt, could lead to more solitary confinement or other punishment.*

I took a chance on the offer, however, and worded my message in such a way that, if it was not changed, my mother could feel some assurance it came from me. My message was indeed sent as written, and she received word from nineteen short-wave operators in the United States who had picked it up. My message was, as the title of my article (Klare, 1995) in the references says, my way of "Keeping in Touch." Needless to say, my mother believed for the first time I really was alive.]

Luckily, I had a fair amount of memorized poetry available, since I had practiced certain verses not long before being confined. Some came from school days and others in connection with driving the tractor on the farm where I lived in the preceding years. I found I could relieve some of the tedium of long days cultivating corn or operating the combine in the wheat fields by reciting verses. To help my memory along I often looked up poems and re-read them before the day's work or during the noon break.

I favored rhyming poetry since I could be more certain of my memory that way, but other poems struck my fancy and I recited all I could recall. One of my favorites was Henley's "Invictus," since "Out of the night that covers me . . ." reflected my position, and I felt I must maintain "an unconquerable soul." Fortunately, however, I also liked the free verse of

Walt Whitman celebrating freedom, and still recall that snatches of his poetry gave me comfort.

[*Here is a sample of what I recited in Dulag Luft and then wrote in one of my blue books a bit later in Stalag Luft One. Blue books were the small booklets provided to POWs by the Red Cross after solitary confinement; I have written about them in the article entitled "Blue Books" listed in the references (Klare, 1996). The verse below is from Walt Whitman's "Song of the Open Road," one of my favorites.*]

From this hour, freedom! From this hour I ordain myself loosed of all limits and imaginary lines,
Going where I list, my own master, total and absolute.
Listening to others, considering well what they say,
Pausing, searching, receiving, contemplating;
Gently, but with an undeniable will
Divesting myself of the holds that would hold me.

I inhale great draughts of air:
The East and the West are mine, the North and the South are mine.
I am larger than I thought,
I did not know I held so much goodness.

Reciting poetry did not begin to fill the entire day (or critical part of the night), however. I discovered several other activities I could engage in when it was light enough to do so. One was to make use of the sign in the cell warning about destruction of property; I could make new words from the letters, which grew out of my interest in crossword puzzles. The irony of the sign had struck me when I first saw it: there was almost nothing to destroy, for one thing, and why would anyone want to make his facilities any more unpleasant by destroying what few comforts there were? For another, what did the Geneva Convention on treatment of prisoners say on this subject anyway? An inspector, if one were to visit, would doubtless find more to criticize in German treatment than in prisoner destructiveness.

I came up with another activity, one that fit in with the statistical training I had completed recently while a student at the University of Minnesota. Lying on my bunk during the long days, I spent many hours staring at the ceiling, so I devised an approach that reduced the boredom. I counted the nails in the ceiling to get a total, then used several sampling methods to estimate this total from the sample values. I recall feeling happy that the workmen who had built the cell did not pay careful attention to the ordering and spacing of the nails, thus making sampling far more interesting.

Despite my best efforts, time seemed to drag on unpleasantly. I might have added the regular activity of pacing up and down in my cell, but my ankle and knee hurt too much for that. I did make a disturbing discovery when examining my cell one day, however. Standing on the stool I found strokes made in the dusty dirt on the window frame by a previous occupant of the cell. The area where the two halves of the window came together provided a narrow ledge on which I found what appeared to be a record of days someone had spent in solitary. The slash marks totaled a disturbing 28. I seemed to recall that the Geneva Convention limited the permissible number to 30, but I was hoping not to be in solitary confinement anywhere near that long.

Somehow I had never given much thought to the importance of social relationships in maintaining mental health, but soon recognized its significance. The only humans I saw in solitary were the enemy guards, and they were not friendly. They delighted in telling me "Vor you der vor ist ofer" (For you the war is over) shortly after arriving and several times later. Beyond that they limited their meetings with me to the necessary operations of calling out and providing food and liquid and permitting me to make the trek to the latrine.

About the only other words of near-English from the one guard who could converse with me in English were not pleasantries. I was reminded, as noted when I asked for medical attention or books, that my treatment would consist of a long rest in the cell. I might have tried to converse in German with other guards but did not wish to advertise the fact I could speak and understand the language fairly well (though not perfectly). I was already afraid this knowledge would be used against me in some way during interrogation.

By the end of around a week in solitary I began to worry about my recurring, circular thinking. Putting all my concerns together led to a weakening of my resolve to limit my answers in the coming interrogation to the required name, rank, and serial number. I got to the point of feeling that if they would only let me out of the cell and begin interrogating me I would tell them most anything they wanted to know. After all, I felt, how would the American government ever know what I had said? My concern grew when I heard German numbers being called out occasionally in the hall. I somehow realized these probably indicated the cells of prisoners who were being taken for interrogation. I longed to hear the number of my own cell called out.

[*As might be expected, prisoners reacted in different ways to solitary confinement. Flammer (1978, p. 60) states, "With seemingly endless hours ahead and no fixed subject on which to concentrate, mental discipline was next to impossible. The same thoughts began to repeat themselves, dropping into the mind as relentlessly as the drops of water which fell at regular intervals from the damp ceiling. Unwanted fears kept reasserting themselves." Again (p. 60), "The majority of those who were alone for any length of time came through the experience without any serious harm. A few went mad. A very few developed an inner strength from the ordeal."*]

[*Flammer (p. 60) also comments that a person might come to feel that "nothing he said or did would ever be known to anyone, except of course the enemy," so why hold back. "Accordingly, a man was responsible only to himself. He was fighting alone, against another world, with no one except his captors knowing whether he was dead or alive." Wilson (1998) provides another excellent description of the emotional trauma of captivity.*]

At last the desired number was called out, indicating I would be taken for interrogation. My first reaction was anxiety, soon followed by a determination not to tell anything other than name, rank, and serial number. I recall thinking to myself something like "Those sons of bitches. I won't tell them a damn thing. Let them quiz me; I won't break." I also tried to think of something, anything, that I might use to distract my interrogator if an opportunity arose. There was not much time for such thoughts, since an armed orderly soon opened my door and motioned for me to come out and go down the long corridor with him.

[*I have found several diagrams of the cell plan at Dulag Luft, but the one used at the War Crimes Trial of the commanding officers of the Center (Cuddon, 1952) is perhaps the most reliable. According to this diagram, my cell could have numbered somewhere in the forties, since I recall a fairly long walk to the latrine, which was near the end of the long main corridor. Oddly enough, considering the emotional feeling involved, I can no longer recall the exact number.*]

MILITARY INTERROGATION

The orderly took me from my cell down the long corridor and knocked on a door. Upon hearing the German command "Herein!" he opened the door and ushered me inside a well-furnished room with a German officer seated behind the desk. The orderly and I both saluted and he announced me as "Kriegsgefangener Klare" (Prisoner of War Klare). The officer was about middle age, perhaps fifty, with well-combed dark hair and dark eyes and of serious mien. His uniform was immaculate, with several medals, and he wore polished jackboots, which I noticed when he stood up to acknowledge the orderly's and my own salute. I was quite familiar with Luftwaffe officer rank and immediately realized he was a major. This high rank surprised and frightened me—I had already observed the vanity and power of German officers, even lieutenants. Why might a person of such high rank be interrogating me, a lowly second lieutenant?

[*A picture of the person I feel certain was my interrogator appears in both Toliver (1978, p. 315) and Merkki (nd). A major named Waldschmidt (first name unavailable), he is described in Toliver as a professor of Indiology at Gottingen University and was said to be one of the best of the bomber section interrogators. Since I was a bomber navigator, his specialty was appropriate to my case. I could find no*] listing of the complement of the Center in my sources, but figures given for the number of staff varies from 270 (50 officers, 100 enlisted men and 120 other support personnel; Dulag Luft, 1944) to 300 total (Bailey, 1981). Whatever the number, rank as high as major was rare; even the commandant was only an oberstleutnant (lieutenant colonel) according to both Toliver (1978) and Dulag Luft (1944). This adds support that Major Waldschmidt was my interrogator.]

After our salutes, the major dismissed the orderly who brought me and who closed the door as he left. The major motioned for me to sit down in a chair placed across from his desk, facing a window, and took his own seat behind the desk. His first words, in clear American-accented English, were to call me by my full name and rank, and to ask me if I had enjoyed my Cook's Tour of Germany. I recognized that the term "Cook's Tour" referred to the old but still popular guided plan for tourists in Europe. Since the major would have known about my mode of travel after being shot down, his remark was clearly meant as a joke, but I was too anxious to appreciate it. My "tour" was indeed "guided," but "guarded" would have been an even better description.

He seemed to be trying to put me at ease, doubtless for more serious questions to follow. My failure to respond except to say "No, sir" after a pause must therefore have been disappointing. Next he offered me an American cigarette, which was a more direct strategy; I accepted, and he lit it for me.

The major then commented on the fact that I had an ankle injury, which surprised me since I had thought my refusing food had no effect. He said he was sorry no medical attention could be given to it, but said that medical facilities were limited and that they had to give priority to more serious cases. He asked whether the injury occurred when I bailed out of my burning B-17 and landed in Wesermünde County.

I realized, after hesitating, that if I answered with a truthful positive answer it would be a beginning confirmation of military information for him. Instead, I said that I could give only my name, rank, and serial number. His response was to say he really wanted to help me out and needed the information in order to be certain that I was not a spy. He said it would be to my advantage to cooperate so that my military role as only a downed American flier and not a spy would be clear.

I wondered if he knew of the earlier spy accusation, or whether this was simply an approach for eliciting information that he might have used with any stubborn prisoner. He said he also knew that I had not completed the Red Cross form, and once again commented that my lack of cooperation was only hurting me. He asked for verification of my parents' names and address, which he said was needed to let the Red Cross know how to communicate with them. Verification? How could he have gotten such information? Once again I felt that this was just the ruse we had been warned against back at the base in England if we were shot down. I again said I could give him only my name, rank, and serial number.

When he asked our target for December 31, I said I could not tell. He thereupon began telling me information about it that was highly detailed and accurate. He knew we had attacked the synthetic oil plant at Hamburg and that we had been shot down shortly after. I was surprised, and my expression might have given me away. How could he have known this about our particular airplane? Had other crew members talked while being interrogated? Perhaps I had shown my feelings, since he continued by saying that I should not underestimate Germany's intelligence capabilities.

He followed this comment by saying he already knew a great deal, and got out a file from his desk drawer with such information. He began with more facts about the mission on which I had been shot down, correctly identifying both primary and secondary oil targets. He said, correctly, that I had come from the 100th Bomb Group base in Thorpe Abbotts in England; he even referred to it as the "Bloody Hundredth," an appellation sometimes used for the Group in England because of its many casualties. He pointed out that twelve of our group's B-17s had gone down that day.

I, of course, could not know whether this number was correct or not, but from what I had been able to observe that day, was beginning to believe he knew a great deal more about our mission than I realized. He made several other comments about the base in England which suggested that he also knew more details about the base than I did. Where and how, I wondered again, could he have gotten the information?

[*Major Waldschmidt was indeed correct about the number of B-17s from the Bloody Hundredth that had failed to return that day as well as other details of the battle on December 31, as I have discovered since World War II (Freeman, 1981; Klare, in press a).*]

Next, he commented that he already knew a great deal about me personally. He said I had been a student at the University of Minnesota before entering the service and commented that the Gophers (the football team) had fared poorly that fall, which was the case. He knew my hometown, my parents' names, even my grandparents' names. He listed the bases in the United States where I had been trained, and when and where I had received my wings as a navigator and my commission as a second lieutenant. To say I was astounded would be an understatement; I was puzzled about how he could possibly have gotten such detailed personal information. Could my crewmates have talked about me? If so, what else could they have confided? I began to feel it would make little difference if I gave the major information well beyond my name, rank, and serial number.

[*A number of sources since World War II have described how this information was collected and organized, e.g., Bailey (1981), Dillon (1995), Foy (1981), Murphy (2001), and others. The best and most detailed description comes from*

Hanns Scharff himself in the book by Toliver (1978) and in his own account (Scharff, 1950). He says information was collected in a bureau called Beute und Nachrichten Abteilung (roughly translated as information through booty). He credits a woman known as Frau Biehler as being integral in the bureau, collecting with her staff every scrap of material recovered from downed fliers, alive or dead. In addition, she is said to have maintained a complete, continuous history of every airforce unit in every country of the Allies.

The Press Section of this bureau also received, from agents abroad, home-town newspapers from all over the United States. In addition to stories about fliers and where and when they completed their training, even photographs were often included. Much of this information apparently traveled through the neutral Span-ish embassy and that way entered the files.

In addition to this rich source of information, there was said to be a contin-uous flow into the files from interrogators. This often included transcripts of conversations with prisoners, taken down mechanically without their knowledge. These transcripts were said to be fitted into the dossiers of the various units by a very effective system of cross-indexing. Information was also collected from indi-vidual Germans, said to be everyone from flak post personnel to civilians, when-ever an Allied plane was downed or prisoners were captured. Another integral per-son also mentioned by Scharff was a former lecturer at Heidelberg University named Bert Nagel, who became an expert on building files on various air force stations.

A delay for collation of this material was instituted while the prisoner was in his cell before he was interrogated. The material was presented as a file to the interrogator before a prisoner was called in for his interview. The detail available was often overwhelming, down to whether or not the prisoner was a smoker, par-ticularly a heavy smoker, so that this information might be used in his handling. By 1944, the prisoner files of the interrogators were described as bulging.]

It was in this atmosphere that the major began asking technical ques-tions of me. One of those I remember concerned why Information Friend or Foe (IFF) transmission between aircraft had been curtailed. I said, hon-estly, that I did not know. He said that as a navigator I should know and could tell him as an indication I was not a spy and thus not compromise my military integrity. Once again, I simply said I did not know, which was fortunate since I had been told back at the base in England not to lie, at least not in an obvious way, which could get one in trouble. I did have an idea why IFF had been restricted, related to the use of this information by Ger-man fighter controllers. But since I had no official information on this mat-ter I could honestly maintain my protestation of ignorance.

Other questions were along the line of why we had a togglier rather than a bombardier on our crew. Was it because of the high number of casu-alties in combat? Was it because most bombardiers were not very accurate? How were targets marked if toggliers simply dropped the bombs when the lead plane with the bombardier could not be seen? I either said I could not tell or protested my innocence, since in most cases I honestly did not have detailed information of the sort that he wished.

He next asked why changes had been made in Very High Frequency (VHF) transmissions between aircraft in formations. This put me on the spot, since here I did in fact have recent information. I said I could not say, that I must restrict my information to name, rank, and serial number. This was, I suppose, a giveaway to a clever interrogator, since I did not come right out and say I did not know.

[*Records I have located about training films and lectures at the base in England during my time there in December, 1944 (Klare, in press b) confirm that a lecture was in fact held on VHF security. The instructor, Major Bowman of S-2 (Intelligence), actually used documentary evidence captured from Germans on the continent of what had been gained through lack of VHF security. We were told that VHF communication between aircraft during combat should be restricted to necessary information with no friendly chat or discussion.*]

During the IFF and VHF exchanges, particularly, I had been trying to think of something that might seem to be a legitimate query rather than simply a way to distract the major from asking further questions. I recalled once again the probable vanity of a German officer of major rank, especially one whose dress and demeanor so clearly seemed to suggest pride in rank. Looking directly at him, I asked about how to tell officer rank, in the guise of wishing to act in a militarily correct manner. At that, he went into the details of officer rank, covering first the highest level down to the lowest. He also covered the noncommissioned ranks, and commented that while a prisoner in Germany I was to respond properly to commands from soldiers at this level as well as the commissioned level.

During this explanation I was searching my mind for another reasonable query to raise. With a quick glance earlier I had noted the large maps on two walls, which I realized were a map of Germany and a map with the military airfields in England. Since the major had mentioned a Cook's tour earlier, I asked whether he could tell me, or show me on the map of Germany, our present location. The major led me to the map and pointed out where we were, in the town of Oberursel, a suburb of Frankfurt. He also pointed out the surrounding area, indicating the presence of the Taunus Mountains beyond. In addition he traced the route of my journey from landing by parachute to the Center. He then also took me over to the map with air bases in England and pointed out the 100th base at Thorpe Abbotts. From what he had told me earlier I almost felt like asking him if he had been stationed there himself at one time.

[*I would like to believe that my queries about rank and location actually played into the major's vanity sufficiently to divert him from further interrogation. I may have saved myself more serious pressure for further information, and could have tricked him into wasting interrogation time. However, information I*

have already mentioned suggests that Major Waldschmidt was one of the clever-
est of the bomber crew interrogators. Many of the interrogators were highly skilled
and prided themselves on this. Hubert Zemke, one of the top American fighter
aces of World War II as well as Allied commandant of Stalag Luft I (see Free-
man 1991 b), was thoroughly interrogated after he had been shot down. Bailey
(1981, p. 18) reports Zemke as saying that Scharff, his interrogator, was so crafty
at eliciting information "that it might even be dangerous just to talk about the
weather with him." Considering interrogators' skills, it may well be, therefore,
that the major already had enough information about IFF and VHF procedures
as well as other technical and military material. He may have needed no more
from me to be sure of the reasons for such procedures. At any rate, my queries
did seem to direct attention away from me, and thus shorten the uncomfortable
technical questioning.]

At this point there was a knock on the door and the orderly appeared
once again to announce and present the next prisoner for interrogation. The
major told the orderly to take me to a new cell, the word "Gestapo" adding
greatly to my anxiety. Had I infuriated the major with my answers? With
my questions? I could only wonder what might be coming next, and why.

POLITICAL INTERROGATION

The orderly took me from the major's interrogation room down the
corridor and out of the large building where I had been held since arriving
at Dulag Luft. We went through a gate and just outside the perimeter fence
to a much smaller building. I was taken to a cell that was larger and much
cleaner than my earlier cell, and there was no unpleasant odor to contend
with. The cell had double bunks, and on each was a much plumper straw-
tick mattress with a cleaner blanket than the one I had before during solitary confinement. Was this really a Gestapo building? If so, why was it better? Could it mean better treatment—or worse?

[Even today it seems strange to say I was in a Gestapo building, yet I have
good reason to believe it was. I have located two diagrams of the Center that include
such a building just outside the perimeter fence. One, labeled "Dulag, Oberursel,
1942–43," shows a building 21 called "Interrogation and Prison Block for Gestapo
Nicknamed 'The Shelter.'" The diagram represents the Center as it was early in
the war, when the number of POWs being captured and interrogated was rela-
tively small. The number given in Cuddon (1952) and Flammer (1972) for the year
1942 was 3,000. By 1943 the number had grown to 8,000, and by 1944, when
the air war was at its height, the figure increased to 29,000. The Center was enlarged
over the years as shown in a diagram labeled "Dulag, Oberursel, December 1944."
This would have been shortly before I became a prisoner, and the diagram is thus
appropriate to my period of incarceration. The building in question is in the

same location as in the earlier diagram, and is called "Gestapo Offices and 'Cooler' for POWs Being Interrogated by the Gestapo."]

After the orderly locked me in and left, I examined my surroundings. I tried the lower bunk for comfort first, then clambered into the upper, which I selected as the more desirable because I could look directly through the cell's one small window. I had also noticed that the window seemed to have a handle for opening; I tried it, and to my delight the window swung open inwardly. There were bars on the outside of the window, but after being in the old cell, with no opportunity to see the outside world at all, it was a great pleasure to be able to look out again into the sunny but cold air.

My next surprise was the improved quality of the food. The diet was basically the same as previously, but the black bread had a thicker coating of either margarine or jam: I could easily taste it. Also, the soup provided at the noon meal was more in the nature of stew than the earlier watery mixture. Water was itself more readily provided, as was the ersatz coffee, by a guard who was also more quickly available to take me to the latrine when desired. My greater comfort could not, however, keep me from dreading the interrogation or worse I was sure to come. It seemed just a matter of when, why, and how.

Looking outside I could see, beyond some fields and buildings, a range of mountainous hills. From what the major had told me and from my own knowledge of the area as a navigator, I took them to be the Taunus Mountains. I fully enjoyed the view and kept the window open as much as possible until the cold air would force me to close it. My new surroundings could temporarily take my mind off the threat of being in a Gestapo prison and facing some unknown treatment.

[*The location of the building outside the perimeter fence is important to my story for two reasons. First, this location permitted me to see the Taunus Mountains from my cell window, since they lie to the north and west of the Center. The location thus again confirms for me that it was the Gestapo building that I was in. Second, several sources (e.g., Dillon, 1995; Toliver, 1978) point out that the Luftwaffe was reluctant to turn prisoners over to the Gestapo even though that was often used as a threat with recalcitrant airmen. Thus, the location outside the perimeter apparently represents the original desire of the Luftwaffe to have as little to do with the Gestapo as possible, especially where interrogation was concerned. Gestapo agents were apparently attached to the Center from its beginnings, but they never played a role in Center operations on a regular basis. They did play a part in certain cases, however, such as prisoners who evaded capture for a time, especially if they were helped by the underground and were found in civilian clothes rather than military uniform.*]

When my day of interrogation did come, it was again a surprise. My interrogator himself came to get me rather than an orderly. Unlike the major, he was dressed in civilian clothes, but was roughly about the same age and, like the major, was armed. He began the interview in a friendly way, inquiring about my welfare. He said that because of the war Germany could not offer me better quarters or diet. After all, he said, both were superior to what the brave German soldiers were getting at the front.

He offered me an American cigarette and lighted it for me. Since I had been on a severely restricted diet for some time by then, a small number of puffs began to make me feel faint and I extinguished it. That small matter seemed to have gotten me off to a poor start with my interrogator, since his demeanor seemed to register disgust at my wasting a good cigarette.

[*The significance of being offered a cigarette by both my previous and by my new interrogator may seem odd now. During the war, however, cigarettes were prized possessions in Europe generally, and in Germany particularly, especially American cigarettes. Tobacco factories in the United States operating at full capacity could not keep up with worldwide demand. Many fliers were heavy smokers (see Kaplan & Smith, 1983, p. 67) and cigarettes were confiscated when POWs were searched after capture. Smokers were, of course, likely to miss cigarettes at such tense times, and their importance to morale is shown by the fact they came in all Red Cross parcels given to POWs later (see Carlson, 1997 and Kaplan and Smith, 1983 for the contents of American Red Cross parcels given to prisoners). As a smoker myself, to be offered an American cigarette was, therefore, a gesture meant to cause me to let down my guard. And since interrogators' supplies of American cigarettes must have been very limited, to waste one was almost unforgivable.*]

After commenting about my background, my interrogator began talking about the "Godless Communists" in the Soviet Union and how uncultured they were. He mentioned the ways Germans were superior, and almost spat out the word "Godless" and also his references to the "Bolshevik Communists." He said Germans were much more like Americans than the Russians were, and that many Americans had actually come from Germany, as he mentioned my ancestors had. He said the United States would live to regret it if Germany was defeated because the Russians would attack Britain and the United States if Germany and the rest of Europe were overcome. He seemed genuinely puzzled as to why the United States and Britain had sided with the Godless Communists and attacked Germany. Now was the time, he said, to support Germany in the struggle.

This warning about the Soviet Union's intentions led to his encouragement for Americans, and clearly me, to consider joining with Germany in the fight against the Godless Communists, the Bolsheviks. He said that the road would be harsh since I would face the same dangers as the heroic German soldiers faced. He did say, however, that I could become part of the German service corps if I preferred. He emphasized that the rewards of joining with Germany in either role would be very satisfying and the world would be grateful when the Bolsheviks were defeated.

[*It may seem surprising with today's perspective to hear that many Germans felt it was still possible to win the war so late in January 1945, but Beevor (2002) provides clear evidence for this. Also, a German broadside given to me encouraged "Soldiers of the British Commonwealth!" and "Soldiers of the United States of America!" to join with Germany in the fight with the "barbaric asiatic East." The German efforts were aimed more directly at British than at American soldiers, and it is known that at least 30 or so British prisoners joined the Germans (West, 1964; Bailey, 1981) at some point. An outfit known first as the Legion of Saint George and later as the British Free Corps was set up to encourage this. Adnet (2001) also says that there were contingents of both French and Spanish fighting with the German armies, and Beevor (2002, p. 241) mentions Danes, Norwegians, Swedes, Finns, and Estonians in the 11th SS Division called Nordland. Several hundred thousand Russian prisoners were also said to have joined the Germans in order to fight Stalin (Bailey, 1981, p. 20).*

Was the German effort to recruit American POWs to the German cause successful? I have been able to find a record of only one American POW who joined the Germans (Toliver, 1978, p. 247ff, hardback edition). Some few others may also have done so, however; Foy (1981) cites a Red Cross figure of over 99% of, yet not all, American prisoners returning home. An all-out German counterattack in late 1944, the so-called Battle of the Bulge, seemed destined to turn the war around, yet most Americans realized that the Allies would be victorious eventually. An almost fanatic belief in German victory (Beevor, 2002) must have been what kept interrogators like mine at their almost hopeless job.]

I showed no interest in joining the German military under any conditions and made that clear. Even apart from my allegiance to the United States and hatred for Nazi policy, I indicated it would have been the utmost folly since in addition I felt sure the war could not last much longer and Germany would be defeated. My interrogator did not agree with that evaluation, but still returned to his earlier approach. Since Germany had so much in common with the United States in religious belief, culture, science, and art, the United States itself should be attacking the Godless Communists and supporting Germany. The Bolsheviks were a savage, barbaric nation, he said, whose rulers mistreated and killed their own people as well as the Germans. What had Germany done to deserve the treatment it was getting from the Allies?

Since this tirade had gone on for a time, I became courageous enough to say there were several reasons for this. One was attacking and overrunning neighboring countries, which he defended as necessary to protect mistreated Germans in those countries. I then mentioned the abuse and slaughter of the Jews in Germany and nearby countries. This angered him immediately, but he countered with American mistreatment of African Americans. I had no good defense for this, but it was clear that the session was not going as the interrogator had hoped. On my part, I made no further attempt to convince him that Germany's behavior could not be excused or overlooked. After all, he had the gun and he was angry.

By this time the interrogator must have known that he could not succeed in his effort to convince me to support the German effort either directly or indirectly. At any rate, the session was quickly over, and he took me to a room with piles of flyers' boots where other prisoners were also arriving from somewhere else. We were told to quickly put on a pair of boots and prepare to march. Little time was allotted for seeking out a pair of proper size. I ended up with a pair larger than desirable, but felt fortunate because some other prisoner probably ended up with boots too small, making marching difficult or even painful for him.

Even for me, the march to the next camp was not easy, since I had to manage a combination of lifting my feet and sliding them along using a left knee and ankle that were still painful. But I was out of the Center at last and had been told that I was on my way to a regular prison camp for the remainder of the war.

A march of about 56.5 kilometers took me and a group of about 30 other prisoners to Wetzlar, a temporary camp, where, on arrival, we were given hot drinks, food, and a chance to rest. I recall two initial impressions. First, seeing the familiar word "Zeiss" on a factory building as we entered the city, which from my interest in photography I knew must refer to the fine Zeiss lenses for Leica cameras made there. Second, scalding my throat drinking the hot chocolate that was so welcome after the long, cold march.

We were photographed and fingerprinted for German record purposes and various physical measurements such as height and weight were taken. Also, items of personal information were solicited, including name and address for next of kin. Several POWs refused to provide this kind of information, but most of us gave it willingly because the American commandant for POWs was present at the time. Since he was a POW himself and an Air Force colonel and did not discourage us from doing so, it seemed reasonable to comply then in contrast to the circumstances of the Red Cross interview.

We were also given articles of clothing, some of which fit, along with shaving equipment and a Red Cross food parcel in preparation for the coming trip to a permanent prison camp. This was the first such parcel most of us had seen, and the food looked irresistible, especially the small chocolate bar. We were cautioned, however, not to eat any of the food then since it would have to last for the entire trip. We were told it would be a dangerous trip of unknown duration because of the state of German transportation at the time. Happy as I was with the change in circumstances, I was left with many questions about the experiences I had faced.

[*How long I may have spent in solitary confinement in the Center is not clear, but I do have a rough idea. I know that I entered on January 3, 1945 because of the three memorable life-threatening events that day mentioned earlier. I also know that I was shipped on January 20 in a Forty and Eight boxcar (see Adnet, 2001) from Wetzlar to Stalag Luft I, the permanent POW camp in Barth, Germany. A few intervening days were spent in Wetzlar before going to Barth, so my best estimate is two weeks in solitary confinement and interrogation.*

I am certain the date of shipment was January 20 because I was able to find a copy of the military travel orders with my name on them in the files at the Washington National Records Center. They were declassified for me and I found them correct except for several typographical errors; even my prisoner number, 7556, is correctly listed. I still have my POW dog tags bearing this number and the inscription STALAG LUFT 1. The orders I found were in English, which puzzled me and suggested they were bogus. However, the librarian at the Records Center said German officials wanted to take back to Germany the originals of certain materials. They were said to have translated the travel orders and certain other such materials into English in return. Further evidence of the authenticity of the travel orders comes from the fact that of the 60 POWs listed, 20 of us ended up in the same room in Stalag Luft I for the remainder of the war.]

ANSWERS

As Frank Murphy (2001) puts it in his book, much of what happened to a particular combat flier in World War II can best be relegated to chance, to the "luck of the draw." Answers to the questions of "why" beyond the reality of military orders are hard to come by, and speculation may become mere storytelling. Perhaps searching out such factual information as "when" and "how," which Murphy accomplishes so well, may seem the best one can do.

However, my curiosity about the rationale for perplexing experiences could not be satisfied without an attempt to find answers for myself. Much of what happened surrounding my interrogations puzzled me, and I have been searching for answers to these questions since. In doing so here, I have tried to separate those experiences I can best consider matters of chance from those for which there may be plausible answers.

This difference can be shown in asking the question of why I was interrogated in the first place. At one level of explanation it was because I was shot down, along with eight other crew members. But why did *our* B-17 happen to go down? Roger Freeman's semiofficial records (1981, pp. 410–411) show that we were not alone: 12 aircraft from our 100th Bomb Group failed to return to base that day. I have searched for as many descriptions of the relevant air battle at Hamburg as I could find in order to get an idea why the number lost, 12 out of the 36 attacking the target, was so high.

Nilsson (1946) and Le Strange (1989) have provided a number of details about the mission, and I have also examined debriefing reports from crews that returned to base on December 31 and that are now stored at Bolling

Air Force Base (Klare, in press a). I now know, for example; the position of our B-17 in the larger formation; when some of the other B-17s went down; the lack of US fighter protection; the heavy concentration of German flak guns at the target; the nature of the German fighter attacks; and so on. But instead of one good reason why we were shot down, the number of possible contributors is both too large and uncertain to designate one. Thus the answer to why our B-17 was shot down is best left to chance.

Similarly, why did one of the soldiers who captured me and spared my life win out over another who wished to kill me? I could simply attribute this to good fortune. But on another level of explanation, it could also be because I did not have a pistol at the time. Since I cannot investigate further now, that answer will have to do.

Again, why did a particular Luftwaffe captain protect the nine of us from a mob in Fulda before we reached the Luftwaffe Interrogation Center? I can hypothesize that this was a matter of a fellow flier protecting even enemy comrades, which was known to happen in World War II as it did in World War I. Or perhaps it was a strong sense of duty, but I can never hope to discover a satisfactory answer today. A chance explanation will have to do.

When my own personal questions from then on arose, the search for answers could be more productive. Until the nine of us entered the Interrogation Center at Oberursel, Germany on January 3, 1945, our experiences were generally similar. The other eight remained in the Center only briefly, however, before being sent on to a permanent prison camp for the remainder of the war. This I know, because I was sent to the same permanent camp, Stalag Luft One, after the two other officers in the crew, the pilot and copilot, had already arrived; I met them there. The six enlisted crew members were similarly sent on quickly to a permanent camp for noncommissioned personnel.

Why was I the one kept on in solitary confinement and interrogated? When was the decision to hold me made? Why did my interrogations take the turns they did? Did the reasons change over time? Assembling the bits and pieces of information I had at that time with what I have gathered since World War II provides some of the "answers." I must label them thus because they are not the only possible ones. They are, at least, based on the best evidence I have been able to uncover, they remove some aspects of chance, and they make sense.

The first question concerns why only one person from a combat crew was kept on at the Interrogation Center. At earlier periods during World War II all surviving members of crews were held in solitary confinement and interrogated, according to Hanns Scharff (Toliver, 1978) and other sources. Once the number of downed fliers increased from 3,000 in 1942 to 29,000 in 1944 (see Flammer, 1972 and others), the Center became too crowded to hold entire crews. If there was no special reason to hold a particular crew member, officers became the choice. Both Scharff (Toliver, 1978, p. 358) and Dillon (1995, p. 59), citing Army Air Force Intelligence Summaries, report that information was more readily obtained from commissioned officers as a class than from noncommissioned officers. Several reasons, such as susceptibility to flattery, background, and treatment, are mentioned.

As the Center facilities became overburdened, often only one of the four commissioned officers in most bomber crews was kept on for interrogation. As noted earlier, our crew did not have a bombardier and therefore we had only three. Instead, a gunner trained as a togglier dropped the bombs when he saw a lead bombardier drop his bombs. A lead bombardier might well have been held if our crew had had one, because of knowledge of special target information, equipment used, etc.

Why I was held for interrogation rather than the pilot or copilot is not certain, though I believe I now have some reasonable answers. Navigators usually have more route and target information than pilots, and the military questions asked of me suggest that getting such information may be one reason I was held. Another was the fact I understood the German language, which by then had become known; neither the pilot nor the copilot had such knowledge. This meant I could have been a planted spy or, more likely, at least could be threatened as a possible spy. This tactic was known to have been used when also pressing other POWs to provide answers during interrogation.

Foy (1981) and Flammer (1972) have further pointed out that reactions of POWs during the Red Cross interviews were important in decisions about how to interrogate a particular POW. The pilot and copilot must have been given Red Cross interviews just after arriving at the Center as I was, but they were sent on to the permanent camp. Thus the impression I made during the Red Cross interview could also have played a part in the decision to interrogate me rather than one of them. I cannot know the answer for certain, but I do know certain relevant personal observations about my appearance were probably made and recorded, as indicated below.

In any case, at some point during my confinement a decision must have been made concerning how to interrogate me. The collection and use of detailed information about downed fliers for this purpose is well documented by Scharff (in Toliver, 1978), Foy (1981), Dillon (1995), Murphy (2001), and others. My file was available to the major who conducted the military interrogation, as I have mentioned, and as his personalized comments about me indicated. He even knew that I was a smoker at the time. But why did he not press further for military information than he did?

It seemed to matter little that I refused to answer detailed questions about the mission of my crew; the major appeared to realize he knew as much and probably more than I did. Also, the chief military questions, about the curtailing of IFF-type and VHF-type communications, may almost have been formalities. He could have correctly assumed this was because comments by fliers during combat often unnecessarily revealed information of use by Luftwaffe intelligence. Further confirmation may not have been needed.

I was surprised and pleased that, instead of further military questions asked of me, the major so readily answered *my* questions about Luftwaffe military rank and geographic location in Germany. At the time I thought I had misled or even outwitted him, but I doubt the likelihood of that, as I have mentioned. As noted earlier, the major was described (Toliver, 1978) as one of the best of the bomber section interrogators, so that seems unlikely. The most I probably could have accomplished was to use up some interrogation time that might have been devoted to further military grilling. But even that seems unlikely because the major could have sent me back to my solitary cell and recalled me later for interrogation if he had wanted more such information.

I now believe the major had a different rationale, at least by that point in time. He may well have taken my questions to be an indication—or an added indication—of some degree of sympathy with the German cause. He already knew of my knowledge of the German language. He knew my name, Klare, began with a "k" rather than a "c" which is typical of Germanic as opposed to English spelling of such a word. He even knew my mother's maiden name (Familienname der Mutter) was a Germanic-sounding "Launer." He may well also have known that my grandfather and grandmother were born in Germany, since his other information about me seemed so complete.

The possibility I might have, or be persuaded to have, sympathy for the German cause gets further support from another source. I was able to locate and take my so-called prisoner card from the files at Stalag Luft I shortly after May 1, 1945 when I was liberated. The first section contains expected identifying data, but the second section ("Nahere Personalbeschreibung") contains intimate personal data. The latter information could well have been carried forward from an earlier period, perhaps the Red Cross interview. The hand-written items on the card indeed suggest that information was entered at different times.

It is this kind of information on the card that is especially curious. Since the card is a standard form (see Merkki, nd, for an example), it must have been collected from other POWs as well as me. Was it just a matter of such physical information being of general interest in Germany and perhaps other countries at that time? Or was there another reason based on racial considerations?

Why such information would have been needed for identification purposes, say in an escape attempt, is puzzling. After all, the card already contains my picture from front and side and my thumb print. Perhaps the notation that my eyes were blue (Augen, blau) and my hair was blond (Haare, blond) might also be of some potential use for identification, but very little. I now believe there was indeed another possible purpose for gathering such information: for classification, i.e., to see whether a POW might or might not fit an "Aryan" versus a "Jewish" stereotype.

This could well have been the purpose for gathering the additional information about my other bodily characteristics, at least. Why else would straight nose shape (*Nase, gerade*), oval head shape (*Schadelform*, oval), and facial appearance (*Gesichtsform*, oval) be recorded? These descriptions would have added little if any useful identification information, but nose shape for example, however unreliable it might be as an indicator, would instead fit the classification assumption.

The only characteristic which might have contradicted this "Aryan" versus a "Jewish" classification in my case is that I was circumcised as a baby, a Jewish practice. This is not entered on my card, but could easily have been noted during one of my several strip searches. Perhaps the fact that circumcision was much more common in the United States than in Europe at the time would have rendered this distinction, as is true of many of the others, of little actual validity. This classification purpose seems highly probable, nevertheless, since German authorities often attempted to separate Jewish from non-Jewish POWs. It seems extremely unlikely that an attempt would have been made to persuade a Jewish POW to support the German cause, but does suggest why an attempt may have been made in my case.

In sum, my personal characteristics plus my questions to the major and my name and German heritage may have been among the bases for him to send me on to a political interrogation by the Gestapo officer. The increased interest of the Germans in recruiting POWs to their cause was shown by the broadside mentioned earlier. Also, by early 1945 political questions were sometimes asked during other interrogations (Dillon, 1995). Putting all this information together today, I have what seems to me a rationale for answers to my questions of *why* that initiated my quest, especially why *me*. And these answers will have to do, since finding unquestionable answers so long after the events occurred will no longer be possible—if indeed they ever were.

REFERENCES

Adnet, J. (2001). *When I see a "Forty-and-Eight. . . ."* Colorado Springs, CO: Adnet Tech.
Bailey, R. H. (Ed.). (1981). *Prisoners of war: World War II.* Alexandria, VA: Time-Life Books.
Beevor, A. (2002). *The fall of Berlin 1945.* New York: Viking Penguin.
Carlson, L. H. (1997). *We were each other's prisoners.* New York: Basic Books.

Cuddon, E. (Ed.). (1952). *Trial of Erich Killinger, Heinz Junge, Otto Behringer, Heinrich Eberhardt, Gustav Bauer-Schlichtegroll* (The Dulag Luft Trial). London: W. Hodge. War Crimes Trials Series, Vol. 9. Also includes a copy of the "Proceedings of a Military Court for the Trial of War Criminals" covering the above trial.

Dillon, C. F. (1995). *A domain of heroes.* Sarasota, FL: Palm Island Press.

Dulag Luft: American prisoners of war in Germany. (1944). Washington, DC: Military Intelligence Service, War Department, 15 July.

Ex-POW Bulletin. (2002). American prisoners of war in World War I, World War II, Korea, Vietnam, Persian Gulf, Somalia, Bosnia, Kosovo, and Afghanistan, March, 21–23.

Flammer, P. M. (Ed.) (1972). Dulag Luft: The Third Reich's prison camp for airmen. *Aerospace Historian, 19,* 58–62.

Foy, D. A. (1981). "For you the war is over": The treatment and life of United States Army and Army Air Corps personnel interned in POW camps in Germany, 1942–1945. Ph.D. dissertation, University of Arkansas.

Freeman, R. A. (1981). *Mighty Eighth war diary.* London: Jane's Publishing Company.

Freeman, R. A. (1991a). *Experiences of war—The American airman in Europe.* Osceola, WI: Motorbooks International.

Freeman, R. A. (1991b). *Zemke's Stalag: The final days of World War II.* Washington, D.C.: Smithsonian Institution Press.

Kaplan, P., & Smith, R. A. (1983.) *One last look: a sentimental journey to the Eighth Air Force heavy bomber bases in World War II England.* New York: Abbeville Press.

Klare, G. R. (1995). Keeping in touch. *Ex-POW Bulletin,* October, 25–26.

Klare, G. R. (1996). Blue books. *Ex-POW Bulletin,* November, 35–36.

Klare, George R. (in press a). The Bloody Hundredth's last big battle. *World War Two.*

Klare, George R. (in press b). USAAF Station No. 139, December 1944. *Splasher Six.*

Le Strange, R. (1989). *Century bombers: The story of the Bloody Hundredth.* Thorpe Abbotts, England: 100th Bomb Group Memorial Museum.

Merkki. (nd). The Interrogators link in World War II—Prisoners of war—Stalag Luft I. Retrieved from http://www.merkki.com/kriegies.htm.

Missing Air Crew Reports, Nos. 11365–11367. (1945). Report of capture of enemy air forces. January 30: Dulag Luft.

Murphy, F. D. (2001). *Luck of the draw: Reflections on the air war in Europe.* Trumbull, CT: FNP Military Division.

Nilsson, J. R. (1946). *The story of the Century.* Beverly Hills, CA: John R. Nilsson.

Scharff, H. J. (1950). Without torture. *Argosy, 38,* 87–90.

Toliver, R. F. (1978) *The interrogator: The story of Hanns Scharff, Luftwaffe's master interrogator.* Fallbrook, CA: Aero Publishers.

West, R. (1964). *The new meaning of treason.* New York: Viking Press.

Wilson, G. W. (1998). The enigma of a POW by an ex-POW. *Ex-POW Bulletin,* January, 22–23.

3

The Third Degree and the Origins of Psychological Interrogation in the United States

RICHARD A. LEO

INTRODUCTION

On August 1, 1930, Christine Colletti was murdered and left lying on the side of an abandoned road with five bullet wounds (e.g., Leo, 1994). Shortly after learning of his wife's death the next day, Tony Colletti, an 18-year-old Cleveland resident, accompanied plainclothes detectives to police headquarters for what he was told would be routine questioning. During the car ride to the station, Detectives Corso and Welch told Colletti that they knew "what really happened," instructing Colletti to "come clean" and tell them about the murder. Colletti responded, as he would continue to do many times over the next two days, that he did not know what the detectives were talking about, explaining that he had last seen his wife the night before and was as surprised as everyone else to learn of her murder.

At the station house during the next 26 hours, Colletti was questioned continuously in relays, lied to, threatened, yelled at, cursed, deprived of food and water, made to stand for hours, forced to stay awake, slapped, slugged with bare fists, stripped naked, and beaten with a rubber hose until

RICHARD A. LEO • Department of Criminology, Law and Society, University of California, Irvine, Irvine, California 92697-7080 (E-mail: rleo@uci.edu). I thank Dan Lassiter and Welsh White for helpful comments and Brynn Nodarse for helpful research assistance.

he no longer denied killing his wife and finally agreed to sign a confession statement acknowledging guilt.

In the beginning of Colletti's interrogation, Detective Hogan plied him with sympathy while commenting on Christine's bad reputation in the neighborhood. Hogan did not blame Colletti for killing his wife, he said; rather, he would have done the same thing in Colletti's place. After twenty minutes of polite questioning, however, Detective Cody stormed into the interrogation room, slamming two guns down on the table and stating angrily (though falsely) that the weapons had been found at Colletti's house and were used to kill Christine Colletti. When Colletti again denied the police accusations of guilt, detective Cody replied: "I'm going to get permission to abuse this fellow like they do in Detroit, hang him up by his feet, beat him up and kick him in the testicles—that will make him talk" (Leo, 1994, p. 2). Eventually Colletti would be physically assaulted and beaten, though not exactly in the manner Cody had threatened. But first Colletti was transferred between rooms at the Cleveland Police Department and questioned incommunicado in relays by Detectives Corso, Welch, Cody, Wolf and Hogan.

The detectives made Colletti stand facing, but not touching, a wall for hours as they continuously questioned and accused him, slapping Colletti every time he appeared to fall asleep. The detectives denied Colletti's requests for water and food, and did not permit Colletti to sit down or lean against the wall. Welch repeatedly struck Colletti with his fists on both sides of Colletti's body just below the ribs, and continually slapped Colletti in the back of the head, causing Colletti's face to strike the wall many times. Although the rooms changed and the detectives moved in and out, the physical assaults and deprivations continued for hours. The detectives repeatedly slapped Colletti in the back of the head and the face; they continuously hit Colletti (sometimes two detectives at once) on both sides of his body; they yelled and cursed at Colletti; and they threatened him with further violence if he did not confess, insisting that they would eventually make him talk. But Colletti continued to deny that he had killed his wife.

After hours of relentless grilling and frequent physical assaults, the detectives again moved Colletti to another room, and this time made him strip and lie down naked on a table. One of the detectives held Colletti's left arm with one hand and pushed his head downward with the other hand, while another detective held his right arm, and a third detective held his legs. Corso then pulled out a two-and-a-half-foot-long piece of rubber hose and proceeded to beat Colletti over his bare back and the soft hollows above his ribs for approximately an hour, intermittently asking him: "Will you talk?" Each time Colletti responded that he had nothing to say, again asserting his innocence. With his back, kidneys and sides swollen and bruised, Coletti finally stated: "I will say what you want me to say if you let up, stop beating me." As he got up from the table, Colletti added: "I don't know what you want me to tell you, but you can make up a statement and I will sign it."

Then, for the first time in more than 24 hours, the detectives provided Colletti with food and water. He was subsequently taken to another interrogation room to wait alone with two of the detectives as his statement was being typed up. When he told them he would not sign it, one of the detectives responded: "If you don't sign it, we'll give you the works worse than we did before." Shortly afterward, two detectives returned to the interrogation room and laid the typewritten paper in front of Colletti, informing him that it contained what he had told them. Colletti hesitated momentarily, but then quickly signed the statement without even first reading it. He was then treated by a police nurse and police doctor for his physical injuries, and subsequently taken to the jail. Only when he read the local newspaper the next day did Colletti discover the contents of the confession statement he had signed. The Cleveland Police Department subsequently denied beating or mistreating Colletti, claiming instead that his welts and bruises had been caused by sleeping on his side.

By the standards of the time, there was nothing unusual about the manner in which Cleveland detectives obtained a confession from Tony Colletti (Hopkins, 1931; Lavine, 1930; National Commission on Law Observance and Law Enforcement, 1931; hereinafter referred to as the Wickersham Report). Rather, Colletti's interrogation was in many ways representative of police methods as they were generally practiced in the early 1930s in the United States; frequently, detectives used far more violent and protracted methods to extract admissions of guilt (Hopkins, 1931; Lavine, 1930; Leo, 1992). What had come to be known in American popular culture as the "third degree"—the infliction of physical pain or mental suffering to extract information—was widely and systematically practiced in American police stations in 1930. Tony Colletti's case remained unremarkable for yet another reason: it never became the subject of an appellate court ruling or published court decision, and, as in virtually every instance of the third degree in that era, the detectives were never disciplined or punished for their extralegal actions. In short, American police routinely employed coercive interrogation practices at the beginning of the fourth decade of the twentieth century.

Yet only 10 years later, W.R. Kidd, a former Berkeley, California police lieutenant, would publish the first police interrogation training manual in American history, condemning third degree practices as "vicious and useless" (Kidd, 1940, pp. 45–46):

Third degree should never be used by the police because:

1. It does not produce the truth. Under sufficient torture, a man will tell you anything you want to know. If you build your case on this "confession" you may find in court the man could not possibly have committed the crime.

2. Evidence so obtained is not admissible in court, and defense attorneys are quick to develop the facts surrounding the securing of the statement.
3. Public confidence in the police is shattered if knowledge of such methods is publicized. Unless the suspect dies, it is difficult to prevent such publicity. If he dies, a terrific public protest is inevitable.

Under third degree, only three things can happen to the suspect:

1. He will tell anything desired.
2. He will go insane if the torture is severe enough.
3. He will die.

Perhaps the greatest harm done by third degree methods lies in the eventual harm to the department. Once the public is convinced such methods are used, it becomes extremely difficult for the police to convict anyone, no matter how guilty nor how good the police case. Judges and juries are ready to believe the defense contention that third degree methods were used. The case goes out the window. The police, unable to obtain convictions, take it out "first hand" on the criminals, usually with the nightstick, and the cycle becomes more and more vicious.

In the decade separating Tony Colletti's case and the publication of the first American police interrogation training manual, the third degree had become a national scandal: numerous media accounts and journalistic exposes, several Supreme Court decisions, and a well-known government commission report (the "Report on Lawlessness in Law Enforcement" from President Herbert Hoover's National Commission of Law Observance and Law Enforcement, which came to be popularly known as "The Wickersham Report" after its chair, former attorney general, George Wickersham; see earlier comment) all had condemned strong-arm interrogation methods and called for their immediate reform. Included in the chorus of criticism were many police leaders and trainers whose larger agenda was to professionalize the occupation of policing. In the 1940s and 1950s, several more interrogation training manuals—all exhorting detectives to avoid third degree practices altogether—would appear and be widely circulated among the nation's police departments. Whereas in the 1920s many police leaders and detectives had publicly defended third degree interrogation methods as necessary for controlling crime, by the 1940s police leaders universally condemned the third degree as immoral under all circumstances. With the spread of so-called "scientific" forms of crime detection as well as new training and education requirements, American police soon came to perceive the third degree not only as unethical and illegal, but also as less effective at eliciting confessions than modern interrogation techniques and thus ultimately as dispensable. As one FBI agent aptly noted, "The special agent questioning a prisoner uses no special compulsions . . . The third degree isn't necessary when you've got the facts. Special agents get the facts" (Purvis, 1936, p. 102).

The third degree, once widespread and systematic in American police departments, has long since been rooted out and become the exception, rather than the norm, in contemporary police work. Although direct evidence frequently has been difficult to come by, third degree interrogation methods appear to have declined dramatically in the 1930s and 1940s, and further still in the 1950s, though violence sometimes persisted in smaller and more rural departments. By the middle of the 1960s, however, the revolution in interrogation practices seemed complete: Police methods appeared to become entirely psychological in nature. Indeed, as the President's Commission on Criminal Justice and the Administration of Justice declared in 1967: "Today the third degree is virtually non-existent" (Zimring & Frase, 1979, p. 132). Police interrogators in the 1960s were no longer criticized for the use of force or duress or extended incommunicado detention, but instead for failing to properly announce the judicially created rights to silence and counsel prior to commencing any custodial questioning. Although today's media occasionally report police violence and physical abuse during custodial questioning, police critics and human rights groups agree that third degree interrogation practices occur very infrequently in contemporary the United States today.

In this chapter, I will describe and analyze third degree interrogation in nineteenth- and early twentieth-century America. My goal is not merely to document the history of the third degree in the United States but to deepen our understanding of the historical backdrop and larger context in which modern psychological interrogation emerged in the 1940s. Although the third degree is, for the most part, a relic of the distant past, its demise represents a crucial turning point in the history of American police investigation. To fully understand the evolution, character, and logic of contemporary psychological interrogation practices, it is essential to take a closer look at the history and logic of third degree interrogation in the United States. For modern psychological interrogation grew out of the third degree and, in many ways, has been a response to the excesses, criticisms, and contradictions of third degree interrogation. Modern psychological interrogation and the third degree are, therefore, historically and logically intertwined. By studying the third degree, we gain a deeper understanding of the roots, context and, contradictions of contemporary police interrogation.

I will begin with a detailed description and analysis of the various kinds and types of third degree interrogation. It is important to understand both the physical and psychological components of the third degree. After canvassing the varieties of third degree interrogation, I will locate the third degree in its historical context. I will then discuss how the ideology and practice of so-called "scientific" lie detection and psychological interrogation—as manifested in the early interrogation training manuals—came to replace the third degree following the Wickersham Commission's Report in the 1930s. Both practically and ideologically, American police sought to overcome the taint of the third degree scandals by creating human lie detectors and psychological manipulators who could more effectively hide the interrogation process from public scrutiny and thus more legitimately elicit admissions of guilt and more effectively help prosecutors win convictions than their earlier counterparts.

THE THIRD DEGREE

The "third degree" is an overarching term that refers to a variety of coercive interrogation strategies, ranging from psychological duress such as prolonged confinement to extreme physical violence and torture. As Ernest Jerome Hopkins (1931) wrote in the heyday of the third degree: "There are a thousand forms of compulsion; our police show great ingenuity in the variety employed" (p. 194). Although there were many interrogation techniques involving violence and duress, there was also considerable overlap in third degree methods. There were purely physical techniques, purely psychological techniques, and many techniques that incorporated both physical and psychological components. Whether physical, psychological or both, some of the techniques were simple and straightforwardly coercive while others were more sophisticated and orchestrated. Regardless, the third degree, in its myriad forms, contained a master psychological logic—the infliction of assault and terror—in order to elicit compliance and extract admissions. To better understand the overlapping forms and logic of coercive interrogation in early American policing, we can divide the third degree into several different subcategories. Each type of third degree interrogation (and often more than one at a time) was routinely and systematically practiced in most American police stations through at least the early 1930s.

PHYSICAL FORCE AND PHYSICAL ABUSE

Direct Physical Abuse

Most fundamentally, coercive interrogation entailed direct and explicit use of physical violence. Suspects were beaten under the kneecaps and on the knees, across the abdomen, the throat, the head, the shoulders, above the kidneys, on the buttocks, in the pit of the stomach, across the hands and thighs, and on the legs; kicked in the face, crotch, stomach, abdomen, torso, ribs and shins (sometimes while another officer was holding down or stomping the other foot and for which some departments had special instruments); clubbed with nightsticks and blackjacks; hit with pistol butts, leather saps loaded with lead, slabs of wood, chairs, and baseball bats; whipped with rubber hoses and leather straps; beaten on the soles of bare feet with copper-bound rulers; and punched across the body and in the face, most commonly with clenched fists, sometimes with brass knuckles, less frequently with boxing gloves (*Harvard Law Review*, 1930; Hopkins, 1931; Lavine, 1930; Wickersham Report, 1931). Sometimes suspects would be "roughed up" and showered with blows while they were handcuffed (or their hands were held or tied behind their backs), sometimes kicked and stamped on by a group of officers, sometimes clubbed and felled from behind with no forewarning (Lavine, 1930). Variations included holding up or hanging a (typically handcuffed) suspect over the top of an open door and pretending that he was a human punching bag, taking two or three running steps across the room and striking the suspect in the pit of his stomach, clubbing suspects repeatedly at the point of the knee jerk reflex in order to cause temporary paralysis, and the "triple blow" method of three direct punches struck directly over the heart. Suspects were knocked onto the floor, knocked across the room, knocked down flights of stairs and sometimes knocked unconscious (Leo, 1994; Sutton, 1976; Wickersham Report, 1931).

The injuries suspects received from direct physical assaults frequently (though not always) left physical marks. Some police beatings (referred to in police jargon as "hospital cases") were so vicious that suspects required immediate medical aid, and some suspects spent days, even weeks, recovering from their injuries. Like the police methods themselves, the injuries from third degree violence were varied and numerous. One reads of broken ribs, arms, hands, and noses; bruised and discolored backs, legs, arms and faces; lacerated and bloodied flesh, sometimes cut to the bone; broken, loosened and knocked out teeth; concussions, deep scalp wounds, and fractured skulls; and in a few instances gouged out eyes (*Harvard Law Review*, 1930; Lavine, 1930; Murphy, 1929; Wickersham Report, 1931; Villard, 1927). In rare cases suspects were beaten so severely that they subsequently died in custody or in jail (Ageloff, 1928). Police reporters and prison personnel frequently viewed healthy individuals entering police stations in good shape and subsequently leaving with bloodied clothing, bruises, cuts, and swollen faces (Murphy, 1929; Wickersham Report, 1931). Judges sometimes asked suspects to remove articles of clothing, and observed that their bodies looked like raw meat (Leo, 1994). One Magistrate interviewed by the Wickersham Commission for example complained that some suspects would come into the court with their faces so bandaged that only their eyes showed (Leo, 1994).

Although third degree violence was widespread, as documented by the Wickersham Commission's investigations, rarely were non-police personnel allowed to witness actual interrogations. New York reporter Emanuel Lavine (1930, 1936), however, spent twenty-five years observing the police in action, including custodial interrogations of criminal suspects. Lavine reported that the brute application of physical force—what the police referred to as a "shellacking," "massaging," or "workout"—was routine and systematic during stationhouse questioning, estimating that seventy percent of criminal cases were solved by confessions wrung from in-custody suspects. Lavine (1930) witnessed one suspect, who, with his head pulled back, was repeatedly and forcibly beaten across the Adam's apple with a blackjack until blood spurted out of his mouth and halfway across the room. In another interrogation, Lavine (1930) observed two suspects who were first beaten with a lead pipe, and then transferred to another police station, where they were beaten by a gang of officers as they lay prostrate on the floor, during which six nightsticks were broken. Lavine (1930) also witnessed police officers who would press both of their fists inward against a suspect's jaw with such force that it dislocated, and in some instances, broke the bone. The more intransigent the suspect, noted Lavine, the more physical punishment they received. Above all, however, Lavine repeatedly emphasized the banality of police brutality during interrogation: "There is nothing, from the police point of view, exceptional or startling in the application of the third degree; it is simply a part of the normal routine" (Lavine, 1930, p. 5).

Lavine's grisly and detailed account of rampant third degree violence is corroborated by the first-hand accounts of other sources, including other police reporters who observed violent interrogations, suspected criminals receiving the third degree, and the police officers themselves who administered it. Like numerous police reporters interviewed by the Wickersham Commission, Sedgwick (1927), for example, observed that "blow after blow [was given the prisoners] from the rubber hose, black jacks, and nightsticks. The prisoners fall to the floor. The blood pours from their faces. They spit and cough blood" (p. 667). Willie Sutton (1976), a well-known thief, described one of his many experiences with third degree interrogation years later in his autobiography:

> Blackjacks came lashing out at me from around the whole perimeter. All around me they were swinging and cursing. A telephone book came down on my head with such force that lights seemed to go popping all around me . . . After I had been ordered to strip, my hands were cuffed behind my back and I was picked up and thrown on top of the table with my stomach sticking up. There were six detectives . . . they started to beat me methodically from my private parts all the way up to my neck. Then they turned me over and beat another tattoo on my back. When they were finished, my skin was completely black. I was one solid contusion, front and back. A slab of quivering pain. And then they turned me over and started all over again. Unbearable! (pp. 110–111)

Other documented forms of direct physical abuse used during interrogation included rubbing lighted cigars against a suspect's feet, arms, neck, or bare chest (Lavine, 1930; O'Sullivan, 1928); torturing a suspect with lighted matches, sometimes burning his skin with red hot pokers (Leo, 1994); tying a suspect's hands around a hot water pipe in the station house or placing a suspect's body against a furnace, sometimes badly burning a suspect's flesh (Murphy, 1929; O'Dwyer, 1987); lifting, kicking, squeezing, or twisting a suspect's testicles, sometimes at regular intervals, causing severe pain, fainting, and in at least one instance emasculation (Hopkins, 1931; Wickersham Report, 1931); blindfolding suspects while administering punishment (*Harvard Law Review*, 1930); hanging a suspect by his thumbs, a thumb and a foot, or by his neck from a rafter until he lost consciousness (Hopkins, 1931; Leo, 1994); forcing a suspect to remove his shoes and climb criss-crossed iron stairways with sharp points, causing his feet to bleed (Larson, 1932; Leo, 1994); banging a suspect's head against a wall during questioning (Wickersham Report, 1931); applying acid to a suspect's genitals (Hopkins, 1931); pressing a penknife or pins under a suspect's fingernails (Murphy, 1929); and, in one instance, enlisting a dentist to grind down and drill into the nerves of a suspect's molars (Lavine, 1930).

Despite the blanket denials by many police leaders, detectives sometimes wrote or spoke publicly about the unrestrained violence they administered during interrogation. Michael Fiaschetti (1930a, 1930b, 1930c) wrote newspaper editorials and magazine articles describing his violent practices, which sometimes involved the use of sawed-off baseball bats and caused blood to be spattered on the walls and ceiling of interrogation rooms. William Severyns, a retired Police Chief, regularly wrote newspaper articles describing the brutal third degree practices of Seattle detectives (Villard, 1927). Cornelius Willemse, a New York Captain of detectives and prolific popular author wrote (1931) that he had beaten up hundreds of criminals "with fist, blackjack, and hose" during custodial interrogation (p. 354). In sum, criminal suspects were regularly beaten, whipped, punched, kicked, and mauled by their interrogators. Sometimes the beatings lasted for hours on end and were administered by multiple officers.

Deniable Physical Abuse

Many physically or psychologically coercive interrogation tactics were intended to be deniable in a court of law, for police well knew that visible marks might arouse the sympathy of judges and juries, or perhaps even cause the district attorney not to use the confession at all. The most famous of these tactics was the use of a rubber hose—which did not break the skin and therefore tended not to leave visible physical marks—to beat a confession out of a reluctant suspect (Wickersham Report, 1931). A variation of this tactic, known as "the taps," involved tying a suspect to an armchair and then striking him on the side of the head at thirty-second intervals. Although the blows were not hard enough to bring on unconsciousness and although the welts disappeared within a few hours, they caused considerable pain and thereafter left the point of contact sensitive for as long as several months (Lavine, 1930; Franklin, 1970). Although the rubber hose was certainly the most well known, and probably the most common method of inflicting pain without leaving marks, police also used garden hoses, pieces of tire, blackjacks soaked in water or wrapped in a handkerchief or covered with soft leather, and sausage-shaped sandbags lined with silk to accomplish the same effect (Johnson, 1979; O'Sullivan, 1928; Wickersham Report, 1931). Suspects were also poked in the ribs with a blackjack or flogged with telephone books, the force of which frequently knocked men down, if not temporarily unconscious (Franklin, 1970; Wickersham Report, 1931). Sometimes a suspect was seated on a bench between two detectives who questioned him alternately, jarring the suspect with an elbow to his ribs, a shove with the heel of their hands to his chin, or a slap on the suspect's face each time he provided a negative answer (Leo, 1994). Another common method was hitting a suspect with a "fist to the wind," (i.e., blow to the solar plexus) not only because it weakened the suspect without leaving marks but also because the suspect quickly recovered (Leo, 1994). Other prominent forms of deniable coercion included administering tear gas on a suspect; choking a suspect with a necktie; bringing a suspect to the morgue to view and touch the body of the individual whom they were accused of murdering (Black, 1927; Larson, 1932; Wickersham Report, 1931; Willemse, 1931); bending a suspect's fingers or twisting his wrists or arms backwards (Henderson, 1924); forcing a suspect to stand up for hours on end, often while manacled (Wickersham Report, 1931); and, of course, threats of harm, which I will discuss separately below.

In addition to these methods, detectives sometimes used specific strategies to conceal their coercions. For example, interrogators often focused on beating certain areas of the body—such as the back, the pit of the stomach, or the kidneys and above the hipbones—that were less likely to blister or bleed (Booth, 1930; Larson, 1932; Wickersham Report, 1931). An unwritten rule in many police departments was to avoid hitting suspects above the shoulders precisely because physical marks were more likely to show. Sometimes detectives delayed letting a doctor see a suspect to give the bruises time to disappear. Sometimes detectives intentionally disguised their identity—by forcing a suspect to stand facing a wall or by wearing masks—so that they could not be identified in court. And sometimes the arresting officer or detective would turn the "rough work" over to another detective, so that he could truthfully assert in court that he had neither touched the suspect nor seen him harmed by other police (Hopkins, 1931).

Other documented forms of deniable physical abuse included: placing ropes or towels around the neck of a bound suspect that were sufficient to choke him (Larson, 1932; Leo, 1994; *New Republic*, 1930); placing a large wooden box over the suspect's head and then releasing tear gas into the box (Leo, 1994); dragging, pulling, or lifting a suspect by their hair, sometimes pulling it out of their head and stuffing it in their mouths (Hopkins, 1931; Lavine, 1930; Murphy, 1929); forcing a suspect to strip and placing him in an interrogation cell with sub-freezing temperatures (Booth, 1930; Murphy, 1929; Willemse, 1931); and stripping a suspect and immersing him into a tub filled with crushed ice and cold water (O'Sullivan, 1928).

Orchestrated Physical Abuse

The infliction of pain or anguish during interrogation was sometimes more subtle and elaborate than the direct application of brute force, though no less coercive. The famous Sweat Box treatment dates back to the Civil War and was a standard interrogation tactic in some police departments (Franklin, 1970; Haller, 1976). This involved placing a suspect sometimes for hours or days at a time in a small, dark cell adjoined by a stove in which miscellaneous materials were used to stir a fire that produced scorching heat and pungent odors. Sickened, perspiring, and not able to endure the rising temperature, the suspect was compelled to confess in order to escape these unbearable conditions (Sylvester, 1910; Wickersham Report, 1931). The Water Cure consisted of holding a suspect's head in water until he almost drowned; or thrusting a water hose into his mouth or down his mouth; or forcing a suspect to lay on his back (if not already strapped to a cot or slab) while pouring water into his nostrils, sometimes from a dipper, until he was nearly strangled (O'Sullivan, 1928; Wickersham Report, 1931).

While the Water Cure represents a modern day variation of the method of water torture that was popular during the Middle Ages, police interrogators relied on modern technology as well. Another method of torture was to force suspects to walk barefoot on an electrically wired mat or floor carpet, causing sparks to fly and the suspect to scream and dance with agony until he confessed or fainted (Villard, 1927). A variation of this method was to strap a suspect into a makeshift or real electric chair and administer electric shocks until the suspect confessed (*Harvard Law Review*, 1930; *International Police Magazine*, 1911; *Los Angeles Evening Express*, 1929; Wickersham Report, 1931). In one city, police invented a technique colloquially known as "the electric monkey," consisting of a storage battery connected to a step-up device with two terminals: one pole was put against the suspect's spine, and another pole was held in the suspect's hands as currents were charged through his body (Hopkins, 1931).

Another ingenious instrument of third degree torture was the so-called "cannon ball," a tactic that involved placing a heavy cannon ball several feet above the floor in a box that was fastened to a wall. Police closed the box with a sliding door, to which a trap was affixed and annexed to a cord. The trap, when sprung, opened the door and released the cannon ball. The suspect would be bound and placed upon the floor immediately under the box so that if the door opened the cannon ball would fall directly on his head and crush it. One of the suspect's legs was then elevated at right angles to his body, and the cord attached to the spring was tied around his ankle, so that if he moved his leg toward the floor at all the trap would be sprung and the cannon ball released. When placed in this position the suspect was taunted by police, who insisted that he was weakening, and thus the cannon ball would soon be released and crush his head (*Los Angeles Evening Express*, 1929; Villard, 1927).

Perhaps the most well-known interrogation tactic in American culture is the so-called "Good Cop/Bad Cop" act or "Mutt and Jeff" routine, in which a pair or team of detectives attempt to extract a confession by alternating between hostile and sympathetic appeals to the suspect. The "Good Cop/Bad Cop" act used to be routinely violent, typically involving the use of physical force as well as psychological appeals. Long after his conviction, a suspect described this technique in detail to a police reporter who was subsequently interviewed by the Wickersham Commission (Leo, 1994):

> He [the reporter] stated that Schlager's confession was obtained by alternate beatings and 'sympathy,' over a period of two days or more . . . Schlager told him that he was not allowed to sleep, but that policemen would enter his cell at night, in the dark, and use their fists, elbows and feet. They would disappear, and then would enter an officer named Burns—described as a grey haired, kindly-looking man—who posed as Schlager's "friend." Burns would hear Schlager's complaint of mistreatment and express indignation. "Who were they? Tell me and I'll report them—I'll have them thrown off the force." Schlager could not identify them because of the darkness. Burns would promise an investigation; also he brought Schlager coffee, cigarettes, etc., and then would disappear. Soon afterward the strong-arm squad would enter his cell again and "put him through" some more; then Burns would come in again . . . [after two to four nights] the man was worn down and finally confessed to Burns. (p. 34)

PSYCHOLOGICAL ABUSE AND DURESS

Incommunicado Interrogation

According to the Wickersham Report, the most common form of coercive interrogation consisted of prolonged, incommunicado questioning under conditions of extreme psychological pressure. The purpose of incommunicado interrogation was to elicit a confession while hiding suspects from friends, family, and especially, their attorneys and the courts. Suspects were detained for long periods—usually twenty-four to ninety-six hours at a time, less frequently for one to two weeks—and questioned in relays without cease, sometimes without pause for rest or food or even a chance to sit down (Wickersham Report, 1931). Sometimes suspects were not even booked prior to questioning; sometimes their arrests were concealed from the police blotter for days at a time so that no attorney could locate them (a common police practice that was known as "losing" the suspect); sometimes police misled counsel or friends as to the suspect's place of detention; sometimes police charged suspects with a different unsolved felony case every forty-eight hours; and sometimes suspects were forced or tricked into signing affidavits disavowing their attorneys altogether (Hopkins, 1931; Lavine, 1930; Wickersham Report, 1931). With such tactics, police frequently succeeded in delaying a suspect's arraignment before a magistrate for days, even weeks, at a time. Although defense attorneys sometimes filed *habeaus corpus* writs requesting permission to see their clients, judges often delayed the operation of the writ (and thus delayed the time at which the suspect must be returned) so as to permit police more time to obtain confessions (Hopkins, 1931).

During incommunicado interrogation detectives often "grilled" and "sweated" suspects in exhaustive relay questioning that frequently involved severe verbal bullying of the accused. The overriding purpose of incommunicado interrogation was to elicit a confession by inducing extreme exhaustion and fatigue. One common and well-known tactic during incommunicado questioning was to shine a bright, blinding strobe light continuously on a suspect's face, though sometimes alternating it on and off. Another strategy was to require a suspect to remain standing upright for hours on end, slapping or jolting him whenever his knees sagged or he started to fall asleep (Wickersham Report, 1931). In some cities, suspects were frequently transferred between a dozen or more police stations, generally for two to three days at a time (or until there was a risk that an attorney might find them), an experience that could last up to six weeks and usually left suspects in terrible physical condition (Clark & Eubank, 1927; Wickersham Report, 1931). During such trips, suspects were often physically beaten, provided with short rations of food and water, not allowed to wash, and forced to sleep on hard benches or cement floors. Suspects were confined in overcrowded "incommunicado" or "third degree" cells that were cold, dark, damp, filthy, window-less, and sometimes infested with cockroaches, mosquitoes or rats (Hopkins, 1931; Limpus, 1939; Wickersham Report, 1931). In sum, suspects were held in solitary confinement or in crowded and unsanitary cells for days and weeks at a time until they confessed. The frequent police practice of incommunicado interrogation essentially amounted to illegal kidnapping of the accused.

Food, Sleep, and Other Deprivations

Related to incommunicado interrogation was the use of physical duress to induce admissions and confessions, particularly through the deprivation of food, drink, sleep, or toilet facilities. By preying on a suspect's physical dependencies, a skillful interrogator could break down resistance to confession. A suspect's food and drink could be withheld for days at a time; a suspect could be kept awake to the point of extreme exhaustion, or regularly woken or harassed after brief periods of sleep. Another tactic was to keep drugs—ranging from tobacco to heroin—from an addict until he confessed (Larson, 1932; Lavine, 1930; Wickersham Report, 1931). According to Willemse (1931):

> A drug addict is easy. Bring him into your office after he has been deprived for a long period of the drug he craves. Wild for a sniff or a jab, he sees on your desk a package of cocaine, heroin or morphine. "A Sniff when you open up, not before!" Hours of that treatment, while he gets wilder by the minute, his whole body crawling for a shot. He breaks in the end, always. (p. 351)

Police not only provided drugs to addicts as a reward for confession, but also provided addicts with drugs (most commonly alcohol and marijuana) prior to interrogation to induce admissions (Booth, 1930; Leo, 1994). A variation on this tactic was to starve a suspect and then place before him an elaborately prepared meal, permitting him to eat only after he confessed (Clark & Eubank, 1927; Larson, 1932; O'Sullivan, 1928). More commonly, police used so-called "truth-serum" drugs to induce confessions from suspects. Typically police directed physicians to inject suspects with scopolamine hydrobromide, morphine, chloroform or sodium amytal (Hopkins, 1931). In one city, police arranged for physicians to examine suspects prior to questioning, tell the suspect he had an incurable disease, and then subsequently administer a shot "to help" the suspect (Leo, 1994). While these so-called "truth-serum" drugs initially anesthetized suspects, police believed that as the drug began to wear off it produced a "twilight sleep" that simultaneously depressed the brain's creative capacities while leaving memory intact, thus eliminating the possibility of lying in response to questions (Mulbar, 1951). Although it prompted suspects to be talkative, once the "truth-serum" drug had worn off altogether the suspect supposedly could not recall anything he had told the police (Gottschalk, 1961). For many years, leading police trainers and researchers at the Scientific Crime Detection Laboratory in Chicago experimented with various "truth-serum" potions as a means of extracting confessions in detective work (Leo, 1994).

Explicit Threats of Harm

The coercive power of threats rests on the psychological intimidation and fear they produce. Suspects were often threatened with death or severe bodily injury: they were hung out of windows or down staircases (sometimes upside down and handcuffed or manacled at the ankles), threatened with mob violence or violence to their family and children, or were told at gunpoint that they would be shot and killed instantly if they did not confess (Hopkins, 1931; Larson, 1932; Lavine, 1930; Wickersham Report, 1931).

As one police official told the Wickersham Commission, "The whole idea was to jump him at the start, make him think he was going to be killed if he didn't talk" (Leo, 1994, p. 44). Lavine (1930) witnessed interrogations in which officers placed a gun against the temple of suspects, discharging blank cartridges until they confessed (known as the "black gun treatment"). Police sometimes also threatened, for example, to place suspects in an electric chair, to pour acid on their bodies, to prod out their eyes with garden forks, or to punch suspects in the face with brass knuckles (Wickersham Report, 1931; Hopkins, 1931). At other times suspects were merely threatened with incommunicado imprisonment or prosecution for additional crimes if they did not confess (Hopkins, 1931; Wickersham Report, 1931). And sometimes the threats remained implicit, as when suspects were told, for example: "You'll stay here for good unless you talk. You know how to get out of here if you want to" (Leo, 1994; p. 44)

Another kind of threat involved mock executions—arranging for the sound of loud screams, groans of agony, the thud of falling bodies, and other bloodcurdling noises to emanate from an adjacent room. This technique was intended to suggest that the suspect would receive comparable treatment if he did not confess (Franklin, 1970) or perhaps that an innocent party would continue suffering until the suspect confessed (Larson, 1932). In this context, many suspects were threatened with physical assault, as the officer rolled up his sleeves, retrieved a rubber hose, or clenched his fists (Wickersham Report, 1931). Willemse (1931) describes this well:

> I rolled up my sleeves and flexed the muscles of my arms and hands. I opened a drawer of my desk. The prisoner could see blackjacks and lengths of rubber hose. A careful selection, and I drew out a long, black piece of hose, testing it in my hands and then with a swish through the air before placing it on top of the desk. A loud moan from the next room, breaking off into sobs. The door opened suddenly. There stood the two detectives, ready for more action. Coats and vests off, shirt-sleeves rolled up, hair disarranged "One minute boys. I'll call you if you're needed!" The sound of groans had swelled. As the door closed again there came a stifled shriek. At last I spoke to the prisoner. (pp. 345–346)

THE THIRD DEGREE IN AMERICAN HISTORY

Following their invention in England, modern police forces emerged in most American cities during the middle of the nineteenth century. Controlled by political machines rather than an independent judiciary, early American police departments typically were brutal and corrupt. Since custodial questioning has always been an invisible or "back room" event in American policing, direct historical evidence about the origins of the third degree, as well as police interrogation practices in the nineteenth century more generally, is extremely difficult to obtain. The term "third degree" appears to have become synonymous with coercive interrogation in popular parlance around the turn of the century (Keedy, 1937), though its usage in police circles dates back at least to the 1870s (Walling, 1887). While there is some debate over the origins of this colloquial term, the "third degree" appears to have originally referred to the rigorous tests necessary to attain the master rank in free masonry and was subsequently transposed in police folklore to signify the third stage of the criminal investigation process, following physical arrest and custodial confinement (Deakin, 1988; Morris & Morris, 1988). Whatever the origins of the term, the third degree is one type of police brutality. Formally, its characteristic features are that (a) it typically occurs during custodial detention; (b) it involves the use of physical force or psychological duress; and (c) its fundamental purpose is to extort admissions and confessions of guilt from criminal suspects.

Due to the paucity of direct historical evidence available on interrogation practices in the nineteenth century, it is unclear whether the third degree was practiced systematically by American police from their inception or became a regular investigative method in the latter decades of the nineteenth century. Although this will remain an open historical question in the absence of better primary sources, there is evidence that the use of some third degree tactics—such as the sweat box, the hanging of suspects by the neck, and the use of incommunicado detention—date back to the middle of the nineteenth century (Franklin, 1970; Sears, 1948; *San Francisco Chronicle*, 1859). In both newspapers and the secondary historical literature, one finds scattered anecdotes and references to the third degree throughout this era yet it is difficult to discern any clear patterns until the final decades of the nineteenth century. Nevertheless, it is likely that coercive interrogation was regularly practiced by American police throughout the nineteenth century both as a method of obtaining evidence and as a method of retribution. Friedman (1993) has noted:

> Thousands of nineteenth-century tramps and thieves were beaten, coerced, arrested, thrown into jail, all without lawyers. They confessed after long stretches of the third degree, and almost nobody uttered a murmur of protest—certainly not the tramps, and thieves; but neither did their advocates, if they had any. (p. 303)

Evidence that the third degree was a routine and systematic police practice becomes clearer toward the end of the nineteenth century. At least one police writer has credited Thomas Byrnes—a well-known New York police officer who was appointed captain in 1870, commanding officer of the detective bureau in 1880, and chief inspector in 1888—with inventing the third degree (Larson, 1932; Editorial, 1910); others have suggested that the term third degree is a play on Byrnes' name (Scheck, Neufeld, & Dwyer, 2000). As Reppetto (1978) has written, Byrnes "was a noted practitioner of the third degree, utilizing both physical beatings and psychological tortures like the sweat box, a small room where the prisoner would be kept for days with no human contact, being fed by an unseen hand" (p. 53). Byrnes regularly employed physical violence on criminal suspects and others who overstepped acceptable social boundaries, so much so that New York police chief George Walling referred to Byrnes' office as a star chamber in which retribution was meted out. Following their interrogation, Byrnes' suspects regularly appeared in Magistrate's courts badly injured, bruised and bandaged, some so weak they could hardly stand (Leo, 1994).

Though Byrnes may have been the most well-known and vocal advocate of third degree practices at the time, he surely was not alone. Newspapers and the popular media frequently reported allegations of third degree violence in the closing decades of the nineteenth century. Moreover, police biographies and autobiographies, as well as journalistic accounts by police reporters and others, provide first-hand observations that the third degree was rampant in New York City and elsewhere from the latter part of the nineteenth century through at least the first three decades of the twentieth century (Clark & Eubank, 1927; Lavine, 1930; Sedgwick, 1927; Willemse, 1931). As one older detective, reminiscing about the era of Thomas Byrnes in New York, told the Wickersham Commission: "The old methods were brutal, and there wasn't any limit" (Leo, 1994, p. 21).

At the turn of the century, the local media would frequently publish allegations or accounts of brutality during interrogation that were virtually always ignored or denied by police departments (Haller, 1976). The third degree did not first become a national issue until 1910, however, when allegations of custodial violence in two cases that were widely reported in the media prompted the United States Senate to appoint a select committee to investigate custodial abuses by federal law enforcement agencies (*Journal of American Institute of Criminal Law and Criminology*, 1912). Although public perceptions of the third degree had roused their concern in preceding years, police leaders reacted to the appointment of the senate committee with much concern and discussion at the Annual meeting of the International Association of Chiefs of Police (the leading professional police organization of the time) in 1910. Although some participants spoke of the need for tough methods in apprehending criminals, most police chiefs, notably President Richard Sylvester of Washington, D.C., denied the existence of third degree practices altogether and attributed "this time worn and antiquated unfair criticism" to "the product of sensations and romances" (Dilworth, 1976, p. 72). Nevertheless, the IACP adopted a resolution to "go on record as stating it is their aim and intention to at all times condemn such practice and to punish those guilty, if possible." As Walker (1977) has noted, the police chiefs mounted a scattershot defense which, ironically, included not only denying the use of third degree methods but also blaming private detectives for existing abuses, just as later police writers would attribute the existence of allegations of third degree methods to the fabrications and exaggerations of "shyster" defense attorneys, sensationalizing journalists and the accused suspects themselves (Mathewson, 1929; Van Wagner, 1938).

The Senate Select Committee to Investigate the Administration of the Criminal Law by Federal Officials similarly mounted a scattershot defense, reporting that (a) convincing evidence of brutality would be difficult to obtain because no witnesses were present at police questioning; (b) their sole source of information on police practices came from interviewing federal officials; and (c) even had they discovered the existence of police abuses, Congress possessed the power to legislate only against third degree practices employed by federal, not state, officials. The Senate committee seemed especially impressed by the testimony of then Attorney General George Wickersham, who (ironically, as it would later turn out) testified that he believed no third degree practices existed among federal officials.

Nevertheless, in response to the heightened media attention and congressional investigation into police abuses, several states legislatively enacted their own statutes against the third degree: Louisiana in 1908; Colorado and Washington in 1909; Indiana, Montana and Nevada in 1911; and Kentucky in 1912 (Keedy, 1937; Wickersham Report, 1931). The third degree had been a crime at common law in some places, and by time of the Wickersham Commission Report in 1931, 27 states carried such statutes on the books, some of which also made illegal any willful delays by police in bringing an arrested suspect promptly before a magistrate. Yet, these statutes remained largely symbolic, for only rarely was a guilty officer or detective actually convicted under such a statute (*Harvard Law Review*, 1930). In the 1910s, for example, not a single police official was prosecuted under one of these statutes, despite the fact that third degree interrogation methods had been rampant during the entire decade (Chafee, 1931).

The two decades following the IACP meetings and Senate Committee's investigation appear to have been the heyday of the third degree in American history, a situation seemingly caused by changing crime patterns, notably the rise of gangland violence and a thriving criminal underworld following Prohibition, and, correspondingly, the nation's first declared war on crime. In response to a perceived threat of increasing crime, numerous crime commissions and crime surveys were established and undertaken in the 1920s. Together, these crime commissions, as Douthit (1975) has noted, influenced policing in at least three significant ways:

> First, they encouraged a climate of attitudes and ideas emphasizing crime control as the primary function of police forces and giving rise to a 'war against crime.' Second, they encouraged the use of the concept of efficiency as the principal criterion for the evaluation of police policies and practice, the same criterion by which

other parts of the criminal justice system came to be evaluated. Third, they emphasized the need for state and national co-ordination and leadership in the struggle against crime. (p. 318)

During these same two decades (1910s and 1920s), the third degree was both widely practiced by police and frequently publicized by the media and other civic organizations (Chisolm & Hart, 1922). The suspicion of third degree methods was always in the air, and in some cities police complained that they were perpetually on the defensive against charges of custodial improprieties by citizens and the press. In the muckraking tradition of the Progressive era, newspapers regularly reported allegations of police abuses, and repeatedly decried violent police interrogation practices in popular editorials, graphically describing the disfiguring injuries that sometimes followed victims of intensive interrogations. Plays were written about the third degree and performed in theaters. In detective fiction and motion pictures the third degree was treated as a standard police practice. Bar association committees, civil liberties groups, and grand juries investigated custodial police abuses and issued reports. Sometimes police officers themselves joined the fray by publicly defending and justifying their third degree methods in news stories, articles and books (e.g., Fiaschetti, 1930a, 1930b, 1930c; Willemse, 1931). Popular sentiment concerning police interrogation practices culminated however in 1931 with the publication of volume eleven of the Wickersham Commission Report, *Report on Lawlessness in Law Enforcement*, which created a national scandal by exposing third degree interrogation methods as a widespread and systematic practice among American police across the country.

The history of third degree interrogation would change dramatically in the decades following the Wickersham Report. Some police departments initially attacked the legitimacy of the Wickersham Commission report and the accuracy of their findings, including the IACP which denounced the report as "the greatest blow to police work in the last half century" during its annual meetings in 1932 (Leo, 1994), and subsequently formed a special committee to refute the findings of the Wickersham Commission's report (Fogelson, 1977). Ironically, though, as Zachariah Chaffee, one of the authors noted, the Wickersham Report "was greeted by the police with two answers which they regarded as conclusive: first, there wasn't any third degree; and second, they couldn't do their work without it" (Smith, 1986, p. 10).

Following the Wickersham Report, police departments would begin to reform their arrest and investigative practices with greater levels of training as the occupation of policing became increasingly professionalized in subsequent decades. Although force and duress had been common police interrogation tactics through the first three decades of this century, the use of coercive methods began to decline in the 1930s and 1940s. To be sure, the decline was uneven; third degree methods persisted in some places longer than others. Nevertheless, by the mid-1960s custodial police questioning had appeared to become psychological in nature. In less than two generations of American policing, the third degree, once a common police practice and later a national disgrace, had virtually disappeared from American policing. Allegations of third degree interrogation methods in America recur from time to time (e.g. Conroy, 2001; White, 2001), but they have become relatively infrequent (Leo, 1992).

TURNING AWAY FROM THE THIRD DEGREE: THE ORIGINS OF MODERN INTERROGATION

The dramatic revelations of coercive interrogation practices in the 1930s caused a national uproar that led police leaders and trainers to emphasize increasingly professional forms of policing and "scientific" methods of crime detection as a means of enhancing their status among the public. Thoroughly documented, the Wickersham Report revealed that police brutality in general, and the third degree in particular, was practiced extensively in police departments across the country. Its findings were immediately popularized by journalist Ernest Jerome Hopkins' *Our Lawless Police*, as well as by many national newspaper and magazine stories. Although journalists, grand juries, legislative committees, bar associations, and civil liberties' groups had all leveled such charges against police in the past, none provoked nearly as much public controversy or exercised nearly as great an impact on public attitudes as the influential Wickersham Report (Walker, 1980).

The graphic revelations of routine police misconduct represented a threat to the institutional legitimacy of police. Police administrators, chiefs and supporters quickly realized the need to eliminate flagrant abuses in order to enhance their status among the public. Police chiefs could no longer brazenly deny that the third degree existed, as some had previously done. Accordingly, police became increasingly concerned with their public image, especially in the media. The professional model of policing, long encouraged by progressive reformers, gained ascendance in police circles. Reform-oriented police chiefs and leaders capitalized on the changing atmosphere to enact or enforce departmental policies against abusive police behavior.

Following the unsettling revelations of the Wickersham Report, J. Edgar Hoover immediately launched both an internal and external attack on third degree practices. Hoover actively promoted more professional (i.e., non-abusive) forms of interrogation, realizing not only that public perceptions of police abuse undermined the image of policing necessary for its success, but also that it undercut the ultimate goal of conviction. To this end, the FBI emphasized "scientific" forms of criminal investigation—which was reflected in such innovations as the crime laboratories, fingerprinting technology, national identification records, police journals and the Uniform Crime Reports—so as to render coercive interrogation altogether obsolete. As Hoover noted (Frank & Frank, 1957):

> Third degree methods, the ill-trained officer might think, perhaps a severe beating, will force a confession. But the trained officer, schooled in the latest techniques of crime detection, will think otherwise—he will go to work, locating a latent fingerprint, a heel-print in the mud, or a toolmark on the safe. (p. 185)

It is in this historical context that police interrogation training manuals began to appear in America. Although *general* police training manuals date back to shortly after the inception of urban police departments in the nineteenth century, *interrogation* training manuals did not emerge until the early 1940s. The first interrogation manual published was Kidd's *Police Interrogation* (1940), soon followed by Inbau's pioneering, *Lie Detection and Criminal Interrogation* (1942). Several other training texts appeared in the coming years—notably, Mulber (1951), O'Hara (1956), and Arthur and Caputo (1959)—as interrogation manuals began to redefine the practice and ideology of custodial police questioning. The early interrogation manuals were a response to a perceived legitimacy crisis in policing generated by popular revelations of police abuses and improprieties. Drawing on the rhetoric, symbols and cultural authority of science, these manuals articulated, for the first time, a professional ideology of police interrogation that sought to replace third degree practices with psychological methods. These manuals were thus part of the larger project of police reform and professionalism already underway in policing during the early and middle decades of the twentieth century (e.g. Fogelson, 1977; Walker, 1977).

The new interrogation manuals have served educational, socialization, and ideological functions for the police. First, these manuals have educated professional detectives about morally appropriate and inappropriate questioning behavior, thereby defining professional standards for legitimate police interrogation practices. From their inception, police interrogation training manuals have uniformly condemned the physically and psychologically coercive interrogation tactics associated with the third degree. By the early 1940s, police trainers and leaders viewed the third degree as unacceptable in all circumstances. By counseling police against third degree methods, the manuals became an internal mechanism through which the police profession sought to eradicate—primarily through increased education and training—all third degree interrogation practices.

Second, the interrogation training manuals instructed police detectives in the new "scientific" techniques of interrogation, techniques that relied on increasingly subtle and sophisticated psychological strategies. As we will see below, the authors of the interrogation manuals have expanded and refined their repertoire of psychological techniques considerably over the years. The purpose of these interrogation methods has been not only to elicit confessions, but also to train interrogators how to detect deception and read into the psyche of criminal suspects—in other words, to create human lie detectors and psychological manipulators. Significantly, the police manuals asserted that the psychological methods they advocated were, in fact, far more effective at eliciting truthful admissions than the traditional physical methods they sought to replace. With the development of "scientific" techniques of criminal detection and the shift from physical to psychological interrogation methods, police reformers argued that violent interrogation tactics were thus no longer necessary to obtain confessions. Moreover, the manuals argued that these psychological methods—unlike the traditional third degree—could not, and thus would not, induce an innocent person to falsely confess. The new psychological interrogation techniques advocated by the manuals have offered police a functional alternative to traditional third degree practices.

Third, the interrogation training manuals have not only defined the professional standards for interrogation behavior, but they have also educated police about the changing (and sometimes rather complicated) law of criminal procedure that regulates police interrogation. The earlier manuals focused almost exclusively on the development of the Supreme Court's case-by-case "voluntariness" standard (Kamisar, 1980; White, 1998). After 1966, the manuals also instructed police on the law of pre-interrogation warnings, and the myriad of legal issues generated by *Miranda* and its progeny. White (1979) has argued that police interrogation manuals have set the standards of legitimate police interrogation practices in the absence of clear guidance from the courts. But this statement is only half correct. The manuals have also set the standards for legitimate police practices even with clear (or relatively clear) guidance from the courts. For the interrogation training manuals have interpreted and taught the police how to apply the courts' rulings, usually correctly but sometimes incorrectly (Kamisar, 1980; White, 1998). The interrogation training manuals and courses have been the medium through which investigators acquire their knowledge of the constitutional law of criminal procedure.

The interrogation training manual has thus become the primary means of professional socialization through which generations of police detectives have learned the ethics, psychology, and law of police interrogation. The interrogation manuals writers have not only responded to changing social norms, but they have also created new standards of professional behavior for police interrogators. The manuals are essentially etiquette guides in lie detection and psychological manipulation for police interrogators; they have taught detectives norms of civility as well as seemingly effective and (for the most part) legal questioning methods. The manuals have transformed the manners and customs of detectives by teaching them to attend to the process and subtleties of interrogation, not merely the outcome of obtaining a confession. Although the psychological methods they advocate may be highly manipulative and deceitful (and sometimes even psychologically coercive), the manuals have implored detectives to treat their suspects with dignity, sympathy, and respect. In so doing, they appear to have contributed to the decline of the third degree in America.

These training manuals created a specialized, written culture of police interrogation that helped lay the basis for claims to professionalism in the occupation of policing. Like the larger movement for professional reform of which they were a part, the interrogation manual writers sought to remove incompetence, inefficiency, corruption, and brutality from their ranks in order to enhance the public image and effectiveness of police. The interrogation training manuals have created a specialized body of knowledge over which police command exclusive jurisdiction, and thus represent a strategy for marking their professional boundaries. Police reformers sought autonomy not only from political machines, but also from the courts that sometimes regulated their behavior. The manuals in effect attempted to assert ownership over the problem of police interrogation. Reflecting a greater degree of specialization within policing, the interrogation training manuals thus sought to remove the controversy of police interrogation practices from the public realm. The movement for police professionalism has largely succeeded in this effort, for the courts, as Weisberg (1961) long ago pointed out, are not so much concerned with regulating police interrogation practices as they are with providing remedies for the victims of improper police procedures. Historically, the law of confessions has been almost exclusively concerned with either the issue of voluntariness or *Miranda* warnings (White, 2001). Outside of these two areas, the law of confessions has avoided laying down many clear guidelines, thus permitting the police profession for the most part to set its own standards and internally regulate its own behavior.

To enhance their claim to professionalism the manual writers claimed to create a "science" (which, as we will see, is really a pseudo-science) of police interrogation. Previously, detectives had conceived of interrogation as an art, a skill that involved a high degree of intuition and could only be learned through experience rather than through textbooks or classroom instruction (Carey, 1930). The new interrogation training manuals, however, began to conceive of interrogation as a "science": that is, as a structured method based on tested empirical data that, if applied as taught, would yield valid, reliable, and predictable results. The interrogation manuals thus not only trained police in increasingly subtle and sophisticated interrogation methods that gradually came to replace the third degree, they also articulated a professional vision of police interrogation that, as part of the project of professionalism within policing more generally, drew on the rhetoric, symbols, and cultural authority of science to confer legitimacy on controversial police practices.

THE EVOLUTION OF MODERN POLICE INTERROGATION: CREATING HUMAN LIE DETECTORS AND PSYCHOLOGICAL MANIPULATORS

THE HISTORY AND PRACTICE OF BEHAVIORAL LIE DETECTION

Throughout human history men have attempted to detect deception by observing physiological changes in the behavior of criminal suspects during interrogation. Ancient and religious societies frequently relied on torture or trials by ordeal to adjudicate guilt and innocence. The polygraph, or so-called lie-detector, seemingly stands in contrast to earlier methods; proponents advertise it as an enlightened, scientific instrument capable of accurately detecting truth and deception. Yet the lie-detector has its origins in, and continues to bear striking similarities to, the trial by ordeal. In one well-known ordeal, for example, the ancient Hindus required a suspect to chew and then spit out a mouthful of rice. If the suspect successfully spit out the rice, he was judged innocent; but if grains stuck to his mouth, he was found guilty. Examples of similar ordeals are numerous (Larson, 1932; Trovillo, 1938, 1939). The polygraph and the "rice test" (as well as other such ordeals) share the same underlying premise: that the act of lying is accompanied by involuntary physiological reactions indicative of criminal guilt.

At the same time, however, the "science" of lie-detection is a distinctively twentieth century phenomenon, a unique product of our modern, secular age (e.g., Lykken, 1998; Kleinmuntz & Szucko, 1984). Whatever its ability to ferret out innocence and guilt, the polygraph is a testament to the triumph of scientific ideology in American police work. The invention of the polygraph and the spread of scientific crime detection in the early twentieth century represented the dawn of a professional age in policing, marking the transition between an era in which detectives routinely relied on third degree violence to one in which they could now boast of more civil and humane methods of criminal investigation. Although it has always been and continues to be little more than a method of intimidating custodial suspects into confessing, the polygraph was the historical precursor (and remains an adjunct) to modern, psychologically oriented methods of police interrogation.

The lie-detector is a multifaceted, seemingly complicated machine that may appear formidable to its subjects. The polygraph consists of a pneumograph, psychogalvanometer, and cardiophygmograph, which are connected to electrically driven ink pens and a moving chart that graphically registers changes in the subject's physiological responses. In the typical polygraph examination, one rubber belt or tube is strapped around a suspect's stomach and another around his chest or abdomen; a blood pressure cuff is stretched around the person's bicep; and metal electrode wires are fastened to the ends of his fingers. Together these attachments measure autonomic nervous system signs of arousal, recording changes in blood pressure, depth and rate of breathing, pulse rate and strength, skin conductivity and temperature, and palmar sweating. Despite the apparent mechanical sophistication of the polygraph, however, the theory of scientific lie-detection remains surprisingly simple. The act of lying induces fear and anxiety in the subject, causing internal tensions that in turn produce involuntary and clearly measurable physiological responses.

As with lying, identifiable symptoms of truth-telling (and thus innocence) can also be observed in the facial expressions, body movements, eye contact, attitudes, posture, grooming gestures and general behavior of suspects during questioning. Truthful suspects, for example, are "composed and very direct while answering questions," "usually very glad to be given an opportunity to prove their innocence," and display an "attitude of genuine confidence in both the instrument and the examiner." Innocent subjects are "often at ease," "light-hearted," "talkative," "cooperative and sincere," and "not overly polite or solicitous." To be sure, just as the polygraph may register inconclusive physiological responses, so too do we find inconclusive behavior symptoms (i.e., common to both liars and truth-tellers), such as anger, impertinence, quietness, and displaying an interest in the polygraph (Inbau & Reid, 1953; Reid & Inbau, 1977). According to its proponents, the lie-detector detects truth and deception as accurately as, sometimes even more so than, other forms of scientific evidence admitted in civil and criminal trials (Reid & Inbau, 1977). Joseph Buckley, a contemporary proponent of the polygraph adds, "compared to other procedures, there's nothing more accurate" (Bureau of National Affairs, 1985, p. 1230).

Although the nominal purpose of the polygraph test is to diagnose the subject as "truthful" or "deceptive" with greater accuracy than one could achieve without examination, the primary function of lie-detectors has always been, and continues to be, to induce confessions. The polygraph exam (or, more accurately, the polygraph examiner) elicits admissions by playing on the psychological fears of exposure the suspect may experience as a result of the lie-detector—sometimes prior to taking the test, sometimes as the tubes and wires are being strapped onto his body, but probably most often after he has "failed" the test. To succeed at obtaining inculpatory admissions, the examiner must convince the subject that the polygraph is infallible, so that the subject will feel overwhelmed by the futility of his continued denials of guilt. The examiner tells the subject that the lie-detector has diagnosed him as "deceptive," that the examiner thus knows the truth, and because the machine never makes mistakes the subject might as well just confess, perhaps adding that it would clearly be in the subject's best interest to do so under the circumstances. The polygraph thus becomes a tool of persuasion and manipulation during the subsequent interrogation process. One of the early leaders in the field of lie-detection estimated that 60–85% of suspects diagnosed as "deceptive" by a polygraph eventually confessed (Lee, 1953; Reid & Inbau, 1977). But as Gudjonsson (1992) notes, "the rate at which suspects confess after being requested to take a polygraph test seems dependent on at least two factors: the perceptions the subject has of the polygraph and its effectiveness, and the skills of the examiner in eliciting a confessions during a post-test interview" (p. 190).

Historically, the modern lie-detector machine was invented to overcome the problems associated with the third degree in America: August Vollmer, the well-known Berkeley Police Chief and prominent spokesperson for police professionalism, directed John Larson to construct a lie-detector test specifically to rid police of the impulse to, or perceived need for, brutality during interrogation (Carte & Carte, 1975). Early police textbook authors acknowledged that one of the virtues of the polygraph was to reduce third degree practices on criminal suspects (e.g., Inbau & Reid, 1953). In addition to emphatically counseling its readers against third degree violence, Inbau and Reid (1953) informed their readers that a suspect will not be fit for a lie-detector test "after undergoing extensive interrogations based upon frequent and constant accusations of guilt—and particularly when such interrogations are accompanied by physical abuse or threats of physical harm administered in an effort to obtain a confession" (p. 70). To this day the polygraph remains a powerful psychological prop, a tool of persuasion and manipulation whose main purpose is to induce inculpatory admissions.

The polygraph is thus not so much an accurate truth verifier or lie-detector as an adjunct to interrogation, and ultimately a sophisticated instrument of intimidation and control in contemporary police work. The polygraph has remained effective because it creates an aura of scientism and expertise, a higher (and thus seemingly more legitimate) claim to truth by police. The polygraph relies on a police-generated myth of infallibility for its efficacy in inducing confessions. In the process, the polygraph turns its subjects inside out, pretends to read their mind (after all the physiological responses measured by the polygraph are not visible) and seeks to penetrate into their thoughts and expose their deceits. The polygraph, an examiner may tell his subject, may even be used to detect deception that is out of the subject's conscious awareness (Gudjonsson, 1992).

Although it remains little more than a mechanism to induce confession, the polygraph is historically significant for offering police an alternative to the third degree, laying the basis for modern, psychologically-oriented methods of interrogation. While the practice of lie-detection is as old as human history, only in the twentieth century has it been elevated to a "science." The sociological significance of the polygraph in contemporary police work is not that it is has been exposed as a pseudo-science and discredited by its academic critics, but rather that the lie-detector has become the medium through which police interrogators have ideologically aligned themselves with modern science and technology in an attempt to confer legitimacy on interrogation practices and further their claims to professionalism.

DEVELOPING A "SCIENCE" OF HUMAN LIE DETECTION AND PSYCHOLOGICAL INTERROGATION

The Inbau-Reid Training Manuals: 1942 to 2001

Fred Inbau was a pioneer in the field of interrogation, fashioning the first sophisticated interrogation manual for police out of his own experience at the Scientific Crime Detection Laboratory of the Chicago Police Department and later refining and extending these methods while a Professor of Law at Northwestern University. Inbau, like his mentor Dean Henry Wigmore before him, opposed third degree interrogation tactics. In the first edition of *Lie Detection and Criminal Interrogation* Inbau (1942) attempted to establish a scientific basis for police interrogation in order to eradicate the use of threatening or abusive tactics from interrogation. As Skolnick (1982) has written: "[*Lie Detection and Criminal Interrogation*] was a reformist document, representing a kind of dialectical synthesis between the polarities of third degree violence and civil liberties for protection of human dignity: Such a synthesis would have been progressive in the 1930s" (p. 47).

Both Inbau and Reid were, indeed, progressives by the political standards of the 1930s, and their seemingly well-intentioned training materials appear to be at least partially responsible for the decline of third degree practices by American police in the 1940s and 1950s. Inbau and Reid taught police not only that the use of force and duress is unacceptable, but also that it is no longer necessary to effectively elicit confessions. From the beginning, Inbau importuned interrogators to avoid tactics that may lead an innocent person to confess, recognizing that both physical and psychological coercion may produce false confessions.

During the last 60 years, *Criminal Interrogation and Confessions* (Inbau & Reid, 1962) has become the definitive police training manual in the United States, if not the Western world. First published in 1942 under the title *Lie Detection and Criminal Interrogation*, this training book has been rewritten into two series (hence the two different titles), with three editions in the first series and four (so far) in the second, totaling seven different manuals altogether (1942, 1948, 1953, 1962, 1967, 1986 and 2001). As the Supreme Court (*Miranda v. Arizona*, 1966; *Oregon v. Elstad*, 1985; *Stansbury v. California, 1994*), legal commentators (Kamisar, 1980; Weisberg, 1961; White, 1979; White, 2001) and social scientists (Gudjonsson, 2003; Kassin, 1997; Leo, 1994) have noted, these manuals provide an important chapter in the history of American interrogation practices and ideology during the last sixty years. In the remainder of this chapter, I will focus on the Inbau-Reid manual not because it is necessarily the best or most effective police interrogation training manual (see also Buckwalter, 1983; Gordon & Fleisher, 2002; Hess, 1997; Holmes, 2003; Macdonald & Michaud, 1992; Rabon, 1992; Royal & Schutt, 1976; Rutledge, 1996; Walters, 2003; Yeschke, 1993; Zulawski & Wicklander, 2002), but because it is the most well-known and influential in the United States. Thousands of American police are trained by the Inbau and Reid materials each year (Irving & Hilgendorf, 1980; Leo, 1994; Zimbardo, 1971) and empirical studies of police work confirm that American detectives employ many of Inbau and Reid's tactics and techniques in practice (Leo, 1996; Simon, 1991; Wald, Ayres, Hess, & Whitebread, 1967).

THE EVOLUTION OF "SCIENTIFIC" INTERROGATION: CREATING HUMAN LIE-DETECTORS

The Behavioral Analysis Interview

The first edition of *Lie Detection and Criminal Interrogation* (Inbau, 1942), as with both editions to follow, is divided into two main parts: one on the polygraph, the other on the methods and law of criminal interrogation. Eventually both sections were revised into separate books: *Truth and Deception* (1966, 1977) and *Criminal Interrogation and Confessions* (1962, 1967, 1986, 2001). The third edition of *Criminal Interrogation and Confessions* (1986) was, according to the authors, "basically an entirely new book" (Inbau, Reid, & Buckley, 1986). Though it rearranged and replicated much of the material in earlier volumes, the third edition (1986) contained dramatic changes and significant advances in the evolution of interrogation methods by Inbau and his co-authors. The fourth, and most recent, edition has updated and extended the materials presented in the third edition.

In the third edition (1986), Inbau et al., for the first time developed a diagnostic method with which they claim police can infer the truthfulness or deceptiveness (and hence the probable innocence or guilt) of suspects prior to commencing formal interrogation—the so-called "Behavioral Analysis Interview." According to Inbau and his co-authors, the Behavioral Analysis Interview consists of a structured set of non-investigative, pre-interrogation questions that are designed to evoke particular behavioral responses from which the interrogator can ascertain the suspect's guilt or innocence. They suggest approximately 15 questions to pose to the suspect, ranging from general questions (such as why does the suspect think someone would have committed the crime) to specific ones (such as would the suspect be willing to take a polygraph). According to Inbau et al., guilty suspects typically react defensively and with discomfort to these questions; they equivocate, stall, and provide evasive or noncommittal answers. Guilty suspects will, for example, state that they do not know why they are being questioned, have not thought about the motive behind the offense, will not eliminate any individuals from suspicion, will not reveal their suspicions, will not take a polygraph, and will recommend only lenient punishment for the actual offender. By contrast, Inbau et al., assert that innocent suspects produce cooperative, direct, and spontaneous responses to these questions.

In deciding whether the suspect is answering truthfully or deceptively to these questions, the interrogator is instructed to focus primarily on the suspect's behavioral responses rather than the actual content of his answers. In their introductory and advanced training seminars, Reid & Associates advise interrogators to treat as guilty (and thus formally interrogate) any suspect whose answers to four or more of the fifteen questions appear deceptive to the interrogator.

Interrogators are further instructed to diagnose truthfulness or deception in the pre-interrogation phase of questioning from the suspect's responses to general and background questions concerning the offense under investigation. The interrogator is taught how to directly observe and evaluate the meaning of the suspect's behavioral, verbal, and nonverbal reactions to external, anxiety-inducing stimuli. The investigator can infer guilt from the following *verbal responses:* specific denials, avoidance of harsh language, delayed or evasive or qualified answers, either unusually strong or unusually weak memory, interjection of irrelevant or digressive issues into the conversation, a request for repetition of questions, mental blocks, a subdued tone of voice, reinforcing denials with oath-taking or religious references, excessive politeness, laughter accompanying answers, and a desire to leave the interrogation in a hurry. Inbau et al. (1986, 2001) argue that guilt can also (and more accurately) be inferred from the following *behavioral* responses (i.e., body language) to questioning: abrupt body movements (such as shifting posture, movement of chair away from interrogator, slouching in one's chair, attempts to stand up or leave the room), grooming and cosmetic gestures (such as wringing one's hands, stroking the back of one's head or hair, picking or biting one's fingernails, shuffling or tapping one's feet, brushing or picking lint from one's clothing, and adjusting or cleaning one's glasses), and supportive gestures (such as placing one's hand over the mouth or eyes while speaking, crossing one's arms or legs, sitting on one's hands, hiding one's feet under the chair, holding one's forehead with one's hand, or placing one's hands under or between one's legs).

Inbau et al. (1986, 2001) warn interrogators to search out deviations from the suspect's normal behavior patterns and that only behavior responses occurring simultaneously with, or immediately after, the suspect's answers can be reliable indicators of truth or deception. The totality of the verbal, nonverbal, and behavior responses elicited during the Behavioral Analysis Interview and background questioning provide, according to Inbau and his co-authors (1986, 2001), a composite identification of the suspect's truthfulness or deception, and thus his likely innocence or guilt. If the suspect is deemed truthful (and thus probably innocent) on the basis of his verbal, nonverbal and behavioral responses to the series of general, background, and non-investigative questions, he is let go; if the suspect is deemed deceptive (and thus probably guilty), he is formally interrogated.

The Behavioral Analysis Interview is premised on the same behavioral assumptions and underlying theory as the so-called lie-detector: The Behavioral Analysis Interview teaches interrogators that it is their job to act, in effect, as a human polygraph—an endeavor that may be fraught with even more potential for error than the lie detector itself (e.g., Ekman & O'Sullivan, 1991; Kassin & Fong, 1999; Lykken, 1998). The Behavioral Analysis Interview is represented by the authors as a scientific advance in the field of interrogation. As we have seen, the lie-detector is an instrument that measures several physiological changes (heart rate, blood pressure, respiration, electrodermal reactivity) in response to questions from an examiner. As with the polygraph, in the Behavioral Analysis Interview an individual's stress reactions are said to be manifest in their behavior symptoms, verbal responses, and nonverbal reactions to investigative questioning. Inbau et al. (1986, 2001), argue that any deviation from the suspect's normal style of speech, physical mannerisms, gestures, or eye contact may be indicative of deception and thus guilt. For example, the idealized deceptive suspect typically displays the following stress reactions: a high degree of nervousness, defensiveness, evasiveness, equivocation, gross body movements, fidgetiness, tension-releasing gestures, uncontrollable sighs, labored breathing, variation of facial expressions, rapid and erratic posture changes, and a shifty look in the eyes. If these behavioral changes occur immediately following questioning and throughout the interview, Inbau et al. (1986, 2001) argue that they are valid and reliable measures of deception.

The style-based diagnostic techniques that Inbau et al. (1986, 2001), advocate in the Behavioral Analysis Interview are premised on the same underlying theory as the polygraph: that the act of deception produces regular and discernable stress reactions in normally socialized individuals. Like the polygraph, the Behavioral Analysis Interview asks the interrogator to detect deception on the basis of verbal, nonverbal, and behavioral deviations from a vaguely specified norm. Because no physiological or psychological response unique to lying (and never present in truthfulness) has ever been discovered, the theory of the polygraph and the Behavioral Analysis Interview remains *prima facie* implausible, leaving both diagnostic methods especially prone to problems of interpreter bias, validity, reliability and false positive outcomes. To support their claims about the Behavioral Analysis Interview, Inbau and Reid (1986, 2001) cite a growing body of academic literature on the psychology of deception, as well as data that Reid & Associates have acquired from interrogating thousands of suspects over the years.

As numerous social scientists have pointed out (Gudjonsson, 2003; Kassin & Fong, 1999; Moston, 1991; Ofshe & Leo, 1997a, 1997b;), however, Inbau and Reid (1986, 2001) misrepresent the academic support for their psychological theories: the Behavioral Analysis Interview is not supported by any research evidence. Moreover, the data that Reid and Associates cite as support for the efficacy of the Behavioral Analysis Interview have never been made public, and (assuming they even exist) they would appear to be little more than an accumulation of unsystematic, *post hoc* observations intended to verify their own preconceptions. As Lykken (1998) has argued, Inbau and Reid's (1986) method and data contain their own self-fulfilling prophecies. In sum, the Behavioral Analysis Interview, like the polygraph, cleverly provides interrogators with an allegedly scientific method for justifying their hunches, intuitions, and preconceptions. Just as the lie-detector was intended as a functional alternative to the third degree, so too has the Behavioral Analysis Interview become a functional alternative to the polygraph. In fact, the interrogation training industry even admits as much: that the Behavioral Analysis Interview was invented as an "acceptable substitute for" the lie-detector in situations where it was either too costly, too time-consuming, or not legally permitted (Wicklander, 1980, 1979).

Neuro-Linguistic Programming

"Neuro-Linguistic Programming" is a theory of how people process information and communicate (Bandler & Grinder, 1979; Brooks, 1989; Lewis & Pucelik, 1990; O'Conner & Seymour, 1990; Richardson, 1987). Taken literally, Neuro-Linguistic Programming refers to the nervous system through which our sensory information is processed (neuro), the language systems through which our neural representations are given meaning (linguistic), and the mental programs we use in our neurological system to store and recall information (programming). Founded by two New Age hypnotists in the late 1970s, Neuro-Linguistic Programming has, according to its police advocates, been subsequently adopted in the fields of psychotherapy, business relations, sports, sales, television evangelism, teaching, and military intelligence (e.g. Bandler & Grinder, 1979). Police trainers have also incorporated the theory of Neuro-Linguistic Programming into their "science" of interrogation (e.g. City of Oakland, 1999). Like the Behavioral Analysis Interview, Neuro-Linguistic Programming is a method of detecting truth and deception (again equated with innocence and guilt) on the basis of behavioral responses to non-accusatory questions. Neuro-Linguistic Programming is thus another psychological method through which police interrogators are trained to become human lie-detectors. But Neuro-Linguistic Programming is more than that, for police trainers also advertise it as a method through which to establish rapport with criminal suspects and, through the strategic use of language, to subconsciously manipulate the suspect into confessing.

According to the theory of Neuro-Linguistic Programming, people have three representational systems or "modalities" (sometimes referred to as cognitive maps) through which they subconsciously process information and experience their environment: visual (sight), auditory (sound), and kinesthetic (feeling). In the process of communication, the theory goes, every person experiences one sensory processing mode as dominant, to the virtual exclusion of the other two. Some people process information primarily through the sense of sight (classified as "visual"), others through the sense of sound (classified as "auditory"), still others through the sense of feeling (classified as "kinesthetic"). If the interrogator can discern which type of processing mode the suspect primarily relies on in understanding and reacting to his environment, then the interrogator can tailor his approach to the suspect's method of learning, thus maximizing the potential for communication and manipulation. According to the theory of Neuro-Linguistic Programming, by relating to the suspect's mode of learning, the suspect subconsciously feels that the interrogator is like him, enabling the suspect to relax, trust the interrogator, and confide in him. The purpose of relating to the suspect in his mode of information processing is thus to subconsciously overcome the suspect's instinctive defense mechanisms, establish rapport, detect truth and deception, extract information, and ultimately to manipulate him into confessing.

The police interrogator is taught to identify which of the three representational systems the suspect uses by carefully listening to how he communicates, and in particular by paying attention to the words and images he uses to describe his experiences. The interrogator thus begins by asking the suspect neutral, non-threatening questions to determine the primary "sensory modality" through which he or she experiences the world and processes information. For example, the interrogator may ask the suspect questions such as, "What did you like about your last car?" or "How many letters are in the word 'Mississippi,' and how do you know that?" Interrogators then discern the suspect's primary system of information processing by analyzing the images the suspect uses to describe his experiences:

individuals who process information through the sense of sight will talk in visual images; people who process information through the sense of sound will speak in auditory images; and people who process information through the sense of feeling will talk in kinesthetic images.

According to Neuro-Linguistic Programming, a relationship exists between the positioning and movement of the eyes and the brain's sensory process mechanisms. Although they are told to ascertain the suspect's neural processing mode through written or spoken communication, interrogators are also taught that one can easily and reliably determine the suspect's predominant system of information processing by watching and studying the suspect's eye movements, which become, quite literally, windows into the suspect's soul. According to the theory of Neuro-Linguistic Programming (Rhoads & Solomon, 1987):

> A visually oriented person will look upward to the right or left 45 degrees from center when thinking. In doing so, he is seeing something about the item he is trying to recall. A sound-oriented person's eyes will move straight across, right or left, as he hears the information being requested or some sound associated with the item he seeks. A sound-oriented person will frequently hear his own voice giving him the answer he seeks, and when this occurs the eyes are moving down and to the person's left. A feeling-oriented person will look down and to the right as he attempts to identify a kinesthetic sensation related to the item in question. A person who looks straight up or down from center is delaying as the mind selects which area to access. (pp. 39–40)

According to police trainers, these sensory-driven eye processing patterns ring true 95% of the time, and, furthermore, cut across cultural, economic, and educational distinctions.

Another behavioral indicator of a subject's "programming patterns" is a person's hand gestures. Visually-oriented people are said to frequently use quick and animated hand gestures while talking, often near the neck level. By contrast, auditorily-oriented people are said to keep their gestures below the shoulder in a more fluid and precise manner, frequently pointing directly to their ear when asking you to explain something. A kinesthetically oriented person is said to use slower and more deliberative gestures that remain near the stomach level.

Once he diagnoses the suspect's sensory orientation mode as either visual, auditory, or kinesthetic the interrogator can begin to establish rapport with the suspect by selecting words and drawing on images that correspond to the suspect's primary mode of information processing. "Feeling-oriented" words or phrases, for example, include "I can grasp that idea" or "I know what you're going through"; "Sound-oriented" words or phrases, for example, include "I hear what you're saying; listen to this; tell me what you mean;" and "sight-oriented" words or phrases, for example, include "I see what you mean; picture this; or look at it this way."

By analyzing the suspect's eye movements in relation to his primary sensory orientation, the interrogator is told he can determine whether the suspect is lying or responding truthfully. For example, if a visually-oriented person looks up and to the left, he is most likely telling the truth; but if his eyes look up and to the right or if he is staring straight ahead and not focused, he is most likely lying. Similarly, a auditorily-oriented person will look straight across and to his left when telling the truth, but straight across and to his right when lying; and a kinesthetically-oriented person will look down and to the right when telling the truth but will look away from that area when lying. In addition, interrogators are instructed to ask suspects neutral, non-threatening questions to establish a baseline for the suspect's eye movements, following the same underlying logic of the polygraph and Behavioral Analysis Interview: once a pattern of eye movement has been established, a movement in the opposite direction is believed to indicate deception. Symptoms such as a break in eye contact, looking away at the ceiling or floor, pupil dilation, closed eyes, squinting eyes, and rapid blinking of the eyes are considered likely indicators of deception. Police trainers claim that this method has a higher than 90% accuracy rate, while maintaining that a person's eye movements are both involuntary responses and expressive of his underlying motivations.

In sum, Neuro-Linguistic Programming purports to teach interrogators to figure out how their suspects are mentally programmed, and then to use the knowledge of the suspect's neurological and sensory programming during interrogation to establish rapport, extract information, detect deception, and ultimately elicit confessions. Interrogators are taught that the programming process has taken place since birth in everyone but remains unconscious: Children are believed to be primarily kinesthetic until they acquire language, and then become primarily auditory until they begin to read, after which they become visual. More generally, Neuro-Linguistic Programming police trainers estimate that 45–60% of the population process information primarily through their visual sense, 20–45% through their auditory sense, and 10–15% through their kinesthetic sense. There is no credible evidence to support these numerical estimates or, for that matter, any of the grand assertions advanced by proponents of Neuro-Linguistic Programming (such as the ability to read into someone's mind and infer truth-telling and deception from their eye movements, for example). None of Neuro-Linguistic Programming's grand claims have ever been experimentally or empirically verified, and no evidence meeting minimal scientific standards as ever been offered in support of Neuro-Linguistic Programming's validity as a diagnostic instrument of truth and deception or any kind of mental programming. Like both the polygraph and the Behavioral Analysis Interview, Neuro-Linguistic Programming is partially oracular, a throwback to pre-modern forms of physiological lie detection.

THE EVOLUTION OF "SCIENTIFIC" INTERROGATION: CREATING PSYCHOLOGICAL MANIPULATORS

The Inbau-Reid Methods of Interrogation

From the early 1940s to the present, interrogation training manuals have sought to teach police how to manipulate, deceive and elicit confessions of guilt from reluctant custodial suspects. By today's standards, the early interrogation training manuals seem psychologically primitive; the more recent manuals have become increasingly sophisticated and process-oriented. A quick look at the evolution of Inbau manual from 1942 to the present easily illustrates the point. In *Lie Detection and Criminal Interrogation* (1942), Inbau prescribed 19 trial and error interrogation tactics, each of which he assigned to a letter of the alphabet. This scattershot, laundry-list approach lacked a sequential or unifying logic or organization. Techniques A through I constitute the "Sympathetic Approach," which is intended to be effective during the interrogation of emotional offenders "whose feelings have produced in them a feeling of remorse, mental anguish, or compunction" (Inbau, 1942, p. 79). The interrogator is instructed to display confidence in the suspect's guilt (Technique A); to invoke circumstantial evidence as probative of the suspect's guilt (Technique B); to point out the suspect's psychological and physiological symptoms of guilt (Technique C); to sympathetically advise the suspect that anyone could have committed a similar offense under similar conditions (Technique D); to recast the offense so as to minimize its moral seriousness (Technique E); to condemn the suspect's victim, accomplice, or anyone else onto whom blame may be legitimately placed (Technique F); to extend friendly gestures and advice, urging the suspect to confess for the sake of his conscience (Technique G); to exaggerate the accusations against the suspect (Technique H); and to inquire about details involved in the offense (Technique I).

For so-called "non-emotional offenders," Inbau (1942) recommended the "Factual Analysis Approach." This approach consists of five techniques: the interrogator is instructed to point out the futility of his resistance (Technique J); to challenge the suspect's honor, or appeal to his pride by selective flattery (Technique K); to call attention to the serious consequences, as well as the futility, of continuing his offensive behavior (Technique L); to seek an admission about another offense as leverage for eliciting a confession for the offense under question (Technique M); and to play co-offenders against one another by suggesting that the suspect's co-offender has already confessed, and that the suspect will receive full punishment for both of their deeds unless he too confesses. There are five additional techniques for both emotional and non-emotional offenders: the interrogator is instructed to inquire if the suspect knows why he has been taken in for questioning (Technique O); to elicit detailed information about the suspect's activities before, during, and after the offense in question (Technique P); to acquire from the suspect everything that he knows about the commission of the offense, the victims, and the suspects (Technique Q); to ask the suspect about facts suggestive of his guilt as if they were not already known by the interrogator (Technique R); and to ask the suspect pertinent questions as though the correct answers were already known to the interrogator (Technique S).

By contrast, the modern version of Inbau et al., manual (1986, 2001) has reorganized the interrogation techniques it advocates from the earlier individualized, trial and error or scattershot approach to a "Nine-step'" model of systematic and unfolding pressure, persuasion, deception and manipulation. The "Nine-step" method is designed to elicit a confession by breaking down a suspect's resistance, causing him to feel trapped and hopeless, and offering him inducements (i.e., reasons to confess) that appear to improve his situation by minimizing his culpability if he complies with the interrogator's demand for confession and, conversely, make his situation worse if he holds to denial (Inbau et al., 1986, 2001; Ofshe & Leo, 1997a, 1997b).

According to the nine-step method, the interrogator begins by accusing the suspect of the crime (Step 1). The purpose here is to set the tone of the interrogation, as well as to disarm the suspect. The interrogator then develops psychological "themes" or scenarios of how the underlying event could have occurred that, according to Inbau et al (1986, 2001), serve morally to excuse or justify the suspect's behavior (Step 2) but may also serve to excuse it altogether and render it non-criminal or non-punishable (e.g., Ofshe & Leo, 1997a, 1997b). This is the most important stage of the interrogation process. Inbau et al., recommend different "themes" for each type of crime. In the next step, the interrogator is instructed to weaken and suppress the suspect's denials, with the goal of altogether shutting down the process of denial (Step 3). In Step 4, the interrogator overcomes (and reverses the meaning of) the suspect's emotional, factual or moral objections to the interrogator's assertions, turning the suspect's stated objections back against him in the form of continuing "theme" development. Next, the interrogator is instructed to retain (largely through physical gestures) the attention of the suspect, who by now should be withdrawn and confused (Step 5). The interrogator handles the suspect's passive and downcast mood by shortening and embellishing the psychological "themes" presented in Step 2, concentrating on the development of one more compelling "theme" in particular (Step 6). In Step 7, the interrogator confronts the suspect with the so-called "alternative question," which consist of two choices (one good, one bad) that account for how the suspect committed the underlying activity or offense. The good choice or "theme" suggests minimal or no moral condemnation and/or minimal or no punishment, while the bad choice or "theme" suggests harsher moral condemnation and/or harsher punishment by the criminal justice system. The suspect is encouraged to choose the good or minimizing alternative, which is a natural extension of the theme developed in Step 2 and refined in Step 6, or else he will receive the bad or maximizing alternative. The interrogator then enjoins the suspect to orally reveal the details of the offense (Step 8). Finally, the suspect's oral statements are converted into a written confession of guilt (Step 9).

In the modern version of the Inbau-Reid manual (1986, 2001), the interrogation techniques are presented as a sophisticated social psychological process model. The Nine-Step method of interrogation consolidates and expands earlier interrogation techniques into a *modus operandi:* An unfolding temporal logic emerges, through which the suspect's active resistance is neutralized as he is transformed into a passive actor who has been persuaded by the interrogator's messages and is eventually manipulated into confessing (or at least to agreeing to a minimizing "theme") to having committed the underlying act with an exculpatory motive. The Nine-Step social psychological process model of interrogation contains a sequential logic of influence, persuasion, and manipulation (and some would argue coercion) that methodically exerts pressure on the suspect to comply with the demands of the interrogator and ultimately to confess. The psychological techniques underlying the Nine-Step model of interrogation are, according to its authors, designed to increase the level of anxiety the suspect experiences when he denies the detectives' accusations, while at the same time reducing the suspect's perception of the external consequences of confessing (Jayne, 1986). According to Inbau et al. (1986, 2001) the interrogator accomplishes the first task by utilizing anxiety-enhancing techniques that direct statements at the suspect's perception of himself and his denials. The interrogator also increases the suspect's anxiety by not allowing the suspect to engage in tension-relieving activities (e.g., smoking), by not allowing the suspect to verbalize his denials, and by not allowing the suspect to vent his anger at anyone or anything other than himself. The interrogator accomplishes the second task by offering the suspect the defense mechanisms of rationalization and projection, which Inbau et al., (1986, 2001) argue should function to distort or deny the suspect's reality. According to the Inbau et al. (1986, 2001) the breaking point that delivers the confession occurs when the suspect's expectation changes from initially believing that confessing is the worst thing he can do to eventually being persuaded (as a result of theme development and presentation of the alternative question) that—given his anxiety-ridden and hopeless situation, the possible *negative* framing of his actions, and the likely *positive* consequences of admission versus denial—it is actually in his best interest to confess.

The point here is to not to critique the Inbau-Reid method of interrogation, though numerous social scientists and scholars have roundly and extensively criticized Inbau et al. (e.g. Gudjonsson, 1992; Gudjonsson, 2003;

Kassin, 1997; Kassin & Fong, 1999; Kassin & McNall, 1991; Wrightsman & Kassin, 1993; Ofshe, 1989; Ofshe & Leo, 1997a, b). Rather, the point is to illustrate how increasingly sophisticated the police training manuals have become in their attempt to turn away from the third degree and turn detectives into psychological manipulators. As we have seen, the evolution of psychological interrogation had its origins in the rampant use of, and scandalous reaction to, third degree police practices in the 1920s and 1930s. Yet the connection between the third degree and modern psychological interrogation remains. Despite the fact that the era of third degree interrogation has long since passed and use of physical techniques is exceptional, the Inbau et al., manual (2001) continues to inveigh against the use of third degree interrogation tactics in the very same language that it did more than 60 years ago when Inbau published the first edition of his manual.

Interrogation Profiling

Interrogation profiling is another so-called "cutting edge" and "scientific" strategy police trainers teach in their interrogation seminars and courses. While efforts to determine deviance through the observation of behavioral traits and characteristics have a long history (Underwood, 1979), the use of profiles by criminal justice agencies is a relatively recent phenomena, beginning in 1968 when the Federal Aviation Administration, Department of Justice, and Department of Commerce compiled a profile of potential skyjackers (Becton, 1987; Risinger & Loop, 2002). Since 1968, the use of profiles has become an increasingly popular law enforcement tool, most notably with the Drug Courier Profile invented by a Federal Drug Enforcement Agent in 1974 and now used extensively in airports across the country (Cloud, 1985). Other profiles used in contemporary law enforcement include the hijacker profile, the drug smuggling vessel profile, the stolen car profile, the stolen truck profile, the alimentary-canal smuggler profile, the battering parent profile, the poacher profile, and the serial killer profile, as well as profiles used to identify serial rapists, child molesters, and arsonists (Becton, 1987). In recent years, "racial" profiling has been a subject of much newspaper coverage and controversy.

Criminal profiling is a relatively new development in the teaching of police interrogation (MacDonald & Michaud, 1987, 1992). The purpose of criminal profiling in interrogation is not so much to identify criminals *per se* (as in more traditional offender profiling) or to detect deception (as in the methods of the Behavioral Analysis Interview and Neuro-Linguistic Programming). Rather, the purpose of criminal profiling prior to interrogation is to identify the underlying psychological traits of the criminal suspect that led him to commit the crime, and subsequently to apply specially-adapted techniques that interrogators believe will enable them to more effectively persuade the suspect to confess.

Reid & Associates teaches interrogators how to profile suspects into one of four categories ("real need" crimes, "lifestyle" crimes, "impulse" crimes, and "esteem" crimes) according to the set of psychological needs the suspect is trying to fulfill by committing the crime. According to Reid & Associates "Real Need" criminals offend to satisfy a real need, typically a situation in which a suspect's livelihood or physical safety has been threatened. Common "real need" crimes include: theft, embezzlement, insurance fraud, receiving bribes, arson for profit, burglary and robbery. "Lifestyle" criminals offend to maintain or protect a social status. Common "lifestyle" crimes are said to include theft, embezzlement, fraud, drug sale, burglary, armed robbery, and shoplifting. "Impulse" criminals offend as a result of intense emotional feelings. Common "impulse" crimes include homicide, assault, rape, child abuse, vandalism, and hit and run. "Esteem" criminals offend to reassure themselves of their worth and security. Common "esteem" crimes include drive-by shootings, rape, child molesting, and indecent exposure.

As taught by Reid & Associates, the interrogator profiles the criminal suspect by bringing a "profile sheet" to the interrogation and asking the suspect five pre-interrogation interview questions: (1) What has the suspect been told is going to happen to the person who committed the crime? (2) What did the suspect think should happen to the person who committed the crime? (3) Did the suspect think the person who did commit the crime deserves a second chance? (If yes, under what circumstances?) (4) What should happen to the victim for saying this about you? (5) Why wouldn't the suspect have committed the crime? The interrogator then interprets the content of the suspect's answers to these questions (Reid, 1991b).

Interrogators are taught that "real need" offenders are usually first time offenders who are desperate; their crime is an opportunistic or emotional one; it is singular, and it rarely involves an accomplice. "Lifestyle" offenders are typically hard workers but flashy dressers, with outgoing personalities, generally well-liked and not usually suspected of a crime. They are usually higher social status and very cunning individuals who live beyond their means; and they commit premeditated offenses, which are ongoing crimes that rarely involves accomplices. "Impulse" offenders typically act spontaneously; have an aggressive personality; and they exhibit poor judgment, which may have been clouded during the commission of the crime. "Esteem" offenders attempt to intimidate or frighten their victims; their crime is opportunistic and premeditated; it may involve an accomplice; and the suspect frequently commits the crime to prove his self-worth.

The first step in interrogation profiling, then, is to identify the personality characteristics of the offender and the need he was trying to fulfill by committing the crime. The next step is to choose techniques of manipulation that appeal to the very same psychological needs that, according to the theory of the interrogation profile, motivated the suspect to offend in the first place. For example, techniques that emphasize "the suspect was acting out of character" or "bring up desirable traits about the suspect" are effective with "real need" criminals; techniques that "minimize the seriousness of the crime" or "make reference to the evidence against the suspect" are effective with "lifestyle" need criminals; techniques that "explain the suspect's original intent or blame the victim's actions" are effective for "impulse" need offenders; and techniques that "minimize the use of psychological force" or "minimize the frequency of the act" are effective with "esteem" need offenders (Reid, 1991b).

These techniques, because they are based on the interrogation profile, are taught as an effective method with which to psychologically manipulate the suspect into confessing. Like the polygraph, the Behavioral Analysis Interview and Neuro-Linguistic Programming, interrogation profiling draws on the rhetoric, symbols and cultural authority of science. And like these other, so-called "scientific" methods, the interrogation profile lacks any supporting evidence or empirical validation.

INTERROGATION TRAINING IN THE CLASSROOM

Every year tens, if not hundreds, of thousands of officers and investigators are taught "state of the art" interrogation techniques, as well as the law of confessions, at specialized police training courses across the United States. Many are taught by in-house training programs in their own (usually large, urban) police departments; others are trained in courses put on by local community colleges or criminal justice centers; many receive instruction from federal law enforcement training agencies and academies; and still others are taught by well-known private interrogation training firms such as Reid & Associates (a private lie-detection and interrogation training firm founded in 1947 by John Reid).

The interrogation seminar and weeklong training course is a recent phenomenon in American law enforcement. While specialized interrogation training manuals first appeared in the early 1940s, specialized interrogation training seminars and courses did not come into existence until 1974, more than thirty years later. Although popular revelations of physically coercive methods motivated the writing and dissemination of specialized interrogation training manuals among police professionals in the 1940s, third degree violence had long since disappeared as a common police practice by the mid-1970s. Instead, specialized interrogation training courses represented an effort by police trainers and leaders to develop increasingly professional practices in response to the popular controversies generated by the *Miranda* decision, which once again drew popular attention to police interrogation methods. To be sure, many urban police have received *general* instruction in interrogation methods and the law since the 1930s and

1940s as part of their basic academy training. But *specialized* interrogation training courses did not appear until 1974 when Reid & Associates began offering introductory courses. Since then, interrogation training has been a regular feature of detective training, and has become institutionalized in police work more generally. Just as police leaders and trainers have increasingly relied on interrogation manuals in recent decades, so too have they increasingly turned to specialized training programs to teach police investigators professional interrogation skills and strategies (Hart, 1981). In thirty years, the interrogation training course has spawned an international, multimillion dollar industry.

Perhaps it was not surprising that just as Inbau pioneered the leading interrogation training manual in law enforcement more than sixty years ago, so too would Reid, Inbau's longtime collaborator, establish the leading private interrogation training firm, which subsequently pioneered the first interrogation training seminars and courses in the United States. Since 1974 Reid & Associates has, according to their website (http://www. reid.com/) trained more than 150,000 thousand law enforcement personnel, including police from Canada, Mexico, England, Europe, Asia, and the Middle East. The interrogation methods fashioned by Inbau and taught by Reid & Associates have been emulated by other training programs. As with the Inbau and Reid interrogation training manual, Reid & Associates have become the most influential training center for professional interrogators in the United States. Reid & Associates advertise that these courses are "on the cutting edge of the most sophisticated and updated material on interrogation offered anywhere" and that their students "will receive training from instructors" who are "considered some of the best interrogators in the world" (Reid, 1994).

Interrogation training seminars and courses serve several functions. Most obviously, they train police officers and investigators in the increasingly subtle and sophisticated psychological methods of interrogation, thus increasing police efficiency. These specialized courses also instruct interrogators in the law of confessions, teaching them those interrogation tactics which are legally permissible and those which are not. Additionally, the courses certify police detectives as professionals who command exclusive control over a specialized body of knowledge. Accordingly, these courses certify the expertise of trained investigators, offering them credentials that testify to their advanced interrogation skills upon completion of the course. These courses thus advance the cause of police professionalism. Not surprisingly, these specialized training courses largely replicate the information presented in the training manuals. For example, Reid (1991a, 1991b) devotes most of the class time to teaching the Behavioral Analysis Interview and Nine-Step method of interrogation, just as Inbau et al. (1986, 2001) devote most of their text to these areas as well. However, the courses also depart from the texts by teaching their subjects in a less formal manner, drawing on more eclectic sources (such as publications, handouts, word of mouth, first-hand experiences and observations, and other lectures and seminars), and they are supplemented with videotapes, role-playing exercises, and group discussion. In addition, many of today's police interrogation training courses teach "state of the art methods" of behavioral lie detection or psychological manipulation that are not mentioned in manuals.

CONCLUSION

As we have seen, American police routinely employed coercive interrogation methods during much of their history. Early American police were not oriented to universalistic or abstract norms that condemned the routine use of violence, but rather to arbitrary and particularistic ones that supported the use of third degree practices as a regular part of daily investigative police work (Haller, 1976). In the absence of formal training and a professional identity, perhaps it is hardly surprising that early American police—who had regularly resorted to violence to solve many of their problems—employed physical force and duress during the questioning of criminal suspects.

The turn away from the third degree can be traced directly to the invention of the polygraph, which established the ideological and theoretical foundations for the "scientific" police interrogation practices later espoused by police interrogation training manuals and courses. The so-called lie detector was first introduced nearly a century ago as a more efficient and sophisticated method of establishing guilt than the third degree. Contemporary investigators are taught that the Behavioral Analysis Interview, Neuro-Linguistic Programming and interrogation profiling are, like the lie-detector, scientifically legitimate methods of detecting truth and deception and thus innocence and guilt.

Historically a response to the physically coercive practices of the "third degree," the interrogation techniques recommended by early interrogation manuals such as Kidd's *Police Interrogation* (1940) and Inbau's, *Lie Detection and Criminal Interrogation* (1942) were initially designed to minimize involuntary confessions. Opposed to police strong-arm methods, Inbau and Reid have been pioneers in fashioning modern interrogation methods that do not rely on physical threat or abuse. In recent years, the interrogation techniques advocated by Inbau and Reid have been substantively transformed from a grab bag of trial and error stratagems with no unifying or underlying logic to a highly sophisticated and systematic set of structured techniques. An individualized, scattershot format has been reorganized into a Nine-Step social psychological process model of interrogation that, as we have seen, operates according to a patterned logic of influence, persuasion, and manipulation. The Nine-Step method consolidates and expands earlier interrogation techniques into a *modus operandi:* An unfolding temporal sequence emerges through which the suspect's active resistance is neutralized as he is transformed into a passive actor who is persuaded by the interrogator's messages. The Nine-Step method emphasizes that interrogation is a lengthy and repetitive process in which the interrogator establishes psychological control over the suspect and gradually elicits a confession by raising the suspect's anxiety levels while simultaneously lowering his perception of the consequences of confessing.

The United States Supreme Court in *Miranda v. Arizona* (1966) excoriated the Inbau and Reid manuals for exploiting the weaknesses of criminal suspects and compelling confessions through psychologically oppressive techniques. The high court failed to appreciate the extent to which Inbau and Reid have advanced the ideology and the practice of police interrogation beyond the abusive practices of the third degree. Yet in the more than thirty-five years since *Miranda* was decided, Inbau and his co-authors have devised, extended and refined the kinds of subtle and sophisticated interrogation methods and ploys that the Supreme Court once seemed to condemn. The Behavioral Analysis Interview has turned the interrogator into a human polygraph, cloaking his subjective hunches about deception in the mantle of scientific legitimacy, while the Nine-Step method, equally mired in the aura of science, has trained interrogators to employ influence, manipulation, and persuasion to systematically break down the resistance of custodial suspects and induce confession. Despite the "scientific" rhetoric of police leaders and trainers, each of these methods of human lie-detection and psychological manipulation—beginning with the polygraph and extending to the Behavioral Analysis Interview, the Nine-Step method, Neuro-Linguistic Programming, and interrogation profiling—lack any scientific grounding. They are based on psychological assumptions that are *prima facie* implausible, they have not been corroborated by empirical evidence meeting minimal scientific standards, and evidence for their validity and reliability remains weak, if not altogether non-existent. The evidence alleged in support of these methods has typically consisted of little more than a series of unsystematic, *post hoc* observations designed to verify the authors own preconceptions, arguably their own self-fulfilling prophecies (Lykken, 1998). A diagnosis of deception (guilt) or truthfulness (innocence) based on the style of the suspect's behavioral responses or his eye movements during questioning rests, ultimately, on little more than the subjective hunches and personal judgments of the investigator. There is, in short, no reason to believe that their diagnostic value is any better than chance. Rather than comprising any kind of science, these diagnostic methods can more accurately be described as pseudo-science, as the folklore and myth of the contemporary culture of police interrogation in America, and ultimately as a throwback to benign forms of the trial by ordeal.

What is sociologically significant about the interrogation training manuals and seminars is not that they are founded on pseudo-scientific knowledge, but rather that Inbau, Reid and others have articulated and disseminated a professional ideology of interrogation that has sought to confer legitimacy on controversial police practices by invoking the cultural authority of modern science and technology. In Becker's (1963) terminology, Inbau and Reid have been "moral entrepreneurs," crusading reformers who have succeeded in establishing a new set of informal rules and practices for interrogators that have sought to legitimize police power both as the instrument and ideology of a professional mandate. Inbau and Reid's manuals and courses have trained generations of police in methods of interrogation that do not rely on physical force or explicit coercion for their efficacy. Inbau and Reid have long held not only that the third degree is unethical, but also that modern, psychological methods of interrogation are more effective at eliciting confessions.

The instrumental goal of modern, "scientific" interrogation methods is to create effective human lie-detectors and psychological manipulators. The aim of the psychological strategies that came to replace the third degree is, on the one hand, to teach interrogators to see through their subjects, to uncover the suspect's conscious and unconscious deceits and to read their minds; and, on the other, to break down the suspect's resistance and then elicit his (seemingly voluntary) compliance with the persuasive demands of the interrogator. The interrogation training industry has created a pseudo-science of behavioral detection and psychological manipulation that seeks to see through the self, to render it visible and to "program" it into confessing while at the same time rendering the psychological methods of interrogation—in contrast to the third degree— altogether invisible. Unlike the third degree, psychological interrogation is intended to deceive the suspect about the very essence of the custodial interaction: to represent the interrogator as the suspect's friend who is looking out for the suspect's best interest, to gather his trust and then to exploit his weaknesses and fears through a preplanned sequence of tricks and inducements that are designed to undermine the suspect's self-interest. In creating human lie detectors and psychological manipulators, contemporary interrogation has not only banished the third degree, but it has also taught police "to manipulate without the appearance of manipulation" (Cialdini, 2001, p. 12)—creating a seemingly flawless form of deception in the interrogation room while at the same time legitimizing an interrogation process that not too long ago was embroiled in political, legal and social scandal.

Acknowledgments: I thank Dan Lassiter and Welsh White for helpful comments and Brynn Nodarse for helpful research assistance.

REFERENCES

Ageloff, H. (1928, November 28). The third degree. *New Republic.* p. 28.

Arther, R. O., & Caputo, R. (1959). *Interrogation for investigators.* New York: Copp.

Bandler, R., & Grinder, J. (1979). *Frogs into princes: Neurolinguistic programming.* Moab, Utah: Real People Press.

Becker, H. (1963). *Outsiders: Studies in the sociology of deviance.* Glencoe: Free Press.

Becton, C. L. (1987). The drug courier profile: 'all seems infected that th' nfected spy, as all looks yellow to the jaundic'd eye.' *North Carolina Law Review, 65,* 417–479.

Bingham, T. A. (1910). Administration of criminal law: Third degree system. *The Annals of the American Academy,* 11–15.

Black, J. (1927). *You can't win.* New York: Macmillan.

Bohn, W. F. (1910). The sweating or third degree system. *Annals of the American Academy of Political and Social Science, 36,* 9.

Booth, B. (1930). Confessions and methods employed in procuring them. *Southern California Law Review, 4,* 83–102.

Brooks, M. (1989). *Instant rapport.* California: Warner.

Buckwalter, A. (1983). *Interviews & interrogations.* Boston: Butterworth.

Bureau of National Affairs (1985, August). *Polygraphs in employment, part V: The experts debate the issues.* (No. 1127, Washington, D.C.: U.S. Government).

Carey, A. (1930). *Memoirs of a murder man.* Garden City: Doubleday.

Carte, G., & Carte, E. (1975). *Police reform in the united states: The era of August Vollmer, 1905–1932.* Berkeley: University of California Press.

Chafee, Z. (1931, November). Remedies for the third degree. *Atlantic Monthly.* pp. 621–630.

Chisolm, B. O., & Hart, H. H. (1922). Methods of obtaining confessions and information from persons accused of crime. *The Fifty-First Congress of the American Prison Association* (pp. 3–19). New York City: Russell Sage Foundation.

Cialdini, R. (2001). *Influence: Science and practice.* Boston: Allyn and Bacon.

City of Oakland, Police Department (1999). *Advanced interviewing techniques.* Unpublished interrogation training manual.

Clark, C. L., & Eubank E. (1927). *Lockstep and corridor: Thirty-five years of prison life.* Cincinnati: University of Cincinnati Press.

Cloud, M. (1985). Search and seizure by the numbers: The drug courier profile and judicial review of investigative formulas. *Boston University Law Review, 65,* 843–920.

Conroy, J. (2000). *Unspeakable acts, ordinary people: The dynamics of torture.* Berkeley: University of California Press.

Deakin, T. J. (1988). *Police professionalism: The renaissance of American law enforcement.* Springfield, Illinois: Thomas.

Dilworth, D. C. (1976). *The blue and the brass: American policing, 1890–1910.* Gaithersburg, MD.: International Association of Chiefs of Police.

Editorial (1910). Thomas Byrnes and the 'Third Degree.' *Bench and Bar, 21,* 91–93.

Ekman, P., & O'Sullivan, M. (1991). Who can catch a liar? *American Psychologist, 46,* 913–920.

Fiaschetti, M. (1930a). The third degree as a cop sees it, *New York World,* p. 7.

Fiaschetti, M. (1930b, March 8). Forced convictions, *New York Telegram,* p. 1.

Fiaschetti, M. (1930c). *You gotta be rough: The adventures of detective Fiaschetti of the Italian squad.* New York: Doubleday, Doran.

Fogelson, R. (1977). *Big-city police.* Cambridge: Harvard University Press.

Frank, J., & Frank, B. (1957). *Not guilty.* New York: Doubleday.

Franklin, C. (1970). *The third degree.* London: Robert Hale.

Friedman, L. (1993). *Crime and punishment in American history.* New York: Basic.

Gordon, N., & Fleisher, W. (2002). *Effective interviewing and interrogation techniques.* San Diego: Academic Press.

Gottschalk, L. A. (1961). The use of drugs in interrogation. In A. Biderman & H. Zimmer (Eds.), *The manipulation of human behavior* (pp. 96–141). New York: Wiley.

Gudjonsson, G. H. (1992). *The psychology of interrogations, confessions and testimony.* New York: Wiley.

Gudjonsson, G. H. (2003). *The psychology of interrogations and confessions: A handbook.* New York: Wiley.

Haller, M. H. (1976). Historical roots of police behavior: Chicago, 1890–1925. *Law & Society Review, 10,* 303–323.

Hart, W. (1981, March). The subtle art of persuasion. *Police Magazine, 7–17.*

Harvard Law Review (1930). The third degree. *Harvard Law Review, 43,* 617–623.

Henderson, G. (1924). *Keys to crookdom.* New York: Appleton.

Hess, J. (1997). *Interviewing and interrogation for law enforcement.* Cincinnati: Anderson.

Holmes, W. (2003). *Criminal interrogation: A modern format for interrogating criminal suspects based on the intellectual approach.* Springfield, Illinois: Thomas.

Hopkins, E. J. (1931). *Our lawless police: A study of the unlawful enforcement of the law.* New York: Viking Press.

Inbau, F. E. (1942). *Lie detection and criminal interrogation.* Baltimore: Williams & Wilkins.

Inbau, F. E. (1948). *Lie detection and criminal interrogation.* (2nd ed.). Baltimore: William & Wilkins.

Inbau, F. E., & Reid, J. (1953). *Lie detection and criminal interrogation.* (3rd ed.). Baltimore: Williams & Wilkins.

Inbau, F. E., & Reid, J. (1962). *Criminal interrogation and confessions.* Baltimore: Williams & Wilkins.

Inbau, F. E., & Reid, J. (1967). *Criminal interrogation and confessions.* (2nd ed.). Baltimore: William & Wilkins.

Inbau, F. E., Reid, J., & Buckley J. P. (1986). *Criminal interrogation and confessions* (3rd ed.). Baltimore: Williams & Wilkins.

Inbau, F. E., Reid, J., Buckley, J. P., & Jayne, B. (2001). *Criminal interrogation and confessions.* (4th ed.). Gaithersburg, Maryland: Aspen.

International Police Magazine (1911, August). Police methods and their critics. p. 9.MAG

Irving, B., & Hilgendorf, L. (1980). Police interrogation: The psychological approach. *Royal Commission on Criminal Procedure Research Study No. 1.* London: HMSO.

Jayne, B. (1986). The psychological principles of criminal interrogation. In F. E. Inbau, J. Reid, & J. P. Buckley (Eds.), *Criminal interrogation and confessions.* Baltimore: Williams & Wilkins.

Johnson, D. R. (1979). *Policing the urban underworld: The impact of crime on the development of the American police, 1800–1887.* Philadelphia: Temple University Press.

Journal of American Institute of Criminal Law and Criminology (1912). The Third Degree., 2, pp. 605–607.

Kamisar, Y. (1980). *Police interrogation and confessions: Essays in law and policy.* Ann Arbor: University of Michigan Press.

Kassin, S., & McNall, K. (1991). Police interrogation and confessions: Communicating promises and threats by pragmatic implication. *Law and Human Behavior, 15,* 233–251.

Kassin, S. (1997). The psychology of confession evidence. *American Psychologist, 52,* 221–233.

Kassin, S., & Fong, C. (1999). I'm innocent: Effects of training on judgments of truth and deception in the interrogation room. *Law and Human Behavior, 23,* 499–516.

Keedy, E. (1937). The third degree and legal interrogation of suspects. *University of Pennsylvania Law Review, 85,* 761–777.

Kidd, W. R. (1940). *Police interrogation.* New York: Basuino.

Kleinmuntz, B., & Szucko, J. (1984). Lie-detection in ancient and modern times: A call for contemporary scientific study. *American Psychologist, 39,* 766–776.

Larson, J. A. (1932). *Lying and its detection: A study of deception and deception tests.* Chicago: University of Chicago Press.

Lavine, E. (1930). *The third degree: A detailed and appalling expose of police brutality.* New York: Garden City.

Lavine, E. (1936). *Secrets of the metropolitan police.* Garden City: Garden City.

Lee, C. D. (1953). *The instrumental detection of deception: The lie-test.* Springfield: Thomas.

Leo, R. A. (1992). From coercion to deception: The changing nature of police interrogation in America. *Crime, Law and Social Change: An International Journal, 18,* 35–59.

Leo, R. A. (1994). *Police interrogation in America: A study of violence, civility and social change.* Unpublished Doctoral Dissertation. University of California, Berkeley.

Lewis, B., & Pucelik, F. (1990). *The magic of nlp demystified.* Portland: Metamorphous Press.

Limpus, L. W. (1939). *Honest cop: Lewis J. Valentine.* New York: E.P. Dutton.

Los Angeles Evening Express (1929, June 7). Confessions to be doubted: Many secured by torture. p. 3.MAG

Lykken, D. (1998). *A tremor in the blood: Uses and abuses of the lie detector* (2nd ed.). New York: Plenum Press.

Macdonald, J., & Michaud, D. (1987). *The confessions: Interrogation and criminal profiles for police officers.* Denver: Apache Press.

Macdonald, J., & Michaud, D. (1992). *Criminal interrogation.* Denver: Apache Press.

Matthewson, D. (1929). The technique of the American detective. *The Annals of the American Academy, 146,* 214–218.

Miranda v. Arizona, 384 U.S. 436 (1966).

Morris, W., & Morris, M. (1988). *The Morris dictionary of word and phrase origins.* (2nd ed.). New York: Harper & Row.

Moston, S. (1992). Truth or lies: are police officers able to distinguish truthful from deceptive statements? *Policing, 8,* 26–39.

Mulbar, H. (1951). *Interrogation.* Springfield, Illinois: Thomas.

Murphy, C. J. (1929). Third degree: Another side of our crime problem. *Outlook, 151,* 522–526.

National Commission on Law Observance and Law Enforcement. (1931). *Report on lawlessness in law enforcement.* Washington: United States Government Printing Office.

New Republic (1930, March 19). American Torquemada. p. 13.

O'Connor, J., & Seymour, J. (1990). *Introducing neuro-linguistic programming.* London: Harper Collins.

O'Dwyer, W. (1987). *Beyond the golden door.* Jamaica, N.Y.: St. Johns University Press.

Ofshe, R. (1989). Coerced confessions: The logic of seemingly irrational action. *Cultic Studies Journal, 6,* 6–15.

Ofshe, R., & Leo, R. A. (1997a). The social psychology of police interrogation: The theory and classification of true and false confessions. *Studies in Law, Politics and Society, 16,* 189–251.

Ofshe, R., & Leo, R. A. (1997b). The decision to confess falsely: Rational choice and irrational action. *Denver University Law Review, 74,* 979–1122.

O'Hara, C. E. (1956). *Fundamentals of criminal investigation.* Springfield, Illinois: Thomas.

Oregon v. Elstad, 470 U.S. 298 (1985).

O'Sullivan, F. D. (1928). *Crime detection.* Chicago: O'Sullivan.

Purvis, M. (1936). *American agent.* New York: Garden City Publishing.

Rabon, D. (1992). *Interviewing and interrogation.* Durham, N.C.: Carolina Academic Press.

Reid, J. E., & Inbau, F. E. (1977). *Truth and deception: The polygraph ("lie-detector") technique.* (2nd ed.). Baltimore: Williams & Wilkins.

Reid, J. E. (1991a). *The Reid technique: Interviewing and interrogation.* Unpublished course booklet.

Reid, J. E. (1991b). *The Reid technique of specialized interrogation strategies.* Unpublished course booklet.

Reid, J. E. (1994). The Reid technique of interviewing and interrogation. Promotional brochure.

Reppetto, T. A. (1978). *The blue parade.* New York: Free Press.

Rhoads, S. A., & Solomon, R. (1987). Subconscious rapport building: Another approach to interviewing. *The Police Chief, 19,* 39–41.

Richardson, J. (1987). *The magic of rapport.* California: Meta Publications.

Risinger, M., & Loop, J. (2002). Three card monte, monty hall, *modus operandi* and "offender profiling": Some lessons of modern cognitive science for the law of evidence. *Cardozo Law Review, 24,* 193–285.

Royal, R. F., & Schutt, S. R. (1976). *The gentle art of interviewing and interrogation: A professional manual and guide.* New Jersey: Prentice-Hall.

Rutledge, D. (1996). *Criminal interrogation: Law and tactics.* Nevada: Copperhouse.

San Francisco Chronicle (1859, March 27). Confessions of prisoners. p. 1.

Scheck, B., Neufeld, P., & Dwyer, J. (2000). *Actual innocence: Five days to execution and other dispatches from the wrongly convicted.* New York: Random House.

Sears, D. W. (1948). Legal consequences of the third degree. *Ohio State Law Journal, 9,* 514–524.

Sedgwick, A. C. (1927. The third degree and crime. *The Nation, 124,* 666–667.

Simon, D. (1991). *Homicide: A year on the killing streets.* Boston: Houghton Mifflin.

Skolnick, J. H. (1961). Scientific theory and scientific evidence: An analysis of lie detection. *Yale Law Journal, 70,* 694–728.

Skolnick, J. H. (1982). Deception by police. *Criminal Justice Ethics,* 40–54.

Smith, D. L. (1986). *Zechariah Chafee, Jr.: Defender of liberty and law.* Cambridge: Harvard University Press.

Stansbury v. California, 511 U.S. 318 (1994).

Sutton, W. (1976). *Where the money was.* New York: Viking Press.

Sylvester, R. (1910, May 10–13). A history of the 'sweat box' and 'third degree.' Proceedings of the international Association of Chiefs of Police, 17th Annual Convention. Reprinted in J. H. Wigmore (1913), *The principles of judicial proof* (pp. 550–551). Boston: Little, Brown.

Trovillo, P. V. (1938). A history of lie-detection. *American Journal of Police Science, 29,* 848–881.

Trovillo, P. V. (1939). A history of lie-detection. *American Journal of Police Science, 30,* 104–119.

Underwood, B. (1979). Law and the crystal ball: Predicting behavior with statistical inference and individualized judgment. *Yale Law Journal, 88,* 1408–1448

Van Wagner, E. L. (1938). *New York Detective.* New York: Dodd, Mead.

Villard, O. G. (1927, October). Official lawlessness: The third degree and the crime wave. *Harpers Magazine, 155,* 605–624.

Wald, M., Ayres, D. W., Hess, M. S., & Whitebread, C. H. (1967). Interrogations in new haven: The impact of Miranda. *The Yale Law Journal, 76,* 1519–1648.

Walker, S. (1977). *A critical history of police reform: The emergence of professionalism.* Kentucky: Lexington.

Walker, S. (1980). *Popular justice: A history of American criminal justice.* New York: Oxford University Press.

Walters, S. (2003). *Principles of kinesic interview and interrogation* (2nd ed.). Boca Raton: CRC Press.

Walling, G. (1887). *Recollections of a New York chief of police.* New York: Caxton.

Weisberg, B. (1961). Police interrogation of arrested persons: A skeptical view. In C. R. Sowle (Ed.), *police power and individual freedom* (pp. 153–181). Chicago: Aldine.

White, W. S. (1979). Police trickery in inducing confessions. *University of Pennsylvania Law Review, 127,* 581–629.

White, W. S. (1998). What is an involuntary confession now? *Rutgers Law Review,* 2001–2057.

White, W. S. (2001). *Miranda's waning protections: Police interrogation practices after Dickerson.* Ann Arbor: University of Michigan Press.

Wicklander, D. (1979). Behavioral interviews to a confession. *Police Chief, 10,* 40–42.

Wicklander, D. (1980). Behavioral analysis. *Security World, 13,* 141–61.

Willemse, C. (1931). *Behind the green lights.* New York: Alfred A. Knopf.

Wrightsman, L., & Kassin, S. (1993). *Confessions in the courtroom.* Newbury Park: Sage.

Yeschke, C. L. (1993). *Interviewing: A forensic guide to interrogation.* Springfield, Illinois: Thomas.

Zimbardo, P. (1971). Coercion and compliance: The psychology of police confessions. In C. Perruci & M. Pilisuk (Eds.), *The triple revolution* (pp. 492–508). Boston: Little, Brown.

Zimring, F. E., & Frase, R. (1979). *The criminal justice system: Legal materials.* Boston: Little, Brown.

Zulawski, D., & Wicklander, D. (2002). *Practical aspects of interview and interrogation* (2nd ed.). Boca Raton: CRC Press.

————————4————————

"You're Guilty, So Just Confess!"

Cognitive and Behavioral Confirmation Biases in the Interrogation Room

CHRISTIAN A. MEISSNER AND
SAUL M. KASSIN

In *Principles of Police Interrogation*, Van Meter (1973) described the qualities of a good interrogator, which included such constructs as *integrity, self-respect*, and *professional attitude*. In addition, Van Meter suggested that individual *prejudices* should be left outside of the interrogation room, as a good interrogator must be *impartial*. He further elaborated:

> I have told you to keep the purpose of the interrogation in mind, and to strive for the confession from your suspect. But you must remember that the person that you are talking to might *not* be guilty. . . . Maintain an impartial attitude throughout the interrogation, and you will not be put in the position of having to make excuses. After all, the courts try the person; you are only an investigator for the court, not the person who has to make the decision of guilt or innocence. By remaining impartial, you can also keep yourself on the sidelines, so to speak, and be in a better position to analyze the suspect's reactions, your words and actions, and the facts in the case. You cannot think straight if you prejudge the person or if you become so personally involved in the case that you develop likes and dislikes. I have seen interrogators personally involved with a suspect, and they usually become very sensitive to the suspect and all that he says. This personal sensitivity often leads to harsh words and useless conversations with the suspect. (pp. 32–33)

CHRISTIAN A. MEISSNER • Department of Psychology, Florida International University, Miami, Florida 33199 (meissner@fiu.edu)   SAUL M. KASSIN • Department of Psychology, Williams College, Williamstown, Massachusetts 01267 (skassin@williams.edu)

While based largely upon his personal experiences in the field, Van Meter's cautions to the interrogator appear to ring true given recent psychological research on the role of *investigative bias* in the elicitation of coerced and sometimes false confessions. As will be discussed in the present chapter, this research indicates that a predisposition to presume suspects "guilty" may set into motion a process of confirmatory hypothesis testing in which evidence of deception is perceived and coercive interrogation techniques are applied. Such a bias toward presuming guilt may thereby limit the diagnostic value of an interrogation and increase the likelihood that a false confession is ultimately obtained.

A body of social science research has investigated the processes involved in police interviews, interrogations, and the elicitation of admissions and confessions (Conte, 2000; Davis & O'Donohue, in press; Gudjonsson, 1992, 2003; Kassin, 1997; Kassin & Wrightsman, 1985; Leo & Ofshe, 1998; Ofshe & Leo, 1997; Wrightsman & Kassin, 1993). Although the incidence of *false* confessions is unknown, there exist a disturbing number of documented cases in which defendants confessed and later retracted these confessions, but were convicted at trial and sometimes sentenced to death—only later to be exonerated by DNA or other forms of irrefutable evidence (Bedau & Radelet, 1987; Leo & Ofshe, 1998; Scheck, Neufeld, & Dwyer, 2000). Leo and Ofshe (1998) found that 73% of defendants were convicted at trial in cases that contained evidence of confessions later proved to be false. Researchers for The Innocence Project have also found that roughly a quarter of all DNA exoneration cases contained full or partial confessions, apparently false, in evidence (http://www.innocenceproject.org/).

Confessions have such powerful and rippling effects within the criminal justice system that researchers have investigated the personal and situational factors that lead people, both guilty and innocent alike, to confess in response to various police interrogation practices. For example, research shows that "minimization" tactics, by which interrogators normalize and suggest moral justification for the crime in question, lead people to infer that leniency would follow from confession, even in the absence of an explicit promise (Kassin & McNall, 1991). Other laboratory studies have shown that the presentation of false evidence—an interrogation tactic that has been sanctioned by the United States Supreme Court (*Frazier v. Cupp*, 1969), is recommended by those who train interrogators for law enforcement (Inbau, Reid, Buckley, & Jayne, 2001), and is commonly used (Leo, 1996a)—can lead innocent people to confess to acts they did not commit and even, at times, to internalize an erroneous belief in their own guilt (Kassin & Wrightsman, 1985; Kassin & Kiechel, 1996). Follow-up studies have replicated this laboratory effect, even when the stakes are raised (Horselenberg, Merckelbach, & Josephs, 2003), and have shown that children are more vulnerable to the effect than adults (Redlich & Goodman, 2003).

In light of a long history of documented false confessions, as well as recent controlled studies designed to identify why they occur, it is important to know whether judges, juries, and appellate courts adequately consider the individual and situational factors that put the accused at risk. The American judicial system relies upon the trial judge to determine if a confession is voluntary and reliable enough to be admitted into evidence, while the jury determines what weight, if any, should be afforded to that statement in reaching a verdict. However, studies have shown that confession evidence is the most potent form of incrimination, even more so than positive eyewitness identifications (Kassin & Neumann, 1997). Furthermore, research has shown that while jurors are sensitive to the extent to which confessions are voluntary or coerced, they invariably exhibit an increased conviction rate whenever confessions appear in evidence, even when they perceived these confessions to be coerced and when they claimed not to have been influenced by that information in reaching their verdicts (Kassin & Wrightsman, 1980, 1985; Kassin & Sukel, 1997). In short, confession evidence is highly potent and incriminating in court. It is also a troubling source of error in the annals of wrongful convictions.

As illustrated by van Meter's (1973) manual on interrogation practices, some early approaches to interrogation purported an "ethical framework" in which an interrogator's primary objective was to obtain evidence from suspects through the use of techniques that were not overly obtrusive or aggressive. Within this framework, judges and juries—not the police—are deemed the arbiters of guilt and innocence. In recent years, however, a vast number of law enforcement professionals in North America have been trained in an alternative framework, namely the Reid Technique (Inbau et al. 2001). Essentially, this approach involves a two-staged process in which: (1) a non-accusatorial interview of a witness or prospective suspect is conducted that is designed to assess truth and deception, followed by (2) a nine-step custodial interrogation of the suspect that is designed to elicit both an admission of guilt and a detailed post-admission narrative—the so-called full confession. It is at this second stage that the Reid Technique departs from van Meter's approach, in its advocacy of such tactics as isolation, positive confrontation, the interruption of denials, the presentation of false evidence, minimization, and various tactics for converting admissions into written narrative statements. Inbau et al. (2001) also note that the stage is set for interrogation once the investigator has reached a personal determination of *guilt*. In their words, "An interrogation is conducted only when the investigator is reasonably certain of the suspect's guilt" (p. 8).

Highly persistent and aggressive methods of interrogation increase the risk of false confessions, so it is important to know what factors might trigger judgments of deception and guilt, whether such judgments are accurate, and what effect such judgments might have on the interrogation that follows. This chapter explores recent lines of research addressing these questions. Our working thesis is that crime investigations are like all other human hypothesis-testing situations and are contaminated by social and cognitive bias. Basic research in non-forensic contexts has long shown that once people form an initial belief or expectation, they unwittingly search for, interpret, and create subsequent information in ways that verify these existing beliefs, while overlooking data that are contradictory (Nisbett & Ross, 1980; Trope & Liberman, 1996). In the present chapter, we discuss factors that influence the processes of interviewing and interrogation, and the elicitation of confessions. We then discuss the impact of *Miranda* warnings, videotaping requirements, and other proposed safeguards for the accused who might find themselves in an interrogation room.

INTERVIEW-BASED JUDGMENTS OF TRUTH AND DECEPTION

Justifying the use of heavy-handed and often deceptive tactics, many law enforcement professionals believe that they can determine in advance of interrogation whether a suspect is guilty or innocent. Sometimes the police formulate these hypotheses on the basis of rumors, witness reports, and physical or circumstantial evidence discovered during an investigation. In these instances, reason would dictate that the stronger the evidence is, the more likely investigators are to presume the suspect guilty.

Although the process is rational, it does not shield investigators and their suspects from error. Consider, for example, the recent re-investigation of the infamous 1989 Central Park jogger case in which a young woman was brutally beaten, raped, and left for dead. Defying the odds, she managed to survive, but she was—and still is—amnesic for the incident (Meili, 2003). Soon thereafter, solely on the basis of police-induced confessions, five boys, 14 to 16 years old, were convicted of the attack and sentenced to prison. At the time, it was easy to understand that detectives aggressively interrogated the boys, some of whom were "wilding" in the park that night (Sullivan, 1992). Yet based on a recent confession by a convicted serial rapist whose DNA was found in semen at the crime scene, the boys' convictions were vacated, their confessions apparently false (Kassin, 2002; *New York v. Wise*, 2002; Saulny, 2002).

The implications of making false inferences of deceit, based upon faulty evidence or a pre-interrogation interview, can be devastating to an innocent suspect. Consider the military trial of *U.S. v. Bickel* (1999; cited in Meissner & Kassin, 2002), in which one of us testified as an expert witness. In this case, a confession to rape was extracted by five agents who used persistent and highly aggressive techniques despite a lack of evidence against the defendant. When asked to explain why they interrogated the defendant with such conviction, one investigator said that he showed "signs of deception based on the training we have received . . . Some examples of body language is that he tried to remain calm but you could tell he was nervous and every time we asked him a question his eyes would roam and he would not make direct contact, and at times he would act pretty sporadic and he started to cry at one time" (p. 470). Correctly, we believe, this defendant was acquitted at trial.

There are many other instances, too, such as the case of Tom Sawyer, in Florida, where investigators accused him of sexual assault and murder, interrogated him nonstop for 16 hours, issued threats, and extracted a confession likely to have been false. The confession was suppressed by the judge and the charges were dropped. The reason Sawyer became a prime suspect was that his face flushed and he appeared embarrassed during an initial interview, a behavioral reaction interpreted as a sign of deception. What investigators did not know was that Sawyer was a recovering alcoholic with a social anxiety disorder that caused him to sweat profusely and blush a deep red in evaluative social situations (Leo & Ofshe, 1998). In another recent case, 14-year-old Michael Crowe and his friend Joshua Treadway were coerced during lengthy and highly deceptive interrogations into confessing to the stabbing death of Michael's sister Stephanie. The charges against the boys were later dropped when a local vagrant who was seen near the victim's home that night was found with her blood on his clothing. Why were these boys targeted in the first place? It seems that Crowe had become a prime suspect right from the start because the detectives assigned to the case believed he had reacted to his sister's death with inappropriately little emotion (http://www.courttv.com/trials/tuite/).

So, how do police investigators make interview-based judgments of truth and deception, and how well do they perform? What, if any, are the effects of training and experience on such judgments? One might expect that experience in law enforcement would both influence overall judgment tendencies and activate stereotypes, or "profiles," that associate deception and criminality with specific categories of individuals. Investigators may also be influenced in their judgments by fellow investigators, superiors, or social and political pressures from the community. Several studies now provide convincing evidence for an *investigator bias*, a tendency to perceive interview suspects as guilty.

Although detecting deception is an inherently difficult task, it is considered a critical skill for law enforcement professionals. Hence, in *Criminal Interrogations and Confessions*, Inbau et al. (2001) advise investigators in Behavior Analysis, in which they recommend the use of various verbal cues (e.g., qualified or rehearsed responses), nonverbal cues (e.g., gaze aversion, frozen posture, slouching), and behavioral attitudes (e.g., anxious, unconcerned, guarded) as indicators of deception. According to John E.

Reid and Associates, investigators trained in the use of these techniques can learn to distinguish truth and deception at an 85% level of accuracy (http://www.reid.com/service-bai-interview.html).

Consistently, however, psychological research has failed to support the claim that individuals can attain such high average levels of performance in making judgments of truth and deception. Rather, studies have shown that people perform at no better than chance levels when attempting to detect deception (DePaulo, Stone, & Lassiter, 1985; Memon, Vrij, & Bull, 2003; Vrij, 2000), that training programs produce only small and inconsistent improvements in performance compared with a control condition (Bull, 1989; Kassin & Fong, 1999; Porter, Woodworth, & Birt, 2000; Vrij, 1994; Zuckerman, Koestner, & Alton, 1984), and that police investigators and others with relevant on-the-job experience perform only slightly better than chance, if at all (Bull, 1989; DePaulo, 1994; DePaulo & Pfeifer, 1986; Ekman & O'Sullivan, 1991; Ekman, O'Sullivan, & Frank, 1999; Garrido, Masip, & Herrero, 2004; Koehnken, 1987; Porter, Woodsworth, & Birt, 2000).

One might argue that judgment accuracy in laboratory experiments is low because the investigators who participate are being asked to detect truths and lies that were given in low-involvement, low-stake situations. However, Vrij and Mann (2001) showed police officers videotaped press conferences of family members pleading for help in finding their missing relatives. Some of these family members had killed their own relatives, yet even in this high-stakes situation the investigators did not exceed chance level performance at detecting deception. One might also argue that investigators would make more accurate judgments of truth and deception when they conduct the interviews as opposed to when they merely observe sessions conducted by others. In fact, however, research does not support this notion. Buller, Strzyzewski, and Hunsaker (1991) had observers watch videotaped conversations between two other participants, one of whom was instructed to lie or tell the truth, and found that observers were more accurate in their assessments of the target than were those who engaged in the conversation. More recently, Hartwig, Granhag, Stromwall, and Vrij (in press) had some police officers interview college students who were guilty or innocent of committing a mock crime, while others observed videotapes of these interviews. Overall levels of accuracy did not exceed chance-level performance, and those who conducted the interviews were even less accurate than those who merely observed them. In short, while the law enforcement community assumes, often with great confidence, that investigators can use verbal and nonverbal behavioral cues to make highly accurate judgments of truth and deception, there is little evidence in published studies to support this claim (for a recent meta-analysis of presumed cues to deception, see DePaulo et al., 2003).

In a series of recent studies using forensically relevant materials, we have examined the extent to which police training triggers a presumption of guilt, leading investigators to interpret suspects' interview behavior through a confirmatory lens, thereby increasing the tendency to make false positive judgments of deception at high levels of confidence. In one study, Kassin and Fong (1999) trained some student participants, but not others, in the detection of truth and deception, before obtaining their judgments of mock suspects. This study was unique in two ways. First, some participants were trained in the popular Reid Technique, which has been used in the training of tens of thousands of law enforcement personnel. Second, judgments were made for a set of forensically relevant videotapes depicting brief interviews and denials by individuals who were truly guilty or innocent of committing one of four mock crimes (breaking and entering, shoplifting, vandalism, and a computer break-in). As in past studies conducted in non-forensic settings, the results showed that observers were generally unable to distinguish between truthful and deceptive suspects better than would be expected by chance. In addition, those who underwent training were less accurate than naïve controls—though trained participants were more confident and cited more reasons as a basis for these judgments. Closer inspection of these data further indicated that the training procedure triggered a response bias toward guilt.

Kassin and Fong's (1999) study suggests the disturbing possibility that police training in the detection of truth and deception leads investigators to make prejudgments of guilt, with high confidence, that are frequently in error. Does special training, as provided by the Reid Technique, create a response bias, making people overly sensitive to various non-diagnostic indicators of deception? From a practical standpoint, these provocative data are importantly limited by the fact that the observers were college students, not police detectives, and their training was condensed, not offered to those with prior experience as part of professional development.

To address these issues, Meissner and Kassin (2002) conducted both a meta-analysis and a follow-up study to examine the performance of experienced investigators. As a first step, we examined the extant literature for evidence of investigator bias. We suggested that previous studies may have overlooked patterns of response bias because researchers tended to examine overall judgment accuracy and not independently test performance on truthful and deceptive trials. We further suggested the use of signal detection theory to distinguish between accuracy in detecting deception, via a measure of "discrimination accuracy," and a tendency to perceive targets as overly truthful or deceitful, via a measure of "response bias" (e.g., Green & Swets, 1966; MacMillan & Creelman, 1991). We identified four studies that had compared investigators and naïve participants and two that manipulated training in deception detection. Across studies, we found that investigators and trained participants, relative to naïve controls, exhibited a proclivity to judge targets as deceptive rather than truthful.

In light of the evidence of an investigator bias, we sought to test the effect in police samples from the United States and Canada. Using the videotapes from the Kassin and Fong (1999) study, which depicted the interviews and denials given by guilty and innocent mock suspects, we compared experienced investigators to the trained and naïve student participants of the previous study. We found that the investigators exhibited no better than chance-level accuracy in their judgments, a response bias toward judging the suspects deceptive, and significantly greater confidence when performance was compared with the previous naïve sample of students. Within our sample of investigators, both years of interviewing experience and specialized training correlated significantly with the response bias, but not with accuracy. Apparently, the pivotal decision to interrogate suspects on the basis of their interview behavior is based on judgments that are confidently made, but biased and frequently in error.

Can investigators distinguish true and false confessions? Indeed, is it generally true—as assumed by those who see judges and juries as a safeguard against erroneous convictions—that people are adept at identifying as false the confessions of innocent suspects? In a recent study, Kassin, Meissner, and Norwick (2003) tested a common collateral assumption about the ability to detect truth and deception in an interrogation setting, namely that "I'd know a false confession if I saw one." To examine this question, and to compare the performance of police investigators and lay people, we recruited and paid male prison inmates in a state correctional facility to take part in a pair of videotaped interviews. Each inmate was instructed to give a full confession to the crime for which he was in prison ("Tell me about what you did, the crime you committed, that brought you here"). To ensure that all confessions contained the same ingredients, each free narrative was followed by a standardized set of ten questions concerning who, what, when, where, how, and other details. In a second videotaped interview, each inmate was provided with a skeletal, 1–2 sentence description of a true crime described by a preceding participant and was instructed to concoct a false confession ("I'd like you to lie about it and make up a confession as if you did it"). Using this yoked design, the first inmate's true confession became the basis of the second inmate's false confession, the second's true confession became the basis of the third's false confession, and so on. The order in which inmates gave true and false confessions was counterbalanced across sessions.

Using this procedure, we created a stimulus videotape that depicted 10 different inmates, each giving a single confession to one of five crimes: aggravated assault, armed robbery, burglary, breaking and entering, and automobile theft and reckless driving. Although the statements were not explicitly paired for presentation, the tape as a whole contained five true confessions and their false confession counterparts. In light of research showing that people are better judges of truth and deception when they use auditory cues rather than less diagnostic visual cues (Anderson, DePaulo, Ansfield, Tickle, & Green, 1999; DePaulo, Lassiter, & Stone, 1982), we also created audiotapes of these same confessions. Two groups of subjects served as judges in this study: college students and police investigators from Florida and Texas, more than two thirds of whom had received training in interviewing and interrogation. The results closely paralleled those obtained for judgments of true and false denials. From the videotapes, neither students nor the investigators performed significantly better than chance, though once again investigators were significantly more confident in their judgments. Consistent with past research, accuracy rates were higher among subjects who listened to audiotaped confessions than among those who watched the videotapes. Importantly, only the students exceeded chance level performance in this condition—though, once again, the investigators were more confident.

Using a signal detection framework to separate discrimination accuracy from response bias, performance in both subject samples was assessed in terms of "hits" (the proportion of guilty suspects whose confessions were correctly identified as true) and "false alarms" (the proportion of innocent suspects whose confessions were incorrectly identified as true). This analysis showed that investigators did not differ from the students in their hit rate, but they exhibited significantly more false alarms. When the estimates were combined into aggregate measures of discrimination accuracy and response bias, the results revealed an investigator bias effect, with police predisposed to believe both the true and false confessions. This bias was particularly evident among those with extensive law enforcement experience and among those who had received specialized training in interviewing and interrogation. Importantly, this response bias did not predispose police to see deception per se, but to infer guilt—an inference that rested upon a tendency to believe false confessions.

Why does law enforcement experience and training increase the tendency to see deception and guilt, and elevate confidence, while failing to improve detection accuracy? We assume that experienced and trained detectives approach the task with a working hypothesis, a presumption of guilt that activates a process of cognitive confirmation. This pseudo-diagnostic hypothesis-testing approach may be initiated by prior experiences, base rates, and stereotypes, as well as social-motivational factors that reward the collection of incriminating evidence. Depending upon the consistency of the evidence with the proposed hypothesis, such a process can elicit high confidence estimates that are unrelated to accuracy. The investigator may also fail to consider the reliability or predictive validity of the so-called indicators of deceit that they observe. It is often difficult to distinguish verbal or nonverbal cues to deception from those independently associated with nervousness, anxiety, or ambivalence—states that are highly probable in an interrogation room (Bond & Fahey, 1987; DePaulo et al., 2003). Prior conceptions, stereotypes, or "profiles" may also be particularly influential in police investigative work. Even more problematic, research has shown that when cognitive resources are limited (possibly due to time constraints or various social pressures) or when a theory is held in great confidence, individuals may neglect to gather evidence altogether and instead rely upon prior beliefs or expectancies in reaching a conclusion (Darley & Fazio, 1980; Hilton & Darley, 1991; Snyder, 1992). Investigators in our sample provided some hint of such an effect, as they generated significantly fewer cues to deception (when compared with our student sample) as a basis for their decision.

BEHAVIORAL CONFIRMATION IN THE INTERROGATION ROOM

Investigator response biases during the pre-interrogation interview increase the likelihood that innocent suspects will be interrogated by detectives who presume guilt, often with a high degree of certainty (Inbau et al., 2001). A second problem is that the presumption of guilt may influence an investigator's conduct while interrogating his or her suspects (Mortimer & Shepherd, 1999). Thus, consistent with Inbau et al. (2001), an interrogation might be thought of as a theory-driven social interaction led by an authority figure who holds a strong a priori belief about the target and who measures success by his or her ability to extract an admission from that target. For innocent people initially misjudged, one would hope that investigators would remain open-minded enough to monitor both the suspect and the situation, and to reevaluate their own beliefs (as suggested by Van Meter, 1973). However, research suggests that once an individual forms a belief, they often unwittingly create behavioral information that verifies that belief. This phenomenon—variously referred to by the terms self-fulfilling prophecy, interpersonal expectancy effect, and behavioral conformation—was first demonstrated by Rosenthal and Jacobson (1968) in their classic study of teacher expectancy effects, with similar results later obtained in military, business, and other organizational settings (McNatt, 2000).

The behavioral confirmation process was first demonstrated in a controlled laboratory experiment by Snyder and Swann (1978), who brought together pairs of participants for a "getting-acquainted" interview. The interviewers were led to believe that their partners were introverted or extraverted, after which they selected interview questions from a list. Two key results were obtained. First, interviewers adopted a confirmatory hypothesis-testing strategy, selecting introvert-oriented questions for the introvert (e.g., "Have you ever felt left out of a social group?") and extravert-oriented questions for the extravert ("How do you liven up a party?"). Second, interviewers unwittingly manufactured support for their beliefs through the questions they asked, which led neutral observers to infer that the interviewees truly were introverted or extroverted, according to expectation. Other laboratory experiments have further shown that behavioral confirmation is the outcome of a three-step chain of events, by which: (1) a perceiver forms a belief about a target person; (2) the perceiver unwittingly behaves toward that person in a manner that conforms to that belief; and (3) the target responds in turn, often behaving in ways that support the perceiver's belief (for reviews, see Darley & Fazio, 1980; Nickerson, 1998; Snyder, 1992; Snyder & Stukas, 1999).

Can a presumption of guilt influence the way police conduct interrogations, perhaps leading them to adopt a questioning style that is confrontational and highly aggressive? If so, can these behaviors lead innocent suspects to become anxious and defensive, thereby providing pseudo-diagnostic support for the presumption of guilt and increasing the risk of eliciting a coerced false confession? In light of research on the behavioral confirmation bias, it is important to know if this process is at work in the interrogation room. Akehurst and Vrij (1999), for example, found that increased movement among police officers triggered movement among interviewees, behavior that is interpreted as suspicious. Thus, behavioral confirmation may come about rather unwittingly during an interrogation.

Recently, Kassin, Goldstein, and Savitsky (2003) investigated whether a presumption of guilt might influence the conduct of student interrogators, the behavior of their suspects, and ultimately the judgments made by neutral observers. This study was conducted in two phases. In Phase I, suspects stole $100 as part of a mock theft or they took part in a related but innocent act, after which they were interviewed via headphones from a remote location. Other subjects, participating as investigators, were led to believe that most suspects in the study were truly guilty or innocent of the mock theft. These sessions were audiotaped for subsequent analysis and followed by post-interrogation questionnaires. In Phase II, observers listened to the taped interviews, judged the suspect as guilty or innocent, and rated their impressions of both sets of participants.

Overall, the results indicated that investigators who were led to expect guilt rather than innocence asked more guilt-presumptive questions, more frequently judged the suspect to be guilty, used more interrogation techniques, tried harder and exerted more pressure on suspects to confess, and made innocent suspects sound more defensive and guilty to observers. Consistently, the most pressure-filled interrogation sessions, as rated by all participants, were those that paired investigators who *presumed guilt* with suspects who were *actually innocent.* Observers who listened to the tapes later perceived the suspects in the guilty expectations condition as more defensive and as somewhat more guilty. In short, these results suggested that the presumption of guilt, which underlies all interrogation, sets in motion a process of behavioral confirmation by which expectations influence an interrogator's behavior, and ultimately the judgments of judges, juries, and other neutral observers. Although these results were obtained in a laboratory paradigm, they may well *under*estimate the risks incurred by innocent suspects in criminal justice settings in which (a) detectives are trained to have confidence, unfounded as it is, in their ability to divine guilt from a suspect's interview behavior; (b) police are specially trained in the use of psychological interrogation techniques; (c) police are motivated by career aspirations to solve cases; (d) police typically pressure suspects over the course of hours, not mere minutes, of interrogation; and (e) the presumption of guilt is a self-generated hypothesis—a condition that exacerbates confirmation biases (Haverkamp, 1993).

MINIMIZING COGNITIVE AND BEHAVIORAL CONFIRMATION PROCESSES

Cognitive and behavioral confirmation biases present a precarious dilemma both for the integrity and diagnostic value of police interviews and interrogations, and for the well being of innocent suspects subjected to the process. Given this potential for harm, we consider the following possible corrective mechanisms: (1) *Miranda* rights that suspects enjoy as a means of protection from interrogation, (2) a requirement that questioning of suspects be videotaped in its entirety, and (3) a reconstrual of the purposes, functions, and rules that regulate the conduct of interrogation.

MIRANDA: AN ADEQUATE SAFEGUARD?

There is one procedural safeguard in place to protect the accused from the presumption of guilt that accompanies interrogation. In the landmark case of *Miranda v. Arizona* (1966), the United States Supreme Court ruled that police must inform all suspects in custody of their Constitutional rights to silence and to counsel (similar "rights and warning" requirements are utilized in Canada). A number of subsequent rulings carved out exceptions to this rule and limited the consequences for noncompliance (e.g., *New York v. Quarles,* 1984; *Harris v. New York,* 1971; *Michigan v. Harvey,* 1990)—developments that have led legal scholars to question the extent to which police are free to disregard *Miranda* (Clymer, 2002; White, 2001). In an important symbolic decision, the Supreme Court recently upheld the basic warning-and-waiver requirement in the case of *Dickerson v. United States* (2000). In some respects, however, the requirement may not have much practical effect (Leo, 2001; White, 2001). For example, research shows that juvenile suspects do not fully comprehend or know how to apply the rights they are given (Grisso, 1981, 1998; Redlich, Silverman, Chen, & Steiner, this volume), and the same is true of adults who are mentally retarded or inexperienced within the criminal justice system (Everington & Fulero, 1999; Fulero & Everington, 1995, this volume).

Given the inherently coercive nature of a police interrogation, it would seem that a vast majority of suspects might exercise their constitutional rights to silence and to counsel and avoid the perils of an interrogation; however, research suggests the opposite tendency. Based on naturalistic observations of live and videotaped interrogations, Leo (1996b) found that four out of five suspects routinely waive their rights and submit to questioning (see also Leo & White, 1999). Studies in Great Britain suggest a similar, if not higher, waiver rate (Baldwin, 1993; Moston, Stephenson, & Williamson, 1993; Softley, 1980). One possible explanation for this tendency is that police employ tactics designed to obtain waivers just as they do confessions. Indeed, Leo (1996b) observed that police investigators often overcome the warning-and-waiver requirement by strategically establishing rapport with the suspect, offering sympathy and an ally, and minimizing the process as a mere formality, thus increasing perceived benefits relative to costs. In some jurisdictions, such as California, investigators are specifically trained in how to get suspects to talk "outside *Miranda*"—even after they have invoked their rights. Statements taken in this manner cannot be used in the state's case in chief at trial. However, such "off the record" disclosures (e.g., as to the whereabouts of physical evidence, names of witnesses, or identities of accomplices) may then be used both to generate other admissible evidence and to impeach the defendant at trial if he or she testifies (Philipsborn, 2001; Weisselberg, 2001).

A second possibility is suggested by individual differences among actual suspects. As was previously observed in Great Britain, Leo (1996) found that people who have no prior felony record are far more likely to waive their rights than are those with a history of criminal justice "experience." In light of known recidivism rates in criminal behavior and the corresponding base rate assumption that people without a criminal past are less likely to commit future crimes (Zamble & Quinsey, 1997), this difference suggests the hypothesis that innocent people in particular may be at risk to waive their rights. In a recent study, Kassin and Norwick (in press) tested this hypothesis in a controlled laboratory setting. Seventy-two participants who were guilty or innocent of a mock theft of $100 were apprehended for investigation. Motivated to avoid additional commitments of time, they were confronted by a neutral, sympathetic, or hostile male "detective" who sought a waiver of their *Miranda* rights. The results showed that although the detective's demeanor had no effect, participants who were innocent were significantly more likely to sign a waiver than those who were guilty—by a striking margin of 81 to 36 percent. Naively believing in the transparency and power of their own innocence to set them free, most of the innocent participants waived their rights even in the hostile detective condition, where the risk of interrogation was apparent.

VIDEOTAPING OF INTERROGATIONS: AN IDEA WHOSE TIME HAS COME

Several years ago, a national survey revealed that approximately one third of all large police and sheriff departments in the United States videotape at least some interrogations, particularly in cases of homicide, rape, and aggravated assault (Geller, 1993). Although Inbau et al. (2001) have long opposed the videotaping of interrogations, and whereas the FBI prohibits it, the practice has many advocates (Cassell, 1996; Drizin & Colgan, 2001; Gudjonsson, 2003; Leo, 1996; Wrightsman & Kassin, 1985). In Great Britain, the Police and Criminal Evidence Act of 1986 mandated that all suspect interviews and interrogations be taped (see Gudjonsson, 2003). In the United States, Minnesota and Alaska have videotaping requirements, the result of state Supreme Court rulings, and Illinois recently joined, as a result of new legislation (at least for homicide cases, see Davey, 2003). Other states may well follow suit.

There are a number of presumed advantages to a policy of videotaping all interviews and interrogations in their entirety. First, a videotape provides an objective and accurate record of what transpired, which is a common source of dispute at suppression hearings and at trial between detectives and suspects. Questions about whether and when *Miranda* rights were administered and waived, whether detectives shouted or physically intimidated the suspect, whether promises or threats were made or implied, and whether the details within a confession emanated from the police or suspect, are among the many issues that would be resolvable by a videotaping requirement. A related advantage is to increase the fact-finding accuracy of judges and juries. Provided that entire sessions are recorded and that the camera adopts a "neutral" perspective that focuses on both the accused and the interrogators (Lassiter & Geers, this volume; Lassiter, Geers, Handley, Weiland, & Munhall, 2002), judges and juries would likely make more accurate judgments when they see not only the confession but the conditions under which it was given and the source of the details it contained. Consistent with other research on the detection of truth and deception, we have found that lay people and police alike have difficulty distinguishing between true and false confessions (Kassin, Meissner, & Norwick, 2003). A preliminary study of how people perceive actual cases with taped confessions, in which the defendant's guilt or innocence is now known, suggests that seeing the interrogation may well lower the conviction rate among mock jurors who watch innocent false confessions without lowering the conviction rate among those exposed to guilty true confessions (Kassin, Leo, Crocker, & Holland, 2003).

Importantly, and more relevant to the purpose of this chapter, a videotaping policy would likely have an important prophylactic effect—namely, to deter police from using highly confrontational, deceptive, and psychologically coercive interrogation tactics (similarly beneficial, it will deter frivolous defense claims of coercion). Videotaping may also reduce the observed tendency among investigators to engage in biased, confirmatory interrogation strategies. Over the years, psychological research has shown that when people feel publicly accountable for decisions, they exhibit less bias in their hypothesis testing strategies (Tetlock & Boettger, 1989). In short, the presence of a camera, and the scrutiny that it implies, may help to increase the diagnostic value of interviews and interrogations and protect the innocent from false confessions.

NEW FRAMEWORKS FOR INTERROGATION

It may be unreasonable to set a normative model of hypothesis testing as a standard for investigators who are pressured to solve crimes by their departments and surrounding communities, and who often develop suspects on the basis of information that is incomplete, unreliable, and fraught with error. It is also important to recognize that the investigator biases described in this chapter, like the use of stereotypes in social perception, are not necessarily willful or conscious. Rather, they are a likely a cognitive byproduct of a law enforcement culture that values crime control over due process. Hence, Meissner and Kassin (2002) found that investigator biases in judgments of truth and deception were positively correlated with experience and training. It is also important to realize that these biases are unlikely to self-correct as a result of feedback, which is seldom available to permit a diagnostic evaluation of their beliefs. Still, a number of corrective steps can be taken to minimize the risks.

First, it is important to acknowledge that certain populations of suspects are uniquely vulnerable to influence and the production of false confessions. Several years ago, Kassin and Wrightsman (1985) introduced a taxonomy of false confessions that distinguished among those that are voluntary, coerced-compliant, and coerced-internalized. This categorization scheme has provided a useful framework for the study of false confessions and has been both used and refined by others (see Gudjonsson, 1992, 2003; Inbau et al., 2001; McCann, 1998; Ofshe & Leo, 1997; Kassin, 1997). This scheme has also suggested that individuals may be vulnerable to manipulation if they are characteristically predisposed to exhibit compliance or interrogative suggestibility. Youth, a lack of intelligence, cultural upbringing, and anxiousness or various psychological disorders that impair cognitive and affective functions present unique sources of vulnerability. Not surprisingly, large numbers of false confessions have been documented in recent years involving children, juveniles, and people who were mentally retarded (for a full discussion of individual differences, see Gudjonsson, 2003). It is therefore important that investigators identify high-risk individuals for purposes of interviewing and interrogation, and understand their potential vulnerability in high-pressure situations.

Second, police investigators and prosecutors should routinely review and analyze the statements they take in a genuine effort at external corroboration. A full confession is not a mere admission, but a post-admission narrative in which suspects recount what they did, how, when, where, with whom, and even why. Analyzing confessions involves a three-step process (Kassin, 2002). The first step concerns the *conditions* under which the statement was made and the extent to which coercive forces were present. These may include forces inherent in the suspect (e.g., age, intelligence, and mental state), the physical conditions of detention, and the use of promises, threats, and other social influence techniques during interrogation. The second step requires analysis of the extent to which the statement contains *details* that are internally consistent and accurate in relation to known crime facts (see Hill, 2003). Finally, the third step concerns a requirement of *attribution* for the source of details within the confession. A confession has diagnostic value if it contains details knowable only by the perpetrator that were not derivable from secondhand sources such as newspaper accounts, crime photographs, overheard conversations, and leading interrogation questions. In short, a confession can prove guilty knowledge to the extent that it is "generative," furnishing police with information not already known or leading to evidence not previously available (e.g., a body or weapon).

Third, psychological research in both forensic and non-forensic contexts indicates that certain conditions of custody and interrogation can increase the risk that guilty and innocent people alike would decide to confess in response to interrogation (Hilgendorf & Irving, 1981; Ofshe & Leo, 1997). For example, isolation can heighten the stress of being in custody, especially after extended periods of time, and hence the incentive to escape (Zimbardo, 1967); fatigue and sleep-deprivation heighten susceptibility to influence and seriously impair complex decision-making ability (Blagrove, 1996; Harrison & Horne, 2000); maximization, often bolstered by the presentation of false evidence, can increase compliance, internalization, and memory confabulation among innocents as well as those who are guilty (Kassin & Kiechel, 1996; Horselenberg, Merckelbach, & Josephs, 2003; Redlich & Goodman, 2003); and minimization can lead people to infer that leniency is forthcoming upon confession, thus serving as the functional equivalent of an explicit promise (Kassin & McNall, 1991).

The problem with these conditions and techniques is that they are indiscriminant, having the power to influence both guilty and innocent suspects. Although it is premature to recommend a research-based approach to interrogation, we think it is important to be explicit about the goal: namely, an approach that is "surgically precise" in its impact so that confessions are drawn from those who are guilty, but not from those who are innocent. With this goal in mind, consider the common and understandable practice of confronting suspects with incriminating evidence. Research shows that a suspect's perception of the strength of the evidence is a highly significant predictor of whether he or she decides to confess (Moston, Stephenson, & Williamson, 1992). Since links to a crime via physical traces, eyewitnesses, and alibis are, by nature, more prevalent for guilty suspects than for innocents, confrontation should have corresponding differential effects, drawing confessions only from guilty suspects trapped by other evidence. But now consider the impact of exaggerating or lying to a suspect about the evidence, either explicitly or by implication (e.g., in the form of an alleged failed polygraph, fingerprint, hair sample, eyewitness, or accomplice confession)—a tactic commonly found in false confession cases, suggested by Inbau et al. (2001), and sanctioned by the U.S. Supreme Court (Frazier v. Cupp, 1969). The presentation of false evidence is a non-surgical tactic that can be used without discrimination and with influence equally upon both guilty and innocent suspects alike. The simple result of such manipulation is to elicit anxiety and, under certain stressful circumstances, an admission that is not perfectly diagnostic of guilt.

Finally, new approaches to interrogation that radically depart from the norm of current practice should be explored. Over the past two decades, the British have altered their approach to interrogation, largely in response to wrongful convictions in cases with documented false confessions. The problem prompted a Royal Commission on Criminal Procedure in 1981, inspired several studies of police interrogation (Irving, 1980; Irving & Hilgendorf, 1980; Softley, 1980), and resulted in the 1984 Police and Criminal Evidence Act (PACE). PACE forced police to identify suspects who may be vulnerable and to record interrogations for subsequent evaluation by the courts. Research conducted in Great Britain after implementation of PACE has suggested that although interrogations have become less coercive, the confession rate has not been affected (Irving & McKenzie, 1989).

Despite the impact of PACE, a number of coercive interrogations were observed, which prompted a Royal Commission on Criminal Justice Report (1993), the adoption of a new "culture" of interrogation practices, and the development of a PEACE model of interviewing (Preparation and Planning, Engage and Explain, Account, Closure, and Evaluate; see Gudjonsson, 2003;

Milne & Bull, 1999; Bull & Milne, this volume). At the heart of this approach, and in sharp contrast to the confrontational Reid Technique, is an ethical and inquisitorial frame of mind (Mortimer & Shepherd, 1999). Overall, PEACE proposes a formal interrogation in which the purpose is clearly communicated to the suspect, rights are properly administered, rapport is established, and a "conversation" is engaged between the lead investigator and suspect. More an interview than an interrogation, the primary purpose of this conversation is to gather information, not to elicit a confession (Milne & Bull, 1999; Shepherd, 1986). Research is needed to examine the influence of such an approach on police, suspects, and observers, and to test the hypothesis that it offers an effective and feasible alternative to the more guilt-presumptive, confrontational approaches to interrogation (see Bull & Milne, this volume, for preliminary findings in this regard).

REFERENCES

Akehurst, L., & Vrij, A. (1999). Creating suspects in police interviews. *Journal of Applied Social Psychology, 29,* 192–210.

Anderson, D. E., DePaulo, B. M., Ansfield, M. E., Tickle, J. J., & Green, E. (1999). Beliefs about cues to deception: Mindless stereotypes or untapped wisdom? *Journal of Nonverbal Behavior, 23,* 67–89.

Baldwin, J. (1993). Police interviewing techniques: Establishing truth or proof? *The British Journal of Criminology, 33,* 325–352.

Bedau, H. A., & Radelet, M. L. (1987). Miscarriages of justice in potentially capital cases. *Stanford Law Review, 40,* 21–179.

Blagrove, M. (1996). Effects of length of sleep deprivation on interrogative suggestibility. *Journal of Experimental Psychology: Applied, 2,* 48–59.

Bond, C. F., Jr., & Fahey, W. E. (1987). False suspicion and the misperception of deceit. *British Journal of Social Psychology, 26,* 41–46.

Bull, R. (1989). Can training enhance the detection of deception? In J.C. Yuille (Ed.), *Credibility assessment* (pp. 83–99). London: Kluwer Academic.

Buller, D. B., Strzyzewski, K. D., & Hunsaker, F. G. (1991). Interpersonal deception: II. The inferiority of conversational participants as deception detectors. *Communication Monographs, 58,* 25–40.

Cassell, P. G. (1996). Miranda's social costs: An empirical reassessment. *Northwestern University Law Review, 90,* 387–499.

Clymer, S. D. (2002). Are police free to disregard Miranda? *Yale Law Journal, 112,* 447–552.

Conte, R. (2000). The psychology of false confessions. *Journal of Credibility Assessment and Witness Psychology, 2(1),* 14–36.

Darley, J. M. & Fazio, R. H. (1980). Expectancy confirmation processes arising in the social interaction sequence. *American Psychologist, 35,* 867–881.

Davey, M. (2003). Illinois Will Require Taping Of Homicide Interrogations. New York Times, July 17, 2003, Section A , page 16.

Davis, D., & O'Donohue, W. (in press). The road to perdition: "Extreme influence" tactics in the interrogation room. In W. O'Donohue, P. Laws, & C. Hollin (Eds.), *Handbook of forensic psychology*. New York: Basic.

DePaulo, B. M. (1994). Spotting lies: Can humans learn to do better? *Current Directions in Psychological Science, 3,* 83–86.

DePaulo, B. M., Lassiter, G. D., & Stone, J. I. (1982). Attentional determinants of success at detecting deception and truth. *Personality and Social Psychology Bulletin, 8*, 273–279.

DePaulo, B. M., Lindsay, J. J., Malone, B. E., Muhlenbruck, L., Charlton, K., & Cooper, H. (2003). Cues to deception. *Psychological Bulletin, 129*, 74–112.

DePaulo, B. M., & Pfeifer, R, L. (1986). On-the-job experience and skill at detecting deception. *Journal of Applied Social Psychology, 16*, 249–267.

DePaulo, B. M., Stone, J. I., & Lassiter, G. D. (1985). Deceiving and detecting deceit. In B.R. Schlenker (Ed.), *The self and social life* (pp. 323–370). New York: McGraw-Hill.

Dickerson v. United States, 120 S. Ct. 2326 (2000).

Drizin, S. A., & Colgan, B. A. (2001). Let the cameras roll: Mandatory videotaping of interrogations is the solution to Illinois' problem of false confessions. *Loyola University Chicago Law Journal, 32*, 337–424.

Ekman, P., & O'Sullivan, M. (1991). Who can catch a liar? *American Psychologist, 46*, 913–920.

Ekman, P., O'Sullivan, M., & Frank, M. G. (1999). A few can catch a liar. *Psychological Science, 10*, 263–266.

Everington, C., & Fulero, S. M. (1999). Competence to confess: Measuring understanding and suggestibility of defendants with mental retardation. *Mental Retardation, 37*, 212–220.

Frazier v. Cupp, 394 U.S. 731 (1969).

Fulero, S. M., & Everington, C. (1995). Assessing competency to waive Miranda rights in defendants with mental retardation. *Law and Human Behavior, 19*, 533–543.

Garrido, E., Masip,. J., & Herrero, C. (2004). Police officers' credibility judgments: Accuracy and estimated ability. *International Journal of Psychology*.

Geller, W. A. (1993). Videotaping interrogations and confessions. *National Institute of Justice: Research in Brief*. Washington, DC: U.S. Department of Justice.

Green, D. M., & Swets, J. A. (1966). *Signal detection theory and psychophysics*. New York: Wiley.

Grisso, T. (1981). *Juveniles' waiver of rights: Legal and psychological competence*. New York: Plenum.

Grisso, T. (1998). *Forensic evaluation of juveniles*. Sarasota, FL: Professional Resource Press.

Gudjonsson, G. H. (1992). *The psychology of interrogations, confessions, and testimony*. London: Wiley.

Gudjonsson, G. H. (2003). *The psychology of interrogations and confessions: A handbook*. West Sussex, England: Wiley.

Harris v. New York, 401 U.S. 222 (1971).

Harrison, Y., & Horne, J. A. (2000). The impact of sleep deprivation on decision making: A review. *Journal of Experimental Psychology: Applied, 6*, 236–249.

Hartwig, M., Granhag, P. A., Strömwall, L. A., & Vrij, A. (in press). Police officers' lie detection accuracy: Interrogating freely vs. observing video. *Police Quarterly*.

Haverkamp, B. E. (1993). Confirmatory bias in hypothesis testing for client-identified and counselor self-generated hypotheses. *Journal of Counseling Psychology, 40*, 303–315.

Hilgendorf, E. L., & Irving, M. (1981). A decision-making model of confessions. In M. Lloyd-Bostock (Ed.), *Psychology in legal contexts: Applications and limitations* (pp. 67–84). London: MacMillan.

Hill, M. D. (2003). Identifying the source of critical details in confessions. *Forensic Linguistics, 10*, 23–61.

Hilton, J. L., & Darley, J. M. (1991). Constructing other persons: A limit on the effect. *Journal of Experimental Social Psychology, 21*, 1–18.

Inbau, F. E., Reid, J. E., Buckley, J. P., & Jayne, B. C. (2001). *Criminal interrogation and confessions* (4th ed.). Gaithersberg, MD: Aspen.

Horselenberg, R., Merckelbach, H. & Josephs, S. (2003). Individual differences and false confessions: A conceptual replication of Kassin and Kiechel (1996). *Psychology, Crime, and Law, 9*, 1–18.

Irving, B. (1980). *Police interrogation. A case study of current practice. Research Studies No. 2*. London: HMSO.

Irving, B., & Hilgendorf, L. (1980). *Police interrogation: The psychological approach. Research Studies No. 1*. London: HMSO.

Irving, B., & McKenzie, I. K. (1989). *Police interrogation: the effects of the Police and Criminal Evidence Act*. London: Police Foundation of Great Britain.

Kassin, S. M. (1997). The psychology of confession evidence. *American Psychologist, 52*, 221–233.

Kassin, S. (2002). False confessions and the jogger case, *New York Times*, November 1, 2002, p. A31.

Kassin, S. M., & Fong, C. T. (1999). "I'm innocent!" Effects of training on judgments of truth and deception in the interrogation room. *Law and Human Behavior, 23*, 499–516.

Kassin, S. M., Goldstein, C. J., & Savitsky, K. (2003). Behavioral confirmation in the interrogation room: On the dangers of presuming guilt. *Law and Human Behavior, 27*, 187–203.

Kassin, S. M., & Kiechel, K. L. (1996). The social psychology of false confessions: Compliance, internalization, and confabulation. *Psychological Science, 7*, 125–128.

Kassin, S., Leo, R., Crocker, C., & Holland, L. (2003, July). Videotaping Interrogations: Does it enhance the jury's ability to distinguish true and false confessions? Paper presented at the Psychology & Law International, Interdisciplinary Conference, Edinburgh, Scotland.

Kassin, S. M., & McNall, K. (1991). Police interrogations and confessions: Communicating promises and threats by pragmatic implication. *Law and Human Behavior, 15*, 233-251.

Kassin, S. M., Meissner, C., & Norwick, R. (2003, July). The post-interrogation safety net: "I'd know a false confession if I saw one." Paper presented at the Psychology & Law International, Interdisciplinary Conference, Edinburgh, Scotland.

Kassin, S. M., & Neumann, K. (1997). On the power of confession evidence: An experimental test of the fundamental difference hypothesis. *Law and Human Behavior, 21*, 469–484.

Kassin, S. M., & Norwick, R. J. (in press). Why suspects waive their *Miranda* rights: The power of innocence. *Law and Human Behavior*.

Kassin, S. M., & Sukel, H. (1997). Coerced confessions and the jury: An experimental test of the "harmless error" rule. *Law and Human Behavior, 21*, 27–46.

Kassin, S. M., & Wrightsman, L. S. (1980). Prior confessions and mock juror verdicts. *Journal of Applied Social Psychology, 10*, 133–146.

Kassin, S. M., & Wrightsman, L. S. (1985). Confession evidence. In S. M. Kassin & L. S. Wrightsman (Eds.), *The psychology of evidence and trial procedure* (pp. 67–94). Beverly Hills, CA: Sage.

Koehnken, G. (1987). Training police officers to detect deceptive eyewitness statements: Does it work? *Social Behavior, 2*, 1–17.

Lassiter, G. D., Geers, A. L., Handley, I. M., Weiland, P. E., & Munhall, P. J., (2002). Videotaped confessions and interrogations: A simple change in camera perspective alters verdicts in simulated trials. *Journal of Applied Psychology, 87*, 867–874.

Leo, R. A. (1996a). Inside the interrogation room. *The Journal of Criminal Law and Criminology, 86*, 266–303.

Leo, R. A. (1996b). Miranda's revenge: Police interrogation as a confidence game. *Law and Society Review, 30*, 259–288.

Leo, R. A. (2001). Questioning the relevance of Miranda in the twenty-first century. *Michigan Law Review, 99*, 1000–1029.

Leo, R. A., & Ofshe, R. J. (1998). The consequences of false confessions: Deprivations of liberty and miscarriages of justice in the age of psychological interrogation. *Journal of Criminal Law and Criminology, 88*, 429–496.

Leo, R. A., & White, W. S. (1999). Adapting to *Miranda*: Modern interrogators' strategies for dealing with the obstacles posed. *Minnesota Law Review, 84*, 397–472.

MacMillan, N. A., & Creelman, C. D. (1991). *Detection theory: A user's guide*. New York: Cambridge University Press.

McCann, J. T. (1998). A conceptual framework for identifying various types of confessions. *Behavioral Sciences and the Law, 16*, 441–453.

McNatt, D. B. (2000). Ancient Pygmalion joins contemporary management: A meta-analysis of the result. *Journal of Applied Psychology, 85*, 314–322.

Meili, T. (2003). *I am the Central Park jogger: A story of hope and possibility.* New York: Scribner.

Meissner, C. A., & Kassin, S. M. (2002). "He's guilty!": Investigator bias in judgments of truth and deception. *Law & Human Behavior, 26*, 469–480.

Memon, A., Vrij, A., & Bull, R. (2003). *Psychology and law: Truthfulness, accuracy and credibility.* London: Jossey-Bass.

Milne, R., & Bull, R. (1999). *Investigative interviewing: Psychology and practice.* New York: Wiley.

Michigan v. Harvey, 494 U.S. 344 (1990).

Miranda v. Arizona, 384 U.S. 336 (1966).

Mortimer, A., & Shepherd, E. (1999). Frames of mind: schemata guiding cognition and conduct in the interviewing of suspected offenders. In A. Memon & R. Bull (Eds.), *Handbook of the psychology of interviewing* (p. 293–315). Chichester: Wiley.

Moston, S., Stephenson, G. M., & Williamson, T. M. (1992). The effects of case characterisation suspect behaviour during questioning. *British Journal of Criminology, 32*, 23–40.

Moston, S., Stephenson, G. M., & Williamson, T. M. (1993). The incidence, antecedents and consequences of the use of the right to silence during police questioning. *Criminal Behavior and Mental Health, 3*, 30–47.

New York v. Quarles, 467 U.S. 649 (1984).

New York v. Wise et al., Affirmation in Response to Motion to Vacate Judgment of Conviction, Indictment No. 4762/89 (December 5, 2002).

Nickerson, R. S. (1998). Confirmation bias: A ubiquitous phenomenon in many guises. *Review of General Psychology, 2*, 175–220.

Nisbett, R. E. & Ross, L. (1980). *Human inference: Strategies and shortcomings of social judgment.* Englewood Cliffs, NJ: Prentice-Hall.

Ofshe, R. J., & Leo, R. A. (1997). The social psychology of police interrogation: The theory and classification of true and false confessions. *Studies in Law, Politics, and Society, 16*, 189–251.

Philipsborn, J. T. (2001). Interrogation tactics in the post-Dickerson era. *The Champion,* January/February 2001, pp. 18–22.

Porter, S., Woodworth, M., & Birt, A. R. (2000). Truth, lies, and videotape: An investigation of the ability of federal parole officers to detect deception. *Law & Human Behavior, 24*, 643–658.

Redlich, A. D., & Goodman, G. S. (2003). Taking responsibility for an act not committed: The influence of age and suggestibility. *Law and Human Behavior, 27*, 141–156.

Rosenthal, R., & Jacobson, L. (1968). *Pygmalion in the classroom: Teacher expectation and pupils' intellectual development.* New York: Holt, Rinehart, & Winston.

Royal Commission on Criminal Justice Report (1993). Cmnd. 2263. London: HMSO Saulny, S. (2002). Why confess to what you didn't do? *The New York Times,* December 8, 2002, Section 4.

Scheck, B., Neufeld, P., & Dwyer, J. (2000). *Actual innocence.* Garden City, NY: Doubleday.

Shepherd, E. (1986). The conversational core of policing. *Policing, 2*, 294–303.

Snyder, M. (1992). Motivational foundations of behavioral confirmation. *Advances in Experimental Social Psychology, 25*, 67–114.

Snyder, M., & Stukas, A.(1999). Interpersonal processes: The interplay of cognitive, motivational, and behavioral activities in social interaction. *Annual Review of Psychology, 50*, 273–303.

Snyder, M. & Swann, W. B., Jr. (1978). Hypothesis-testing processes in social interaction. *Journal of Personality and Social Psychology, 36*, 1202–1212.

Softley, P. (1980). *Police interrogation. An observational study in four police stations. Home Office Research Study No. 61.* London: HMSO.

Sullivan, T. (1992). *Unequal verdicts: The Central Park jogger trials.* New York: Simon & Schuster.

Tetlock, P. E. & Boettger, R. (1989). Accountability: A social magnifier of the dilution effect. *Journal of Personality and Social Psychology, 57*, 388–398.

Trope, Y. & Liberman, A. (1996). Social hypothesis testing: Cognitive and motivational mechanisms. In E. Higgins & A. Kruglanski (Eds.), *Social psychology: Handbook of basic principles* (pp. 239–270). New York: Guilford Press.

Van Meter, C. H. (1973). *Principles of police interrogation*. Springfield, IL: Thomas.

Vrij, A. (1994). The impact of information and setting on detection of deception by police detectives. *Journal of Nonverbal Behavior, 18*, 117–132.

Vrij, A. (2000). *Detecting lies and deceit: The psychology of lying and the implications for professional practice*. London: Wiley.

Vrij, A., & Mann, S. (2001). Who killed my relative? Police officers' ability to detect real-life high-stake lies. *Psychology, Crime, & Law, 7*, 119–132.

Weisselberg, C. D. (2001). In the stationhouse after *Dickerson. Michigan Law Review, 99*, 1121–1167.

White, W.S. (2001). *Miranda's* failure to restrain pernicious interrogation practices. *Michigan Law Review, 99*, 1211–1240.

Wrightsman, L.S., & Kassin, S.M. (1993). *Confessions in the courtroom*. Newbury Park, CA: Sage.

Zamble, E., & Quinsey, V. L. (1997). *The criminal recidivism process*. New York: Cambridge University Press.

Zimbardo, P.G. (1967, June). The psychology of police confessions. *Psychology Today, 1*, 17–20, 25–27.

Zuckerman, M., Koestner, R., & Alton, A. O. (1984). Learning to detect deception. *Journal of Personality & Social Psychology, 46*, 519–528.

5

The Police Interrogation of Children and Adolescents

ALLISON D. REDLICH, MELISSA SILVERMAN, JULIE CHEN, AND HANS STEINER

For delinquents, law enforcement is the doorway to the juvenile justice system. Once a juvenile is apprehended for a law violation, it is the police officer who first determines if the juvenile will move deeper into the justice system or will be diverted (Snyder & Sickmund, 1999, p. 111).

Every year, there are substantial numbers of juveniles who come into contact with police and the legal system. In 2000, 2.4 million juveniles (17 years or younger) were formally arrested, 32% (758,208) of whom were aged 14 years and younger (Snyder, 2002). Many more children interact with law enforcement but are not officially arrested. And, as the above quote indicates, what occurs during the police interaction can have a significant impact on juveniles' further passage into the legal system.

Whether the crime is a non-serious misdemeanor or a serious felony, the police usually question persons suspected of committing the acts. During this questioning period, the police may use various manipulative and potentially coercive techniques to get suspects to incriminate themselves.

ALLISON D. REDLICH • Policy Research Associates, Inc., 345 Delaware Avenue, Delmar, New York 12054 (aredlich@prainc.com).   MELISSA SILVERMAN • Stanford University School of Medicine Department of Psychiatry and Behavioral Sciences, Stanford, California 94305-5719.   JULIE CHEN • Stanford University School of Medicine Department of Psychiatry and Behavioral Sciences, Stanford, California 94305-5719.   HANS STEINER • Stanford University School of Medicine Department of Psychiatry and Behavioral Sciences, Stanford, California 94305-5719.

Currently, there is little empirical information about how children are questioned when suspected of committing crimes. In contrast, there is a wealth of knowledge about how children are questioned in forensic interviews when suspected of being the victim of or witness to crimes (e.g., Poole & Lamb, 1998). The number of wrongful arrests and convictions involving juveniles and questionable police methods is unacceptable: of 125 proven false confession cases compiled by Leo and Drizin (2003), an alarming 33% involve juveniles. Most recently, the case of the juveniles who falsely confessed to, and were subsequently convicted and imprisoned for the 1989 Central Park jogger rape case has come to light and a heightened focus is being placed on how juveniles are treated by our nation's police officers (Kassin, 2002).

The purpose of this chapter is to describe the relevant law and research that has been conducted on children and interrogations and children and confessions, as well as to raise awareness of what issues need to be addressed. After first briefly describing modern-day police interrogation, we describe the extant information on youthful interrogations. We then draw from the large literature on child victim/witnesses to make inferences about the abilities of child suspects in regard to forensic interviews, and about the possible dangers of using questionable police interrogation techniques with children and teens.

CONTEMPORARY POLICE INTERROGATION

In the past 50 years, police interrogation techniques have moved from heavy-handed intimidation, shine-a-bright-light-in-your-face tactics to ones relying on psychological manipulation (Gudjonsson, 2003; Kassin, 1997; Leo, this volume). When a person is suspected of a crime, s/he may be brought into the police station to be interrogated. Before a formal interrogation begins, the police will usually "interview" the person to determine if they want to go ahead with the "interrogation." Thus there is a thin line between the interview and the interrogation, but one method of distinguishing the two is the reading of the *Miranda* warning. Before an interrogation can begin, the suspect must be made aware of the right to have a lawyer present and the right against self-incrimination. For a police interrogation to proceed, the suspect must waive *Miranda* rights, and for this waiver to stand up in a court of law, it must be made knowingly, intelligently, and voluntarily (see Fulero & Everington, this volume for a discussion of these criteria). Robin (1982) contends that "[Juveniles'] low status in relation to their adult interrogators, societal norms concerning youthful obedience to authority, children's greater dependence upon adults, and their lower threshold of intimidation" are coercive factors present in juveniles' decision to waive *Miranda* rights (p. 225).

Police interrogations are indeed "inherently coercive" situations (*Miranda v. Arizona*, 1966). The main objective is to get the suspect to confess guilt and to reach this objective police use an array of psychologically oriented techniques (Inbau, Reid, Buckley, & Jayne, 2001; Leo, this volume). Kassin and McNall (1991) classify these techniques into two types: minimization and maximization. Minimization techniques are those that mitigate the offense or lessen the strength of the evidence, such as feigning sympathy, friendship, or understanding, and flattering suspects (e.g., "Only someone as smart as you could have pulled this off"). Maximization techniques are those that exaggerate the strength of the evidence and use a strong-arm approach, such as intimidation and veiled threats. Additionally, the police are allowed to use "trickery and deception" (e.g., telling suspects they have an eyewitness or fingerprints on the weapon when they do not) to obtain statements of guilt (*Frazier v. Cupp*, 1969).

Like *Miranda* waivers, confessions must be voluntary to be admissible in court. Confessions that are considered coerced are ones that were offered under threat of punishment or promise of leniency, or through actual or threatened physical harm. These guidelines were established to minimize the chances of a false confession arising. However, when false confessions arise, they are often due to a combination of overly manipulative police interrogation techniques and inherent vulnerabilities of the suspect (e.g., heightened suggestibility, mental handicaps) (see Fulero & Everington, this volume; Leo and Ofshe, 1998). A commonly noted vulnerability to false confession is youthfulness. There are numerous case examples of juveniles being coerced into confessing criminal acts they did not commit (Leo & Drizin, 2003).

POLICE INTERROGATION OF JUVENILES

Currently, there is little direct information available on the interrogation of youthful suspects. There is some evidence to support the hypothesis that juvenile offenders are more likely than adults to confess to their crimes. For example, Ruback and Vardaman (1997) examined rates of confessions in a subset of juveniles and found that 84% confessed to some or all of the charges against them. In contrast, Leo (1996b) found that 64% of adult suspects in his sample fully or partially confessed. It is also believed that juveniles are more likely to falsely confess voluntarily (which is distinct from false confessions obtained via coercion) to protect friends or relatives (Gudjonsson, 2003; McCann, 1998). Information that is available on juvenile suspect interviews can be gleaned from three general sources: (1) interrogation training manuals; (2) court decisions; and (3) extant empirical studies of child interrogations.

Interrogation Training Manuals

The leading instruction manual on police interrogations (Inbau et al., 2001) teaches new investigators to interrogate under an assumption of guilt. In contrast, in forensic evaluations of alleged child maltreatment victims, interviewing under the assumption that the abuse occurred is strongly advised against. This kind of suggestive interviewing leads to confirmation bias, testing of a single hypothesis (i.e., that the abuse occurred) and an increased possibility for false reports (Bruck, Ceci, & Hembrooke, 1998). Thus, working under the assumption that youthful suspects are guilty may increase the likelihood of false confession (see Kassin, Goldstein, & Savitsky, 2003; Meissner & Kassin, this volume).

The authors of the leading interrogation manual also suggest using the same psychologically oriented themes with juvenile suspects as used with adult suspects, in addition to other themes specific for juveniles (e.g., restless energy and availability of temptations). Inbau et al. (2001) advise trainees to exercise caution when evaluating the behavioral responses (which is in itself problematic with adults, see Kassin, 1997) of youths, but without further explanation and training, this advice may be ineffectual.

The manual also has suggestions regarding parents' role during the interrogation process, if they are required by the State to be present. Specifically, Inbau et al. (2001) write, "A parent who is present during the interrogation should be advised to refrain from talking, confining his or her function to that of an observer" (p. 301). Then, the authors advise where parents should sit and to proceed as if investigators were alone with the suspect. Perhaps because of these instructions and/or because of parents' possible ignorance of interrogation, there are instances in which parents can have a detrimental effect on a juvenile's interview. Instead of advising their children to remain silent, parents will sometimes urge their children to tell the truth and defer to the police officer's authority (Grisso & Ring, 1979; Robin, 1982). In the Central Park jogger case, parents and other family members were present during the questioning and false confessions were still elicited. When the suspect is a juvenile, we recommend having attorneys' presence required either in lieu of or in addition to parents.

In another police interrogation training guide (Macdonald & Michaud, 1992), in regard to questioning youthful suspects, an experienced detective is quoted as saying, "I can interrogate and the kid doesn't know he is being interrogated. . . . .I don't say I'm a detective. I tell them my name and that I've been assigned this matter" (p. 43). Although it is likely that the point the detective was trying to make was that he does not attempt to intimidate child suspects, his advice may also have the negative consequence of de-stressing the significance of the situation. If a child suspect does not realize he is being interrogated by the police and that anything he says can later be used to convict him, then that child is likely to not appreciate the adversarial nature of the police interrogation and the consequences of his words and actions in the interrogation room. Importantly, in legal matters, it is often what the suspect perceives to be true that is crucial rather than what is true (e.g., *Rhode Island v. Innis*, 1980).

LEGAL DECISIONS

Although there have been many decisions handed down by the courts on the topics of juvenile interrogations and confessions, we briefly describe (in chronological order) four noteworthy decisions (for a more detailed discussion, see Huang, 2001; Kaban & Tobey, 1999). The first two decisions, both of which predate *Miranda v. Arizona* (1966), favor juvenile defendants. In *Haley v. Ohio* (1948), a case involving the interrogation of a boy accused of robbery and murder, the Supreme Court overturned the original conviction stating "A 15-year-old lad, questioned through the dead of night by relays of police, is a ready victim of the inquisition. Mature men possibly might stand the ordeal from midnight to 5 A.M. But we cannot believe that a lad of tender years is a match for the police in such a contest" (pp. 599–600). In *Haley*, the Justices argued whether youthful suspects have the maturity and wherewithal to provide *voluntary* confessions when faced with the force of police authority.

In the second case, *Gallegos v. Colorado* (1962), the Court upheld their earlier decision in *Haley* and stated that a 14-year-old boy "cannot be compared with an adult in full possession of his senses and knowledgeable of the consequences of his admission. . . . Adult advice would have put him on a less unequal footing with his interrogators" (p. 54). The original conviction of the boy in *Gallegos* was also overturned. Both *Haley* and *Gallegos* emphasized the youthfulness and immaturity of teenaged defendants.

The third decision is a landmark case in juvenile justice, *In re Gault* (1967), a case involving a 15-year-old prank caller who received undue punishment. Here, the Court criticized the informality of juvenile courts and maintained that juveniles are entitled to several (but not all) of the same Constitutional rights as adults. Interestingly, it is unclear where the Court in *Gault* stood on the issuance of *Miranda* warnings to juveniles. On one hand, the Court states "We are not concerned with the procedures or constitutional rights applicable to the pre-judicial stages of the juvenile process." But, on the other hand, the Court later states "It would indeed be surprising if the privilege against self-incrimination were available to hardened criminals but not to children." Generally, after *Gault*, the courts held that juvenile suspects, like adult suspects, must be made aware of their Constitutional rights prior to police questioning (Robin, 1982).

The final case, *Fare v. Michael C.* (1979), concerned a 16-year-old convicted of murder who had asked for his probation officer during his interrogation. The California Supreme Court overturned his conviction citing
that the youth was indeed invoking his Constitutional rights. However, the
U.S. Supreme Court reversed this ruling claiming the California Court interpreted *Miranda* too broadly. Thus, statements made by suspects who ask
to see their probation officers or social workers are not protected. Importantly, research has shown that juveniles are more prone than adults to confuse their right to an attorney with the non-right to a social worker (Grisso,
1981; Redlich, Silverman, & Steiner, 2003).

In sum, whereas early Courts stressed a defendant's youthfulness,
later, more conservative Courts rejected the notion of special protections
for young suspects. Today, most states have adopted the "totality of circumstances" approach explicitly adopted for juveniles in *Fare v. Michael
C.* (1979). Although age is usually a consideration in this approach, it is
generally not afforded more or less weight than other factors (Kaban &
Tobey, 1999).

EMPIRICAL STUDIES

There is a dearth of scholarly research on youth interrogations. One
reason for this may be because of the ethics involved in accusing participants, especially children, of a wrongdoing in the laboratory. Another potential reason concerns the ecological validity of experimental paradigms and
whether confessing to mock crimes generalizes to actual crimes. The authors
know of four studies investigating children, interrogations, and confessions. Two studies focus on interrogation understanding/behaviors, and
two focus on false confessions. The first study to investigate youths' understanding and appreciation of the interrogation situation generally, and of
interrogation rights specifically was Grisso's (1981) seminal research on
juveniles' comprehension of *Miranda* rights. He discovered that juvenile
detainees aged 14 and younger were significantly less likely to comprehend their interrogation rights compared to older teens and adults. Additionally, intelligence was strongly correlated with rights understanding.
This is noteworthy because many juvenile offenders are of low intellect (see
Grisso et al., 2003).

The second study examined youths' hypothetical decision-making
capabilities in interrogation scenarios. Within a larger study on legal competence, Grisso and his colleagues (2003) questioned nearly 1,400 community and detained youths and young adults about the "best choice" for a
vignette character during a police interrogation—choices included confess to the offense, deny the offense, or refuse to speak. About 50% of 11–13-
and approximately 45% of 14–15-year-olds chose confession as the best

option. Rates were significantly lower for 16–17-year-olds (~30%) and young adults (~20%). There were no significant differences in regard to gender, ethnicity, community/detainee status, intelligence, or socioeconomic status. Thus a person's age was the only factor studied to significantly influence decisions to confess. Frequencies of *Miranda* waivers (Grisso, 1981) and confession rates among youthful offenders (e.g., Ruback & Vardaman, 1997) support the potential for these findings to generalize to actual interrogations.

In the third study, Redlich and Goodman (2003) used a false confession paradigm originated by Kassin and Kiechel (1996) to compare the likelihood of false responsibility-taking among pre-teens, teens, and young adults. Specifically, participants from three age groups—12- and 13-year-olds, 15- and 16-year-olds, and young adults—were led to believe that they caused a computer to crash, losing important data, when in fact, none had. Additionally, half of the participants were presented with false evidence indicating they committed the mock crime. Results indicated that younger participants, particularly those presented with false evidence, were more likely to take responsibility for crashing the computer. Younger participants were also more likely than older participants to falsely take responsibility without question or comment. Although Redlich and Goodman's findings are intriguing, at this point in our knowledge, it is still unclear whether juveniles are more likely than adults to falsely confess to actual crimes.

The final study included younger participants; specifically children aged 5 to 8 years. Prompted by a false confession case in Chicago in 1998 involving 7- and 8-year-old boys, Wood et al. (2000) examined the influence of reinforcement on children's likelihood of providing false guilty knowledge and false confessions. In the Chicago case, the police detective reportedly offered the boys McDonald's Happy Meals (Possley, 1998), an act criticized by the media and theorized to contribute to the boys' false confession to the murder of an 11-year-old girl. In the Wood et al. study, child participants were visited in their classroom and asked to play with a toy. On a separate day, a new visitor appears and claims that the toy is missing. Children were randomly assigned to the control condition (asked suggestive questions) or to the reinforcement condition (also asked suggestive questions but reinforced for positive responses; e.g., "Thanks!"). Preliminary results revealed that in comparison to children who did not receive reinforcement, children in the reinforcement condition—especially the youngest children—were more likely to report knowing specific details about the toys disappearance (i.e., false "guilty knowledge") and were more likely to falsely claim that they had taken the toy.

In summary, the current empirical data that are available on youthful interrogations only scratch the surface of the amount that needs to be known. In contrast to the lack of studies on children as suspects, hundreds of studies have been conducted on children as victims and witnesses. Although it is arguable whether children who commit crimes are qualitatively similar to children who are victimized by crime, we have seen no research comparing characteristics (e.g., intelligence, psychosocial maturity) of same-age child victim/witnesses and child suspects. From a developmental standpoint, it is illogical to think that child suspects/defendants differ from child victim/witnesses. Indeed, a large percentage of child defendants were once child victims themselves. Next, we draw on the immense literature on child victim/witnesses to theorize about the capacities of child suspects.

CHILDREN'S AND ADOLESCENTS' ABILITIES
IN FORENSIC INTERVIEWS

Within the literature on child victim/witnesses, several consistent findings have emerged that are relevant to child suspects. First, in regard to forensic interviews, age is negatively related to accuracy, completeness, and consistency, and positively related to suggestibility (see Ceci & Bruck, 1993; Goodman, Emery, & Haugaard, 1997; Quas, Goodman, Ghetti, & Redlich, 2000 for reviews). Briefly, with age, we are continually developing our cognitive, social, and emotional skills. As we get older, we have increased ability to engage in hypothetical and logical decision-making, to reliably remember and report events, to extend our thinking into the future and consider the long-term consequences, and to engage in advanced social-perspective taking. These are abilities that can certainly influence performance during forensic interviews.

Although the majority of child victim/witness studies have focused on the differences between preschool children and older children, there is some evidence concerning older children. For example, Richardson, Gudjonsson, and Kelly (1995) compared the suggestibility of juvenile offenders (mean age = 15.5 years) and adult offenders (mean age = 30.1 years) and found that juveniles were more suggestible (in response to receiving negative feedback) than adults (see also Warren, Hulse-Trotter, & Tubbs, 1991). Importantly, suggestibility has been linked with decreased understanding of *Miranda* rights (Everington & Fulero, 1999; Redlich et al., 2003) and with false confession (Ofshe, 1992; Redlich & Goodman, 2003). Regardless of whether suspects are guilty or innocent, it is likely that suggestible persons are more apt to confess in response to psychologically oriented interrogation tactics.

Second, research on child victim/witnesses has revealed that younger children have less knowledge and understanding of legal terms than older children and adults (Carter Bottoms, & Levine, 1996; Saywitz, Jaenicke, & Camparo, 1990). Saywitz, Nathanson, and Snyder (1993) reported that 8- to 11-year-olds generally believed that judges were omniscient (e.g., could tell when witnesses were lying) and were the sole decision-makers. Twelve- to 14-year-olds had a better understanding of the legal system but were still confused about the roles of judges and juries. As noted above, nearly three-quarter of a million juveniles aged 14 years and younger were formally arrested in 2000 (Snyder, 2002) and countless others who interacted with police. Thus, there are potentially substantial numbers of juveniles who are subjected to court procedures and terminology they do not fully under-stand. Indeed, research has shown youths' understanding of legal concepts to be deficient compared to adults (Grisso, 1997). In their comprehensive study on adolescents' competence to stand trial, Grisso et al. (2003) found that 11–13- and 14–15-year-old detainees were significantly less able to understand legal terms and concepts and less able to reason appropriately about legal decisions than 16–17-year-olds and young adults. Clearly, an understanding of legal terms and appreciation for legal procedures is imper-ative to the interrogation situation.

A third area of child victim/witness research informative to child sus-pect interviewing is research on the use of suggestive and other types of inappropriate questioning (Garven, Wood, Malpass, & Shaw, 1998). There is much evidence to support that suggestive and leading questions more often leads to inaccurate and false reports than open-ended and non-sug-gestive questioning (e.g., Ceci & Bruck, 1993; Ceci, Loftus, Leichtman, & Bruck, 1994). Again, however, much of the research has focused on pre-school and school-age children, who are less likely than adolescents to come into contact with police as suspects. Nonetheless, there is research on ado-lescents (Pezdek, Finger, & Hodge, 1997), and adults accepting false beliefs about non-experienced personal events (e.g., Hyman & Billings, 1998; Lof-tus & Pickrell, 1995).

One adjunct area of research to false beliefs is imagination infla-tion. In this research, participants who are asked to systematically imag-ine false events become more confident that the event occurred (Garry, Manning, Loftus, & Sherman, 1996). In several cases of false confession, similar techniques (e.g., asking suspects to make up how they would have committed the crime) have been used and highly criticized as the main contributing factor to wrongful arrests or convictions (e.g., case of Paul Ingram, Ofshe, 1992; Rolando Cruz's "dream statement"). We have not seen research investigating how children or adolescents react to such techniques in the interrogation room or in the laboratory in an accusa-tory context. Based on the findings from studies of children incorporat-ing false beliefs and stereotyped information, we would hypothesize that using similar procedures could lead some children and teens into accepting culpability for transgressions they did not commit (i.e., coerced-internal-ized false confessions; Kassin, 1997).

Finally, the supportiveness of interviewers has been examined as a factor affecting child victim/witnesses' reports. Results have been less consistent depending upon what aspects of support and contexts are studied. Carter et al. (1996) examined the effect of social support on children's accuracy and resistance to suggestion in the forensic context. They found that when children were interviewed by friendly, supportive interviewers (e.g., smiled, made eye contact, sat with a relaxed posture), errors and suggestibility decreased in comparison to intimidating, non-supportive interviewers (e.g., did not try to establish rapport, minimal eye contact and smiling) (see also Goodman, Bottoms, Schwartz-Kenney, & Rudy, 1991).

Garven and her colleagues (Garven et al., 2000; Garven, Wood, Malpass, & Shaw, 1998) also examined supportiveness of interviewers but were concerned with exaggerated support. That is, they studied the influence of reinforcing children when the children provided answers consistent with the interviewer's focus (i.e., techniques used in the McMartin Preschool case in which hundreds of false allegations of sexual abuse were made). Garven et al. (2000) demonstrated that "reinforcement dramatically increased the rate of making false allegations by children ages 5 to 7 years" (p. 45). As mentioned above, there is also preliminary evidence to suggest that reinforcement can also lead to false allegations against oneself (Wood et al., 2000).

At this point in our knowledge it is unclear whether maximization techniques—where the interrogator would be intimidating and angry—or minimization techniques—where the interrogator would be supportive and sympathetic—are more likely to elicit admissions of guilt from youths in comparison to adults. Interactions between adult suspects and detectives may be different than interactions between juvenile suspects and detectives. Delinquent youths are often diagnosed with Oppositional Defiant Disorder (ODD; characterized by negative, hostile, and defiant behavior) (Teplin et al., 2002), and as such, ODD youths' interactions with police officers may be volatile and unpredictable. In large part, ODD youths do not deal well with authority. The age and authority differential between youthful suspects and police interrogators is likely to enhance the possibility of obtaining self-incriminating statements (both true and false), but definitive research is needed (Grisso et al., 2003).

In short, the research on child victim/witnesses is far more advanced than the research on child suspects. Although scientists are beginning to learn more about the abilities of (Grisso et al., 2003) and attitudes towards child defendants (Ghetti & Redlich, 2001; Stalans & Henry, 1994), there is still much to be learned about children and adolescents who are accused of and prosecuted for crimes.

PRELIMINARY STUDY ON INTERROGATION
OF ADOLESCENTS AND YOUNG ADULTS

To our knowledge, there are no systematic data on what children and adolescents actually experience when talking to the police about crimes they are suspected of committing. Inbau et al. (2001) claim that the principles of adult interrogation "are just as applicable to the young ones" (p. 298), but do the police in fact use the same interrogation techniques they use with adults? Also, how do juveniles perceive these interactions? Do teens recognize the techniques as compliance-gaining tactics, or, for example, actually believe that the police officer is trying to befriend them? As part of a larger study comparing juveniles' and young adults' legal capabilities, we asked participants who had interactions with the police a series of questions about their perceptions of what occurred. This portion of the study was conducted in a semi-structured interview format and was intended as a pilot measure to further understanding of juveniles' experiences with the police. The data are qualitative in nature and should be reviewed as such. The main study, which is described in more detail in Redlich et al. (2003) examined relations between understanding and appreciation of *Miranda* rights, competency to stand trial, age, and suggestibility.

PARTICIPANTS

Participants were 35 individuals (69% male): 18 juveniles (aged 14 to 17 years) and 17 young adults (aged 18 to 25 years). They were recruited from a local high school, a community center, and through newspaper advertisements. The ethnic breakdown was as follows: 60% European American, 23% African American, 6% Asian American, and 11% "Other"/Mixed background. Participants were paid $20.00 for their involvement.

PROCEDURES

After completing the main part of the study, participants were asked if they ever had any interactions with the police in which they were suspected of committing a crime, and if so, the number of police interactions. Next, for those participants that had been involved with the police, questions were asked about the police interview (e.g., where did it occur, how long did it last, how many police officers questioned you, etc.), the *Miranda* warning, and admissions of guilt. Interviews were audiotaped and later transcribed.

For those with more than one police interaction, a system was developed for targeting one interaction to answer questions about. The system was prioritized by 1) severity of crime/ interaction (i.e., the situation most closely matching an actual interrogation), and 2) length of time since the interaction had occurred. The majority of people had five or fewer interactions and targeting one was not difficult (e.g., more than one-third had only one interaction).

RESULTS

A total of 68.6% (n = 23) had answered that they had interactions with the police as suspects. Of these participants, the number of police interactions ranged from one interaction (38%) to more than 30 interactions (5%). The crimes ranged from minor offenses (e.g., prank call) to moderately serious offenses (e.g., underage drinking and shoplifting) to severe offenses (e.g., attempted burglary, sexual assault, robbery). A subset (n = 11; 47.8% of police interaction sample) had claimed to have been formally arrested.

For the majority (78%) of police questioning incidents that were discussed, the person was a juvenile when the questioning occurred. Twenty-two percent were age 13 years or younger, 17% age 14 or 15 years, 39% were 16 or 17 years, and 22% were between 18 and 23 years. None of the participants had gone to the police on his/her own. In about 35% of the cases, the police came to the person's home or school for questioning. The majority of questioning took place at the "scene of the crime" (e.g., on the curb or in a parking lot) or continued from the scene to the police station. Forty-two percent were eventually questioned at the police station. Furthermore, most of the questioning was brief. Most (82%) were one hour or less, with the longest interview lasting approximately three hours, although one person claimed to have been kept at the police station for 15 days.

Slightly less than half (42%) of the police questioning took place late at night, after 11:30 pm; the rest occurred at various times during the day. Approximately half of the participants (48%) had been using alcohol or drugs just prior to questioning. Importantly, intoxication has been noted as a vulnerability factor increasing the chance of false confession (Kassin, 1997). And finally, no participant, including the 11 participants who had been arrested, had a lawyer present during questioning, although a portion of this finding can be explained by the location and relative informality of the interviews.

Of the 11 participants who had been arrested, two invoked their right to silence, although only seven could clearly remember being read their *Miranda* rights. Another participant claimed not to have been arrested but did recall having been read his Miranda rights. He was 12 years at the time of the police interaction and in regard to his *Miranda* warning stated:

> So, basically [the police officer] brought us in, separated all of us, read us our rights in the car, which I understand those more now, but at that time, I had no clue what any of that stuff meant. They didn't really say, they don't explain your

rights at all, they just read them. Then, they just started questioning me, so obviously, I just answered their questions because I was a scared little seventh grader, didn't know what to do. Even the way they read you your rights, regardless of whether you know you really have a choice or not, it just seems like you have to talk to them. It's kind of just your instinct that you feel like if someone isn't speaking, they're obviously withholding something. So, it kind of just shows that you're guilty even though it doesn't.

The myth about the innocent not needing to invoke their rights is clearly present in this participants' statement. Kassin and Norwich (in press) found that 80% of innocent participants in a mock crime situation waived their rights because they believed innocence was their shield.

During the semi-structured interview, it was discovered that many of the same techniques police use with adults (Kassin & McNall, 1991; Leo, 1996a, 1996b) were mentioned by participants as ploys the police had used with them. When asked if they thought the police were trying to trick or frighten them, 35% and 43% answered in the affirmative, respectively. Table 1.1 lists several police interrogation techniques and accompanying examples from participants. It's important to note that most examples were spontaneous and not in response to direct questions.

Perhaps most noteworthy are the examples of implied promises from the police to go home if they tell the police what they want to hear. In several false confessions cases involving juveniles and other at-risk suspects, the false confessors have claimed that the police made similar promises to them and that these promises were a main motivation for the false confession (see Drizin, this volume). Indeed, one 15-year-old boy charged with 12 counts of sexual battery claimed the only reason he talked to the police was because he wanted to go home (see Table 1). In this specific case, the boy spent three days in juvenile hall, was then on house arrest and went to court four times concerning this matter.

There were also other examples of minimization and maximization techniques. When asked directly if the police ever told him things would be easier on him if he confessed, one 16-year-old's response was "Yeah, that's their main lie." When asked to expand on this, he stated "They just make it seem like that they already have everything completely figured out. And if you want to get yourself in the clear, you can just agree to their story." Another boy when asked if the police *promised* leniency for being cooperative, he stated "I don't know about that; in so many words, if you cooperate"—an example of an implied tactic that pragmatically translates into an illegal police interrogation tactic (Kassin & McNall, 1991).

Although the findings reported in this preliminary study are intriguing, we would again like to emphasize the qualitative nature of the data. Clear interpretations of the data are limited by several factors. The sample is small and the types of police interaction are widely variable. Further

TABLE 1. Examples of Police Interrogation Techniques from Preliminary Data

Police technique	Age at time of police interaction	Suspected crime/charge	Examples
Good-cop/ bad-cop routines	16	Possession and use of drugs	"The girl cop was playing the bad cop and then the guy was the good cop. He's like 'You know, if it was just me and the chief of police wasn't there, I'd let you go.' He was trying to be all buddy-buddy. We were like 'Yeah, right.'"
Already know you're guilty/ need your side	16	Felony conspiracy, vandalism, organized gang activity	"The cop called me and 'Sure you don't want to come in? I have a statement from one of your friends.' And I knew that was the way they manipulate. 'We already have evidence so if you don't want to clear your name, go ahead.'" ….."They [the police] just make it seem like that they already have everything completely figured out. And if you want to get yourself in the clear, you can just agree to their story."
Threats	15	Trespassing/ miscellaneous crimes	"That's another thing. That they [the police] threaten kids with a lot of things, and tell them that they can do things to them to make them talk. Because they assume the kids don't know all their rights, and what they can and can't do." … "He [the police officer] threatened that if I didn't tell him what he wanted to know, he would take me to juvie [juvenile hall] when he had no right to take me to juvie."
Easier on you if you cooperate/ confess	16	Possession and use of drugs	"Either get it over in this little period of time, or we can spread it out. Impound your car, do this, do that, take you here, take you there, go to juvie [juvenile hall]. And it will suck or else you can cooperate and just deal with your parents. Alright, much rather just get it over with now."
Flattery/ sympathy/ friendship	20	Drug-related offenses	"He was trying to befriend me in the sense that he was trying to make me feel calm, that I'm not going to get hit that hard …"
	15	Sexual battery	"Tried to make it seem like he [the police officer] was relating to me."

Trickery/ deception	15	Trespassing/ miscellaneous crimes	"They lie a lot.... ... They just make up, just add in little details that weren't there just to incriminate you even more."
	16	Felony conspiracy, vandalism, organized gang activity	"They [the police] kept asking me questions like 'Who threw the rock?' Little things about the case so I could say it. This cop said 'Who threw the rock?' I said 'I dunno, I'm not saying anything." He said 'You don't know who threw it?' Then I'm like 'I'm not saying anything.' He's like 'If you weren't guilty, you would say what rock?' He's like 'How'd you know there was a rock?'"
Implied promises to be let go/ go home	16	Felony conspiracy, vandalism, organized gang activity	"Just tell us what happened and we'll let you go." .... "Alright, just tell me what happened, we'll go home to our families and go to sleep." [what police officer allegedly said to juvenile]
	15	Sexual battery	"He [the police officer] said if I cooperate, I'd get out of there, just tell him the truth and be able to go home.. ......"Only reason I talked was because I wanted to get out of there."
	18	Robbery	"They [the police] said if I would find the [stolen] purse, then they would let me go"

more, the length of time between the time of the police interaction and the time of the study was not standardized. Some of the participants were young adults talking about their police interactions when they were juveniles, and had introspective capabilities that were presumably different from adolescent participants. In sum, we view the data as interesting fodder for future, more systematic studies.

CONCLUSIONS

Based on interrogation training manuals, exceptional case studies, and findings from the preliminary study reported above, there is tentative evidence to claim that police interrogators question adult and youthful suspects with the same psychologically oriented techniques. Certainly more systematic studies need to be conducted for definitive conclusions, but to date, there is no contrary evidence in refute of this claim. When we extrapolate findings from the forensic interviewing of child victim witnesses to child suspects, there is cause for alarm. Specifically, techniques such as the assumption of guilt, pursuit of a single hypothesis, imagination requests (or "inviting speculation," Garven et al., 1998), and deliberate misleading of interviewees, have resulted in increased false reports and internalized suggestions among children, adolescents, and adults. Because there are individual differences in acceptance rates, a profitable next step would be to investigate why some persons are more or less prone to false confession and false internalization than others.

The study of the interrogation of children and adolescents is still in its infancy. However, there is much to be gained from examining the literature—and the progression of the literature—on child victims and child witnesses. There are many interesting and informative parallels. For example, a strong emphasis was placed on videotaping all forensic interviews with children (e.g., McGough, 1994) and on establishing standardized guidelines for the police, social workers, and medical personnel who interviewed children who alleged abuse (Poole & Lamb, 1998) to eliminate many of the same problems identified in questionable interrogations. Of course, there are differences in the questioning of child suspects and child victim/witnesses, such as the emphasis placed on the motivation to lie and the evidence that needs to be gathered. But, the likely developmental similarities between child suspects and victims and the mass of related research findings on the forensic interviewing of child victim/witnesses suggest that adult interrogation techniques are not suitable for children, particularly those younger than 15 years. The potential to elicit false confessions from child and adolescent suspects and the concomitant consequences are formidable enough that the risk should not be overlooked.

Today there exist numerous reforms and accommodations (Bruck et al., 1998; Goodman, Quas, Buckley, & Shapiro, 1999) for child victim/witnesses in part due to the large body of research on their abilities, their limitations, and attitudes towards them. Armed with a similar amount and breadth of research on child suspects, the potential exists to change and improve the methods police use to question youths and other vulnerable populations accused of committing crimes.

Acknowledgments: This research was supported in part by grants from the TCWF Violence Prevention Initiative—Academic Scholars program to Drs. Redlich and Steiner. We would like to thank Huy Dang and Nicole Hernandez, and the community organizations that allowed us to use their facilities to recruit participants and collect data. Correspondence and request for reprints can be addressed to Dr. Allison D. Redlich at the above address or by e-mail).

REFERENCES

Bruck, M., Ceci, S. J., & Hembrooke, H. (1998). Reliability and credibility of young children's reports: From research to policy and practice. *American Psychologist, 53*, 136–151.

Carter, C. A., Bottoms, B. L., & Levine, M. (1996). Linguistic and socioemotional influences on accuracy of children's reports. *Law and Human Behavior, 20*, 335–358.

Ceci, S. J., & Bruck, M. (1993). Suggestibility of the child witness: A historical review and synthesis. *Psychological Bulletin, 113*, 403–439.

Ceci, S. J., Loftus, E., Leichtman, M., & Bruck, M. (1994). The role of source misattribution in the creation of false beliefs among preschoolers. *International Journal of Clinical and Experimental Hypnosis, 62*, 304–320.

Everington, C. & Fulero, S. M. (1999). Measuring understanding and suggestibility of defendants with mental retardation. *Mental Retardation, 37*, 212–220.

Fare v. Michael C., 442 U.S. 707 (1979).

Frazier v. Cupp, 394 U.S. 731 (1969).

Gallegos v. Colorado, 370 U.S. 49 (1962).

Garry, M., Manning, C. G., Loftus, E. F., & Sherman, S. J. (1996). Imagination inflation: Imagining a childhood event inflates confidence that it occurred. *Psychonomic Bulletin and Review, 3*, 208–214.

Garven, S., Wood, J. M., Malpass, R. S., & Shaw, J. S. (1998). More than suggestion: The effect of interviewing techniques from the McMartin preschool case. *Journal of Applied Psychology, 83*, 347–359.

Garven, S., Wood, J. M., & Malpass, R. S. (2000). Allegations of wrongdoing: The effects of reinforcement on children's mundane and fantastic claims. *Journal of Applied Psychology, 85*, 38–49.

Ghetti, S., & Redlich, A. D. (2001). Reactions to youth crime: Perceptions of accountability and competency. *Behavioral Sciences and the Law, 19*, 33–52.

Goodman, G. S., Bottoms, B., Schwartz-Kenney, B., & Rudy, L. (1991). Children's testimony about a stressful event: Improving children's reports. *Journal of Narrative and Life History, 7*, 69–99.

Goodman, G. S., Emery, R. E., & Haugaard, J. J. (1997). Developmental psychology and law: Divorce, child maltreatment, foster care, and adoption. In I. E. Sigel & A. Renninger (Eds.), *Handbook of child psychology: Vol. 4. Child psychology in practice* (5th ed., pp. 775–874). New York: Wiley.

Goodman, G. S., Quas, J. A., Bulkley, J., & Shapiro, C. (1999). Innovations for child witnesses: A national survey. *Psychology, Public Policy, and the Law, 5,* 255–281.

Grisso, T. (1981). *Juvenile's waiver of rights: Legal and psychological competence.* New York: Plenum.

Grisso, T. (1997). The competence of adolescents as trial defendants. *Psychology, Public Policy, and the Law, 3,* 3–32.

Grisso, T., & Ring, M. (1979). Parents' attitudes toward juveniles' rights in interrogation. *Criminal Justice and Behavior, 6,* 211–226.

Grisso, T., Steinberg, L., Woolard, J., Cauffman, E., Scott, E., Graham, S., Lexcen, F., Reppucci, N. D., & Schwartz, R. (2003). Juveniles' competence to stand trial: A comparison of adolescents' and adults' capacities as trial defendants. *Law and Human Behavior, 27,* 333–363.

Gudjonsson, G.H. (2003). *The psychology of interrogations and confessions.* Chichester: Wiley.

Haley v. Ohio, 332 U.S. 596 (1948).

Huang, D. T. (2001). "Less unequal footing": State courts' per se rules for juvenile waivers during interrogations and the case for their implementation. *Cornell Law Review, 86,* 437–477.

Hyman, I. E., Jr., & Billings, F. J. (1998). Individual differences and the creation of false childhood memories. *Memory, 6,* 1–20.

Inbau, F. E., Reid, J. E., Buckley, J. P., & Jayne, B. C. (2001). *Criminal interrogation and confessions* (4th ed.). Gaithersburg, MD: Aspen.

In re Gault, 387 U.S. 1 (1967).

Kaban, B., & Tobey, A. E. (1999). When police question children: Are protections adequate? *Journal of the Center for Children and the Courts, 1,* 151–160.

Kassin, S. M. (2002, November). False confessions and the jogger case. (Opinion Editorial) *New York Times.*

Kassin, S. M. (1997). The psychology of confession evidence. *American Psychologist, 52,* 221–233.

Kassin, S. M., Goldstein, C. C., & Savitsky, K. (2003). Behavioral confirmation in the interrogation room: On the dangers of presuming guilt. *Law and Human Behavior, 27,* 187–203.

Kassin, S. M., & Kiechel, K. L. (1996). The social psychology of false confessions: Compliance, internalization, and confabulation. *Psychological Science, 7,* 125–128.

Kassin, S. M., & McNall, K. (1991). Police interrogations and confessions: Communicating promises and threats by pragmatic implication. *Law and Human Behavior, 15,* 233–251.

Kassin, S. M., & Norwich, R. J. (in press). Why people waive their Miranda rights: The power of innocence. *Law and Human Behavior.*

Leo, R. A. (1996a) Miranda's revenge: Police interrogation as a confidence game. *Law and Society Review, 30,* 259–288.

Leo, R. A. (1996b). Inside the interrogation room. *Journal of Criminal Law and Criminology, 86,* 266–303.

Leo, R. A. & Drizin, S. (2003). *Proven false confessions cases.* Retrieved March 7, 2003 from http://www.innocenceproject.org/docs/Master_List_False_Confessions.html

Leo, R. A., & Ofshe, R. J. (1998). The consequences of false confessions: Deprivations of liberty and miscarriages of justice in the age of psychological interrogation. *Journal of Criminal Law and Criminology, 88,* 429–496.

Loftus, E., & Pickrell, J. E. (1995). The formation of false memories. *Psychiatric Annals, 25,* 720–725.

Macdonald, J. M., & Michaud, D. L. (1992). *Criminal interrogation.* Denver, CO: Apache Press.

McCann, J. T. (1998). Broadening the typology of false confessions. *American Psychologist, 53,* 319–320.

McGough, L. (1994). Videotaping children's accounts. In L. McGough (Ed.), *Child witnesses: Fragile voices in the American legal system* (pp. 189–232). New Haven, CT: Yale University Press.

Miranda v. Arizona, 384 U.S. 436 (1966).

Ofshe, R. J. (1992). Inadvertent hypnosis during interrogation: False confessions due to dissociative state; mis-identified multiple personality and the satanic cult hypothesis. *The International Journal of Clinical and Experimental Hypnosis, XL,* 125–156.

Pezdek, K., Finger, K., & Hodge, D. (1997). Planting false childhood memories: The role of event plausibility. *Psychological Science, 8,* 437–441.

Poole, D. A., & Lamb, M. E. (1998). *Investigative interviews of children: A guide for helping professionals.* Washington, DC: American Psychological Association.

Possley, M. (1998, August). How cops got boys to talk. *Chicago Tribune.* Chicago, IL.

Quas, J. A., Goodman, G. S., Ghetti, S., & Redlich, A. D. (2000). Questioning the child witness: What can we conclude from the research thus far? *Trauma, Abuse, and Violence, 1,* 223–249.

Redlich, A. D., & Goodman, G. S. (2003). Taking responsibility for an act not committed: The influence of age and suggestibility. *Law and Human Behavior, 27,* 141–156.

Redlich, A. D., Silverman, M., & Steiner, H. (2003). Factors affecting pre-adjudicative and adjudicative competence in juveniles and young adults. *Behavioral Sciences and the Law, 21,* 1–17.

Rhode Island v. Innis, 446 U.S. 291 (1980).

Richardson, G., Gudjonsson, G. H., & Kelly, T. P. (1995). Interrogative suggestibility in an adolescent forensic population. *Journal of Adolescence, 18,* 211–216.

Robin, G. D. (1982). Juvenile interrogation and confessions. *Journal of Police Science and Administration, 10,* 224–228.

Ruback, R. B., & Vardaman, P. J. (1997). Decision making in delinquency cases: The role of race and juveniles' admission/denial of the crime. *Law and Human Behavior, 21,* 47–69.

Saywitz, K., Jaenicke, C., & Camparo, L. (1990). Children's knowledge of legal terminology. *Law and Human Behavior, 14,* 523–535.

Saywitz, K., Nathanson, R., & Snyder, L. S. (1993). Credibility of child witnesses: The role of communicative competence. *Topics in Language Disorders, 13,* 59–78.

Snyder, H. N. (2002, November). Juvenile arrests 2000. *OJJDP Juvenile Justice Bulletin.* Office of Juvenile Justice and Delinquency Prevention, Office of Justice Programs, U.S. Department of Justice, Washington, DC.

Snyder, H. N., & Sickmund, M. (1999). *Juvenile offenders and victims: 1999 National report.* Office of Juvenile Justice and Delinquency Prevention, Office of Justice Programs, U.S. Department of Justice, Washington, DC.

Stalans, L., & Henry, G. (1994). Societal views of justice for adolescents accused of murder: Inconsistency between community sentiment and automatic legislative transfers. *Law and Human Behavior, 18,* 675–696.

Warren, A., Hulse-Trotter, K., & Tubbs, E. (1991). Inducing resistance to suggestibility in children. *Law and Human Behavior, 15,* 273–285.

Wood, J. M., Billings, J., Taylor, T., Corey, D., Burns, J., & Garven, S. (2000, June). *Guilty knowledge and false confessions regarding a staged theft: Effects of reinforcement on children's admissions.* Paper presented at the Annual Convention of the American Psychological Society, Miami, Florida.

6

Tales from the Juvenile Confession Front

A Guide to How Standard Police Interrogation Tactics Can Produce Coerced and False Confessions from Juvenile Suspects

STEVEN A. DRIZIN AND BETH A. COLGAN

Children in the United States are regularly subjected to police interrogations. The modern police interrogation, except in rare circumstances, no longer involves the physical abuse, extreme isolation, and sleep deprivation commonly known as the "third degree" but instead involves more psychologically based interrogation techniques (see Leo, this volume). These techniques, which combine "minimization" techniques like feigning friendship, flattery and false sympathy, with "maximization" techniques like lying about or exaggerating the strength of the evidence, are designed with one purpose in mind: to get the suspect to confess guilt. The leading interrogation manual, *Criminal Interrogations and Confessions* (2001) by Inbau, Reid, Buckley, and Jayne instructs police officers to use these same techniques with children and adults.

Inbau et al. (2001) maintain that the use of these methods, which they reduce to a nine-step formula, are not "apt to cause an innocent person to confess" (p. 212). Although this premise has been challenged and studied in cases involving adults (Kassin, 1997; Kassin & McNall, 1991; Kassin & Kiechel, 1996; Leo & Ofshe, 1998; Ofshe & Leo, 1997), because the interrogations of

STEVEN A. DRIZIN • School of Law, Northwestern University, Chicago, Illinois, 60611-3069 (s-drizin@law.northwestern.edu).   BETH A. COLGAN • Attorney at Law, Seattle, Washington 98118 (bethcolgan@stanfordalumni.org)

child suspects are rarely recorded and because the use of these techniques in the laboratory are so anxiety producing that they are not likely to be approved by human subjects review boards, this premise has largely gone unchallenged in cases involving children (Redlich, this volume; Redlich & Goodman, 2003).

In this essay, we analyze several confession cases in which psychologically based interrogation techniques were used on children. From the five cases we discuss, patterns emerge that show how the legal and generally accepted psychological interrogation techniques used by police to interrogate adults can elicit false, or at the very least, coerced confessions from children. These techniques, and the consequences of using them on children, are described below through the stories of Michael Crowe, Anthony Harris, Lacresha Murray, Joshua Treadway, and B.M.B.

The stories of these children are not unique. In our research, we have uncovered dozens of false confessions involving children (Drizin & Colgan, 2001; Drizin & Leo, in press). What makes these narratives unique is that the interrogations of the suspects were recorded in their entirety, giving us a complete record of how police manipulated the children during their interrogations. In this article, we will demonstrate these techniques and their effect on the children who were interrogated, discuss the psychosocial research which suggests that such techniques are problematic for children, and conclude with suggested reforms which will protect children during police interrogations and minimize the risk of obtaining false confessions. At the outset, however, to set a framework for the discussion that follows, we begin with a discussion of the applicable United States Supreme Court law on juvenile confessions.

THE LAW

In *Haley v. Ohio* (1948), the United States Supreme Court first spoke about the difficulties that children face when interrogated by police officers. The Court overturned the murder conviction of a 15-year-old boy, finding that the child's confession was not voluntary. Looking at the interrogation through the eyes of the child, who was subjected to an interrogation while isolated from his family and attorney, the Court wrote:

> He needs counsel and support if he is not to become the victim first of fear, then of panic. He needs someone on whom to lean lest the overpowering presence of the law, as he knows it, crush him. No friend stood at the side of this 15-year-old boy as the police, working in relays, questioned him hour after hour, from midnight until dawn. No lawyer stood guard to make sure that the police went so far and no farther, to see to it that they stopped short of the point where he became the victim of coercion. No counsel or friend was called during the critical hours of questioning. A photographer was admitted once this lad broke and confessed. But not even a gesture towards getting a lawyer for him was ever made. (pp. 599–600)

Fifteen years later, in *Gallegos v. Colorado* (1962), the Court analyzed the interrogation of a 14-year-old boy in a murder case. The interrogation at issue in *Gallegos* was far less coercive than that in *Haley*. Here, there was no prolonged questioning of the boy and the boy was advised of his right to counsel. The boy admitted his role in a burglary and assault almost immediately. While the boy was in the detention center, the victim died, and police approached him for a second interview. Five days after his initial admission, the boy signed a formal written confession to the murder. Despite these less coercive circumstances, the Court still overturned the boy's conviction, placing great emphasis on the fact that the boy's mother was denied access to him and that the boy was left to make the decision to speak to police or stand on his right to remain silent by himself:

> He cannot be compared with an adult in full possession of his senses and knowledgeable of the consequences of his admissions. He would have no way of knowing what the consequences of his confession were without advice as to his rights—from someone concerned with securing him those rights—and without the aid of more mature judgment as to the steps he should take in the predicament in which he found himself. A lawyer or an adult relative or friend could have given the petitioner the protection which his own immaturity could not. Adult advice would have put him on a less unequal footing with his interrogators. Without some adult protection against this inequality, a 14-year-old boy would not be able to know, let alone assert, such constitutional rights as he had. To allow this conviction to stand would, in effect, be to treat him as if he had no constitutional rights. (p. 54)

Five years later, the landmark case of *In re Gault* (1967), again touched upon the rights of juveniles during police interrogations. In the first juvenile interrogation case after *Miranda v. Arizona* (1966), the Court skirted the question of whether and how police should administer *Miranda* rights to juveniles. Instead, the thrust of the decision focused on the basic lack of due process during the juvenile court delinquency proceedings and on giving juveniles most of the same protections as adults, including the right to notice of the proceedings, the right to counsel and the privilege against self-incrimination. Nevertheless, the Court reaffirmed that courts must take "special caution" in evaluating confessions from juveniles, found that no such care existed in the taking of the 15-year-old's admission to making a crank phone call, and reversed his conviction.

The Court's next decision on juvenile confessions and interrogations was *Fare v. Michael C.* (1979), a case involving a 16-year-old who confessed to a murder but asked to speak to his probation officer before confessing. Instead of allowing him to see his probation officer, a team of detectives continued to interrogate the boy for several hours, ignoring his repeated denials, until they obtained a confession. The narrow issue before the Court was whether the request for a probation officer was an invocation of the juvenile's rights to remain silent and to counsel. Expecting the teenager to invoke his legal rights with "adult-like precision" (Feld, 2000), the Court held that his request for his probation officer was not tantamount to a request for a lawyer or an invocation of his right to remain silent. Instead, the Court held that the same "totality of the circumstances" used to determine if adults "knowingly and intelligently" waive their *Miranda* rights should apply to the question of whether a juvenile has waived his rights. In cases involving juveniles, the Court stressed that the "totality of the circumstances test" gave courts the flexibility to consider all relevant factors, including, particularly in juvenile cases, "the juvenile's age, experience, education, background, and intelligence, and into whether he has the capacity to understand the warnings given him, the nature of his Fifth Amendment rights, and the consequences of waiving those rights" (pp. 725–727). Four justices dissented, arguing that the Court's approach in treating juveniles and adults equally, was an abandonment of its earlier position that "the greatest care" must be taken to ensure that juvenile confessions are voluntary.

In the wake of *Fare,* the majority of state courts have adopted the "totality of the circumstances" test when analyzing juvenile interrogations. A minority of courts, however, remaining true to the trilogy of *Haley, Gallegos, and Gault,* have created *per se* rules requiring that any statements taken from children outside of their parents, guardians, or an attorney, are inadmissible against the child in court (Huang 2001; Krzewinski 2002).

The "totality of the circumstances," test, while theoretically affording judges flexibility, in practice, has offered little protection to children. Without bright lines for courts to follow, the end result has been unfettered and unreviewable discretion by judges. In practice, as Feld's research (1984) has shown, when judges apply the test, "they exclude only the most egregiously obtained confessions and then only haphazardly" (p.118). After *Fare,* there are legions of cases in which judges have ignored or paid lip service to the unique vulnerabilities of children in the interrogation process, including their difficulties in understanding their *Miranda* rights and deciding whether to give them up, their diminished social status relative to that of their interrogators, their tendency to comply with authority figures, and in some cases, their suggestibility. The cases of the five children to which we now turn, illustrate how the "totality of the circumstances" test, by failing to give due weight to these developmental factors, has failed to protect children, not only from "knowing and intelligent" waivers, but from coerced and false confessions.

THE CRIMES

The story of each child who is interrogated by the police begins with the commission of a crime, too often the tragic death or injury of another child. For Michael Crowe and his friend Joshua Treadway, it was the death of Michael's sister; for Anthony Harris it was the death of his five year old neighbor; for Lacresha Murray it was the death of an infant left in her grandparents' care, and for B.M.B., it was the alleged rape of his four year old neighbor.

THE MURDER OF STEPHANIE CROWE

January 21, 1998 was in many ways a typical evening for the Crowe family of Escondido, California. Twelve-year-old Stephanie Crowe and her 14-year-old brother, Michael, spent the evening watching a TV program. At approximately 9:25 P.M., Stephanie said good night to her family and went to bed. At 6:30 the next morning, Stephanie's grandmother awoke to the sound of Stephanie's alarm going off. She went to Stephanie's room to wake her, and found her lying in the doorway. Stephanie had been stabbed nine times (Sauer & Wilkens, 1999).

THE DISAPPEARANCE OF DEVAN DUNIVER

On Saturday, June 27, 1998, at approximately 1:30 P.M., 5-year-old Devan Duniver left her mother Lori's home in New Philadelphia, Ohio, to go outside to play. At around 1:45 P.M., Anthony Harris, a 12-year-old boy who lived in the apartment next to the Dunivers, was on his way home from a friend's house. He took a shortcut through an open field surrounding a small wooded area, less than 100 yards from his home. Shortly after 2:00 P.M., Anthony encountered Lori Duniver, who was looking for Devan. She and Anthony spent much of the next several hours searching for Devan together. Mrs. Duniver called the police about her missing child at about 8:00 P.M.

News of Devan's disappearance quickly spread through the neighborhood and hundreds of people joined the search. The search continued throughout the night and the next day. At around 2:30 P.M. on Sunday, June 28, 1998, two emergency medical technicians found Devan's body in a clump of undergrowth behind a fallen tree in the wooded area. A large black plastic bag was on the path nearby. An autopsy performed later that evening by the Stark County Coroner's Office revealed that Devan's death was caused by seven stab wounds to the front of the neck which partially severed her carotid artery. Her hands bore no defensive wounds and there was evidence of a blow to her head and several abrasions and contusions on Devan's body. Because of his proximity to the place where Devan's body was found at the time she disappeared, the police zeroed in on Anthony as a chief suspect (see ABC, 1999; *In re Harris*, 2000).

THE DEATH OF JAYLA BELTON

On May 24, 1996, two year old Jayla Belton was dropped off at the home of 11-year-old Lacresha Murray, where Lacresha's grandparents operated an unlicensed day-care facility. Jayla was tired and feverish, and shortly after arriving she vomited at the lunch table. Lacresha's 18-year-old sister suspected the child had a virus, gave her some over-the-counter medication, and put the child down to sleep in a back bedroom. No one checked on Jayla until late in the afternoon. At that time, Lacresha went back near where the bedroom was located. Her grandfather remembers hearing some thumping which he presumed was the sound of Lacresha playing ball. A short time later, Lacresha emerged from the back of the house and told her grandfather that Jayla had been throwing up and shaking. Eventually, Lacresha and her grandfather took Jayla to the hospital where she was pronounced dead shortly thereafter. An autopsy later revealed that Jayla died of massive injuries; although she had over thirty bruises on her body, the most likely cause of death was a traumatic blow to her liver which broke four of her ribs and split her liver into two pieces. Because Lacresha had been in Jayla's company near the time of her death and the medical examiner opined that the toddler's injuries would have caused death within minutes of their infliction, Lacresha became the target of the police investigation (*In re L.M.*, 1999).

THE ASSAULT OF J.

In May of 1996, in Wichita Kansas, three children—J, a 4-year-old girl, C, her 7-year-old brother, and B.M.B., C's 10-year-old friend—were playing together in a pile of sand in a neighbor's backyard. C and J were burying J in the sand. B.M.B. was pushing sand over to C, who was using his hands to scoop sand in the bucket. When J was buried in the sand up to her knees, she screamed and ran to her house. She was crying when she got to the house and told her mother that "a boy had tried to put his finger up my butt." J's mother started brushing the sand off of her and noticed that there was sand and fresh blood inside J's panties. When she asked J how the sand got there, J told her that "the black man tried to put his finger up her butt." After calling the police, J's mother took her to the hospital where a nurse found a laceration, some broken blood vessels beneath the skin, and sand-like gravel in J's genital area. The nurse found that the injuries were recent and consistent with J's general description of what had happened to her (*In the Matter of B.M.B.*, 1998). Because B.M.B. was black and had been playing with J and her brother in the sandbox, he became the main suspect.

THE INTERROGATIONS

The police who investigate crimes such as these are under tremendous pressure to solve them. In each case discussed herein, the detectives had conducted an investigation which led them to suspect that the children they were interrogating were somehow involved in the crimes. As a result, they entered the interrogation room with a bias against the children's innocence (Meissner & Kassin, this volume). Their interrogations were designed to elicit admissions that matched the information they believed to be true about the crimes. Unfortunately, such interviewer bias can lead police to "attempt to gather only confirmatory evidence and to avoid all avenues that may produce negative or inconsistent evidence" (Bruck, Ceci, & Hembrooke, 1998, p. 140). Interviewer bias played a critical role in the cases of each of the five children discussed below, and in each case had a devastating impact on the lives of the children and their families.

In addition to interviewer bias, certain psychological interrogation techniques were common to the interrogations of the children. Below, we highlight several of these techniques, including multiple interviews, the presentation of insurmountable evidence, the use of rewards or punishment, suggestive questioning, selective reinforcement and repetition, and negative feedback. We then discuss why these techniques are particularly problematic for children.

MULTIPLE INTERVIEWS

Police often begin an interrogation, leave the suspect alone for a period of time, and then return to continue the interrogation; this process could be repeated several times. This is highly problematic for children, because information suggested by the police in earlier interviews is very likely to be incorporated in the child's own narrative in later interviews (Bruck et al., 1998; Myers, 1996).

Michael Crowe, for example, was interrogated on three separate occasions. The first occurred when the Crowe family was taken to police headquarters on the day Stephanie Crowe was found murdered. Each family member, including Michael and Stephanie's ten year old sister, Shannon, was required to take off his or her clothes, piece by piece, and he or she was photographed at various stages of undress. Hours later, Michael was interviewed by police regarding the events of the proceeding night. Michael informed the police that he had awoken at approximately 4:30 A.M. with a headache. Michael stated that he had walked down the hall adjoining Stephanie's bedroom, and had gone to the kitchen to take a Tylenol. After this interview Michael and Shannon were not returned to their parents, but rather were taken to a shelter for abused and neglected children (Sauer & Wilkens 1999).

At approximately 4:30 P.M. the following day, Michael was taken back to police headquarters. Michael was placed in a 14 X 14 foot interrogation room with no outside windows. Over the next three and a half hours, Michael was interrogated by a series of police officers. Unsatisfied by Michael's claims of innocence, the police resumed questioning Michael the following afternoon for an additional six hours (see Crowe Transcripts; Sauer, & Wilkens, 1999).

Michael's 15-year-old friend Joshua, was also subjected to multiple interrogations. The first began at 9:45 P.M. and did not finish until after 8:00 A.M. the following morning. Joshua was interrogated a second time two weeks later; that interrogation lasted 11.5 hours. Details about the knife allegedly used in Stephanie's murder that were told to Joshua during his initial interrogations became essential ingredients to the police questioning and the confession Joshua ultimately gave to police (*see generally* Transcript of Interrogation of Joshua Treadway, Vols. I-II).

The length of Joshua's interrogations likely contributed to his ultimate confession. Many have suggested that limits be placed on the length of interrogations because the longer the interrogation, the more coercive it becomes, and therefore the more likely that it will produce involuntary and false confessions (Perina, 2003; White 1997). Inbau et al. (2001) suggest that interrogations should not last more than four hours. The length of the interrogation may be even more crucial when juveniles are being interrogated. Children and adolescents have a different conception of time; interrogations which last more than four or five hours can seem like an eternity to a child. But in cases involving children, it is important not to place too much weight on the length of the interrogation. What is so striking about the interrogations of B.M.B. (38 minutes), Anthony Harris (a little over an hour), and Lacresha Murray (2.5 hours) is how quickly detectives were able to get them to confess. These children were no match for the seasoned detectives who interrogated them, enabling the detectives to obtain false or coerced confessions from them in a few hours or less.

PRESENTATION OF INSURMOUNTABLE EVIDENCE

A standard police interrogation tactic is that of presenting extensive, and often fictional, evidence implicating the suspect, thereby imparting the notion that the suspect cannot avoid prosecution. Michael's interrogation is a prime example of this technique. At the beginning of Michael's second interrogation, he repeated the version of events he had told the police on the day Stephanie was found murdered. Michael also told the police that he did not know anything about his sister's murder. Michael repeatedly expressed his anguish over his sister's death and the fact that he had been separated from his family. Although his interrogators explained that they were only questioning Michael in order to "eliminate [him] from suspicion," the increasingly aggressive tone of the interrogation suggested otherwise. For example, the police told Michael that hair had been found in Stephanie's hand and suggested that it would prove to be Michael's hair (see Transcripts of Interrogation of Michael Crowe, Vol. I-II).

The police also lied to Michael, declaring that there was a mounting pile of physical and scientific evidence that would prove that he was Stephanie's killer. They told him that investigators had found blood in Michael's room. When he asked where the blood was found the detective stated, "I'm sure you know. It's easy to make mistakes in the dark." Michael was told that the police knew he was lying about walking to the kitchen because it would have been impossible to do so without seeing Stephanie's body (see Crowe Transcripts, Vol. II).

The police continued to lie during Michael's third and final interrogation. For example, the police told Michael that they knew the murderer had to be someone living in the house, because evidence proved that all windows and doors were locked and none had been disturbed. In reality, a sliding glass door to the backyard had been left unlocked (Sauer & Wilkens 1999).

As they had with Michael, the police also lied to Joshua Treadway by telling him that they had conclusive physical evidence that Michael and their friend Aaron had murdered Stephanie and were setting Joshua up to take the fall for her death. They also told Joshua that they could prove that a knife found at his home was used to murder Stephanie. During the interrogation, Joshua told the police he did not believe that the knife was the murder weapon and asked to see his mother. The police ignored their legal duty to allow Joshua access to his mother at that point and stated, "If you want to conclude this conversation, we can do that, okay? But now you're no longer faced with the opportunity of getting the truth from you. 'Cause what's going to happen is once I leave here, the only possible conclusion is that you have a knife that was used to kill a 12-year-old girl and it was there in your bedroom, okay?" (Crowe Transcripts, Vol. II).

The police also subjected both Michael and Joshua to a Computer Voice Stress Analyzer ("CVSA") test (see Crowe Transcripts, Vol. II, pp. 40, 52–61; Treadway Transcript, Vol. I, pp. 34–51; 133–142). A CVSA is used to measure voice tremors, but is of questionable accuracy. Michael was asked a series of questions altering between general subjects (e.g., "Are we in the state of California?") and specific questions regarding Stephanie's murder (e.g., "Do you know who took Stephanie's life?"). The police then went through the test results and told Michael that the results indicated that he was lying. "This machine doesn't know you," they told Michael, "technology doesn't lie." When presented with the test results that suggested he had killed his sister, Michael began to sob uncontrollably. At that point, the police began to suggest that Michael might be blocking out the fact that he, in fact, murdered Stephanie (e.g., Crowe Transcripts, Vol. II.).

Like Michael, Joshua was also given a CVSA test, and was told repeatedly that the test results indicated that he was lying about whether he took a knife from the home of Aaron Houser, a friend of Michael's and Joshua's who was also a suspect in Stephanie's murder. Joshua was subjected to several hours of testing during his overnight interrogation. At one point, his interrogator suggested to him that perhaps Aaron gave him the knife. Exhausted, eager to please his interrogator, and desperate to pass the CVSA, Joshua finally told the police that the Aaron had given him a knife to dispose of on Michael's instructions. After being informed that he had finally passed the CVSA test, Joshua declared, "All right. Oh, praise God. Thank you, God, you saved me. . . . I got to get some sleep." (Treadway Transcripts Vol. I, p. 142).

Joshua's relief was short-lived. Although he passed the test with respect to one question, his admission to disposing of the murder weapon, led another, more heavy-handed detective to re-interview him and challenge him with respect to other answers (Treadway Transcripts Vol. III-V).

REWARD OR PUNISHMENT

Police often follow a description of the insurmountable evidence against a suspect with an offer to help the suspect if he or she confesses. This suggestion of reward, or in the alternative, punishment, is one of the most persuasive techniques that police use in interrogating suspects. Police often limit the options open to the suspect to two: (1) you did it and if you do not confess I cannot help you so you are going to be punished harshly, or (2) you did it and if you do confess, you are a good person and I can help you. Having imparted the notion that the suspect cannot avoid prosecution, the police suggest that the suspect will be better off if he or she confesses (Ofshe & Leo 1997).

This technique was woven throughout the interrogations of Michael, Anthony, Lacresha and Joshua. Perhaps most notable was the explicit manner in which the technique was used by Chief of Police Thomas Vaughn, the officer who interrogated Anthony. Chief Vaughn was an interrogation specialist, certified in the Reid method of interrogation (see Leo, this volume). Chief Vaughn's questions suggested to Anthony that lab analyses were being conducted on the clothes Anthony wore on the day of the crime, and that it would be likely that the victim's blood would be found in the lining of his pockets, and that his shoe prints would be matched to prints found at the crime scene (see Transcript of Interrogation of Anthony Harris). When these efforts to elicit an admission from Anthony were unfruitful, Chief Vaughn told Anthony that he would have to take a Computer Voice Stress Analyzer test, but could avoid it if he confessed. Vaughn stated:

> Okay, 'cause like I said before, I can only help you, if you help me. And we're probably going to know ah, and have, or at least have the test results back in a couple of days from the place where they sent your clothes to, and it's going to say whether there was blood in those clothes or not, and that blood would have

been our victim's here. Ah, and see that would be the point in time that you're sort of stuck. Ah, now it's not that Anthony was forthcoming. He came in, he talked to me, he didn't want to tell me. I'm not going to deny that, I mean it's probably going to be the toughest thing you ever do is if you tell me that you did this. It's going to be tough for your mom to hear too, but your mom can't help you and I can't help you if you're not honest with me, and ah, you know, I will be able to tell once I give the test if you're telling the truth, I'll know that, and again, I would like to know that before I give the test, so that I don't have to send court or the prosecutor's office or anybody else I listed on there that I did the test and Anthony lied to me on this test. That's the worst thing in the world that could happen here. Because put yourself in the judge's shoes or the prosecutor's shoes. He reads this report, here's Anthony who took this test and didn't do good on the test. He didn't say that he did it. He lied about it, so if you were in the judge's shoes, does that put you on looking for some kind of counseling and help that way or just hey, this guy needs to be put away until he's twenty-one cause he's not remorseful, and he didn't care that he did that. Two different kind of people, isn't it? Now if you were the judge which would you want to see, the truthful person or the person that didn't care? (Harris Transcript, p. 9)

Anthony later explained why he confessed to Devan's murder: "I just felt like I was in a maze. I couldn't find my way out. . . . If I said I did it, I'll go home. That's what I thought. But now I know as soon as I said I did something horrible, I'm not going to go home." (ABC, 1999).

Michael was also subjected to this interrogation tactic. At one point a detective explained to Michael, "You're a child. You're 14 years old. Nobody's going to hold you to the same standards that they would some criminal on the street, okay. You're going to need some help through this" (Crowe Transcripts, Vol. III p. 73). At another point when Michael expressed concern that he would be "locked up," the following exchange occurred:

DETECTIVE CLAYTOR: I think we have ways of helping this situation. You know what?

MR. CROWE: What?

DETECTIVE CLAYTOR: I'm not really sure that locking you up is the answer. You know what else?

MR. CROWE: What?

DETECTIVE CLAYTOR: We don't do that to 14-year-olds.

Mr. Crowe: What do you do to them?

DETECTIVE CLAYTOR: We look for understanding, and we try to help. But you know what? It's a two-way street. We put out that effort, we need that effort. The detective went on to remark, "You know, I'm not real sure how familiar you are with this system, but kind of the way it works is if the system has to prove it, yeah, it's jail. If they don't, then its help. . . . [W]here that kind of puts us is in a position of you have these two roads to go here. Which one are we going to go down?" (p. 80)

SUGGESTIVE QUESTIONING

The type of questioning used during an interrogation takes advantage of the suggestibility of children. Police tend not to use open-ended questions which would call for a narrative response in which a child would be allowed to answer based on his or her own knowledge (cf. Bull & Milne, this volume). Rather, police engage suspects by asking questions that force the suspect to choose between set answers (Bruck et al., 1998, p. 140; Lyon, 1999). This type of questioning is problematic because children are likely to choose between the forced-choice answers presented by the police "even when none are correct" (Lyon, 1999, p. 18; see also Grisso, 1987, p. 9). Questions of this nature are also suppositional, in that they assume that some information contained in the question is true. These questions relay to the child that the police believe something to be true, which often leads to a false affirmation of that information by children (Lyon, 1999).

Suggestive questioning was a principle tactic used in Lacresha's interrogation. After eliciting Lacresha's admission that she was the only person in the room where the baby was sleeping on the afternoon of her death, the detectives told her that a doctor "with over twenty years of experience" has found that the baby sustained her injuries during the time that Lacresha was in the room. Throughout the interrogation, Lacresha denied having any knowledge of how the baby was injured, even stating on one occasion, "I didn't do nothing, I promise to God" (Murray Transcript, p.25). Shifting to a more suggestive mode of interrogation, one detective suggested to Lacresha that the baby may have been hurt in an accident, telling Lacresha that perhaps the baby slipped out of her arms while she was carrying her:

> OFFICER 2: Yeh, but nobody else, you know. You might have to, the baby might have been sick and you had him in the arms, or whatever, you might have dropped the baby, uh, and that's perfectly understandable. That happens all the time. I don't know what happened, you see? And you know people are thinking the worst. You're the only person that can clear those things up, and nobody else. (p. 31)

After more prompting, Lacresha finally told the detectives that when she had picked up the baby to take her to her grandfather, the baby fell and hit her head on the floor. The detectives then asked Lacresha if she kicked the baby and after additional encouragement, Lacresha said: "Don't know, maybe . . . I was trying to run back and pick her up, probably I was trying like my feet probably kicked against her side or something" (p. 34). The detectives continued to interrogate Lacresha because her statement did not account for all the bruising on the toddler's body. They prodded her for more details of the beating and repeatedly accused her of not telling the truth. Finally, Lacresha refused to answer any more questions, bringing the interrogation to a halt.

Suggestive questioning was also a key tactic used against Joshua. For example, during Joshua's second interrogation, the interrogating officer stated that he believed Joshua had helped plan the murder. After Joshua denied being in on the planning, the detective kept prodding him for more details of a plan. Joshua first said he had heard Michael and Aaron talk about a plan to kill Stephanie but he never thought that they would actually carry it out (Treadway Transcripts, Vol. IV). Soon thereafter, Joshua admitted to having been involved in the planning. Still not satisfied, the officer suggested that the CVSA was indicating deception with regard to Joshua's answer that he was not involved in the killing.

The police then administered additional CVSA tests, telling Joshua yet again that he had failed. Joshua broke into tears and then stated that Aaron had threatened to kill Joshua and his family if he told what had happened to Stephanie. The police then suggested to Joshua that he had been a lookout. Again, only after this suggestion was made, Joshua's story included a description of his role as a lookout standing outside of the Crowe home. The police later stated, "It's not going to be any bigger problem if you were in the house or if you actually saw what these guys did in there" (Treadway Transcripts Vol. V, pp. 50–51). Joshua then stated that he did go into the house. Over 9 hours into the interrogation, Joshua told the police a detailed story about how the three planned and committed Stephanie's murder. At that point, he was placed under arrest. Joshua then spent the next two hours recounting his story (Treadway Transcript, Vol. V).

The suggestive questioning utilized by police in interrogating Michael was not so straightforward. A significant part of the interrogation was spent convincing Michael that there were "two Michaels"—one good, and one evil. It was the evil Michael, police theorized, that surfaced and killed Stephanie. For the bulk of the interrogation, Michael insisted that he could not confess to the murder, because he had no recollection of any involvement with the crime (Crowe Transcripts, Vol. III). However, it was clear that the "two Michaels" tactic was effective:

DETECTIVE CLAYTOR: You know what you have to do to help the bad part in Michael be understood by the rest of us.
MR. CROWE: (Indiscernible.)
DETECTIVE CLAYTOR: And you know what needs to be done—
MR. CROWE: If that's true, then the other Michael has taken over because I don't know what's going on because I don't remember.
DETECTIVE WRISLEY: You know what, that's possible.
MR. CROWE: It's the most horrible thing in the world. (pp. 71, 104)

However, Michael was still unable to provide the police with any details regarding the murder. The police told Michael that he should use his imagination to describe what he thought the evil Michael might have done (see Fulero, this volume, for a description of similar tactic used in the interrogation of Bradley Page). They asked him to guess what kind of knife would have been used. Michael told the police that he "would have to make up a story" (Crowe Transcripts, Vol. III, pp. 77, 129–30, 142). The story Michael told was as follows:

MR. CROWE: You know, I'll lie. I'll have to make it up.
DETECTIVE WRISLEY: Tell us the story, Michael.
MR. CROWE: You want me to tell you a little story?
DETECTIVE WRISLEY: Tell me the story. What happened that night?
MR. CROWE: OKAY. I'm telling you right now, it's a complete lie.
DETECTIVE WRISLEY: Tell us the story.
MR. CROWE: OKAY. This is true. I am extremely jealous of my sister.
DETECTIVE WRISLEY: Okay.
MR. CROWE: She's always had a lot of friends. We were good friends and stuff like that. She was friends with people my age, I mean with all the popular girls like that. That's true, okay.
DETECTIVE CLAYTOR: You let me know when you get to the lie part.
MR. CROWE: Okay. Here's the part where I'll start lying. That night I got pissed off at her. I couldn't take it anymore, okay. So I got a knife, went into her room, and I stabbed her. After I was done, I pulled her off the bed . . .

*   *   *

DETECTIVE CLAYTOR: How many times did you stab her?
MR. CROWE: This is going to be a lie, three times.

*   *   *

DETECTIVE CLAYTOR: When you went in to do that, Mike, was she on her back or on her stomach or on her side when she was in bed?
MR. CROWE: On her side, that's a lie. I don't know. I told you it was going to be a lie.
DETECTIVE CLAYTOR: Well, tell me what the truth is.
MR. CROWE: The only reason I'm trying to lie here is because you presented me with two paths, one I'm definitely afraid of. I'd rather die than go to jail. (pp. 161–62)

SELECTIVE REINFORCEMENT AND REPETITION AND NEGATIVE FEEDBACK

Police also tend to selectively reinforce the responses of the suspect they are interrogating. They do this by responding positively to information that inculpates the suspect while responding negatively or ignoring information that exculpates the suspect (Bruck et al., 1998; Ofshe & Leo, 1997). This technique is highly effective when used on children, particularly when repeated frequently (Lyon, 1999). In interrogations, questions are often repeated over and over again until the suspect gives the answer that a police officer is hoping to elicit. However, even innocent "children who are asked the same question more than once may assume they gave the 'wrong' answer the first time, and feel pressure to provide the 'right' answer when the question is repeated" (Myers 1996, p. 23; also see Lyon, 1999). In addition, children tend to be more compliant than adults and more eager to please adult authority figures.

Repetitive selective reinforcement was used throughout Michael's interrogations. For example, at one point Michael was asked what he did with the knife used to murder Stephanie. Michael insisted that he had no idea what they were talking about and that he knew nothing about the murder, but the police persisted:

> MR. CROWE [MICHAEL]: Why are you doing this to me? I didn't do this to her. I couldn't. God, God. Why? (Indiscernible). I can't even believe myself anymore. I don't know if I did it or not. I didn't though. (Indiscernible).
> MR. CLAYTOR [DETECTIVE]: Well, I think you're on the right track. Let's go ahead and think through this now.
> MR. CROWE: I don't think—if I did this I don't remember it. I don't remember a thing."
> MR. CLAYTOR: You know what, that's possible. (Crowe Transcripts, Vol. II, pp. 82–86)

Detectives seized on the notion that Michael might have blocked out Stephanie's murder and repeatedly encouraged Michael to believe that he had done so. In contrast, police responded harshly when Michael attempted to discern whether the evidence the police claimed pointed to him was accurate. For example, when police turned the discussion back to the hair found in Stephanie's hand, Michael stated he wanted to know for sure whether the hair was his. The detective responded, "Well, that wouldn't be fair at this point. You know that." (Crowe transcripts, p. 93). As the interrogation wore on, Michael stopped asking questions about the alleged evidence and took on the police's contention that a "bad Michael" had killed Stephanie and that the "good Michael" had blocked out what had occurred. Michael eventually gave a detailed description of hostility toward his sister for overshadowing him at school and home. He told the police of a part of his personality called "Odin" which he believed had killed Stephanie. He stated, "I'm not sure how I did it. All I know is I did it." Although Michael, at that point in time, apparently believed that he had committed the murder, he was still unable to provide the police with any details of the crime (*See generally* Crowe Transcripts).

The use of selected positive reinforcement is often coupled with the repeated use of negative feedback, a technique that is also problematic for child and juvenile suspects. For example, interrogators are trained to cut off a suspect's denials, to preclude the suspect from asserting his innocence and from telling his side of the story. The reason for this stems from what Inbau, et. al call a "fundamental principle of interrogation": "the more often a guilty suspect denies involvement in a crime, the less likely he will be to tell the truth." (Inbau et al., 2001, p.304) This use of negative feedback was the predominant technique used in the interrogation of B.M.B. in connection with the alleged rape of his four year old neighbor.

Over a three-day period, Detective Swanson of the Wichita Police Department attempted to contact B.M.B.'s mother to arrange an interview of B.M.B. On the third day, J's father called Swanson and notified him that B.M.B. would be leaving the next day to spend the summer in Arkansas with his uncle. Without trying to contact B.M.B.'s mother, Swanson went to B.M.B.'s school, picked him up from his fourth-grade class, and told school authorities that he was taking the boy to the Exploited and Missing Child Unit for an interview. The interrogation lasted approximately thirty eight minutes and the statements obtained from B.M.B. led the State to file rape charges against B.M.B (*In the Matter of B.M.B.*).

Time and again, B.M.B. asserted his innocence, and each time the boy denied responsibility, he was told by his interrogator that the question was not whether he had digitally penetrated J but why he had done so:

DETECTIVE SWANSON: Well, let me tell you something, okay? I didn't bring you down here to ask you if you did it. Okay? I brought you down here to tell me why you did it.

*   *   *

DETECTIVE SWANSON: Well, let me ask you something, okay? This is, it's not a matter of if, okay? Something happened and I don't think you meant to hurt the girl, but it did happen. So now what we have to do is we have to deal with what happened.
B.M.B.: Yeah, but I didn't. . . .
DETECTIVE SWANSON: Okay, now listen.
B.M.B.: Touch her.

*   *   *

DETECTIVE SWANSON: I mean I don't think you're a bad kid. I don't think you meant to hurt the girl.
B.M.B.: No, if I did I'm sorry but I didn't know and C was right there, I don't know why he won't tell the truth for me because I didn't touch that girl. If I did, I'm sorry.

DETECTIVE SWANSON: Well, see the doctor says it happened, cause she's
  got, she's got some little cuts down there and it hurt her.
B.M.B.: I didn't go nowhere down there, but on her feet, C was right
  there with me. He was right there standing right next to me.

Finally, after several more of his denials were ignored, B.M.B. admitted that he "might" have touched J by accident. Even then, it was a reluctant admission:

DETECTIVE SWANSON: Okay, B., we were talking before okay? The fact
  of the matter is it happened, it was a mistake. You didn't mean to
  hurt her. Did you? Okay, and I don't think you did. You don't want
  to hurt that girl. Was it this, you were curious or I mean it's, it's
  okay. I'm not going to think badly of you. Like I said, the only thing
  I deal with is the truth. That's the only thing I'm interested in. I
  mean was it an accident?
B.M.B.: I don't see how I could.
DETECTIVE SWANSON: Huh?
B.M.B.: I don't see how I could have touched her though cause all I
  was doing was putting sand on her.
DETECTIVE SWANSON: But your hand touched her down there, didn't
  it? You know, it's okay. You know these things really bother us
  and cause us problems, but if you talk to me and let me know,
  we can help.
B.M.B.: Could have been an accident, or what I don't know I was putting sand on her and that was it. (B.M.B. Transcript, p. 12)

THE AFTERMATH

MICHAEL AND JOSHUA

On the basis of Michael and Joshua's statements, the Escondido police
arrested the two boys and their friend Aaron and charged them with the
murder of Stephanie Crowe. The stories told by Michael and Joshua, however, simply did not match the evidence. No blood or DNA was found on
the knife, nor were Michael or Aaron's fingerprints. The timeline described
by Joshua was inconsistent with alibi evidence provided by Joshua and
Aaron's families. The confessions, however, were introduced as evidence at
a hearing to determine whether the boys should be tried as juveniles or adults.
Although the judge found there was legal sufficiency to transfer the boys
to adult court, she remarked that the boys' statements were "troublesome"
and chastised the police for twisting the boys' words until they admitted to

the crime. Although the issue was not before her, she strongly suggested that the police had coerced the statements from the boys.

In the trial court, Michael and Joshua filed motions to suppress their statements. After viewing the videotapes, the trial court also took issue with the confessions. Michael's entire confession was thrown out because of police statements that Michael would receive "help" if he confessed. Joshua's first statement, given in the overnight interrogation, was thrown out pursuant to a finding that the interrogation was "coercive" because Joshua had been denied sleep and food. The majority of Joshua's second confession was also excluded because he had not been *Mirandized*. The remaining two hours of the interrogation were allowed to be presented against Joshua, but not against Michael or Aaron.

Prior to the trial, however, Joshua's attorney, Mary Ellen Attridge made a stunning discovery. After examining a sweatshirt taken from Richard Tuite, a drifter who had been knocking on doors in the Crowe's neighborhood looking for a girl named Tracy, she noticed spots on the red sweatshirt that looked like blood splatter. She asked that the spots be analyzed by the crime lab. The test results showed that the blood on Tuite's sweatshirt was Stephanie's. The police knew of Tuite, and were aware that he was a schizophrenic who suffered from methamphetamine addiction. Tuite had a history of violent behavior, and was arrested within a few weeks of Stephanie's murder for harassing two girls, ages 12 and 13, by stating, "Tracy, all I want to do is have sex with you" (Sauer & Wilkens, 2002). Although Tuite was picked up immediately following Stephanie's murder, at which point his sweatshirt was inventoried, he was released without being fingerprinted. Once the police zeroed in on Michael Crowe and his two friends, they never considered Tuite a serious suspect. The bombshell discovery that Stephanie's blood was on Tuite's sweatshirt, however, caused prosecutors to dismiss the murder charges against the boys (Sauer & Wilkens 1999). Escondido police officers and San Diego County prosecutors have not, to this day, formally exonerated the boys nor apologized to them. The California Attorney General's Office took over the Crowe case and reinvestigated Stephanie's murder from scratch. The results of their investigation cleared the boys and led to the filing of murder charges against Tuite. In a hotly contested preliminary hearing, Tuite's defense attorneys tried to use the videotaped confession of Joshua to get the charges against Tuite dismissed. In an ironic twist, prosecutors from the Attorney General's Office called University of California at Irvine, Professor of Criminology and Professor of Psychology, Richard A. Leo, a noted expert on police interrogations and false confessions, to the stand to offer his expert opinion that the Treadway confession was unreliable. The trial court found that there was probable cause to proceed to trial against Tuite. It will be up to the jury whether the false confessions of Michael and Joshua will provide Tuite with the reasonable doubt he needs to be acquitted.

The impact of these events on Michael was devastating. He explained in early 2002, "I've changed a lot. I have difficulty being in groups. When I go out, I still hear people say, "That's the guy who killed his sister." I'm shy to the point of being antisocial. So, my number of friends is down to just two: my fiancée and my best guy friend. Most of all though, I haven't yet begun to deal with the loss of my sister. I'm going to need to get over everything else before I can even touch that. But right now, I'm still trapped somewhere in the grief" (Crowe, 2002).

LACRESHA

On the basis of Lacresha's statements, the Travis County, Texas District Attorney's Office charged 11-year-old Lacresha Murray with capital murder in connection with the death of 2-year-old Jayla Belton. In announcing the charges of murder and injury to a child, District Attorney Ronnie Earle declared, "This case appears to be unprecedented in our local history . . . It just shows that Austin is not immune from the hideous malady sweeping the country of children killing children" (Banta, 1996).

In June 1996, Lacresha became the youngest girl ever indicted in Texas for capital murder when a grand jury approved Earle's petition to try her under the juvenile court system's Determinate Sentence Act. Capital murder charges were automatic under Texas law because the victim was under the age of six. Due to her age, Lacresha Murray was ineligible for the death penalty, but she could receive a maximum sentence of forty years in prison, a sentence that Earle vowed to seek on the day the indictment was returned (Obregon, 1996). The prosecution's case against Lacresha rested primarily on the statements she had given to Austin detectives during the controversial two-and-a-half hour taped interrogation.

Before her trial, Lacresha's public defender sought to have her statements suppressed, arguing that Lacresha did not understand her *Miranda* warnings and that the statements were the product of suggestive questioning. The trial court held that Lacresha was not in police custody at the time when the statements were made, and admitted her statements into evidence. At trial, the State's case consisted of the taped interrogation and testimony from medical experts that the injuries sustained by the baby were not accidental in nature and that they occurred within a few hours of her death, the very time period when she was in a room frequented by Lacresha. A psychologist hired by the State testified that Lacresha "could hold her own under police questioning" but told the jury, during cross-examination, that he did not believe that Lacresha intended to kill the baby (Harmon, August 6, 1996). As a result of this testimony, prosecutors backed away from the capital murder charge, urging jurors to convict her of the lesser charge of intentional injury to a child, a charge which also carried

the same maximum sentence of up to forty years in prison. After deliber-
ating for two days, the jury convicted Lacresha of the lesser charges of intentionally injuring a child and criminally negligent homicide (Harmon, August
8, 1996).

Under Texas' Determinant Sentencing Act, the jury could sentence
Lacresha from probation to forty years in prison. They sentenced her to
a twenty-year term. Under the terms of the "blended sentence," Lacresha
would have to spend at least three years in a juvenile prison before becoming eligible for parole. If she was not rehabilitated, she would have to
remain in the juvenile prison until age 21, and could then be transferred
to an adult prison to serve out the remainder of her sentence (Harmon,
August 10, 1996).

Lacresha's conviction was only the first chapter in a legal saga that
was to make many twists and turns. In a rare move, just two months after
presiding over Lacresha's jury trial, Judge John Dietz granted a motion for
a new trial after hearing a day and a half of testimony about the unfairness
of the trial, focusing largely on the ineffective representation provided by
Lacresha's trial attorney. Dietz told the stunned observers in the courtroom
that he was granting a new trial on his own motion, not the defense's motion,
declaring, "this system is an adversarial system, designed to search for the
truth. . . . In this situation, I have to tell you, I have cause to question as to
whether or not justice is served" (Palomo, 1996). District Attorney Ronnie
Earle, in the midst of a hard fought reelection campaign, was so taken aback
by the ruling that he remarked, "Excuse me while I get back up off the floor.
. . . This is a nightmare. You couldn't have shocked me more if you told me
that Jesus Christ came back" (Palomo, 1996).

Prosecutors re-tried Lacresha for the baby's death. The second trial
allowed both sides to correct the mistakes of the first trial. The prosecution
augmented its motive evidence, suggesting that the motive for the killing
was Lacresha's anger at having to clean up the vomit of the baby, who had
been sick when she arrived at the Murray home that morning. A new expert,
Dr. Vincent DiMaio, the Medical Examiner of neighboring Bexar County,
testified that the baby had been stomped to death, telling jurors that the
tread pattern on Lacresha's shoes seemed to match bruises left on the baby's
body perfectly (Harmon, February 4, 1997). The defense, who had failed to
call any expert witnesses at Lacresha's first trial, countered with an expert
of its own, Dr. Linda Norton, a Dallas pathologist, who testified that Jayla
was a chronically battered child. Dr. Norton disagreed with the state's evidence about the time of the injuries, finding that the baby's injuries could
have been inflicted hours before her death and that many of the bruises
were a result of the efforts by doctors in the emergency room to revive her
through CPR. Dr. Norton also disputed the testimony that the two parallel marks on the baby's torso were caused by a shoe, and stated that a broom

handle or belt were more likely to have caused them (Harmon, February 13, 1997). Despite the vigorous defense put on by her new lawyers, Lacresha was convicted a second time of intentionally injuring a child. This time around, however, Judge Dietz sentenced her to twenty-five years in prison, a sentence to which both the prosecution and the defense had agreed (Harmon, February 18, 1997).

After her second conviction, and during its appeal, Lacresha's case became a cause célèbre. Barbara Taft, a legal secretary at a prestigious Austin law firm, quit her job and began working full-time on Lacresha's case. She set up a website and organized monthly marches to protest Lacresha's conviction (Hughes, 1989). *New York Times* columnist Bob Herbert wrote a series of articles, which were highly critical of the role of police and prosecutors in the case, and made a strong argument that Lacresha was innocent (Herbert, November 15, 1998; Herbert, November 26, 1998). The television news magazine show, "60 Minutes" did a piece on the case entitled "Juvenile Injustice?" in which Dr. DiMaio backed away from his testimony that the marks on the baby's torso were a perfect match to the tread of Lacresha's shoe.

On April 15, 1999, the Court of Appeals of Texas reversed Lacresha's conviction, ruling that the trial court had erred when it admitted Lacresha's recorded and written statements into evidence at her trial. The court took issue with the trial court's finding that Lacresha was not in custody at the time of her interrogation, holding that "it is appropriate for Texas courts to consider the age of the juvenile in determining whether the child is in custody" (*In re L.M., 1999*, p.289). The appropriate standard, wrote the court, is "whether, based upon objective circumstances, a reasonable child of the same age would believe her freedom of movement was significantly restricted" (p.289). Looking at this question through the eyes of Lacresha, an eleven year old girl who had never been through the legal system before, who was isolated and alone throughout the interview, who was the target of the police investigation, and who was never told she was free to leave or that she could call her grandparents, the Court ruled that Lacresha was in custody at the time of the interrogation (*In re L.M., 1999*).

On April 21, 1999, after serving three years in state custody for a crime she still adamantly insists she did not commit, Lacresha Murray was freed from the Texas Youth Commission. Prosecutors debated whether to try her for a third time. While they were deciding, Lacresha's defense attorneys proffered new forensic evidence which they claimed established her innocence. The evidence, magnified slides from the baby's autopsy, showed that Jayla's injuries occurred several hours before she died during a timeframe when she was not in Lacresha's care (Quinn 2000). On August 13, 2001, all charges against Lacresha Murray were dismissed. Her long legal nightmare was finally over.

ANTHONY

On the basis of his statements, Anthony Harris, was charged with the murder of Devan Duniver. Because he was only 12 years of age, he was not eligible to be tried as an adult. The key pretrial battle centered around whether Anthony's statements would be admissible. During a suppression hearing, the defense called three expert witnesses, including Dr. Kathleen Quinn, a psychiatrist at the Cleveland Clinic Foundation; Dr. Steven Neuhaus, a clinical psychologist at University Hospitals Health System, who both opined that Anthony could not understand his *Miranda* warnings and was not developmentally mature enough to waive them; and Dr. Richard Ofshe, a sociologist at University of California-Berkeley and an expert on police interrogations, who testified about the coerciveness of the tactics police used to obtain Anthony's confessions (Frankston 1999; *In re Harris*, 2000). Despite this unrebutted testimony, Tuscawaras County Juvenile Court Judge Linda Kate denied the suppression motion, ruling that Anthony was not "in custody" at the time he made incriminating statements, obviating the need for Chief Vaughn to give him *Miranda* warnings, that when Vaughn did read him his rights, Anthony "knowingly and intelligently" gave them up, and that Vaughn's persistent questioning did not constitute undue coercion (*In re Harris*, 2000, p. 6). On March 10, 1999, at the close of a lengthy trial, she adjudicated Anthony delinquent for intentionally causing Devan's death and ordered that he be committed to the Department of Youth Service until his twenty-first birthday (*In re Harris*, 2000). On June 18, 1999, ABC News featured Anthony's case in an episode of its prime-time "20/20" show. The show, which featured interviews with Anthony, his mother, his attorneys and Dr. Ofshe, criticized the Reid Technique used by Chief Vaughn to obtain Anthony's confession, and raised anew serious concerns about the propriety of using these techniques on children and Anthony's innocence (see ABC, 1999).

On June 7, 2000, an Ohio appellate court reversed Anthony's conviction, finding that the juvenile court erred when it denied Anthony's motion to suppress. Looking at the interrogation through the eyes of Anthony, the court found that Chief Vaughn's repeated accusations and refusal to accept Anthony's denials, "conveys to [Anthony] that he had no choice but to submit to Chief Vaughn's will and confess to the murder" (*In re Harris*, 2000, p. 8). In its analysis, the court noted the fact that the State presented no evidence to rebut the findings of the clinicians that Anthony could not understand and intelligently waive his *Miranda* rights, and that Chief Vaughn read Anthony his rights outside of the presence of his mother. Based on those facts, as well as Anthony's age, criminal inexperience, and the "intensity of the interview," the court found that Anthony's waiver of his *Miranda* rights was not knowing and intelligent (*In re Harris*, 2000, p. 11).

Finally, the court zeroed in on several of Chief Vaughn's Reid-based tactics in ruling that the confession was involuntary. These included the use of the minimization technique of telling a suspect that there are two types of people—honest and dishonest—and that only honest people can get help, the threat to use the voice stress analyzer test to prove that Anthony was dishonest and undeserving of Vaughn's help, and the use of suggestive and leading questions to get Anthony to fill in details of the crime in "the post-admission narrative" phase of the interrogation (*In re Harris*, 2000, p. 13–16). "It is important to remember," stressed the court, that Chief Vaughn used these techniques on a twelve-year-old child that was entering the seventh grade" (p. 12).

Without Anthony's statements, the State had no other evidence to link Anthony to the crime. On June 8, 2000, 14-year-old Anthony walked out of a juvenile prison. Judge Kate ordered that he be released pending a decision by the State whether to appeal or to retry Anthony (Ruiz Patton, 2000). Tuscarawas County Prosecutor Amanda Spies Bornhorst filed an appeal asking the Ohio Supreme Court to reinstate the verdict. After the appeal was dismissed by the Ohio Supreme Court (*In re Harris*, 2000; Hagelberg, 2000), the State decided not to retry Anthony.

B.M.B.

On the basis of his statements, B.M.B. was charged with one count of rape in juvenile court. B.M.B's motion to suppress his statements was denied and on March 7, 1997, he was adjudicated delinquent (Lessner, Mar. 8, 1997). Once news of the conviction broke, many people began to call the Wichita Eagle, the paper which broke the story, and area radio stations to find out what they could do to help (Lessner, Mar. 14, 1997; Lessner, May 25, 1997). In an unusual move, the juvenile court judge, Carol Bacon, spoke to a reporter from the Wichita Eagle about the case, stating that although she admitted the statements into evidence, there was ample evidence to convict the boy without the statement, pointing to the fact that a witness saw the boy in the sandpile next to the girl when the girl screamed. She allowed the statement into evidence because she saw "no legal reason" to keep it out. According to Judge Bacon, the police did not abuse their power or trick the boy into confessing and "it wasn't a case of where this boy was retarded or couldn't comprehend English. . . . the boy was very clear in what he said" (Lessner, Mar. 15 1997, p. 8A); Editorial, *Kids Need Some Help When Arrested* 1997, p.8A).

Two new attorneys agreed to take on B.M.B's case for free and filed a motion for a new trial (Lessner, Mar. 21, 1997). At the hearing on the motion for a new trial, the attorneys called Dr. Marc Chaffin, a clinical professor of psychiatry at the University of Oklahoma, the research director at the Center of Child Abuse and Neglect, and co-director of the Adolescent Sex Offender Treatment Program, as an expert on B.M.B.'s behalf. When asked for his opinion on the methods used to obtain B.M.B's statements, Dr. Chaffin stated:

> I've reviewed transcripts of many interviews in several other cases, as well as this one, interviews that I thought were both appropriate and inappropriate. This interview was a difficult one. This transcript was a difficult one to review. I have to say, unfortunately, it's probably the worst I've seen in my career. It was at best, incompetent; at [worst] reprehensible. And I say this with a great deal of difficulty because I'm someone who works with abused children, who works with law enforcement people, who works with people who do this. I'm normally on the other side of cases. This particular interview was beyond the pale. . . .
>
> These are techniques that law enforcement use with adult suspects who are suspected of being sex offenders. They are wholly inappropriate for use with ten year old children. We have reams of research about the effects of coercive questioning, suggestive and leading questioning, pressured situations and the effects these have on children and how its different from the effect they have on adults. Basically, these types of techniques, in my opinion, have no place in any kind of setting in use with children. They would likely lead—in fact, we really from a research perspective don't know the effects of this type of questioning because typically, in the suggestibility and coercive questioning research that's been done, far less pressure has been exerted on children. . . . because people don't think it would be ethical to go this far with children to see what would happen. Even in settings where less pressure, less suggestion and less coercion have been studied, we found substantial numbers of children will agree with things that are factually inaccurate, will give assention to things, will nod and say 'Uh-huh' or will—will essentially agree to things or even come to believe things that are not true. . . . This type of interview technique—if what one wants is a confession, this type of interview technique with ten year old children will get it. It will unfortunately, in my opinion, get it from the guilty and get it from the innocent. I think-my guess would be a substantial number—and I'm not talking about ten percent or fifteen percent. But a substantial number perhaps as many as half, of all children interviewed in this way would have given some minimal agreement to what was being suggested to them with this level of pressure and coercion. (*In the Matter of B.M.B.*, 1998, pp. 1304–1306)

Despite Dr. Chaffin's testimony, the motion for a new trial was denied. B.M.B was placed in the custody of the Department of Social and Rehabilitation Services and institutionalized at a treatment center. Shortly after his arrival there, B.M.B. was sexually assaulted by another teenager who forced B.M.B. to perform oral sex and threatened to kill him if he told the authorities (Lessner, June 25, 1997). News of B.M.B's rape only broadened the coalition of concerned citizens united to free B.M.B. (McCormick, 1997).

On March 13, 1998, the Kansas Supreme Court reversed B.M.B.'s conviction, finding that "we have serious doubts about whether B.M.B. fully understood his constitutional rights or the consequences of waiving them" and that the State failed to show that B.M.B's statement was voluntary (*In the Matter of B.M.B.*, 1998, p. 1312). The Court went much further, however, holding that the traditional "totality of the circumstances test" was insufficient "to ensure that a child under fourteen years of age makes an intelligent and knowing waiver of his rights" (p. 1312).

Instead, the Court created a bright-line rule, preventing the State from using any statements obtained from a juvenile under 14 years of age against the juvenile in court unless the juvenile first had an opportunity to consult with a parent, guardian, or attorney, and both the parent and juvenile were advised of the juvenile's right to an attorney and to remain silent. "We can no longer ignore the immaturity and inexperience of a child under 14 years of age and the obvious disadvantage such a child has in confronting a custodial police interrogation" (p. 1312) wrote the Court; nor could the court tolerate trial courts, like that in B.M.B, paying "lip service" to the factors in the "totality of the circumstances" test and ignoring whether children like B.M.B. comprehend their rights or their situation (pp. 1312–13).

Although his legal victory wiped the rape conviction off of his record, it did not undo the damage done to B.M.B. B.M.B.'s mental health began to deteriorate when he was first held in custody while awaiting his trial. As the youngest child in the juvenile detention center, B.M.B. was placed on a suicide watch after he banged his head on walls and doors, bruising his face and swelling his eyes shut. When his legal victory came, he was still in a mental health facility under constant supervision because of his suicidal tendencies (Lessner, Apr. 3, 1998).

RECOMMENDATIONS

Several possible solutions to the problems of false and coerced confession of juveniles, including the right to have a parent present and the right to counsel during the interrogation process, are contained in the United States Supreme Court decisions of *Haley, Gallegos,* and *Gault.* New psychological research into the competencies of children to understand the *Miranda* warnings and the consequences of waiving them, suggests that the "totality of circumstances" test recommended by the Court in its last interrogation decision, *Fare v. Michael C.,* must be abandoned, or at the very least modified, by the Court. Other solutions, including mandatory videotaping of interrogations and an end to the use of psychological interrogation techniques on children arise from research on the suggestibility of children and on analysis of police interrogation methods and false confession cases which did not exist at the time of *Fare.* These developments, as well as greater understanding of the frequency of wrongful convictions, fueled largely by new DNA technologies, further underscore the need for a reevaluation of the law and practice in the area of juvenile interrogations.

REQUIRING A RECORD OF THE CHILD'S *MIRANDA* COMPREHENSION

Along with the similarity of interrogation techniques used, a common denominator among the interrogations of Michael, Anthony, Lacresha, Joshua, and B.M.B. is that it is unclear whether any of these children understood that they had a right to refuse to answer questions, or to seek the advice of an attorney. For example, although detectives began Lacresha's interrogation by reading her *Miranda* rights off of a pre-printed card, they merely accepted the 11-year-old's simple affirmation that she understood her rights, without ever discerning whether she actually did comprehend their meaning. Lacresha's very limited understanding of criminal matters became obvious later in her interrogation after police had already obtained a confession. Detectives presented a typed statement to Lacresha, asking her, "Can you read pretty good?" "No," she responded, "but I try " (Murray Transcript, p. 47). As she struggled to read the statement, Lacresha asked, "what's that word? Home-a-seed?" The detectives corrected her pronunciation. She then asked again, "Homicide? What's that?" (Murray Transcript p.47) Her question went unanswered, and the detectives continued the interrogation. Like Lacresha, Anthony gave similar one word responses when he waived his Miranda warnings but later claimed he had no idea what the words meant (Harris Transcript, p.1; ABC 1999).

Since the Kansas Supreme Court's decision in *B.M.B.*, there has been a renewed and growing concern about the ability of children to knowingly and intelligently waive their *Miranda* rights (e.g., Myers 1996, p. 27; Kaban & Tobey, 1999). Research conducted on the competence of children in relation to criminal matters has shown that this concern is well-justified, as children are less able than adults to understand the complexities of the criminal justice system (Grisso et al., 2003). Additionally, once in the midst of a custodial interrogation, a child's situation is more precarious than an adult's because children are extraordinarily susceptible to the tactics used by police to elicit information, and therefore more likely to give false confessions (Inbau, 1991; Redlich & Goodman 2003).

Problems arise when children are asked to comprehend what the *Miranda* warnings mean. Children do not comprehend the meaning of a "right" in the same manner that adults do. Research has shown that: "Adults typically see a legal right as an 'entitlement,' which is provided to them by law and cannot be revoked. In contrast, research suggests that children think of a right as 'conditional'—something that authorities allow them to have but that could be retracted" (Grisso 1997, p. 7).

While this is particularly true for young children (Grisso 1997; Shepherd & Zaremba 1995), older delinquent youths, particularly those who are learning disabled (Crawford 1985; Grisso 1997), also tend to have this limited understanding of their rights. In one study, older delinquent youths were found to be significantly less likely to understand the meaning of a "right" than adult offenders. The difference could clearly be seen because:

> When asked what is meant when police said, "You do not have to make a statement and have the right to remain silent," many youths indicated a conditional view of legal rights, such as "You can be silent unless you are told to talk," or "You have to be quiet unless you are spoken to." (Grisso 1997, pp. 7–8; see also Shepherd & Zaremba, 1995, p. 34)

The fact that so many delinquent youths are learning disabled is further complicated by the fact that these disabilities are not likely to be readily identifiable by an observer, such as a police officer. This is in part because a learning disability "is not a form of mental retardation . . . it stems from a disorder in the basic psychological processes that are involved in how an individual uses or understands language" (Shepherd & Zaremba, 1995, p. 32). Additionally, children who have learning disabilities may either inaccurately believe that they have understood the *Miranda* warnings, or try to hide their lack of understanding because of embarrassment (Shepherd & Zaremba, 1995; Johnson, 1997). In either case, the child may tell the police that he has understood, allowing the interrogation to proceed even though a knowing and intelligent waiver has not been made.

When a child nods his head or otherwise affirms that he understands his *Miranda* warnings, police officers often proceed to interrogate the child without testing the extent of the child's understanding. All too often, courts bless this practice. A simple "yes" or an "uh huh" is taken as conclusive proof of a knowing and intelligent waiver. This practice must stop. Police officers and prosecutors who *Mirandize* children should make it standard practice to ask the child to explain back to them what each right means in their own words before proceeding to interrogate the child and should record verbatim these responses. Their failure to do so should be held against them by courts when evaluating whether the child "knowingly and intelligently" waived his rights. Even John Reid and Associates, the company which trains officers in the Reid technique, now states on its website:

> When a juvenile in custody, particularly a youngster under 15 who has not had any prior experience with the police, is advised of his Miranda rights, the investigator should carefully discuss and talk about those rights with the subject (not just recite them) to make sure that he understands them. If it is apparent that the suspect does not understand his rights, no interrogation should be conducted at that time. The same is true for a person who is mentally impaired. (John E. Reid & Associates, 2003, at http://www.reid.com/critic-FALSE.html)

PARENTAL PRESENCE

Another common thread among the interrogations is the absence of parents during the interrogation process. In the cases studied herein, Anthony

Harris and Joshua Treadway were the only children who had contact with their parents during their interrogations. In Anthony's case, his mother followed police officers to the station and remained there throughout his interrogation. However, she was not permitted to be in the room while her son was interrogated and was misled into thinking that the only purpose for his presence was to get a voice stress analyzer test (ABC, 1999). In Joshua's case, he was permitted to meet briefly with his father during his interrogation. When his father entered the room, an obviously distressed Joshua nearly collapsed in his arms. Instead of calling a halt to the interrogation, Joshua's father implored him to continue answering the detectives' questions (Treadway Transcripts Vol. II; CBS, 2000). Michael Crowe's parents, B.M.B.'s parents, and Lacresha's family, were never informed that their children were being interrogated by police officers. B.M.B.'s mother tracked down her son and called the police while her son was being interrogated; instead of stopping the questioning and waiting for her to arrive, police continued interrogating B.M.B. in an effort to gain further admissions from him (*In the Matter of B.M.B.*, 1998).

The failure of police to inform parents of the gravity of their child's situation and to include parents in the interrogation process, as well as the failure of parents to protect their children in those instances when they are present, are common problems. There are legions of reported cases in which police officers interrogate children outside the presence of their parents and countless court decisions allowing statements taken from children outside their parent's presence to be used against the children in court. While a minority of courts have created *per se* rules for excluding such statements, a substantial majority simply view the absence of a parent as but one factor in the "totality of circumstances" voluntariness test (Huang, 2001; Krezewinski, 2002; Kaban & Tobey, 1999). Police officers are willing to take the risk of losing juvenile statements because they know that judges are generally loath to suppress confessions even if parents are absent.

On the other hand, if parents are present during the interrogations or confessions of their children, it is almost certain that courts will find the child's statements admissible. This practice also must change. The mere presence of a parent is often of little use to the child and may, in fact, compound the coercion inherent in the interrogation. In one study analyzing data from more than three hundred police interviews of children, it was found that parents halted interrogations only about 2% of the time. Approximately 16% of the time, they encouraged their children to talk to police. The overwhelming majority of the time (71%) parents did absolutely nothing (Eig, 1999; Grisso & Pomicter, 1977; Kaban & Tobey, 1999).

The fact that parents fail to protect children is not necessarily their fault. Interrogators are trained to make sure parents are passive participants in the interrogation process. For example, Inbau et al. (2001) suggest that to enlist the cooperation of parents, interrogators should "emphasize three primary points: 1) no one blames the parents or views them as negligent in their upbringing of their child, 2) all children at one time or another have done things to disappoint their parents, and 3) everyone—the investigator as well as the parents—has done things as a youth that should not have been done" (p. 301). In light of such training, courts need to look at what role, if any, a parent played during the interrogation instead of reflexively admitting statements taken in the presence of parents. We support parental presence requirements, not because they offer suitable protection for children—they do not—but for two other reasons. First, we believe that parents, who have constitutionally and statutorily protected rights to participate in a variety of life-altering decisions involving their children, should have the same right to participate in the decision of their children to speak with the police. This is particularly important given that the decision to speak to the police can lead to incarceration or even execution of their children (as of this writing, in 21 states, children who are 16 or 17 at the time they commit murder can be sentenced to death). Second, the presence of parents will enable them to be witnesses to the interrogation and may cause police officers to refrain from using the most coercive tactics in their arsenal.

ATTORNEY PRESENCE

Because parents are unable to protect their children during the interrogation process, it is essential that children be permitted access to attorneys before and during any interrogation. Opponents to attorney presence requirements often argue that any good attorney will tell their client not to waive their rights and that will unduly hamper the ability of police to obtain confessions. What these opponents seem to overlook, however, is that every suspect has a *constitutional right not to give a statement.* If being informed by an attorney causes a child to truly understand the importance of his *Miranda* rights and therefore he refuses to waive them, then the Constitution is satisfied. If, however, a child is not allowed the opportunity to speak with an attorney and makes an unknowing waiver, a constitutional violation occurs.

The likelihood that a child will properly invoke his right to an attorney is limited. Since *Fare* individuals subject to custodial interrogation must clearly invoke their right to counsel or to silence (*Davis v. United States,* 1994). Anything less than a clear and unequivocal statement of the words "I want an attorney" is not likely to be seen as an invocation of the right to counsel and a roadblock to further questioning by the detectives. Even those children who have some grasp on the meaning of *Miranda,* when confronted by an aggressive authority figure, are unlikely to assert their rights (Feld, 1999). Therefore, an essential reform would be the passage of legislation requiring police to provide counsel to children prior to the inception of an interrogation (Ceci, 1999).

VIDEOTAPING OF INTERROGATIONS

The saving grace for Anthony, B.M.B, Joshua, Lacresha, and Michael, was that their interrogations were recorded. Without those recordings, the extent to which the police used these techniques, and the extraordinary impact those techniques had on the children's ultimate confessions, may never have surfaced. As of this writing, only three states, Alaska, Minnesota and Illinois, require that police electronically record custodial interrogations of suspects in criminal cases. In both Alaska (*Stephan v. State,* 1985) and Minnesota (*State v. Scales,* 1994), the taping requirement was imposed by decisions of the state supreme courts. In July 2003, Illinois became the first state to legislatively mandate electronic recording of interrogations when Governor Rod Blagojevich signed into law a bill to require recording of interrogations in homicide cases beginning in July 2005 (Mills, 2003). We have called for mandatory videotaping of interrogations in an earlier article and we renew our call again here (e.g., Drizin & Colgan, 2001; Drizin, Aug. 26, 1998; Drizin, Aug. 28, 1998). Videotaping, however, is not a panacea to the problem of false and coerced confessions by children (Schlamm, 1995). In each of the cases discussed in this chapter, the interrogations were taped and in four of the five cases, trial judges ruled that the confessions were voluntary. Despite the United States Supreme Court's repeated pronouncements (*Haley,* 1948; *Gallegos,* 1962, *Gault,* 1967) that age is entitled to significant weight in the "totality of the circumstances" test and that judges are required to take "special care" when evaluating juvenile confessions, judges remain reluctant to suppress statements in serious felony cases. For this reason, in addition to a mandatory videotaping requirement, we propose two further safeguards. In cases in which minimization, maximization, and deception are used in interrogations involving children, any confessions obtained from children should be deemed inadmissible, or at the very least, presumptively inadmissible. If presumptively inadmissible, prosecutors should be required to meet a high burden, either "proof beyond a reasonable doubt" or "clear and convincing evidence," that the confession is both voluntary and reliable, before being allowed to use it against a child at trial. Second, to give meaning to the requirement of "special care," we believe that it is essential that children be allowed to introduce expert testimony on the subject of suggestive interviewing techniques and their effect on the reliability of children's statements in pre-trial motions to suppress. This testimony should also be admissible at trial as should expert testimony on the psychology of false confessions, and the relationship between suggestive techniques and the risk of false confessions (Gudjonnsson, 2003; White, 2003).

PROGRESS IN SEVERAL JURISDICTIONS

Much has been written about the failure of the "totality of the circumstances" test to adequately account for the unique vulnerabilities of juveniles in the interrogation process. To date, research which demonstrates that children do not sufficiently understand their *Miranda* warnings nor the consequences of waiving them (Grisso, 1980), that children, especially younger children, are highly suggestible (Bruck, Ceci & Hembrooke, 1998), and that they tend to be more compliant when pressed by adult authority figures (Grisso et al., 2003; Redlich & Goodman, 2003), has not carried the day in efforts to increase protections for children in the stationhouse. The risk of false confessions, however, has the power to dramatically change this debate and is already making a difference.

In Illinois, for example, evidence that Chicago police officers were routinely torturing suspects into confessing in the 1980's led to suggestions that police be required to record confessions. This recommendation lay dormant, however, until July of 1998, when a high profile false confession case involving two small boys, revived it. In the wake of the infamous Ryan Harris case, a case in which Chicago police officers and prosecutors charged a seven year old and an eight year old boy with the murder of an eleven year old girl, only later to learn that the 8-year-old's inculpatory statements were false, many of the reforms suggested in this article were debated and some of them have been enacted. For example, Illinois enacted a law requiring that all children under age thirteen be provided access to attorneys before they are interrogated in murder and sex cases (Juvenile Competency Commission, 2001).

Stung by criticism of his office's handling of the Harris case, Cook County State's Attorney Richard Devine, appointed a blue-ribbon commission of psychiatrists, psychologists, law enforcement officers, defenders and academics, to study how juveniles are handled in the investigation process. After more than two years of research and study, this Commission recommended even broader reforms, including barring the State from using any uncounseled statements against children under age 17 in any proceedings in which children face potential adult punishments, mandatory videotaping of custodial interrogations of suspects, and increased efforts on the part of police to include parents in the interrogation process (Juvenile Competency Commission, 2001). Public focus on the problem of false confessions, particularly false confessions involving children, was instrumental in the passage of these reforms.

The discovery of false confessions has also spurred reforms in other jurisdictions. In South Florida, a series in the Miami Herald on false confessions and the high profile case of Tim Brown, a mentally retarded teenager who was wrongfully convicted of the murder of a police officer on the basis of a false confession (DeMarzo & de Vise, 2003), led Broward County law enforcement authorities to voluntarily agree to start taping interrogations in a wide range of the most serious felonies (DeMarzo & de Vise, 2002; McMahon, 2003). A series in the Washington Post on false confessions in nearby Prince Georges County, Maryland, led authorities there to institute a taping policy (Witt, 2002; Witt, 2001). In New York, it remains to be seen what the fallout will be in the wake of the Central Park Jogger case, although videotaping and others reforms of the juvenile system are already being debated (Gardiner, 2002; Smith, 2003).

This increased attention to the problem of false confessions gives us hope that real change may soon come to the way in which police officers interrogate children. False confessions aside, we hope that greater scrutiny of the interrogation process will result in increased recognition of the far more common and serious problem of coerced confessions of children. In this regard, we are inspired by what has happened in Minnesota, a jurisdiction which has been taping interrogations for less than nine years. Minnesota courts, with the benefit of tapes and transcripts of juvenile interrogations, have all but outlawed many of the psychological tactics which police officers used to extract the confessions from Anthony, B.M.B, Joshua, Lacresha, and Michael. Minnesota courts have held that police may not use deception or stress-inducing interrogation techniques in obtaining a juvenile's confession (*State v. Garner,* 1980). If deception is used by police, and it "is the kind that would make an innocent person confess," the confession is involuntary and must be suppressed (*State v. Jones,* 1997, p. 324). Confessions have also been suppressed where police made express or implied promises to juveniles (*In re Welfare of D.S.N.,* 2000), such as suggesting that the police will exercise their influence over prosecuting attorneys to obtain counseling or a reduced charge for the suspect or implying that juveniles can go home if they confess. These juvenile confessions were all suppressed as "involuntary" under the "totality of the circumstances" test, suggesting that perhaps the greatest benefit of taping is that when courts are faced with the cold hard facts regarding the way in which police interrogate children, they are forced to once again recognize the unique vulnerabilities of children to these pressures. When these developmental factors are recognized and given their due weight, even the "totality of the circumstances" test, which since *Fare,* has more often than not been a curse for children, can become their shield.

REFERENCES

ABC. (June 18, 1999). 20/20. Transcript #99061802-j11 (Available on LEXIS).

Banta, Bob (May 31, 1996). Girl 11, Arrested in Toddler's Death, Child is Youngest in Recent Memory in Travis County, *Austin-American Statesman,* A1.

Bruck, M., Ceci, S. J., & Hembrooke, H. (1998). Reliability and credibility of young children's reports: From research to policy and practice. *American Psychologist, 53,*136–151.

Cassell, P. G. (1999). The guilty and the "innocent": An examination of alleged cases of wrongful conviction from false confessions. *Harvard Journal of Law and Public Policy, 22,* 523–603.

CBS News. (June 19, 2000). 48 Hours. Transcript (2000 WL 8422824).

Ceci, S. J. (1999). Why minors accused of serious crimes cannot waive counsel. *Court Review, 36,* 8–9.

Crawford, D. (1985). The link between delinquency and learning disabilities. *Judges' Journal, 24,* 23.

Crowe, M. (Dec., 2002). It happened to me. *Jane,* 111.

Davis v. United States, 512 U.S. 452, 458–9 (1994).

DeMarzo, W., & de Vise, D. (May 15, 2003) "I'm Finally Going Home?" Tim Brown is released from prison. *Miami Herald,* A1.

DeMarzo, W. & de Vise, D. (Dec. 22, 2002). Review finds grave flaws in Broward murder cases. *Miami Herald,* A1.

Drizin, S. A. (1998). In the Maelstrom: Children as murder suspects. *Chicago Daily Law Bulletin,* 5.

Drizin, S. A. (Aug. 26, 1998). When little tykes give "Full Confessions." *Chicago Tribune,* 19.

Drizin, S. A. & Colgan, B. A. (2001). Let the cameras roll: Mandatory videotaping of interrogations is the solution to Illinois' problem of false confessions. *Loyola University of Chicago Law Journal, 32,* 337–424.

Drizin, S. A. & Leo, R. A., (in press) The problem of false confessions in the post-DNA world. *North Carolina Law Review, 82.*

Editorial, (Mar. 24, 1997). Kids need some help when arrested. *Wichita Eagle, 8A.*

Eig, J. (January 1999). Making children talk. *Chicago Magazine,* 83.

Fare v. Michael C., 442 U.S 707 (1979).

Feld, B. C. (2000). Juvenile's waiver of legal rights: Confessions, Miranda, and the right to counsel. In T. Grisso & R. Schwartz (Eds.), *Youth on trial: A developmental perspective on juvenile justice* (pp. 105–138). Chicago: University of Chicago Press.

Feld, B. C. (1999). *Bad kids: Race and the transformation of the Juvenile Court.* New York: Oxford University Press.

Feld, B. C. (1984). Criminalizing juvenile justice: Rules of procedure for the juvenile court. *Minnesota Law Review, 69,* 141–276.

Frankston, J. (Jan. 30, 1999). Teen's hearing still on hold; Defense wants to block police search, confession in case against juvenile suspected of killing girl, 5. *Akron Beacon-Journal,* E2.

Gallegos v. Colorado, 370 U.S. 49 (1962).

Gardiner, S. (December 11, 2002). Getting it Right; Experts eye measures to prevent injustices. *Newsday,* A08.

Grisso, T., Steinberg, L., Woolard, J., Cauffman, E., Scott, E., Graham, S., Lexcen, F. , Repucci, N. D., & Schwartz, R. (2003). Juvenile's competence to stand trial: A comparison of adolescents' and adults' capacities as trial defendants. *Law and Human Behavior, 27,* 333–363.

Grisso. T (1980). Juvenile's capacities to waive *Miranda* rights: An empirical analysis. *California Law Review, 68,* 1134–1166.

Grisso, T. (1997). Juvenile competency to stand trial: Questions in an era of punitive reform. *Criminal Justice, 12,* 4–11.

Grisso, T., & Pomicter, C. (1977). Interrogation of juveniles: An empirical study of procedures, safeguards and rights waiver. *Law & Human Behavior, 1,* 321.

Gudjonsson, G. (2003). *The psychology of interrogations and confessions: A Handbook.* West Sussex, England Wiley.

Hagelberg, K. (October 5, 2000). Confession still ruled out: Prosecutors lose final try in Ohio Supreme Court to use boy's statement in New Philadelphia Murder. *Akron-Beacon Journal,* D3.

Haley v. Ohio, 332 U.S. 596 (1948).

Harmon, D. (August 6, 1996). Lesser verdict is pursued in girl's death. *Austin American-States-man*, A1.

Harmon, D. (August 8, 1996). Girl found guilty in toddler's death. *Austin American-States-man*, A1.

Harmon, D. (August 10, 1996). Girl gets 20 years in death of toddler. *Austin American-States-man*, A1.

Harmon, D. (February. 4, 1997). Murray's shoes match marks. *Austin American-Statesman*, B1.

Harmon, D. (February 13, 1997). Witness, toddler had an abusive history. *Austin American-Statesman*, B1.

Harmon, D. (February 18, 1997). Jury finds Murray Guilty in Second Trial. *Austin American-Statesman*, A1.

Herbert, B. (November 15, 1998). In America: A child's confession. *New York Times*, A39.

Herbert, B. (November 26, 1998). In America: Truth in Travis County. *New York Times*, Section 4, 15.

Hughes, P.R. (July 4, 1989) Legal secretary fights for girl, now 15, accused of killing tot. *Houston Chronicle*, p. 22.

Huang, D. T. (2001). "Less unequal footing": State courts' per se rules for juvenile waivers during interrogations and the case for their implementation. *Cornell Law Review, 86*, 437–477.

In re D.B.X., 638 N.W.2d 449 (Minn. App. 2002).

In re Gault, 387 U.S. 1 (1967).

In re Harris, 2000 WL 748087 (Ohio App. 2000).

In re Harris, 736 N.E.2d 25, TABLE, No. 00-1305 (Ohio, Oct. 4, 2000).

In re L.M., 993 S.W.2d 276 (Tex. App. 1999).

In re Welfare of D.S.N., 611 N.W.2d 811 (Minn. App. 2000).

In the Matter of B.M.B., 955 P.2d 1302 (Kan. 1998).

Inbau, F.E., Reid, J.E., Buckley, J.P., & Jayne, B.C. (2001). *Criminal interrogations and confessions* (4th ed.). Gaithersburg, MD: Aspen.

Inbau, F. E. (1991). Miranda's immunization of low intelligence offenders. *Prosecutor: Journal of National District Attorneys Association, 24*, 9–10.

John Reid and Associates, 2003, Retrieved on December 3, 2003 from http://www.reid.com/critic-FALSE.html.

Johnson, G. (1997). False confession and fundamental fairness: The need for electronic recording of custodial interrogations. *Boston University Public Interest Law Journal, 6*, 719–751.

Juvenile Competency Commission. (2001). *Final Report*. Retrieved on December 3, 2003 from http://www.luc.edu/law/academics/special/center/child/JCC.pdf

Kaban, B. and Tobey, A. E. (1999).When police question children: Are protections adequate? *Journal for the Center of Children and the Courts, 151–158.*

Kassin, S. M. (1997). The psychology of confession evidence. *American Psychologist, 52*, 221–233.

Kassin, S. M., & Kiechel, K. L. (1996). The social psychology of false confessions: Compliance, internalization, and confabulation. *Psychological Science, 7*, 125–128.

Kassin, S. M. & McNall, K. (1991). Police interrogations and confessions: Communicating promises and threats by pragmatic implication. *Law and Human Behavior, 15*, 233–251.

Krzewinski, L. M. (2002). But I didn't do it: Protecting the rights of juveniles during interrogation. *Boston College Third World Law Journal, 22*, 355–386.

Leo, R. A., & Ofshe, R. J. (1998). The consequences of false confessions: Deprivations of liberty and miscarriages of justice in the age of psychological interrogation. *Journal of Criminal Law and Criminology, 88*, 429–496.

Lessner, L. (Mar. 8, 1997). Family says boy's confession coerced. *Wichita Eagle*, 1A.

Lessner, L. (Mar 14, 1997). Schools to review policy on police contact: Wichita school board officials are concerned that police officers can question students without notifying their parents. *Wichita Eagle*, 1A.

Lessner, L. (Mar. 15, 1997). Judge statement legal but not needed: Boy waived his Miranda rights during a police interview without his parents present, then admitted fondling the girl. *Wichita Eagle*, 9A.

Lessner, L. (Mar. 21, 1997). New trial sought for boy convicted of rape: Defense lawyers take on controversial case for free. *Wichita Eagle*, 13A.

Lessner, L. (May 25, 1997). Black community rallies around convicted boy, 10. *Wichita Eagle*, 22A.

Lessner, L. (June 25, 1997). Boy 11, attacked in SRS care; Older boy sexually assaults youth who was convicted of fondling a 4-year-old girl. *Wichita Eagle*, 11A.

Lessner, L. (April 3, 1998). Boy won a legal victory but won't be home soon; Wichita child whose rape conviction was set aside is suicidal and in treatment. *Wichita Eagle*, 13A.

Lyon, T. D. (August 1999) Questioning children: The effects of suggestive and repeated questioning. *USC Law School Olin Working Paper No. 99–24* Retrieved on December 3, 2003 from http://ssrn.com/abstract=198069.

McMahon, P., & Friedberg, A. (February 11, 2003). Sheriff to tape felony inquiries. *South Florida Sun Sentinel*, 1A.

McCormick, M. E. (July 12, 1997). Young rapist's plight unites a varied group: The 11-year old boy convicted of rape brought together people usually divided by many differences. *Wichita Eagle*, 9A.

Mills, S. (July 18, 2003) Law mandates taping of interrogations. *Chicago Tribune*, A1.

Miranda v. Arizona, 384 U.S. 436 (1966).

Myers, J. E. B., Saywitz, K., & Goodman, G. (1996). Psychological research on child witnesses: Practical implications for forensic interviews and courtroom testimony. *Pacific Law Journal, 28*, 3–76.

Obregon, E. (June 15, 1996). Girl, 11, should get 40 years, Earle says. *Austin American-Statesman*, B1.

Ofshe, R. J., & Leo, R. A. (1997). The decision to confess falsely: Rational choice and irrational action. *Denver University Law Review, 74*, 979–1119.

Palomo, J. (October 3, 1996), Murray gets retrial in girl's death. *Austin American-Statesman*, A1.

Perina, A. (2003). "I confess." *Psychology Today, 36*, 11.

Quin, L. (Oct. 25, 2000). Microscope might come to Lacresha's aid. *Austin American-Statesman*, A1.

Redlich, A. D., & Goodman, G. S. (2003). Taking responsibility for an act committed: The influence of age and other individual difference factors. *Law and Human Behavior, 27*, 141–156.

Ruiz, P. S. (June 9, 2000). Teenage suspect in child's killing freed on appeal. *The Plain Dealer Cleveland*, 4B.

Sauer, M., & Wilkens, J. (May 11–16, 1999). Part 1: The night she was killed; Part 2: The arrest; Part 3: The knife; Part 4: More arrests; Part 5: In court; Part 6: The bombshell. *San Diego Union Tribune*.

Sauer, M., & Wilkens, J. (May 15, 2002) Crowe slaying suspect battled troubled past; Court records show Tuite's history of drug abuse, mental illness. *San Diego Union Tribune*, A14.

Schlamm, L. (1995). Police interrogation of children and state constitutions: Why not videotape the MTV generation? *University of Toledo Law Review, 26*, 901–935.

Shepherd, R. E., & Zaremba, B. A. (1995). When a disabled juvenile confesses to a crime: Should it be admissible? *Criminal Justice, 9*, 31–35.

Smith, A. (April 30, 2003). Interrogating under video's watchful eye. *Newsday*, A29.

State v. Critt, 554 N.W.2d 93 (Minn. App. 1996), review denied (Minn. Nov. 20, 1996).

State v. Garner, 294 N.W.2d 725 (Minn. 1980).

State v. Hough, 571 N.W.2d 578 (Minn. App. 1997).

State v. Jones, 566 N.W.2d 317 (Minn. 1997).

State v. Scales, 518 N.W.2d 587 (Minn. 1994).

State v. Slowinski, 450 N.W.2d 107 (Minn. 1990).

Stephan v. State, 711 P.2d 1156 (Alaska 1985).

Transcript of Interrogation of B.M.B (May 30, 1996), Case # 96C43540 (on file with authors).

Transcripts of Interrogation of Michael Crowe, Volumes I-III (January 22–23, 1998) (on file with authors).

Transcript of Interrogation of Anthony Harris (January 15, 1998) (on file with authors).

Transcript of Interrogation of Lacresha Murray (May 29, 1996). (Available at: http://www.peopleoftheheart.org/transcript_interrogation.htm).

Transcript of Interrogation of Joshua Treadway Volumes I-V (January 27–28, February 10, 1998) (on file with authors).

White, W. S. (2003). False confessions in criminal cases. *Criminal Justice, 17*, 4–10.

White, W. S. (1997). False confessions and the constitution: Safeguards against untrustworthy confessions. *Harvard Civil Rights & Civil Liberties Law Review, 32*, 105–156.

Witt, A. (June 3, 2001). False confessions, allegations of abuses mar murder cases. *Washington Post*, A1.

Witt, A. (Feb. 1, 2002). Pr. George's police to install video cameras; Interrogation tapings to begin by March 31. *Washington Post*, B4.

7

Mental Retardation, Competency to Waive *Miranda* Rights, and False Confessions

SOLOMON M. FULERO AND CAROLINE EVERINGTON

Persons with mental retardation are encountering the criminal justice system in increasing numbers. Persons with mental retardation who become suspects in criminal cases must deal with issues of competence to waive their right to remain silent upon police questioning, as well as the admissibility of any confession that is made as a result of that questioning. Unfortunately, we have begun to learn that confessions are frequently entered by persons with mental retardation in police interrogations without full understanding of their rights (Atchison & Keyes, 1996). In addition, because of the particular characteristics of those with mental retardation, statements that they may make must also be evaluated closely for reliability, even if their admissibility satisfies legal standards.

SOLOMON M. FULERO • Department of Psychology, Sinclair College, Dayton, Ohio 45402 (sol.fulero@sinclair.edu).   CAROLINE EVERINGTON • Richard W. Riley College of Education, Winthrop University, Rock Hill, South Carolina 29732 (everingtonc@winthrop.edu).

"VOLUNTARY, KNOWING, AND INTELLIGENT":
THE LEGAL ANALYSIS OF WAIVER OF *MIRANDA* RIGHTS

As first articulated in the United States Supreme Court case, *Miranda v. Arizona* (1966), criminal suspects must be provided certain warnings prior to any interrogation, including their right to remain silent, the potential for use of their statements in court proceedings, and the right to legal counsel prior to questioning, at no cost to them if they cannot afford to hire an attorney. The suspect may waive these rights and make a valid statement or confession, if the waiver is made voluntarily, knowingly, and intelligently. These three prongs are the keys to any analysis of admissibility of a criminal defendant's statements.

A second important United States Supreme Court case, *Connelly v. Colorado* (1986), has had important implications for confession law. Connelly approached a police officer and said he had murdered someone and wanted to talk about it. The officer read him his *Miranda* rights; Connelly said he understood them but still wanted to talk about the murder, and made a confession. A court-appointed psychiatrist testified later that the defendant was psychotic and was "following the voice of God" in confessing. The psychosis interfered with his ability to make free and rational choices, but did not prevent him from understanding his rights. The United States Supreme Court ruled that Connelly's confession was not "involuntary," and that "coercive police activity" is a necessary predicate to a finding that a confession was not voluntary. The Connelly case has made it more difficult for persons with mental retardation, because mental confusion alone was not enough to make the confession invalid as being involuntary, unless it could be shown that the police exploited the confusion in some way through "coercive" actions (O'Neill, 2002).

In a case decided in the same year, *Moran v. Burbine* (1986), the United States Supreme Court elaborated a bit on the full analysis to be used. The inquiry as to whether a waiver is "coerced" (that is, whether or not it was "voluntary") has two distinct dimensions:

> First, the relinquishment of the right must have been voluntary in the sense that it was the product of a free and deliberate choice rather than intimidation, coercion, or deception. Second, the waiver must have been made with a full awareness of both the nature of the right being abandoned and the consequences of the decision to abandon it. Once it is determined that a suspect's decision not to rely on his rights was uncoerced, that he at all times knew he could stand mute and request a lawyer, and that he was aware of the State's intention to use his statements to secure a conviction, the analysis is complete and the waiver is valid as a matter of law. (p. 421)

Thus, "coercion" refers to the voluntariness of the waiver of rights. But a statement must also be made knowingly and intelligently. Suspects must have a "full awareness" of the nature of their rights, and of the consequences of waiving them. This, of course, is where the element of mental retardation will first enter into the determination.

In addition, in determining if the waiver is valid, the court must look to the totality of circumstances in which the waiver was given. The "totality of circumstances test" requires that the court consider such factors as IQ, chronological age, suspect's education, suspect's previous experience in the criminal justice system and previous experience with entering a waiver of rights in a confession (O'Neill, 2002). Some (Cloud, Shepherd, Barkoff, & Shur, 2002; O'Neill, 2002) have begun to contend that the totality of circumstances test is unworkable for persons with mental retardation, as the impact of the disability is so great that mental retardation should trump other factors.

In evaluating the validity of a waiver, two things should be considered: (a) the defendant's ability to understand the warnings and (b) the manner in which the rights were given (Grisso, 1986). The validity of waivers entered by persons with mental retardation are suspect in regard to both understanding and voluntariness. First, due to limited cognitive and linguistic abilities of persons with mental retardation, most lack a complete understanding of the *Miranda* warning and, thus, may not realize that a waiver of rights involves possible self-incrimination (Fulero & Everington, 1995; Everington & Fulero, 1999). Second, research on personality characteristics and adaptive skills of persons with mental retardation indicates that persons with mental retardation are more likely to respond to coercion and pressure than the average individual (Ellis and Luckasson, 1985) and that they are highly suggestible to leading questions and false information supplied by others in interrogations (Gudjonsson, 1984; Gudjonsson, Clare, & Rutter, 1994; Perlman, Ericson, Esses, & Issacs, 1994).

This chapter will first examine the research on persons with mental retardation's understanding of *Miranda* and the relevant personality characteristics that make persons with mental retardation more vulnerable in interrogation situations. Second, we will provide suggestions for the forensic evaluation of individuals with mental retardation, and will conclude with suggestions for changes for policy and practice in the criminal justice system.

RESEARCH ON DEFENDANTS WITH MENTAL RETARDATION'S UNDERSTANDING OF THE *MIRANDA* WARNING

The available research indicates that persons with mental retardation have significant problems in the comprehension of the Miranda warning. To date, three studies have investigated persons with mental retardation's understanding of the *Miranda* warning: Fulero & Everington, 1995; Everington & Fulero, 1999; Cloud et al., 2002. All three studies used the series of assessments developed by Grisso (1981, 1986, 1998). The Fulero and Everington (1995) and Everington and Fulero (1999) studies used the *Comprehension of Miranda Rights* tests developed by Grisso (1981, 1986).

COMPREHENSION OF *MIRANDA* RIGHTS TESTS

The *Comprehension of Miranda Rights* (CMR) tests developed by Grisso (1981, 1986) were designed to assess juvenile and adult defendants' understanding of the *Miranda* warning. The CMR battery consists of three tests: (a) *Comprehension of Miranda Rights* (CMR), (b) *Comprehension of Miranda-True False* (CMR-TF), (c) *Comprehension of Miranda Vocabulary* (CMV). The first measure, the CMR, involves the reading of each of the four *Miranda* statements and requests the individual to define each statement in his or her own words. For scoring, Grisso developed a set of criteria in which answers are scored as either 0, 1, or 2. The potential range of scores is 0–8.

The second measure, the CMR-TF, was developed to assess comprehension in a manner that would require no construction of verbal responses. There are a total of 12 items on the CMR-TF, of which half are false and half are true. The participant is given a card on which one of the *Miranda* warning statements is printed. The warning is read aloud. The participant is told that several statements will be read that may "mean the same thing" or that may be different and that he or she will need to indicate if that statement is the same as or different than the original statement. There are three such statements for each of the four *Miranda* statements. Accordingly, the potential score on the CMR-TF can range from 0–12. For example, for the first statement, "You do not have to make a statement and have the right to remain silent," the following three statements are read: "(1) It is not right to tell lies; (2) You should not say anything until the police ask you questions; (3) You should not have to say anything about what you did."

The final measure was the CMV. Grisso identified six words within the warnings that offered potential difficulty for participants: consult, attorney, interrogation, appoint, entitled, and right. The participant is asked to define each in his or her own words, and responses are scored using a format similar to the Wechsler Vocabulary subscale, in which an answer can receive a 0, 1, or 2 point score. The potential range on this measure is 0–12. In 1998, Grisso published a new version of the CMR, entitled *Instruments for Assessing Understanding and Appreciation of Miranda Rights*. This test battery contains the three tests discussed above and a new test, *Function of Rights in an Interrogation*. This test examines the individual's grasp of Miranda in the context of an interrogation.

REVIEW OF THE LITERATURE

In their first study, Fulero and Everington (1995) gave the CMR battery to 54 individuals with mental retardation. The first group consisted of 29 adults with mild-to-moderate mental retardation who lived in the community and attended a sheltered workshop. The second group consisted of 25 individuals with mild mental retardation who were on probation. This second group had a mean IQ score of 65. The study found that the mean scores of both groups with mental retardation were lower than the adult and juvenile populations used in the original CMR studies, indicating significant deficits in understanding appear to exist for this population. While Grisso (1981) argued that although there is no "cutoff point" on the scales for competency, when a juvenile received a zero credit on any one of the four warnings of the CMR, it is suggested that he/she would not meet the standard for sufficient understanding. From two samples of persons with mental retardation tested, Fulero and Everington (1995) found 90% of adults with mental retardation from the workshop setting and 68% of adults with mental retardation on probation did not meet this standard. This is higher than the 55% found in the original juvenile studies conducted by Grisso (1981).

In their second study, Everington and Fulero (1999) gave the CMR to 30 mentally typical offenders and 18 offenders with mild mental retardation. Both groups were on probation at the time of testing. The mean IQ for the persons with mental retardation was 68 (range 59–75). Criminal charges for both groups included misdemeanors and felonies.

The results of this study indicated that probationers who had mental retardation scored significantly lower on each of the CMR tests than the non-retarded group. In this study, significantly more persons with mental retardation (67%) than mentally typical persons (17%) did not meet minimum criteria for competence. In addition, significantly more persons with mental retardation did not understand any of the substantive portions of this warning—the right to remain silent, potential use of statements in a court proceeding, and the right to an attorney before and during questioning. Finally, this study replicated the Fulero and Everington (1995) study with defendants with mental retardation. Mean scores for defendants with mental retardation in this study were close to those obtained in the previous study. These findings suggested to the authors that there is a high likelihood that a person with mental retardation may not understand the notion of self-incrimination or the advising role of the attorney in the interrogation.

The results of this study were troubling as one might assume that the sample in this study—defendants on probation—were likely to be more experienced in criminal justice issues than the typical adult with mental retardation in the community. As this group also experienced difficulties, these are disturbing findings.

The third study examining the understanding of *Miranda* by defendants with mental retardation was conducted by Cloud et al. (2002). In this study, it appeared that the authors used an adaptation of the revised CMR, the *Instruments for Assessing Understanding and Appreciation of Miranda Rights* (Grisso, 1998). Tests for understanding of *Miranda* were given to 49 individuals with mental retardation and 22 mentally typical individuals.

This study contained individuals with a broad range of IQ scores from less than 25 to 88, with a mean IQ of 55.5. A large portion of the study participants (43%) functioned in the moderate range or lower. The participants were taken from community settings and many had not had contact with the criminal justice system. No information was provided on the background of the mentally typical subjects in this study. While the participants with mental retardation were not as representative of persons with mental retardation in the criminal justice system, the results were very similar to those of the previous studies discussed.

The authors found that while people of average intelligence did understand their *Miranda* rights, the group with mental retardation did not always understand the *Miranda* warnings. For example, the comparison of total scores indicates the group with mental retardation achieved an average score of 30% correct compared to 87% for the controls. Regarding vocabulary, the most poorly understood word was "interrogation" (88% of the group with mental retardation failed). Similar to Everington and Fulero (1999), this study found that the individuals with mental retardation did not understand their right to silence—only 22% passed this portion, as compared to 87% for the control group. Similar to Everington and Fulero (1999), these subjects with mental retardation demonstrated a slightly better understanding of the "If you cannot afford an attorney, one will be appointed to you" (34% correct compared to 97% for the control group). On the subtest the authors termed the "Concepts Test," the authors indicated that the individuals with mental retardation performed particularly poorly in regards to their understanding of the function of rights in an interrogation.

The implications of these findings are striking. The three studies show consistent evidence that the majority of persons with mental retardation are unable to meet the knowing and intelligent aspects of this waiver.

CHARACTERISTICS OF PERSONS WITH MENTAL RETARDATION THAT INCREASE VULNERABILITY

Voluntariness is another critical aspect of *Miranda*. Yet we know from research in this area that it is easier to elicit a confession from a person with mental retardation than from a mentally typical individual (Perske, 1994). This can be attributed to several general personality traits found to be present to a greater degree among persons with mental retardation than the general population.

One reason is that because persons with this type of impairment frequently experience repeated failures in social and academic settings, they frequently display "outer-directed" behavior, relying more on social and linguistic cues provided by others (Bybee & Zigler, 1992). In contrast, while mentally typical individuals may also display "outer-directedness" in difficult problem-solving situations, they are better able to discriminate helpful from misleading or inaccurate cues when looking to others for cues (Bybee & Zigler, 1992). Therefore, a person with mental retardation may be more unsure of his or her answer, more easily influenced by others, and will look to the interviewer for clues.

A second characteristic of persons with mental retardation that is relevant to voluntariness is the strong desire to please others, particularly those in authority (Shaw & Budd, 1982). This bias toward providing a "socially desirable" response is so strong that many persons with mental retardation will literally tell the questioner whatever they perceive that he or she wants to hear. Shaw and Budd (1982) found that questions such as "Did you make your bed this morning?" engender a "yes" answer and questions such as "Do you ever forget to brush your teeth?" engender "no" answers regardless of the actual facts.

An additional response bias common with this population is acquiescence. When asked a yes/no question, the person with mental retardation is significantly more likely to answer "yes" regardless of the appropriateness of that response (Sigelman, Winer, & Schoenrock, 1982). This can be referred to as "yes-saying" (Finlay & Lyons, 2002). This tendency is so strong that persons with mental retardation have been observed to provide affirmative answers to absurd questions. For example, in a study with a group of persons with mental retardation in Texas, Sigelman, Budd, Spanel, and Schoenrock (1981) found that 73% answered "yes" to the question, "Does it ever snow here in the summer?" and 44% to the question "Are you Chinese?" Further, Finlay and Lyons (2002) contend that yes-saying is more likely to occur when the linguistic difficulty of the question increases. Yes-saying is also more likely when the person does not have to say they do not know or that they are uncertain of the answer. As the CMR studies show, the language and concepts in these warnings are clearly difficult for persons with mental retardation. Further, police interrogations discourage vague or ambiguous answers.

Finally, people with mental retardation have a great deal of difficulty with what is called "social intelligence" (Greenspan, Switzky, & Granfield, 1996). Social intelligence includes the ability to decipher the motives of others and to act on that information appropriately in complex situations. Deficits in social intelligence cause problems in many ways when people with mental retardation become involved in the criminal justice system (Greenspan, 2003). Persons who exhibit deficits in this area are often labeled by others as gullible and naïve. People with mental retardation are often easier to deceive than the general population. The classic response for a person with mental retardation after being interrogated by police is to state: "They told me if I told them I did it, we could all go home." Finlay and Lyons (2002) suggest that one reason that persons with mental retardation are more prone to acquiescence and confabulation during questioning is that they do not understand the consequences of their actions in the interrogation situation.

RESEARCH ON INTERROGATIVE SUGGESTIBILITY IN PERSONS WITH MENTAL RETARDATION

Responsiveness to leading questions within a criminal interrogation has been examined extensively by Gudjonsson and his colleagues. The *Gudjonsson Suggestibility Scale* (GSS) (Gudjonsson, 1984; Clare, Gudjonnson, Rutter, & Cross, 1994) has been developed to measure "interrogative suggestibility," that is, the responsiveness of the individual to leading questions and to disapproval of others in an interrogation context. Gudjonsson (1990) distinguishes between acquiescence and suggestibility. He explains acquiescence as a form of compliance. In this case, the individual answers "yes" regardless of the content. The individual may not believe the content, but believes a "yes" response is required. In the confessions context, this has been referred to as "coerced-compliant" (Kassin, 1997). In contrast, in suggestibility, the individual accepts the message as true. In the confessions context, this has been referred to as "coerced-internalized" (Kassin, 1997). This is an important distinction which may provide some explanation for the stronger tendency among persons with mental retardation for confabulation in interrogations (Clare & Gudjonsson, 1993).

Studies in England using the GSS scale with persons with mental retardation (Clare & Gudjonsson, 1993; Gudjonsson & Clare, 1995) have found that this group was significantly more likely to display interrogative suggestibility than their average ability counterparts. The findings of Gudjonsson and colleagues were supported by research findings in the United States (Everington & Fulero, 1999). Everington and Fulero gave a modified version of the *Gudjonsson Suggestibility Scale* (GSS) (Gudjonsson, 1984, 1992) to 18 probationers with mental retardation and 30 mentally typical probationers. (These were the same subjects discussed in the CMR study earlier in this text). The results from the suggestibility scale indicated that persons with mental retardation were significantly more likely to be influenced by leading questions and coercion in an interrogation situation than mentally typical individuals. In addition, the study's findings showed that the individuals with mental retardation were much more likely to change or to "shift" their answers when mild disapproval was given.

The high shift scores obtained by the defendants with mental retardation in the Everington and Fulero (1999) study were a disturbing finding since, in this case, defendants were merely told that they had gotten several answers wrong in the previous testing and that they should try harder. Other potentially coercive aspects typically present in a criminal interrogation such as intense prolonged questioning were not present in the testing environment. In addition, the "risk" to defendants in this situation was minimal, as the questions were about a story they had listened to and not about the culpability of their own actions. In actual interrogation situations, more direct coercion is more likely to be used. One can reasonably suggest that if this group of individuals is so suggestible in this low-risk questioning situation, then they might be even more likely to respond to suggestible questions and to "shift" their answers when the pressure is greater.

Finally, Gudjonsson (1984) points out that the GSS measures suggestibility to verbal questions. Certainly, there are also many nonverbal aspects of an interrogation situation that imply coercion and can thus influence responding. As discussed earlier, persons with cognitive and linguistic deficits could be more susceptible to extra-linguistic cues than others. The results of this study, along with previous work, strongly suggest that heightened scrutiny of any statements made by individuals with mental retardation is needed.

SUSCEPTIBILITY TO FALSE CONFESSIONS
IN INTERROGATIONS

While there is no work directly finding that persons with mental retardation are more likely to render false confessions than those without mental retardation, all of the evidence discussed above suggests that this is likely. Persons with mental retardation are susceptible to non-physical forms of coercion, pressure and intimidation by the police that people with normal intelligence can more readily withstand. They are less able to handle the stress and fear of a police interrogation, particularly if the questioning is prolonged. They are also less likely to resist the efforts of an apparently "friendly" police questioner. Their characteristic desire to please figures of authority can lead them to do whatever they think necessary to gain approval.

It is worth noting that even those who train police interrogators acknowledge the dangers of interrogating persons with mental retardation. For example, in the commonly-used manual by Inbau, Reid, and Buckley

(1986), interrogators are cautioned to take into consideration the "intelligence, social responsibility, and maturity" of the suspect. The American Bar Association's Criminal Justice Mental Health Standards (American Bar Association, 1989) recognize the impact of mental retardation on the reliability of confessions as well: "Official conduct that does not constitute permissible coercion when employed with non-disabled persons may impair the voluntariness of statements of persons who are mentally ill or mentally retarded." (Standard 7–5.8, passed by the ABA House of Delegates on August 10, 1988, found in American Bar Association, 1989). And as far back as 1963, a Task Force on Law of the President's Panel on Mental Retardation (cited in Ellis & Luckasson, 1985) suggested that:

> The retarded are particularly vulnerable to an atmosphere of threats and coercion, as well as to one of friendliness designed to induce confidence and cooperation. A retarded person may be hard put to distinguish between the fact and the appearance of friendliness. If his life has been molded into a pattern of submissiveness, he will be less able than the average person to withstand normal police pressures. . . . Some of the retarded are characterized by a desire to please authority: if a confession will please, it will be gladly given. . . . It is unlikely that the retarded will see the implications or consequences of his statements in the way a person of normal intelligence will. (p. 33)

COMPARISONS WITH JUVENILE POPULATIONS

Research with juvenile populations indicates that they are vulnerable to pressure from others and experience similar problems in understanding the *Miranda* warning (Grisso, 1981; Fulero & Everington, 1995; Drizin & Colgan, this volume; Redlich, Silverman, Chen, & Steiner, this volume). Grisso's work, reported in his 1981 book, was a ground-breaking empirical examination of juvenile competency to waive *Miranda* rights. Based on evaluations of hundreds of juveniles and adults in the Saint Louis, Missouri area, Grisso concluded that juveniles less than 15 years of age were generally incompetent to waive their rights to silence and legal counsel. Juveniles aged 15–16 years with IQ scores of 80 or below also demonstrated incompetence to waive their rights to silence and legal counsel. In addition, about half of juveniles aged 15–16 years who have IQ scores above 80 also demonstrated incompetence to waive their rights to silence and legal counsel.

Grisso (1981) suggested that juveniles might benefit from some sort of simplified version of the *Miranda* warnings that would be easier for them to understand. However, there have been several studies of such simplified warnings both here and in the United Kingdom, where there have been relatively recent changes in the law of waiver (see Fulero & Everington, 1995). Unfortunately, these studies have not demonstrated any significant increase in juveniles' abilities to comprehend the warnings.

SUGGESTIONS FOR FORENSIC EVALUATIONS

The results of the studies discussed do provide some empirical data that lend support to concerns that Perske (1991, 1994) and others have expressed regarding confessions made by people with mental retardation. We know that it is easier to elicit a confession from a person with mental retardation than a mentally typical individual (Perske, 1994). Further, these confessions frequently play a central role in the prosecution of the case. As Perske (1994) states: "confessions for heinous crimes continue to be seen in many legal circles as the 'queen of the case'" (p. 377).

However, these findings also can inform forensic assessment. Because of the depth of information needed, it is of critical importance that forensic evaluators should perform a comprehensive clinical assessment (Frumkin, 2000). This clinical assessment should be based on assessments of a defendant's understanding of the *Miranda* warning and measures of intelligence, linguistic abilities, and reading skills. In addition, it should incorporate (a) background information on a defendant's adaptive skills and personality and (b) all available information on the interrogation and confession. Each of these aspects will be discussed separately.

ASSESSMENT OF UNDERSTANDING OF *MIRANDA*

First, the Grisso (1998) test battery (Instruments for Assessing Understanding and Appreciation of *Miranda* Rights) provides an objective measure that can assist forensic psychologists and defense attorneys in determining the validity of the defendant's waiver of rights (Frumkin, 2000). While there are other factors that should be considered in determining whether the statement was made voluntarily, knowingly, and intelligently, performance on this instrument gives information relevant to knowledge and understanding. As courts are increasingly requiring experts to make opinions based on standardized and validated assessment procedures (see Fulero, this volume), this instrument has utility in providing some empirical data regarding the defendant's understanding (Frumkin, 2000). Scores on Grisso tests should be supported with informal questioning of the defendant's knowledge both at the time of the evaluation and at the time of the interrogation. In some cases, the defendant may gain an understanding after the interrogation through repeated conversations with attorney and others (Feinstein, Everington, Derning, & Keyes, in press).

MEASURES OF INTELLIGENCE, LINGUISTIC
ABILITIES, AND READING SKILLS

When making a determination regarding the knowing and intelligent aspects of the waiver, it is important to gather accurate information on the defendant's intellectual functioning, linguistic abilities, and reading skills (Feinstein et al., in press). To meet the standard for the "knowing" aspect of the waiver, the defendant must understand the vocabulary and concepts related to waiver. One piece of information that assists in this determination is the reading level of the defendant. The readability of most *Miranda* statements occurs by the seventh grade (Baroff & Freedman, 1988). The expectation of maximum reading achievement for persons with mental retardation is generally considered fourth to fifth grade (Drew & Hardman, 2000). Many individuals with mental retardation sign a statement that they have read and understand the waiver. If this is the case, it is crucial to determine the defendant's current reading level.

Forensic evaluations rarely include assessment of language skills. However, for individuals with mental retardation, language skills are significantly related to competence abilities (Everington, DeBerge, & Mauer, 2000). Administering assessments which provide normative information on language functioning of adults such as the *Test of Adolescent and Adult Language* (TOAL-3) (Hammill, Brown, Larsen, & Wiederholt, 1994) or the *Peabody Picture Vocabulary Test-Third Edition* (Dunn & Dunn, 1997) can provide important support for both the "knowing" and "intelligent" prongs of the waiver. For example, knowing that defendants have receptive language skills which are more than two standard deviations below the mean for their age can provide support for findings on Grisso tests and can assist in countering charges of malingering. In addition, low receptive language scores can speak to the intelligent aspect of the waiver. The individual may not have the capacity to understand concepts such as "waive" and "right."

Finally, accurate assessment of intelligence is crucial in any evaluation of mental retardation (Feinstein et al., 2003). This information provides support for findings in all other areas. Accepted practice dictates that only global measures of intelligence are appropriate for diagnosing mental retardation (Luckasson et al., 2002). There are three individually administered intelligence tests acceptable for evaluation of mental retardation in adults: *Wechsler Adult Intelligence Scale*—Third Edition (WAIS-III) (1997); *Stanford-Binet Intelligence Scale*-Fourth Edition (Thorndike, Hagen, & Sattler, 1986); Kaufman Adolescent and Adult Intelligence Test (1993).

USING INFORMATION ON ADAPTIVE SKILLS

All evaluations for diagnosing mental retardation must incorporate assessment of adaptive skills (Luckasson et al., 2002). The typical protocol includes standardized assessments of adaptive behavior (Taylor, 1997). While the information gained from these instruments is critical for the diagnosis of the disability, it is less helpful for documentation of the personality characteristics relevant to problems in interrogations. Interviews with family members, peers, employers or teachers can reveal the rich detail, which is so critical in explaining the defendant's actions in the interrogation to the court and attorneys. Information can be gathered on the defendant's tendency to follow others, acquiesce, and problems of social ineptitude. It is helpful for the evaluator to develop an interview protocol. It should be noted that not all defendants display the characteristics of suggestibility, acquiescence, and social difficulty discussed.

INTERVIEW STRATEGIES

Clinical interviews of the defendant should employ questioning strategies that are appropriate for persons with mental retardation. As it is well documented that individuals with mental retardation have a strong tendency for acquiescence and a strong desire to hide their disability (Ellis & Luckasson, 1985), care should be taken by the evaluator to avoid the use of leading or suggestive questions. Because we know that acquiescence increases when questions become more linguistically complex, simple language should be used (Finlay & Lyons, 2002). Defendants should be asked to explain concepts in their own words to insure comprehension.

While it is appropriate to query individuals regarding their abilities and experiences, self-report should never be the sole basis for the assessment of adaptive skills or personality characteristics. Unfortunately, many forensic reports rely solely on defendants' inflated portrayal of their accomplishments or denial of problems as the basis for the documentation of adaptive skills (Everington & Keyes, 1999).

During the interview, it is important to get defendants' accounts of their interrogations, including their perceptions and feelings at the time of the interrogation as well as other facts such as the length of time of the interrogation and persons present. All materials—transcripts, videos, and audio-tapes—should be carefully reviewed.

IMPLICATIONS FOR POLICY AND PRACTICE IN THE CRIMINAL JUSTICE SYSTEM

The findings discussed in this chapter highlight the importance of educating law enforcement officers and other criminal justice professionals. In addition to understanding the characteristics of mental retardation, it is important for officers to be cognizant of the effect of certain types of interrogation techniques. When the individual is suspected of having a disability, efforts should be made to insure that understanding is achieved.

This may be better accomplished by having the defendant explain the meaning of the warning and other critical vocabulary in his or her own words rather than through use of questioning techniques that elicit yes-no responses.

While many advocate the use of *Miranda* statements that are written with simplified vocabulary, research conducted with these warnings indicates these are ineffective with respect to increasing the understanding of defendants with mental retardation (Cloud et al., 2002). In addition, studies on readability of these modified warnings indicates they are not below the seventh grade level of the typical Miranda statements (Baroff & Olley, 1999).

The special educator or mental retardation professional can be an effective resource for the criminal justice professional in providing training on relevant characteristics (Everington & Luckasson, 1989). The Special Offenders Services in Lancaster, Pennsylvania (Wood & White, 1992) is an example of one such program that has instituted statewide training and specialized procedures for law enforcement officials. Training materials such as those developed by McAfee (1999) provide useful guidelines for law enforcement on interrogation of detainees with mental retardation.

There may be a need for changes in interrogation law and practice such as those made in the British system (see Bull & Milne, this volume). In the British system, when a person with a disability is being interrogated, a neutral person is required in the interrogation to ensure that the individual understands the questions and the implications of any statements that he/she makes (Miller, 1996). Also, in Great Britain, all interrogations, regardless of the suspect's mental status, are taped in their entirety, a requirement that has begun to have its advocates in the United States (see Kassin, 1997 for a discussion, and Johnson, 2002 for a similar proposal for juveniles).

Finally, it is revealing that Grisso (1981) believed that his studies on juveniles support the need for extraordinary protections for persons ages 14 or below. Some of the suggestions he proposed include legislation to provide blanket exclusion of confessions by such children, providing automatic legal counsel to them prior to police questioning, or even establishing 14 years as the age below which there is a rebuttable presumption of incompetence to waive *Miranda* rights. Grisso (1981) comments "these juveniles' waiver of rights should be considered valid only when made with the assistance of competent legal advice and advocacy at the time of the rights waiver." Others have proposed similar sorts of safeguards for juveniles (Guire, 2002; Krzewinski, 2002). One cannot help but wonder if similar proposals for special protections (e.g., the neutral person proposed by Miller, 1996, parental presence for juveniles suggested by McGuire, 2002) might not also be applicable where the defendant is a person with mental retardation.

REFERENCES

American Bar Association (1989). *Criminal justice mental health standards*. Chicago, IL: American Bar Association.

Atchison, M., & Keyes, D. (1996). Why Johnny Lee Wilson went to prison. In D. S. Connery (Ed.), *Convicting the innocent* (pp. 118–126). Cambridge, MA: Brookline.

Baroff, G. S., & Freedman, S. C. (1988, April). Mental retardation and Miranda. *The Champion*, 6–9.

Baroff, G. S., & Olley, J. G. (1999). *Mental retardation: Nature, causes, and management*. Philadelphia: Brunner/Mazel.

Bybee, G. S., & Zigler, E. (1992). Is outer directedness employed in a harmful or beneficial manner by students with and without mental retardation? *American Journal of Mental Retardation, 96*, 512–521.

Clare, I., & Gudjonsson, G. (1993). Interrogative suggestibility, confabulation, and acquiescence in people with mild learning disabilities (mental handicap): Implications for reliability during police interrogations. *British Journal of Clinical Psychology, 32*, 295–301.

Clare, I., Gudjonnson, G., Rutter, S. & Cross, P. (1994). The inter-rater reliability of the Gudjonnson Suggestibility Scale (Form 2). *British Journal of Clinical Psychology, 33*, 357–365.

Cloud, M., Shepherd, G. B., Barkoff, A., N., & Shur, J. V. (2002). Words without meaning: The Constitution, confessions, and mentally retarded suspects. *University of Chicago Law Review, 69*, 495–624.

Connelly v. Colorado, 479 U.S. 157 (1986).

Drew, C. J., & Hardman, M. L. (2000). *Mental retardation: A life cycle approach* (7th ed.). Columbus, OH: Prentice Hall.

Dunn, L. M., & Dunn, L. M. (1997). *Peabody Picture Vocabulary Test-Third Edition (PPVT-III)*. Circle Pines, MN: American Guidance Service.

Ellis, J., & Luckasson, R., A. (1985). Mentally retarded criminal defendants. *George Washington Law Review, 53*, 414–493.

Everington, C., DeBerge, K., & Mauer, D. (2000). The relationship between language skills and competence to stand trial abilities in persons with mental retardation. *The Journal of Psychiatry and Law, 28*, 475–492.

Everington, C., & Fulero, S. (1999). Competence to confess: Measuring understanding and suggestibility of defendants with mental retardation. *Mental Retardation, 37*, 212–220.

Everington, C., & Keyes, D. W. (1999). Diagnosing mental retardation in criminal proceedings: The critical importance of documenting adaptive behavior. *The Forensic Examiner*, 31–34.

Everington, C., & Luckasson, R. (1989). Addressing the needs of the criminal defendant with mental retardation: The special educator as a resource to the criminal justice system. *Education and Training of the Mentally Retarded*, 193–200.

Feinstein, J. S., Everington, C., Derning, T., & Keyes, D.(2003). *Individuals with mental retardation: A guide for psychologists*. Philadelphia, PA: Temple University.

Finlay, W., & Lyons, E., (2002). Acquiescence in interviews with people who have mental retardation. *Mental Retardation, 40*, 14–29.

Frumkin, B. (2000). Competency to waive Miranda rights: Clinical and legal issues. *Mental and Physical Disability Law Reporter, 24*, 326–331.

Fulero, S. M., & Everington, C. (1995). Assessing competency to waive *Miranda* rights in defendants with mental retardation. *Law and Human Behavior, 19*, 533–543.

Greenspan, S. (2003). Perceived risk status as a key to defining mental retardation: Social and everyday vulnerability in the natural prototype. In H. N. Switzky & S. Greenspan (Eds.), *What is mental retardation? Ideas for an evolving disability*. Washington, DC: AAMR.

Greenspan, S., Switzky, H. J., & Granfield, J. M. (1996). Everyday intelligence and adaptive behavior: A theoretical framework. In J. W. Jacobson & J. A. Mulick (Eds.), *Manual of diagnosis and professional practice in mental retardation* (pp. 127–136). Washington, DC: American Psychological Association.

Grisso, T. (1998). *Instruments for assessing understanding and appreciation of Miranda rights*. Sarasota, FL: Professional Resource Press.

Grisso, T. (1981). *Juveniles' waiver of rights: Legal and psychological competence*. New York: Plenum Press.

Grisso, T. (1986). *Evaluating competencies: Forensic assessments and instruments*. New York: Plenum Press.

Gudjonsson, G. H. (1984). A new scale of interrogative suggestibility. *Personality and Individual Differences, 5*, 303–314.

Gudjonsson, G. H. (1990). The relationship of intellectual skills to suggestibility, compliance, and acquiescence. *Personality and Individual Differences, 11*, 227–231.

Gudjonsson, G. H. (1992). Interrogative suggestibility: Factor analysis of the Gudjonsson suggestibility scale (GSS2). *Personality and Individual Differences, 13*, 479–481.

Gudjonsson, G. H., Clare, I., & Rutter, S. (1994). Psychological characteristics of suspects interviewed at police stations: A factor-analytic study. *Journal of Forensic Psychiatry, 5*, 517–525.

Gudjonsson, G. H., & Clare, I. (1995). The relationship between confabulation and intellectual ability, memory, interrogative suggestibility and acquiescence. *Personality and Individual Differences, 19*, 333–338.

Gudjonsson, G. H., Rutter, S. C., & Clare, I. (1995). The relationship between suggestibility and anxiety among suspects detained at police stations. *Psychological Medicine, 25*, 875–878.

Hammill, D. D., Brown, V. L., Larsen, S. C., & Wiederholt, J. L. (1994). *Test of Adolescent and Adult Language* (TOAL-3). Austin, TX: PRO-ED.

Inbau, F., Reid, J., & Buckley, J. (1986). *Criminal interrogation and confessions* (3rd ed.). Baltimore, MD: Williams and Wilkins.

Johnson, M. (2002). Juvenile *Miranda* law in New Jersey, from Carlo, 1966 to JDH, 2001: The relevance of recording all custodial questioning. *Journal of Psychiatry and Law, 30*, 3–57.

Kassin, S. (1997). The psychology of confession evidence. *American Psychologist, 52*, 221–233.

Kaufman, A., & Kaufman, N. (1990). *Kaufman Brief Intelligence Test*. Circle Pines, MN: American Guidance Service.

Krezewinski, L. (2002). "But I didn't do it": Protecting the rights of juveniles during interrogation. *Third World Law Journal, 22*, 355–387.

Luckasson, R., Schalock, R.L., Borthwick-Duffy, S., Buntinx, W.H.E., Coulter, D.L., Craig, E.M., Reeve, A., Snell, M.E., Spitalnik, D.M., Spreat, S., & Tasse, M.J. (2002). *Mental retardation: Definition, classification, and systems of supports* (10th ed.). Washington, DC: American Association on Mental Retardation.

McAfee, J. K. (1999). *Individuals with mental retardation and the criminal justice system: A guide for law enforcement personnel*. Philadelphia, PA: Temple University.

McGuire, R. E. (2002). A proposal to strengthen juvenile *Miranda* rights: Requiring parental presence in custodial interrogations. *Vanderbilt Law Review, 53*, 1355–1387.

Miller, A. (1996). Even Galileo confessed. In D. S. Connery (Ed.), *Convicting the innocent* (pp. 87–94). Cambridge, MA: Brookline Books.

Miranda v. Arizona, 384 U.S. 436 (1966).

Moran v. Burbine, 475 U.S. 412 (1986).

O'Neill, T. P. (2002). Miranda's illusion of fairness to mentally retarded. *Chicago Daily Law Bulletin, 5*, 6.

Perlman, N. B., Ericson, K. I., Esses, V. M., & Issacs, B. J. (1994). The developmentally handicapped witness: Competency as a function of question format. *Law and Human Behavior, 18*, 171–188.

Perske, R. (1991). *Unequal justice? What can happen when persons with mental retardation and other developmental disabilities encounter the criminal justice system*. Nashville, TN: Abingdon Press.

Perske, R. (1994). Thoughts on the police interrogation of individuals with mental retardation. *Mental Retardation, 32,* 377–380.

Shaw, J. A., & Budd, E. D. (1982). Determinants of acquiescence and nay saying of mentally retarded persons. *American Journal of Mental Deficiency, 87,* 108–110.

Sigelman, C. K., Budd, E. C., Spanel, C. L., & Schoenrock, C. J. (1981). When in doubt say yes: Acquiescence in interviews with mentally retarded persons. *Mental Retardation, 19,* 53–58.

Sigelman, C. K., Winer, J. L., & Schoenrock, C. J. (1982). The responsiveness of mentally retarded persons to questions. *Education and Training in Mental Retardation, 17,* 120–124.

Taylor, R. L. (1997). *Assessment of individuals with mental retardation.* San Diego, CA: Singular.

Thorndike, R., Hagen, E., & Sattler, J. (1986). *Stanford Binet Intelligence Scale* (4th ed.). Chicago: Riverside.

Wechsler, D. (1997). *Wechsler Adult Intelligence Scale* (3rd ed.). San Antonio, TX: The Psychological Corporation.

Wood, H. R., & White, D. L. (1992). A model for habilitation and prevention for offenders with mental retardation: The Lancaster County (PA) Office of Special Offenders Services. In R. W. Conley, R. Luckasson, & G. N. Bouthilet (Eds.), *The criminal justice system and mental retardation: Defendants and victims* (pp. 153–165). Baltimore, MD: Brooks.

8

Attempts to Improve the Police Interviewing of Suspects

RAY BULL AND BECKY MILNE

In recent decades, court cases in several countries have revealed some police interviewing of suspects to be grossly incompetent. However, few countries seem to have sought to improve this crucial aspect of policing, which is of great importance to society. However, in England and Wales in the last 20 years, the police service and the government have made pioneering attempts at improvement, these attempts largely being based on work by psychologists. This chapter provides an overview of these developments.

Some countries have recently sought to benefit from these developments. For example, in Norway, in 2003, a select group of police officers is being extensively prepared to deliver to police throughout the country a comprehensive training course designed to improve the interviewing of suspects. This training course is very much based on developments in England and Wales.

We will review work in England and Wales concerning the situation prior to compulsory audiotape recording; what audiotape recording revealed; a new ethos and training program; whether the new training achieved its objectives; the views of interviewees/suspects; the supervision of interviews, and a new national framework for investigative interviewing.

RAY BULL • Department of Psychology, University of Leicester, 106 New Walk, Leicester, LE1 7EA, United Kingdom (ray.bull@le.ac.uk).   BECKY MILNE • Institute of Criminal Justice Studies, University of Portsmouth, P01 2QQ, United Kingdom (becky.milne@port.ac.uk).

THE SITUATION PRIOR TO COMPULSORY
AUDIOTAPE RECORDING

Many police forces around the world seem to have tried to train interviewers merely by getting them to observe experienced colleagues. Given that the available research reveals (see below) that most police officers who have not been properly trained are poor interviewers, then merely observing such colleagues will not produce good interviewers. Although such observational learning is relatively cheap, those being observed also lack the skills required to train effectively. Furthermore, the common absence in policing of any valid, reliable, and comprehensive way of evaluating interviewer performance prevents proper recognition of poor versus good role models. If police interviews with suspects are not audio or video recorded, there is no useful way of assessing interviewer performance.

Some police forces, particularly in the United States, have adopted what is usually known as the Reid Technique for the interviewing of suspects (see Leo, this volume). Many aspects of this technique are contrary to the principles of good investigative interviewing jointly adopted in 1992 in England and Wales by the Association of Chief Police Officers and the government (see below). Also, some of the police forces that have adopted the Reid Technique seem to be ignorant of the point made by Reid that this approach was developed for interrogating suspects whose guilt already seems definite or reasonably certain (Memon, Vrij, & Bull, 1998). In England and Wales, at least, prior to most police interviews with suspects, their guilt had not yet been reliably established, even though interviewers often believed prior to the interview that the suspect was the guilty person (Plimmer, 1997).

In 1980, Irving published the first English study of what actually happens in police interviews with suspects. As part of a study for the Royal Commission On Criminal Procedure (i.e., a very extensive and high level inquiry), he sat in on 60 such interviews and reported that the interviewers used several manipulative and persuasive tactics, which included

- minimizing the seriousness of the offense
- manipulating the suspect's self-esteem
- pretending to be in possession of more evidence than they actually had
- pointing out the futility of denial
- telling the suspect that it was in his or her best interest to confess.

The Royal Commission in its 1981 report questioned the use of such tactics and the subsequent *Police and Criminal Evidence Act 1984* sought to rule out the inappropriate use of psychological tactics (and mandated, from

1986, that all police interviews with suspects are audiotape recorded). Some years later, Irving and McKenzie (1989) reported in another observational study that the frequency of the use of such tactics had declined. Interestingly, they pointed out that the frequency of confessions had not decreased. Indeed, the frequencies they had found (of 62% and then 65%) are similar to those found in some other, later studies (e.g., Pearse & Gudjonsson, 1996, found 58%).

WHAT AUDIOTAPE RECORDING REVEALED

A few years later, the Home Office (the relevant part of government) published Baldwin's (1992) comprehensive report on his analysis of several hundred recent police interviews with suspects (which had been audio- or videorecorded). Baldwin (1993, p. 326) noted that before interviews with witnesses were tape-recorded, "the police account of what had transpired in the interview room had to be largely taken on trust." (Interestingly, even though some members of the police service were apprehensive about mandatory audiotape recording of interviews prior to the 1986 implementation, only a few years later, the service came to the view that such tape recording is extremely valuable—a view retained today.)

Baldwin (1993) was of the view that most police officers, prior to audiotape recording, seemed to believe that interviews with suspects are complex and difficult encounters with awkward and aggressive people (some police training around the world also seems based on such beliefs). What he actually found in his analysis of 600 recorded interviews was that "most were short and surprisingly amiable discussions" (Baldwin, 1993, p. 331), with over a third of the suspects admitting culpability from the outset. Perhaps the most crucial of all his pioneering findings was that in only 20 of the 600 interviews did suspects during the course of the interview change from denial/uninvolvement to confession/admittance. Furthermore, "in only nine of these cases was the change of heart attributable to the persuasive skills of the interviewer, and even here only three involved cases of any seriousness" (Baldwin, 1993, p. 333). Thus the majority of the suspects kept to their initial position (i.e., denial, admission, or somewhere in between) throughout the interview. Therefore Baldwin suggested that police training to interview suspects move away from attempting to persuade denying suspects to confess, since, he contented, this is a false view of what is the real agenda.

However, in England and Wales (as in many other countries), police officers believed that the main aim of interviews with suspects was to gain a confession. For example, Stephenson and Moston (1994) found that 80% of the police interviewers they asked indicated that obtaining a confession was usually their main goal and that 70% indicated, just prior to conducting a real interview, that they were already sure of the suspect's guilt (cf. Meissner & Kassin, this volume). Plimmer (1997) also found among his colleagues that gaining confessions was the main aim. However, Williamson (1993), a senior officer playing a major role in trying to bring about fundamental change in the ethos concerning the interviewing of suspects, reported that in his survey, officers said that searching for the truth was a major aim of interviews with suspects.

Like Baldwin's (1993) study, Moston, Stephenson, and Williamson's (1992) study was based on analyzing several hundred tape-recorded interviews with suspects. They found, as had Irving and McKenzie (1989), that the psychologically manipulative tactics noted by Irving (1980) (and still practiced today in some countries) were largely absent. In their place, they noted a confrontational style in which suspects were accused of the alleged offense(s) at the beginning of the interview and asked for their response to such accusations. Not surprisingly, Moston et al. (1992) noted that many interviewees resisted such accusations. The police devoted little of the interview to giving the suspect the opportunity to give a free narrative/open-ended account. Instead, they put accusations to interviewees, hoping they would agree to these accusations. Sometimes these accusations involved mention of actual evidence the police believed implicated the suspect. (In England and Wales the police are not allowed to lie or use trickery about this available evidence.) When such evidence was strong, confessions were more likely. Thus, what primarily influenced confessions was incriminating evidence rather than interviewer skill (though, of course, the appropriate timing and amount of evidence disclosed at any one time is an aspect of good interviewing).

An effect of the strength of evidence was also found by Evans (1993) who noted that of those juvenile suspects who did not confess at or near the beginning of the interview, half did confess later in the interview, usually if the evidence against them was strong. Importantly, Evans found that 77% of suspects readily confessed at or near the beginning of the interview, leaving only a quarter to be possibly affected by interviewer skill (including disclosure of evidence). Evans found that when the evidence was weak, few suspects who started the interview with denial were persuaded to confess. He concluded that this supported the belief that "interviewing techniques and tactics have a limited overall effect on admission rates compared to other factors" (Evans, 1993, p. 35).

McConville and Hodgson (1993) found the most common police interviewing procedure was to tell suspects that because of the evidence against them they should confess. When suspects did not confess the police often then repeatedly made accusations, sometimes in an abusive way.

Pearse and Gudjonsson (1996) also found that in interviews with suspects (conducted in 1991/92) it was rare that suspects would move from denial to admission/confession during an interview (or from one interview to the next). The vast majority of the 58% of suspects who confessed did so at or near the beginning of their interview. The most frequent police technique (75%) was the introduction of evidence.

One way to interpret what these studies of tape-recorded interviews reveal is to realize that most suspects have already decided (with or without legal advice) whether to confess or not in the coming interview and that the proportion who have decided to confess is (surprisingly) large. What appears to influence those who have not yet decided to confess is the strength of evidence revealed against them during the interview, and if the evidence is revealed as strong, some then confess. (Of course, guilty suspects would often be able to tell if the police were revealing false evidence against them and thus deduce that the police case was weak.) Given the key role of evidence, this suggests that the police should be in possession of as much evidence as possible before interviewing, should not reveal this all at the beginning, should seek an account from the suspect, should compare the suspect's account with the unrevealed evidence, should then reveal some of the evidence, and get the suspect to offer an explanation of the discrepancies/contradictions. This is, in part, what the new ethos of police interviewing in England and Wales has been about.

A NEW ETHOS AND TRAINING PROGRAM

In the late 1970s, a Royal Commission on Criminal Procedure was set up partly as the result of a high profile case in which the police had obtained false confessions from youths suspected of murder (Fisher, 1977). (This case has similarities with the Central Park jogger case.) In its 1981 report, this Commission recommended, with regard to the interviewing of suspects, that a readjustment of attitudes and training was required throughout the police service and that "it is equally important to convey to the detective in training a sharper awareness of the psychology of custody and interrogation" (p. 195).

A decade later a senior police officer noted that "little was done for nearly ten years . . . to implement the Commission's intention to develop improved methods of interviewing" (Williamson, 1993, p. 92). In the early 1990s, a major national review of police interviewing took place, jointly organized by the government and the Association of Chief Police Officers (for England and Wales). This review produced new principles of interviewing which emphasized that (Milne & Bull, 1999):

- The role of the police is to obtain accurate information from suspects.
- Interviews should be approached with an open mind.
- Information obtained from the suspect must be compared with what the interviewer already knows.
- The interviewing officer(s) must act fairly.
- Vulnerable suspects must be treated with particular consideration.
- The interviewer need not accept the first answer given.
- Even when the suspect exercises the right to silence, the interviewer still has a right to ask questions in order to try to establish the truth (so long as these questions are relevant and not repetitive).

The 1992 publication of these principles sought to replace "interrogation" by "investigative interviewing" and to change the ethos of interviewers from that of seeking a confession to a search for information—from a blinkered, closed-minded, oppressive, and suggestive interviewing style to one involving open-mindedness, flexibility, and the obtaining of reliable evidence.

Alongside the publication of these principles, came a new interview training program and two relatively short, specially written booklets on interviewing that were issued to all 127,000 officers. The new program standardized for the first time interview training across all police forces in England and Wales. The booklets and the training recommended a five-part model of investigative interviewing that emphasized Planning/preparation; Engaging of and explaining to the suspect; Account from the suspect; Closure; and Evaluation.

Taking the first letter of each of these steps produced the acronym PEACE, which the approach and the training was, and is, called. This new approach also involved the fundamental realization that good interviewing of suspects has many, major similarities with good interviewing of victims and witnesses, for example the obtaining of valid information (Milne & Bull, 1999). This resulted in an emphasis in the new training on the crucial role of psychological knowledge concerning attention, perception, memory, interpersonal behavior, and so on, with these topics being equally important in the interviewing of witnesses and in the interviewing of suspects.

The government (in collaboration with the police service and other relevant organizations), in 1991, commissioned a lawyer (Professor D. Birch) and a psychologist (the first author of this chapter) to write the first working draft of the 1992 official guidance on how to interview child victims/witnesses—the "Memorandum of Good Practice on Video Recorded Interviews with Child Witnesses for Criminal Proceedings" (Home Office & Department of Health 1992; see also Bull, 1992, 1996). This document's section on conducting interviews was very much based on the psychological research available at that time and it adopted the four-phased approach of rapport, free recall, questioning, closure.

It also stated that no interview should be conducted without proper planning. Furthermore, since the *Criminal Justice Act 1991* had permitted that normally interviews with (possible/alleged) child witnesses should be video-recorded, these video recordings allow, for the first time, thorough evaluation of interviewer performances to take place. Thus the four phases (above) plus planning and evaluation closely resemble the five aspects of the PEACE model (the account part of which involves first of all obtaining free recall before asking questions, with the different question types being asked in the correct order—see Milne & Bull, 1999).

The 2002 government update of the "Memorandum of Good Practice" ("Achieving Best Evidence: Guidance for Vulnerable or Intimidated Witnesses, Including Children," Home Office) retains the phased approach and it was largely written by psychologists (including the first author). The PEACE training package has now been updated several times by The National Crime Faculty (2000). Thus, over the last 10 years, there have been several opportunities to re-evaluate the sense of the fundamental realization in the early 1990s that good interviewing of suspects and good interviewing of witnesses share many similarities. Indeed, when one realizes (Pearse & Gudjonsson, 1996) that the vast majority of police suspects in interview (at least in England and Wales) are polite and cooperative (at least to an extent), then such similarities are not surprising. If one's basic approach to interviewing suspects is to believe from the outset they are guilty, to fire accusations at them, and to use psychological coercion, then they may not be polite and cooperative.

However, if the approach is to treat them with the respect any human being deserves, to actively entertain the possibility that they may be innocent, and to avoid psychological coercion, then they may be willing to give a full account, even if they have committed wrong-doing. Indeed, when interviews with suspects are conducted in line with the latter approach, the confession/admittance rate is still found to be around 50% (plus or minus 10%—see below).

Obviously, one crucial aspect of this new approach to the interviewing of suspects is that the information gathering must not be confined to attempting to gain information from the suspect during the interview, but must form a central component of the planning and preparing for the interview. Here arises another psychological issue: the ability of police officers to gather and extract information in an unbiased way prior to interview. Little research has been conducted on this, and the present authors are about to start a collaborative project on the issue. One of our doctoral students (Mortimer, 1994 a, b; Mortimer & Shepherd, 1999) did examine this issue in collaboration with an English police force. She constructed standardized crime files based on five real-life cases. Prior to interview, officers were given one of the files and after unrestricted preparation time, they interviewed the suspect (an actor playing this role). From analysis of the tape-recorded interviews, a consistent pattern emerged. For example, only 41% of the relevant information in the file seemed to have been correctly abstracted. Even when officers rated the evidence available in the file as "weak," their belief (prior to interview) that the suspect "did it" was high. In the interviews, the prior stated investigating aims and objectives were often not enacted, and the interviews usually soon moved from an initial investigatory style to a confirmatory style (i.e., asking the suspect to confirm the evidence the officer had extracted from the file; cf. Meissner & Kassin, this volume). When the suspect blocked this style, the officers often resorted to outright accusation.

In the last ten years, most, but not yet all, operational police officers have gone through the five-day-long PEACE training course. (For more on each of the five steps of PEACE, see Milne & Bull, 1999). By and large, the PEACE ethos was well received by officers, some of whom in their initial two-year police training had earlier experienced training that extensively involved relevant findings from psychology, video-recorded role plays, and feedback evaluations (Bull & Horncastle, 1988, 1989, 1994).

HAS THE NEW TRAINING PROGRAM ACHIEVED ITS OBJECTIVES?

There have been few formal evaluations of the effectiveness of PEACE training. McGurk, Carr, and McGurk (1993) were commissioned to make an evaluation based on four pilot courses conducted prior to the national introduction of PEACE. Their assessment consisted of a knowledge test, plus simulated and real-life interviews pre- and post-training. They concluded that the courses were "effective in producing investigative learning outcomes which . . . should ensure that interviews of . . . suspects are conducted . . . within the codes of practice" (McGurk et al., 1993, p. 27). Given this encouraging evaluation, PEACE training was introduced nationally. (We should note, however, that when people, especially perhaps police officers, know that they are being evaluated, this alone may bring about improvements.)

Since McGurk et al.'s (1993) published evaluation, a number of in-house studies have taken place. For example, in one police force in England, a comparison was made of 30 interviews with suspects conducted by officers who had been PEACE trained with 30 by officers who had not yet been PEACE trained. Each interview was classified as (i) *highly skilled*, (ii) *skilled*, (iii) *average*, (iv) *less skilled*, or (v) *poor*. For the non-PEACE-trained officers, 77% of their interviews were classified as *less skilled* or *poor*, whereas only 34% of the PEACE-trained officers' interviews were classified as such. Surprisingly (or perhaps not—see earlier parts of this chapter), none of the non-PEACE-trained interviews were classified as *highly skilled* and only 3% as *skilled!* For the PEACE-trained officers, the corresponding figures were 10% and 23% (i.e., a third were judged as good). These are interesting findings but, unfortunately, the evaluator of the interviews was not "blind" to which interviews were conducted by non-PEACE-trained officers.

In 1999, Colin Clarke (a serving police officer and psychology graduate) and the second author of this chapter received support from the government's Police Research Award Scheme to conduct a national evaluation of the PEACE course. Six police forces in England and Wales participated in the research, being selected in terms of their size, geographical location, and supervision policy. The resulting report (Clarke & Milne, 2001) was very comprehensive and thus only some of the more essential findings are reviewed here.

The 177 taped interviews with suspects were classified into one of five categories with regard to their outcome:

1. A comprehensive account gathered from the suspect which contained a confession/admission and a detailed account of what happened—17%
2. A confession/admission but little detail of what happened—23%
3. A partial admission to the offense(s) in question—25%
4. Denial of the offense(s)—29%
5. Refusal to answer questions or replied "No comment"—6%

Thus, 40% of the interviews contained a confession, and a further 25%, a partial admission.

Each interview was analyzed in depth (Clarke & Milne, 2001) with regard to the aims and objectives of the PEACE approach. With regard to planning/preparation, the majority of interviews were rated as *adequate*, with few as *very good* or *poor*. For engage/explain, in half of the interviews, the grounds for arresting the interviewee were explained in a clear and professional manner. However, the purpose of the interview was only clearly explained in 12%, and the fact that the interview is an opportunity for the suspect to provide their own version of events was explained in only 9%. Little rapport building was found.

With regard to obtaining an account, the interviewers generally made a good effort to encourage the interviewer to give an account, though subsequent explorations of this account by the interviewer using appropriate summaries and links were relatively rare. Active listening was rated as good in 36%, and half of the interviewers demonstrated clear ability to keep interviewees to relevant topics. In general, interviewers' communication skills were rated as *good*. However, while challenges of the suspects' accounts occurred in most of the interviews in which suspects provided accounts, only a minority of these were rated as being professional (e.g., conducted using evidence). Questioning of the interviewee was rated as *good* in a quarter of the interviews, the mean rating being *adequate*. The question types most often employed were "open questions," and "appropriate closed questions." Leading questions and overtalking occurred relatively rarely. Appropriate use of pauses and silences occurred in only 18% of the interviews. In closure, 75% of interviewers provided the opportunity for the suspect to correct, alter, or add to the interviewer's recapitulation/summary of what the suspect had said. However, the rating of the summary-giving was rather low—only basic summaries were often provided. Only 10% of the interviews were evaluated as possibly breaching the relevant parts of the *Police and Criminal Evidence Act, 1984.*

Clarke and Milne (2001) then compared those interviews conducted by officers who had been on a week's (approximately) full-time PEACE training course with those by officers who had not. (Two-thirds of the sample had been on the course.) Few statistically significant differences were found. This lack of difference may at first glance seem surprising, but the officers who had not been on the course knew about PEACE and had observed PEACE-trained colleagues conducting interviews. Interviews conducted in locations where there was a supervision policy in place (e.g., supervisors listening to tapes of interviews or sitting in on interviews) were in some respects better than interviews where no clear supervision policy existed. Clarke and Milne (2001) concluded, based on a comparison with the findings of pre-PEACE studies (i.e., those reviewed above), that the introduction of PEACE has led to improvement in the ethos and methods of investigative interviewing.

Some other researchers have assessed, in England and Wales, the quality of the police interviews with suspects conducted since the introduction of PEACE. For example, the first author was commissioned by the Home Office (the relevant part of government) to identify what skills-gaps existed in "specialist" investigative interviews with suspects. These interviews were concerned with alleged offenses of a special nature (e.g., child abuse) and/or with interviewees requiring special skills (e.g., a vulnerable person). Each of these audio-taped interviews was assessed by two psychologists with expertise on the topic of investigative interviewing. The assessors independently evaluated the interviews for the overall level of skill demonstrated by the interviewers and for 28 particular skills drawn from the relevant literature (Cherryman & Bull, 1996) and from gathering the views of experienced detectives (Bull & Cherryman, 1995).

Contrary to Baldwin's (1993) concern that different people might not consensually assess the quality of investigative interviews, we found significant inter-assessor agreement not only for overall skill but also for the particular skills. Of the 28 skills, 11 were found significantly to differentiate between the interviews that overall were judged as skilled and those judged as not skilled. Several of these 11 skills relate to the new ethos contained in PEACE (e.g., open-mindedness, flexibility, empathy/compassion, appropriate use of pauses and silences, responds to what interviewee says, communication skill, open questions) though some of them (e.g., flexibility, avoidance of use of closed questions, empathy/compassion) were not often present (i.e., even in the skilled interviews). Furthermore, some of the particular skills that have been the focus of criticism of poor interviewing in the past (e.g., inappropriate interruptions, long/complex questions, overtalking, undue pressure) were found to be rarely present, even in the interviews that overall were judged as not skilled.

In our project, we also asked specialist investigative interviewers which factors most prevented them from carrying out better interviews. The most frequently mentioned factor was not having enough time to prepare properly.

Support for Baldwin's (1993) concern about a possible lack of inter-assessor agreement came from our finding (Cherryman, Bull, & Vrij, 1998a) that experienced police interviewers did not (independently) agree with each other when evaluating a sample of the interviews evaluated by the psychologists. Since these more experienced interviewers were trainers and/or supervisors of investigative interviewing, this lack of agreement is worrying. Cherryman (2000) found that the levels of authoritarianism and of empathy in these trainers/supervisors explained little of the variation in inter-judge agreement. However, Cherryman, Bull, and Vrij (1998b) found that officers who regularly conduct interviews with suspects did (independently) demonstrate inter-judge agreement about the skills of the interviews assessed by the trainers/supervisors, but their judgments were not the same as the psychologists. These officers' judgments of the interviewers' skills were strongly affected by whether or not the interviews contained a confession, even if this confession occurred early on in the interview.

In a more recent study, we asked experienced detectives (in semi-structured interviews) for their comments on the way they conduct interviews with suspects (Soukara, Bull, & Vrij, 2002). They said that

- the available evidence largely determined the style of interview
- the nature of the crime and the individual characteristics of the suspect also influence the style of interview
- preparation for the interview and the social skills of the interviewer are of the utmost importance
- the interview should be a search for the truth rather than a search for a confession.

In addition, 40% of these detectives said that the *Police and Criminal Evidence Act, 1984* had reduced the pressure on the police to gain confessions.

Of course, what interviewers say they do may actually differ from what they do. In order to assess actual interviewer performances, we were able to negotiate access to a large random sample of audio-taped interviews with suspects conducted by officers in the same police force as the respondents to our semi-structured interviews. Eighty of these interviews (concerned with a variety of alleged offenses) have so far been evaluated. Our evaluation involved examining them for the use of 17 tactics reported in the previous international literature on police interviewing of suspects (e.g., Kalbfleish, 1994; Kassin, 1997; Kassin & McNall, 1991; Memon et al., 1998; Pearse & Gudjonsson, 1999; Vrij, 2002).

Interjudge agreement was found among the psychologists (with expertise on investigative interviewing) who independently assessed the interviews for the presence/absence of each tactic. In 39% of the interviews, a confession occurred. The tactics of "intimidation," "situational futility," and "minimization" were never present, and "maximization" occurred in only one interview. These four tactics are among those that are of most concern to psychologists (Memon et al., 1998) and most contrary to the ethos of PEACE. The use of open questions and the appropriate disclosure of evidence occurred in all but one interview. In three quarters of the interviews "positive confrontation," "emphasizing of contradictions," and "challenges account" occurred, these being in line with PEACE. "Repetitive questioning" occurred in 84% of interviews, such repetitive questioning not being in line with PEACE. (The frequency of the other tactics ranged from 44% to 15%—for more on this, see Soukara, Bull, & Vrij, in preparation).

In those interviews in which a confession occurred, contrary to previous findings in England and Wales, these confessions did not largely occur near the beginning of the interview. For those interviews in which the suspect initially denied the allegation but later confessed, the following tactics were present—"disclosure of evidence," "emphasizing contradictions," "showing concern," "challenging account," and "repetitive questioning." Thus the absence in these interviews of tactics that have caused concern to psychologists seems not to have reduced the possibility that suspects during the interview will move from denial to confession.

THE VIEWS OF THE INTERVIEWEES

Almost no published research has contained information gathered from interviewees/suspects concerning the behavior/skill/tactics of police interviewers (but see Klare, this volume). This lack is, perhaps, understandable given the difficulty of gaining access to such suspects, their probable participation rate, and the likelihood that they might purposely provide biased information (especially since, if they participate in such research soon after their police interview, the information they provide would be disclosable in any subsequent court proceedings). Nevertheless, we have been negotiating access to such interviewees for the last six months and expect an outcome soon.

Holmberg and Christianson (2002) asked men in prison for serious crime in Sweden to complete a postal questionnaire about their police interviews (conducted months or years prior). Many of the inmates indicated that their interviewers displayed condemning attitudes, a lack of empathy, and impatience. A notable proportion of them said they had felt insulted as human beings during their interviews. Holmberg and Christianson found that two major interviewing styles were reported, one they described as dominating, and the other as humane. The former style involved "a superficial case-oriented approach, characterized by impatience, aggression, a brusque and obstinate condemning approach, presumably aiming to extort a confession" (Homberg & Christianson, 2002, p. 42). Importantly, they found that those interviewees who had perceived humanitarian attitudes from the interviews were the ones who "were more likely to admit crime" (Homberg & Christianson, 2002, p. 40). They found the dominating style to be associated with suspects denying the offense. (However, we should add that denial may possibly have caused the dominating style, see Meissner & Kassin, this volume.)

SUPERVISION, MANAGEMENT, AND A NATIONAL FRAMEWORK

Clarke and Milne (2001) made 19 recommendations regarding how to improve officers' interviewing skills. These revolve around the three broad areas of guidance, supervision, and training. Interview guidance has now been distributed nationally concerning the importance and requirement of having written plans prior to the conducting of all interviews. With regard to training, one recommendation was that refresher training now focus on obtaining, further developing, and then testing suspects' accounts.

However, the training of practitioners in best practice may well have limited impact if they are not supported by active, informed management and if there is not a comprehensive supervision policy in place. Research (e.g., Stockdale, 1993) has demonstrated that support is important for the transference of new knowledge and skills into the workplace. Furthermore, the more cognitively complex a task, the less able practitioners are to self-monitor and provide self-feedback. Good supervision is thus crucial.

Supervision also allows for quality assurance mechanisms to be in place that may play a role in appraisal and career development (ACPO, 2002). The police service in England and Wales recently developed a set of minimum competencies for investigative interviewing which officers are required to meet (ACPO, 2003). Supervision would provide the opportunity to assess such competencies and to identify developmental needs.

The outcome of supervision also, of course, provides an evaluation of the training itself, which in turn fulfills the cycle of training in that, for example, it should help to identify general skills-gaps in practitioners' performance. It also can help to determine the functional life of a training program and where refresher training is needed.

Another reason Clarke and Milne (2001) suggested for the lack of full transference of PEACE into the workplace was that trainees may have been taught too much too early. One of their recommendations, therefore, was a tiered approach to interview training that developed alongside interviewers' careers. This has now been incorporated into a new ACPO (2002) interviewing strategy that is in the process of being implemented by the ACPO Steering Committee For Investigative Interviewing. The second author of this chapter is a member of this committee, her role being to give scholarly advice regarding psychological principles. The aim of the interviewing strategy is to "increase professionalism in operational policing activity" (p. 2) and to state a national, professional standard for investigative interviewing. The strategy provides a five-tiered approach as proposed by Clarke and Milne (2001), the tiers consisting of:

Tier 1—"foundation" for recruits which focuses on interviewing regarding "volume" crime (e.g., theft)

Tier 2—"investigator" for interviews regarding "serious" crime (e.g., robbery)

Tier 3—"specialist" for interviewers who work on "major" crime (e.g., murder)

Tier 4—"supervisor" for those who supervise/manage interviewers

Tier 5—"advisor" for those who provide an expert consultancy role in their force on matters relating to policy and strategy as well as advising Senior Investigating Officers on difficult matters relating to interviews

These five tiers are associated to the 2003 competencies, and the steering committee has recently provided a National Curriculum for each of the tiers so that the police service can train to and implement them in the coming 12 months. This is a tall order, being costly in terms of time and money. It shows the commitment of the service to further improving this core area of police business. Being discussed now is how standards are to be ensured and maintained. Issues of assessment and university accreditation are also being examined.

REFERENCES

ACPO. (2002). The management and supervision of interviews. National Steering Committee on Investigative Interviewing. Unpublished paper.

ACPO (2003). Investigative interviewing strategy. National Steering Committee on Investigative Interviewing. Unpublished paper.

Baldwin, J. (1992). *Video-taping of police interviews with suspects—An evaluation.* Police Research Series Paper No. 1. London: Home Office.

Baldwin, J. (1993). Police interview techniques. Establishing truth or proof? *British Journal of Criminology, 33,* 325–352.

Bull, R. (1992). Obtaining evidence expertly: The reliability of interviews with child witnesses. *Expert Evidence, 1,* 5–12.

Bull, R. (1996). Good practice for video recorded interviews with child witnesses for use in criminal proceedings. In G. Davies, S. Lloyd-Bostock, M. McMurran, & C. Wilson (Eds.), *Psychology, law and criminal justice (pp. 100–117).* Berlin: de Gruyter.

Bull, R., & Cherryman, J. (1995). *Helping to identify skills gaps in specialist investigative interviewing.* London: Home Office Police Department.

Bull, R., & Horncastle, P. (1988). Evaluating training: The London Metropolitan Police's recruit training inhuman awareness/policing skills. In P. Southgate (Ed.), *New directions in police training* (pp.219–229). London: Her Majesty's Stationery Office.

Bull, R., & Horncastle, P. (1989). An evaluation of human awareness training. In R. Morgan & D. Smith (Eds.), *Coming to terms with policing* (pp.97–117). London: Tavistock.

Bull, R., & Horncastle, P. (1994). Evaluation of police recruit training involving psychology. *Psychology, Crime and Law, 1,* 157–163.

Cherryman, J. (2000). *Police investigative interviewing: Skill analysis and concordance of evaluations.* Unpublished doctoral thesis, University of Portsmouth.

Cherryman, J., Bull, R., & Vrij, A. (1998a). *Investigative interviewing: British police officers' evaluations of real life interviews with suspects.* Paper presented at the Annual Conference of the European Association of Psychology and Law, Krakow.

Cherryman, J., Bull, R., & Vrij, A. (1998b). *British police officers' evaluations of investigative interviews with suspects.* Poster presented at the 24th International Congress of Applied Psychology, San Francisco.

Clarke, C., & Milne, R. (2001). *National evaluation of the PEACE investigative interviewing course.* Police Research Award Scheme. London: Home Office.

Evans, R. (1993). *The conduct of police interviews with juveniles.* Royal Commission on Criminal Justice Report. London: HMSO.

Fisher, H. (1977). *Report of an inquiry by the Hon. Sir Henry Fisher into the circumstances leading to the trial of three persons on charges arising out of the death of Maxwell Confait and the Fire at 27, Doggett Road, London, SE6.* London: HMSO.

Holmberg, U., & Christianson, S. (2002). Murderers' and sexual offenders' experiences of police interviews and their inclination to admit or deny crimes. *Behavioral Sciences and the Law, 20,* 31–45.

Home Office & Department of Health (1992). *Memorandum of good practice for video recorded interviews with child witnesses for criminal proceedings.* London: HMSO.

Home Office & Department of Health (2002). *Achieving best evidence in criminal proceedings: Guidance for vulnerable or intimidated witnesses, including children.* London: HMSO.

Irving, B. (1980). *Police interrogation. A case study of current practice.* Research Study Number 2. Royal Commission on Criminal Procedure. London: HMSO.

Irving, B., & McKenzie, I. (1989). *Police interrogation: The effects of the Police and Criminal Evidence Act.* London: Police Foundation.

Kalbfleisch, P. J. (1994). The language of detecting deceit. *Journal of Language and Social Psychology, 13.* 469–496.

Kassin, S. M. (1997). The psychology of confession evidence. *American Psychologist, 52,* 221–233.

Kassin, S. M., & McNall, K. (1991). Police interrogations and confessions: communicating promises and threats by pragmatic implication. *Law and Human Behavior, 15,* 233–251.

McConcille, M. & Hodgson, J. (1993). *Custodial legal advice and the right to silence.* The Royal Commission on Criminal Justice Research, Research Study No. 16. London: HMSO.

Memon, A., Vrij, A., & Bull, R. (1998). *Psychology and law: Truthfulness, accuracy and credibility.* Maidenhead: McGraw Hill.

Milne, R., & Bull, R. (1999). *Investigative interviewing: Psychology and practice.* Chichester: Wiley.

Mortimer, A. (1994a). *Cognitive processes underlying police investigative interviewing behaviour.* Unpublished PhD thesis. University of Portsmouth.

Mortimer, B. (1994b). Asking the right questions. *Policing, 10,* 111–124.

Mortimer, A., & Shepherd, E. (1999). Frames of mind: Schemata guiding cognition and conduct in the interviewing of suspected offenders. In A. Memon & R. Bull (Eds.), *Handbook of the psychology of interviewing* (pp. 293–315). Chichester: Wiley.

Moston, S., Stephenson, G. M., & Williamson, T. (1992). The effects of case characteristics on suspect behaviour during police questioning. *British Journal of Criminology, 32,* 23–40.

National Crime Faculty (2000). *A practical guide to investigative interviewing.* Bramshill: National Crime Faculty and National Police Training.

Pearce, J., & Gudjonsson, G. H. (1996). Police interviewing techniques at two south London police stations. *Psychology, Crime, and Law, 3,* 63–74.

Plimmer, J. (1997). Confession rate. *Police Review,* 7 February, pp.16–18.

RCCP (1981). *Report of the Royal Commission on Criminal Procedure.* London: HMSO.

Soukara, S., Bull, R., & Vrij, A. (2002). Police detectives' aims regarding their interviews with suspects: Any changes at the turn of the millennium? *International Journal of Police Science and Management, 4,* 110–114.

Soukara, S., Bull, R., & Vrij, A. (In preparation). Do English police officers actually use appropriate tactics when interviewing suspects?

Stephenson, G., & Moston, S. (1994). Police interrogation. *Psychology, Crime, and Law, 1,* 151–157.

Stockdale, J. (1993). Management and supervision of police interviews. Police Research Group Paper No. 5, London: HMSO.

Vrij, A. (2002). "We will protect your wife and child, but only if you confess." In P. van Koppen & S. Penrod (Eds.) *Adversarial versus inquisitorial justice: Psychological perspectives on criminal justice systems* (pp. 55–79). New York: Kluwer.

Williamson, T. (1993). From interrogation to investigative interviewing: strategic trends in police questioning. *Journal of Community and Applied Social Psychology, 3,* 89–99.

Bias and Accuracy in the Evaluation of Confession Evidence

G. DANIEL LASSITER AND ANDREW L. GEERS

The preceding chapters in this volume have focused primarily on how interrogations are conducted and have shed light on which of the standard investigative approaches used by police are most problematic with regard to producing coerced and/or false confessions. In this chapter we move from the interrogation room to the courtroom to consider the question of how confession evidence is evaluated once it is introduced at trial. If trial fact finders (judges and jurors) are in fact good at identifying and discounting problematic confessions—that is, ones that are indeed coerced or false— then the damage caused by errors made in the earlier stages of the criminal-justice process may be contained to some degree. We will review the empirical evidence that speaks to this issue. In addition, we will examine the related question of how evaluations of confession evidence are affected by the format in which it is presented. This issue of presentation format is an especially timely one as many states are currently grappling with how best to capture and later present what transpires during interrogations so as to minimize the possibility of unreliable confessions exerting any influence on trial verdicts.

G. DANIEL LASSITER • Department of Psychology, Ohio University, Athens, Ohio 45701-2979 (lassiter@ohio.edu).   ANDREW L. GEERS • Department of Psychology, University of Toledo, Toledo, Ohio 43606-3390.

CONFESSION EVIDENCE AND ITS EVALUATION

According to law, self-incriminating statements made while in police custody cannot be used as evidence against a defendant until it is determined that such statements were provided freely and intentionally rather than obtained by means of coercion—for example, a threat of punishment or a promise of leniency (Grano, 1993, and Kassin & Wrightsman, 1985, provide discussions of the law pertaining to the use of confessions). Although there is variation across jurisdictions, this issue of voluntariness is usually decided by the presiding judge or ultimately by the jury (see Kamisar, LaFave, & Israel, 1994, or Kassin & Wrightsman, 1985, for more detailed information concerning the procedures for determining voluntariness). In instances of the latter, jurors must come to the conclusion that a confession was given voluntarily, otherwise they are instructed to disregard it entirely (Mathes & DeVitt, 1965).

Although a U. S. Supreme Court decision (*Lego v. Twomey*, 1972) is based on the assumption that jurors are readily capable of differentiating voluntary from involuntary confessions and thereby discounting the latter, the research evidence is far less optimistic. Kassin and Wrightsman (1980, 1981) had mock jurors read a detailed transcript of a criminal trial. In one version of the trial, the defendant was said to have confessed to the crime in response to a threat of punishment and in another version to a promise of leniency. As noted above, the law considers both of these strategies for eliciting confessions coercive. Yet, Kassin and Wrightsman's studies demonstrated that mock jurors were not able to totally disregard confession evidence that resulted from a promise of leniency. More specifically, mock jurors who read that the confession followed a threat of punishment judged both the confession to be involuntary and the defendant to be not guilty, whereas mock jurors who read that the confession followed a promise of leniency judged the confession to be involuntary, but rendered a guilty verdict anyway.

A later study by Kassin and McNall (1991) found that if a confession is elicited by an interrogator's use of a minimization strategy—that is, "a 'soft-sell' technique in which the interrogator tries to lull the suspect into a false sense of security by offering sympathy, tolerance, face-saving excuses, and even moral justification, by blaming a victim or accomplice, by citing extenuating circumstances, or by playing down the seriousness of the charges" (p. 235)—mock jurors tend to react in the same manner as they do to admissions of guilt following promises of leniency, namely judging the confession to be less than voluntary, but still viewing the confessor as largely culpable for the crime. Kassin and Wrightsman (1980, 1981) have labeled this pattern of results the *positive coercion bias* and have noted that it is consistent with studies indicating that individuals tend to view behaviors enacted to secure a positive outcome as more freely and intentionally initiated by an actor than equivalent behaviors enacted to avoid a negative outcome (e.g., Wells, 1980).

In their 1981 experiments, Kassin and Wrightsman attempted to reduce this bias by presenting mock jurors with various forms of judicial instruction: one form directed jurors to ignore a confession they deemed coerced; a second form additionally defined the legal concept of coercion and emphasized the unreliability of such confessions; a third form defined coercion and emphasized the unconstitutionality and unfairness of such confessions; and a fourth form defined coercion and emphasized *both* the unreliability and unfairness of such confessions. Results showed that the first three forms of instruction had no effect either on participants' judgments of voluntariness or on their verdicts. The instruction that emphasized both the unreliability and unfairness of coerced confessions, however, did successfully lower judgments of voluntariness for illegally coerced confessions. Still, the effectiveness of this form of instruction was not complete as verdicts remained unaltered.

Kassin and Wrightsman (1985) made two additional attempts to eliminate jurors' biased appraisals of certain types of confession evidence. First, they changed the timing of the judicial instruction regarding voluntariness from the end of the trial (the usual timing of such instruction) to just before the presentation of the confession evidence. This alteration was suggested by previous findings indicating that judicial instruction may be more effective when delivered prior to the presentation of evidence (Feldman, 1978 cited in Horowitz & Willging, 1984; Kassin & Wrightsman, 1979). Second, unlike their earlier studies that focused on the evaluations of the individual, nondeliberating juror, they instructed six-person, mock juries to collectively discuss the merits of the evidence before rendering a verdict. This change was in response to reports that discussion and the exchange of information among jurors can reduce susceptibility to certain nonevidentiary biases (e.g., Kaplan & Miller, 1978). Neither of these modifications, however, was successful in eliminating the tendency to give inappropriate weight to self-incriminating statements that were legally involuntary.

Kassin and Sukel (1997) continued examining the extent to which trial decision makers fail to discount coerced confessions by investigating whether the magnitude of the pressure exerted during an interrogation influenced verdicts. Participants read one of three versions of a murder-trial transcript. In the high-pressure version, the defendant was described as being handcuffed, verbally abused, and threatened with a weapon during the interrogation in which his confession was obtained. In the low-pressure version, the interrogation was free of the above three elements and the defendant was said to have confessed immediately in response to police questioning. In the no-confession version, the defendant was said to have denied any involvement in the murder all along. Although mock jurors recognized the high-pressure interrogation as clearly coercive, their conviction rate was nonetheless increased compared to the condition in which no confession was introduced. Moreover, a straightforward admonishment from the judge to disregard the coerced confession did not eliminate its tendency to boost guilty verdicts, thereby further demonstrating the power of confession evidence to influence jury decision making even when it logically and legally should not.

The results of these studies unequivocally demonstrate that people do not necessarily evaluate and use confession evidence in the ways prescribed by law. Such findings are especially troubling in light of the 1991 U. S. Supreme Court ruling in *Arizona v. Fulminante.* Prior to this, if in the trial process an error was committed that allowed a coerced confession into evidence and the defendant was convicted, an appeal on behalf of the defendant would automatically nullify the verdict and produce a new trial. In a startling reversal of this long-standing precedent, the Court ruled that the improper use of an involuntary confession in a trial resulting in a conviction is not in and of itself sufficient reason to invalidate the conviction. That is, if other evidence in a particular case was adequate to justify a conviction, then the admission of an involuntary confession could be viewed as "harmless error." There is concern among some legal scholars that this ruling could increase the willingness of prosecutors to introduce as evidence confessions whose voluntary status is dubious (e.g., Kamisar, 1995). Such a possibility, considered together with the above literature, could mean that the problem of unreliable confessions affecting trial outcomes described by Lassiter and Ratcliff (this volume) may only get worse.

PRESENTATION FORMAT OF CONFESSION EVIDENCE: THE GROWING EMPHASIS ON VIDEOTAPE

Until the 1980s, most confession evidence was initially recorded and later presented at trial in either a written or audiotaped format. Today, it is estimated that more than half of the law enforcement agencies in the United States videotape at least some interrogations (Geller, 1992). In three states—Alaska, Minnesota, and most recently Illinois—videotaping interrogations is required. The practice of videotaping police interrogations has many proponents in the legal community as well as in allied fields (Cassell, 1996; Drizin & Colgan, 2001; Dwyer, Neufeld, & Scheck, 2000; Gudjonsson, 1992; Johnson, 1997; Leo, 1996), and it appears to be only a matter of time before the videotaped format becomes the norm for introducing confession evidence at trial. In a report to the National Institute of Justice, Geller (1992) concluded that "the videotaping of suspect statements is a useful, affordable step on the road toward a more effective, efficient, and legitimate criminal justice system" (p. 154). However, despite the seeming objectivity associated with the making and subsequent evaluation of a video-taped interrogation and confession, the scientific literature on illusory causation suggests that the videotaping procedure has the potential to influence judgments in a manner that is unintended and far from salutary.

WHAT IS ILLUSORY CAUSATION AND WHY DOES IT OCCUR?

Illusory causation occurs when people ascribe unwarranted causality to a stimulus simply because it is more noticeable or salient than other available stimuli (McArthur, 1980, 1981; Taylor & Fiske, 1978; Zebrowitz, 1990). In the first systematic demonstration of illusory causation in the social domain, Taylor and Fiske (1975) had observers view a casual, two-person conversation. The vantage point of the observers was varied by seating them in different locations around the two interactants. After the conversation ended, observers rated each interactant in terms of the amount of causal influence he or she exerted during the exchange. The results revealed that greater causality was attributed to whichever person observers happened to be facing, which, of course, was determined by their seating position—an entirely incidental factor that logically should have had no bearing on their causal judgments.

Early attempts to specify a mediator of illusory causation emphasized memory processes (Fiske, Kenny, & Taylor, 1982; Smith & Miller, 1979). Generally, it was argued that salient information tends to be more memorable than nonsalient information, and this difference in memory is responsible for the greater causality ascribed to salient information. Recent studies (Lassiter, Geers, Munhall, Ploutz-Snyder, & Breitenbecher, 2002), however, suggest that illusory causation may have more to do with how people initially pick up or register information from an observed interaction than with how they subsequently remember that information (Newtson, Rindner, Miller, & LaCross, 1978; McArthur, 1980). That is, the point of view from which individuals observe an interaction appears to influence the initial registration or perceptual organization of information from the ongoing interaction, which in turn directly influences causal attributions and related judgments. Because illusory causation seems linked to the earliest stages of information processing, over which people may have somewhat less mental control, there is reason to suspect that this phenomenon will be highly resistant to debiasing attempts (Wilson & Brekke, 1994).

ILLUSORY CAUSATION AND VIDEOTAPED CONFESSIONS

There is no doubt that, under certain circumstances, more accurate assessment of the voluntariness and reliability of confessions can be obtained via the videotape method. Certainly, if interrogators use obviously assaultive coercion, any reasonable observer will recognize the illegitimacy of the confession. However, such third-degree intimidation has been replaced by nonassaultive psychological manipulation (see Leo, this volume) that is not always recognized as coercive but, as research has shown, can nonetheless lead to false admissions of guilt (Kassin & Kiechel, 1996; Leo & Ofshe, 1998). In this age of psychologically oriented interrogation approaches, videotaping interrogations and confessions may not be a surefire preventive against convicting the truly innocent. In the United States and in many other countries (such as Canada, Australia, and the United Kingdom) videotaped interrogations and confessions are typically recorded with the camera focused on the suspect (Geller, 1992; Kassin, 1997). Positioning the camera in this manner seems straightforward and logical because trial fact finders presumably need to see directly what the suspect said and did to best assess the voluntariness and veracity of his or her statements.

The illusory-causation phenomenon, however, suggests the alarming possibility that the default camera perspective taken when recording criminal confessions (i.e., focused on the suspect) could have an unintended prejudicial effect on trial participants' subsequent evaluations of the voluntariness of the confessions. More specifically, observers of a videotaped confession recorded with the camera focused on the suspect, compared with the same confession recorded from a different camera perspective, might be more likely to judge the confession as voluntary (i.e., attributable to the suspect). Considerable empirical data now exist indicating that this is not simply a possibility; it is a reality (Lassiter, 2002; Lassiter, Geers, Munhall, Handley, & Beers, 2001).

EVIDENCE FOR A BIASING EFFECT OF CAMERA PERSPECTIVE ON EVALUATIONS OF VIDEOTAPED CONFESSIONS

In an initial demonstration of the biasing effect of camera perspective, Lassiter and Irvine (1986) had participants view a mock, videotaped confession (regarding shoplifting) recorded with the camera either focused on the "suspect," focused on the "interrogator," or focused equally on the suspect and interrogator. Following the presentation of the confession, participants were asked to indicate the degree to which they believed it was a product of force or coercion. The confession was judged to be the least coerced in the suspect-focus condition, more coerced in the equal-focus condition, and the most coerced in the detective-focus condition.

In a follow-up investigation, Lassiter, Slaw, Briggs, and Scanlan (1992) demonstrated that this *camera perspective bias* generalized across different crimes (i.e., rape, drug trafficking, and burglary) and that the suspect-focus videotapes produced greater perceptions of voluntariness compared to both audiotape and transcript versions of the confessions. This result suggests that the focusing of the camera on the suspect led observers to judge these particular interrogations to be *less* coercive than they would have judged them had the confessions been presented in a more traditional format. Even individuals high in the need for cognition (Cacioppo, Petty, Feinstein, & Jarvis, 1996)—that is, those most inclined to be effortful and critical thinkers—fell prey to the bias. (Recently, Lassiter et al., 2003, reported that evaluations of videotaped confessions by individuals who are particularly adept at reasoning about sophisticated causal relationships—that is, those identified as high in attributional complexity [Fletcher, Danilovics, Fernandez, Peterson, & Reeder, 1986]—are also swayed by the camera's perspective.) Finally, it is important to note that equal-focus videotapes yielded voluntariness assessments that were no different than those based on the audiotape and transcript versions of the confessions.

Lassiter, Beers, Geers, Handley, and Weiland (2002) found that collective deliberation among mock jurors prior to rendering their judgments was not sufficient to obviate the prejudicial effect of camera perspective. In addition, these authors showed that the biasing influence of camera perspective tainted not only assessments of voluntariness, but also perceived likelihood of guilt and sentencing recommendations—perceived likelihood of guilt was greater and recommended sentences were more severe when the suspect-focus videotape of a confession was viewed. In subsequent studies, Lassiter, Beers et al. (2002) attempted to eliminate the camera perspective bias first by forewarning mock jurors that their "judgments could be affected by the angle of the camera" (Study 2), and second by having them engage in a task that forced more of their attention and concentration on the actual content of the videotaped confession, which was the same regardless of the camera perspective (Study 3). Both these procedures, however, failed to diminish the biasing influence of the camera's point-of-view. The mock confessions used in the studies described so far were designed to be short (no longer than 5 min in duration) and to be composites of various elements that have been documented to occur in real interrogations or that police manuals advise should occur. In a fourth and final study, Lassiter, Beers et al. (2002) presented mock jurors with a significantly longer confession (lasting approximately 30 min) that was derived entirely from an actual police interrogation. These changes also yielded no improvement with regard to overcoming the camera perspective bias.

One criticism that could be leveled at the foregoing series of studies is that participants experienced no real sense of accountability for their judgments, and it is for this reason that they were influenced so readily by the trivial factor of camera perspective. According to this argument, if the stakes were raised such that decision makers knew in advance that they would be held accountable for, or had to justify, their judgments to an expert or relevant authority, they would not so readily succumb to the bias. Research investigating the effects of accountability on judgments does suggest that increased accountability can attenuate bias (e.g., Bodenhausen, Kramer, & Süsser, 1994; Tetlock, 1985; Thompson, 1995). However, this literature also provides empirical examples of accountability amplifying bias (e.g., Gordon, Rozelle, & Baxter, 1988; Siegel-Jacobs & Yates, 1996), or having no effect at all on people's judgments (e.g., Simonson & Nye, 1992).

Lassiter, Munhall, Geers, Weiland, and Handley (2001) conducted an experiment that addressed this issue directly. Some participants were made to experience a heightened sense of accountability for their evaluations of a 30-min videotaped confession by informing them that they would subsequently have to justify their assessments of the confession's voluntariness to a judge from the local criminal court. Participants in a relatively low-accountability condition did not receive this information; rather, they were assured that their judgments would be kept confidential. All participants then viewed either a suspect-focus or equal-focus version of the videotaped confession. Although supplementary measures indicated that high-accountability participants processed information contained in the videotaped confession more carefully and thoroughly, the camera perspective bias persisted.

Lassiter, Geers, Handley, Weiland, and Munhall (2002) noted some limitations of the preceding work on videotaped confessions with respect to their external validity. One issue with these studies is that, for the most part, there was no additional evidence for participants to consider other than the confession itself. In real trials, fact finders are likely to be presented with other evidence in addition to the confession. It is conceivable that the presence of other kinds of evidence as well as the inclusion of the usual elements found in a courtroom trial (e.g., the testimony of multiple prosecution and defense witnesses, and opening and closing arguments of the prosecution and defense) could cause a dilution of this prejudicial effect (Visher, 1987). The prior studies also used only college students as mock-trial participants. Some investigators (e.g., Feild & Barnett, 1978) have questioned the use of students as participants in jury-simulation studies. The responses of students, it is argued, may be quite different from those of jury-eligible adults, in which case the generalizability of the findings of studies using student mock jurors is likely to be severely compromised. (Recent reviews of the mock juror/jury literature by Bornstein, 1999, and MacCoun, 1989, however, indicate that the judgments of student and adult mock jurors are comparable.) A final drawback pointed out by Lassiter, Geers et al. (2002) has to do with the fact that participants made their judgments only on continuous rating scales. However, verdicts in actual courtrooms are made in an either/or manner, and it cannot be known for certain that the bias observed with rating scales will still occur with cruder, but more ecologically valid, dichotomous measures (Kerr, 1978).

To address these concerns, Lassiter, Geers et al. (2002) conducted two studies that used an extensive videotaped trial simulation (based on the actual trial of Bradley Page; see Fulero, this volume, for details of Page's legal case) that required from 4 to 5 hours of participants' time, and included the direct testimony and cross-examination of several witnesses, the presentation of physical evidence, prosecution and defense arguments, judicial rulings on points of law, and most of the other trappings associated with such legal proceedings. In Study 1, both nonstudent and student participants were used so that a systematic comparison of their responses could be made. In Study 2, all participants were nonstudent, jury-eligible adults. In both studies, dichotomous measures of participants' judgments were obtained.

Drawing on Kassin and Wrightsman's (1981, 1985) earlier work, Lassiter, Geers et al. (2002, Study 1) also tested the effectiveness of judicial instruction as a means of reducing the influence of camera point of view on mock jurors' voluntariness and guilt judgments. More specifically, two forms of judicial instruction were examined. One form—similar to the version used by Kassin and Wrightsman (1981)—emphasized the need for mock jurors to be cognizant of both issues of reliability and fairness in evaluating confession evidence. This form of judicial instruction was included because, as noted earlier in this chapter, it has been shown to reduce, to a certain degree, the biased evaluation of some kinds of confession evidence. The second form of judicial instruction was the same as the first; however, it further emphasized to mock jurors that they should not allow the perspective from which the confession was videotaped to influence in any way their evaluation of the confession. This form of judicial instruction was included because it more specifically directs mock jurors' attention to the source of the bias and thus provides a strong test of their ability to override the bias when alerted to its existence. Finally, the timing of judicial instruction was varied (before vs. after the presentation of the confession evidence) to determine whether it moderates to any extent the instruction's effectiveness in minimizing the influence of camera perspective on judgments (cf. Kassin & Wrightsman, 1985).

Before discussing the results, it should be noted that participants in these studies showed clear signs of being very engaged in the proceedings. For example, even after 4 hours of participation, many of them chose to stay after the simulation was completed to ask thoughtful questions, gather more information about the actual Page case, and discuss their concerns about bias creeping into real jurors' decisions. This behavior indicates that participants were highly involved and treated the trial simulation very seriously.

As a whole, the data collected by Lassiter, Geers et al. (2002) provide evidence that the camera perspective bias in videotaped confessions can still occur even when ecological validity is relatively high. For the first time, the perspective from which a videotaped confession was recorded was shown to affect mock jurors' verdicts regarding guilt or innocence. This result was obtained in the context of elaborate trial simulations, with jury eligible adults from a variety of communities, regardless of whether participants deliberated collectively, and despite various instructions from the judge designed to minimize any biasing effect of camera perspective.

Konecni and Ebbesen (1979), have argued that psycholegal research "must be concerned with issues of external validity and generalizability to an *unusually high degree*" (p. 40, emphasis added). Or as stated more bluntly by Bornstein (1999), "courts have not welcomed psycholegal research findings with open arms, especially when derived from methods that are neither very realistic nor representative of actual legal processes" (p. 88). A critical goal of the next two experiments to be described was to move the research on the camera perspective bias in videotaped confessions even closer to this unusually-high-degree-of-generalizabilty standard needed to ultimately impact the legal system.

As noted at the outset of this chapter, a judge typically conducts a pretrial hearing to decide on a confession's voluntariness and admissibility. Thus judges are critical gatekeepers in terms of what confession evidence juries are actually allowed to consider. An important question, then, is do judges also succumb to the prejudicial effects of camera perspective? One possibility is that judges will be immune to the camera perspective bias. That is, their knowledge, experience, and understanding of the law pertaining to confessions could insulate them from the prejudicial effects of camera perspective. On the other hand, the findings indicating that the bias has it roots in perceptual processes that are not always controllable, suggest that judges may be no better in resisting the contaminating effects of the confession-presentation format than individuals who are without benefit of extensive legal training and experience.

Guthrie, Rachlinski, and Wistrich (2002) point out that systematic, controlled studies of judicial decision-making are rare. In investigations these researchers conducted on judges' susceptibility to various cognitive illusions (e.g., the hindsight bias and the inverse fallacy), they found that although judges were as susceptible to some illusions as laypersons and other professionals, their relative performance with regard to other illusions was noticeably better. Findings such as these suggest the possibility that judges may be able to overcome the camera perspective bias. A more theoretically based reason for thinking judges may manifest greater resistance to the prejudicial effects of camera perspective can be derived from the Elaboration Likelihood Model (Petty & Cacioppo, 1986). According to this model, people can usually process information either centrally or peripherally. Central processing of information is systematic, effortful, and emphasizes attention to and reliance on the most diagnostic cues—regardless of the difficulty associated with discerning them—for reaching a conclusion. Peripheral processing by contrast is typified by a more heuristic mode of thinking that involves greater attention and reliance on cues that are readily discernable without having to expend much in the way of cognitive resources. Judges, unlike laypersons, may be better at focusing their attentional resources on the cues that are most revealing in terms of reaching an accurate assessment of the voluntariness of a given confession. Although laypersons in several of the previous studies were no doubt highly motivated to reach an accurate assessment, their lack of expertise with deciding the voluntariness question may have made them gravitate to the most salient cues rather than the most diagnostic ones.

To directly test whether judges exhibit the camera perspective bias in videotaped confessions, Lassiter and Diamond (2003) presented judges (who were attending a judicial conference at the University of Illinois College of Law) with either a suspect-focus, equal-focus, or detective-focus version of a mock interrogation and confession regarding a sexual assault. Results revealed that judges' evaluations of the voluntariness of the confession, like those of laypersons previously, were affected by the camera perspective. This was true even for the judges who had the most prior experience dealing with confession evidence (i.e., those who had previous experience as prosecutors, criminal defense attorneys, and trial court judges hearing criminal cases).

Recently, Lassiter, Ratcliff, Ware, and Irvin (2003) noted that the likelihood of the legal establishment paying heed to the scientific evidence for a camera perspective bias could be diminished by the fact that in none of the experiments reviewed so far were participants exposed to actual confessions obtained during real police interrogations. That is, the prior work used mock confessions that were designed to be composites of various elements known to occur in real confessions or that were constructed re-enactments developed from transcripts of actual police interrogations. This type of simulated confession was required in the earlier stages of the research program because of the need to produce multiple camera perspectives of the same confession. However, critics can rightfully say that there were no serious consequences for the simulated "confessors" and therefore whether observers viewing actual videotaped presentations of interrogations and confessions will also manifest the camera perspective bias remains an open question.

As described earlier, audiotapes and transcripts of confessions produce evaluations that are comparable to those obtained with equal-focus videotapes. Based on this pattern of results, Lassiter, Ratcliff et al. (2003)

argued that comparing actual suspect-focus videotapes with audio only and transcript presentations of the same interrogation and confession would constitute a reasonable test of the camera perspective bias under conditions of high external validity. That is, if the bias truly occurs with real confessions, then an actual suspect-focus videotape should produce judgments of greater voluntariness than either an audio only or a transcript presentation.

In a preliminary test of their idea, Lassiter, Ratcliff et al. (2003) had mock jurors view, listen to, or read the actual 25-min interrogation of a young white male accused of sexual assault. The videotape was recorded with the camera positioned behind (and somewhat above) the interrogator and focused directly on the suspect. Supporting the existence of the camera perspective bias in real police confessions, mock jurors judged the confession as more voluntary when presented with the suspect-focus videotape. Consistent with previous findings, judgments based on the audio only and transcript presentations were comparable.

DOES VIDEOTAPING LEAD TO MORE ACCURATE EVALUATIONS OF CONFESSION EVIDENCE?

There is at least an implicit assumption that an actual videotape of an interrogation and confession should make it possible for trial fact finders to assess more accurately the reliability of the confession (cf. Gudjonsson, 1992; Leo & Ofshe, 1998). Yet, such an assumption has not heretofore been empirically tested. The fact that camera point of view has been shown to bias observers' evaluations of a videotaped confession might seem to suggest that just the opposite may in fact be true—that is, videotaping leads to less accurate assessments of reliability. But the presence of a bias in judgment does not necessarily say anything definitive about the accuracy of that judgment (cf. Funder, 1987; Jussim, 1991; Kruglanski & Ajzen, 1983). For example, it has been repeatedly demonstrated that people consistently favor dispositional explanations for an observed other's behavior over situational explanations (Jones, 1979; Ross, 1977). However, the question of whether this attributional bias increases, decreases, or has no effect on the accuracy of causal judgments typically has not been addressed (cf. Funder, 1982; Harvey, Town, & Yarkin, 1981). In a similar manner, the research reviewed so far was designed to allow for an examination of possible judgment bias, but not for an assessment of judgment accuracy. We now turn to the few studies that have specifically attempted to address the important issue of accuracy in the evaluation of videotaped confessions.

Lassiter et al. (2003) have recently examined the effect of camera perspective on the ability of observers to differentiate true from false confessions using materials based on the case of Peter Reilly. Reilly was wrongfully convicted of the manslaughter of his mother based on a coerced and false confession he made to police after intensive interrogation. Two years following his conviction, evidence was discovered that demonstrated that Reilly could not have been the actual killer. As a result, his conviction was overturned and all charges against him were dismissed. A 2.5 hour videotaped simulation of critical aspects of Reilly's trial (including a 40-min videotaped confession) produced voluntariness and guilt judgments that revealed a most interesting pattern: Participants more accurately judged that Reilly was less likely to be guilty and that his confession was less likely voluntary when they viewed an *interrogator-focus* version, as opposed to a suspect-focus or an equal-focus version. It seems that observers were able to detect and/or appreciate better the external pressure to confess experienced by Reilly when the camera perspective made the source of that pressure, the interrogator, visually conspicuous (Arkin & Duval, 1975; Storms, 1973).

Lassiter and Clark (2003) noted that a drawback to the preceding study was that observers viewed only a single, simulated false confession and that there were no non-video presentation formats to allow for an assessment of baseline accuracy. To address these issues, Lassiter and Clark first obtained true and false confessions from several different individuals. Employing a modification of the methods of Kassin and Kiechel (1996) to induce false confessions, pairs of college students worked together on a computer task. The computer ostensibly "crashed" and the "cause" was due either to the actual participant (males in all cases) or a confederate (females in all cases) hitting a certain key. The experimenter questioned the participant about his role in crashing the computer—extracting a true confession in cases in which the participant did hit the critical key (at the urging of the confederate). In instances where the confederate was "guilty," she pleaded with the participant to take the blame so as not to hurt her chances of obtaining a research position with the faculty member conducting the experiment. This method was effective in getting some participants to give a false confession. Participants' confessions were recorded and later presented to new groups of participants whose task was to judge whether a given confession was true or false. The presentation format was systematically varied five ways (participant/suspect-focus video, experimenter/interrogator-focus video, equal-focus video, audio only, and transcript) so as to determine which format promotes the highest degree of judgmental accuracy. The overall results were sobering: Observers were no better than chance at differentiating true from false confessions. However, consistent with the findings of Lassiter, Beers et al. (2003), the participants who saw the interrogator-focus video did relatively better at identifying false confessions than those who evaluated the confessions in one of the remaining four presentation formats.

POLICY IMPLICATIONS OF THE RESEARCH
ON VIDEOTAPED CONFESSIONS

We noted above that many scientific, legal, and political experts have called for the universal adoption of videotaping as a relatively easy and straightforward solution for the problem of some innocent people being induced to incriminate themselves when confronted by standard police interrogation tactics. The research we have summarized, however, indicates that the application of videotaping to solve the problem of coerced or false confessions slipping through the system is not as clear-cut as it might first seem.

As pointed out earlier, in the United States and in many other countries videotaped interrogations and confessions are customarily recorded with the camera lens zeroed in on the suspect. One reason for this particular positioning of the camera is likely the belief that a careful examination of not only the suspects' words but also their less conspicuous actions or expressions, will ultimately reveal the truth of the matter (Geller, 1992). The empirical validity of such beliefs aside, it has been convincingly shown that focusing the video camera primarily on the suspect in an interrogation has the effect of impressing on viewers the notion that the suspects' statements are more likely freely and intentionally given and not the result of some form of coercion. Moreover, the subset of studies showing judgments derived from suspect-focus videotapes significantly deviate from judgments based on "control" media—transcripts and audiotapes—leads to the conclusion that the greater perception of voluntariness associated with suspect-focus videotapes is an unmistakable bias of the most serious kind, that is, one that runs contrary to the cornerstone of our system of justice, the presumption of innocence.

Is it the case, then, that videotaped interrogation and confession evidence should not be used at all in courts of law? No, because the literature does not paint an entirely negative picture with regard to the use of videotaped confessions in the courtroom. For example, it was found that videotaped confessions that focused on both the suspect and the interrogator equally generated judgments that were comparable to those based on more traditional presentation formats, that is, audiotapes and transcripts (Lassiter et al., 1992; Lassiter, Beers et al., 2002). Thus, it is clear that the videotaping procedure per se is not inherently prejudicial. Rather, it is the manner in which the videotaping procedure is implemented that holds the potential for bias. It appears, then, that the advantages associated with the videotape method—for example, a more detailed record of the interrogation is provided to trial participants—can be maintained without introducing bias if an equal-focus perspective is taken by the video camera.

This very approach to preventing the camera perspective bias in video-taped confessions has actually already been adopted in New Zealand. In the early 1990s, the Police Executive Committee of New Zealand approved the videotaping of police interviews/interrogations on a national basis. In implementing this policy, various procedural guidelines were established. One critical issue that had to be dealt with was in which direction to point the camera. One of the authors of "The New Zealand Video Interview Pro-ject" (Lani W. Takitimu, personal communication, November 3, 1993) noted that the seminal research on camera perspective and videotaped confes-sions (Lassiter & Irvine, 1986) led them to opt for showing side profiles of both the Police Officer and the suspect, although they knew, at the time, this was different from the procedures used in parts of Australia, Canada, and the United Kingdom.

Thus, New Zealand made it a national policy that police interroga-tions be videotaped from an equal-focus perspective based on only the first study conducted on camera perspective and videotaped confessions. With the greater wealth of data that now exists, it would be prudent for the United States and the other aforementioned countries to seriously consider adopt-ing a similar policy.

However, those who must make policy decisions regarding the imple-mentation of the videotape method should not preclude the possibility of directing the camera primarily at the interrogator(s) whom a detained sus-pect must face. As the most recent studies on accuracy in evaluating video-taped confessions (Lassiter, Beers et al., 2003; Lassiter & Clark, 2003) sug-gest, this particular camera perspective may hold the greatest potential for facilitating judges and jurors' all-important evaluations concerning the reli-ability of a given videotaped confession.

REFERENCES

Arizona v. Fulminante, 111 S. Ct. 1246 (1991).

Arkin, R., & Duval, S. (1975). Focus of attention and causal attributions of actor and observers. *Journal of Experimental Social Psychology, 11*, 427–438.

Bodenhausen, G. V., Kramer, G. P., & Süsser, K. (1994). Happiness and stereotypic thinking in social judgment. *Journal of Personality and Social Psychology, 66*, 621–632.

Bornstein, B. H. (1999). The ecological validity of jury simulations: Is the jury still out? *Law and Human Behavior, 23*, 75–91.

Cacioppo, J. T., Petty, R. E., Feinstein, J., & Jarvis, W. B. G. (1996). Dispositional differences in cognitive motivation: The life and times of individuals varying in need for cognition. *Psychological Bulletin, 119*, 197–253.

Cassell, P. G. (1996). All benefits, no costs: The grand illusion of Miranda's defenders. *North-western University Law Review, 90*, 1084–1124.

Drizin, S. A., & Colgan, B. A. (2001). Let the cameras roll: Mandatory videotaping of interro-gations is the solution to Illinois' problem of false confessions. *Loyola University Chicago Law Journal, 32*, 337–424.

Dwyer, J., Neufeld, P., & Scheck, B. (2000). *Actual innocence: Five days to execution and other dispatches from the wrongly convicted.* New York: Doubleday.

Feild, H. S., & Barnett, N. J. (1978). Simulated jury trials: Students vs. "real" people as jurors. *Journal of Social Psychology, 104,* 287–293.

Fiske, S. T., Kenny, D. A., & Taylor, S. E. (1982). Structural models for the mediation of salience effects on attribution. *Journal of Experimental Social Psychology, 18,* 105–127.

Fletcher, G. J. O., Danilovics, P., Fernandez, G., Peterson, D., & Reeder, G. D. (1986). Attributional complexity: An individual differences measure. *Journal of Personality and Social Psychology, 51,* 875–884.

Funder, D. C. (1982). On the accuracy of dispositional vs. situational attributions. *Social Cognition, 1,* 205–222.

Funder, D. C. (1987). Errors and mistakes: Evaluating the accuracy of social judgment. *Psychological Bulletin, 101,* 75–90.

Geller, W. A. (1992). *Police videotaping of suspect interrogations and confessions: A preliminary examination of issues and practices* (A report to the National Institute of Justice). Washington, DC: U.S. Department of Justice.

Gordon, R. A., Rozelle, R. M., & Baxter, J. C. (1988). The effect of applicant age, job level, and accountability on the evaluation of job applicants. *Organizational Behavior and Human Decision Processes, 41,* 20–33.

Grano, J. D. (1993). *Confessions, truth, and the law.* Ann Arbor: University of Michigan Press.

Gudjonsson, G. (1992). *The psychology of interrogations, confessions and testimony.* Chichester, England: Wiley.

Guthrie, C., Rachlinski, J. J., & Wistrich, A. J. (2002). Judging by heuristic: Cognitive illusions in judicial decision making. *Judicature, 86,* 44–50.

Harvey, J. H., Town, J. P., & Yarkin, K. L. (1981). How fundamental is the "fundamental attribution error"? *Journal of Personality and Social Psychology, 43,* 345–346.

Horowitz, I. A., & Willging, T. E. (1984). *The psychology of law: Integrations and applications.* Boston: Little, Brown.

Johnson, G. (1997). False confessions and fundamental fairness: The need for electronic recording of custodial interrogations. *Boston University Public Interest Law Journal, 6,* 719–751.

Jones, E. E. (1979). The rocky road from acts to dispositions. *American Psychologist, 34,* 107–117.

Jussim, L. (1991). Social perception and social reality: A reflection-construction model. *Psychological Review, 98,* 54–73.

Kamisar, Y. (1995). On the "fruits" of *Miranda* violations, coerced confessions, and compelled testimony. *Michigan Law Review, 93,* 929–1010.

Kamisar, Y., LaFave, W., & Israel, J. (1994). *Modern criminal procedure* (8th ed.). St. Paul, MN: West.

Kaplan, M. F., & Miller, L. E. (1978). Reducing the effects of juror bias. *Journal of Personality and Social Psychology, 36,* 1443–1455.

Kassin, S. M. (1997). The psychology of confession evidence. *American Psychologist, 52,* 221–233.

Kassin, S. M., & Kiechel, K. L. (1996). The social psychology of false confessions: Compliance, internalization, and confabulation. *Psychological Science, 7,* 125–128.

Kassin, S. M., & McNall, K. (1991). Police interrogations and confessions. *Law and Human Behavior, 15,* 231–251.

Kassin, S. M., & Sukel, H. (1997). Coerced confessions and the jury: An experimental test of the "harmless error" rule. *Law and Human Behavior, 21,* 27–46.

Kassin, S. M., & Wrightsman, L. S. (1979). On the requirements of proof: The timing of judicial instruction and mock juror verdicts. *Journal of Personality and Social Psychology, 37,* 1877–1887.

Kassin, S. M., & Wrightsman, L. S. (1980). Prior confessions and mock juror verdicts. *Journal of Applied Social Psychology, 10,* 133–146.

Kassin, S. M., & Wrightsman, L. S. (1981). Coerced confessions, judicial instruction, and mock juror verdicts. *Journal of Applied Social Psychology, 11,* 489–506.

Kassin, S. M., & Wrightsman, L. S. (1985). Confession evidence. In S. Kassin & L. Wrightsman (Eds.), *The psychology of evidence and trial procedure.* Beverly Hills, CA: Sage.

Kerr, N. L. (1978). Severity of prescribed penalty and mock jurors' verdicts. *Journal of Personality and Social Psychology, 36,* 1431–1442.

Konecni, V. J., & Ebbeson, E. B. (1979). External validity of research in legal psychology. *Law and Human Behavior, 3,* 39–70.

Kruglanski, A. W., & Ajzen I. (1983). Bias and error in human judgment. *European Journal of Social Psychology, 13,* 1–44.

Lassiter, G. D. (2002). Illusory causation in the courtroom. *Current Directions in Psychological Science, 11,* 204–208.

Lassiter, G. D., Beers, M. J., Geers, A. L., Handley, I. M., Munhall, P. J., & Weiland, P. E. (2002). Further evidence for a robust point-of-view bias in videotaped confessions. *Current Psychology, 21,* 265–288.

Lassiter, G. D., Beers, M. J., Geers, A. L., & Munhall, P. J. (2003). [Which camera perspective leads to more accurate evaluations of videotaped confessions?]. Unpublished raw data.

Lassiter, G. D., & Clark, J. K. (2003). [Observers' ability to differentiate true from false confessions as a function of presentation format.]. Unpublished raw data.

Lassiter, G. D., & Diamond, S. S. (2003). [Are judges also affected by the camera perspective bias in videotaped confessions?]. Unpublished raw data.

Lassiter, G. D., Geers, A. L., Handley, I. M., Weiland, P. E., & Munhall, P. J. (2002). Videotaped interrogations and confessions: A simple change in camera perspective alters verdicts in simulated trials. *Journal of Applied Psychology, 87,* 867–874.

Lassiter, G. D., Geers, A. L., Munhall, P. J., Handley, I. M., & Beers, M. J. (2001). Videotaped confessions: Is guilt in the eye of the camera? In M. P. Zanna (Ed.), *Advances in experimental social psychology,* (Vol. 33, pp. 189–254). New York: Academic Press.

Lassiter, G. D., Geers, A. L., Munhall, P. J., Ploutz-Snyder, R. J., & Breitenbecher, D. L. (2002). Illusory causation: Why it occurs. *Psychological Science, 13,* 299–305.

Lassiter, G. D., & Irvine, A. A. (1986). Videotaped confessions: The impact of camera point of view on judgments of coercion. *Journal of Applied Social Psychology, 16,* 268–276.

Lassiter, G. D., Munhall, P. J., Berger, I. P., Weiland, P. E., & Handley, I. M., & Geers, A. L. (2003). *Attributional complexity and the camera perspective bias in videotaped confessions.* Manuscript submitted for publication.

Lassiter, G. D., Munhall, P. J., Geers, A. L., Weiland, P. E., & Handley, I. M. (2001). Accountability and the camera perspective bias in videotaped confessions. *Analyses of Social Issues and Public Policy, 1,* 53–70.

Lassiter, G. D., Ratcliff, J. J., Ware, L., & Irvin, C. (2003). [Does the camera perspective bias manifest with real confession evidence?]. Unpublished raw data.

Lassiter, G. D., Slaw, R. D., Briggs, M. A., & Scanlan, C. R. (1992). The potential for bias in videotaped confessions. *Journal of Applied Social Psychology, 22,* 1838–1851.

Lego v. Twomey, 404 U. S. 477 (1972).

Leo, R. A. (1996). The impact of Miranda revisited. *The Journal of Criminal Law and Criminology, 86,* 621–692.

Leo, R. A., & Ofshe, R. J. (1998). The consequences of false confessions: Deprivations of liberty and miscarriages of justice in the age of psychological interrogation. *The Journal of Criminal Law and Criminology, 88,* 429–496.

MacCoun, R. J. (1989). Experimental research on jury decision-making. *Science, 244,* 1046–1050.

Mathes, W. C., & DeVitt, E. J. (1965). *Federal jury practice and instructions.* St. Paul, MN: West Publishing.

McArthur, L. Z. (1980). Illusory causation and illusory correlation: Two epistemological accounts. *Personality and Social Psychology Bulletin, 6,* 507–519.

McArthur, L. Z. (1981). What grabs you? The role of attention in impression formation and causal attribution. In E. T. Higgins, C. P. Herman, & M. P. Zanna (Eds.), *Social cognition: The Ontario symposium* (Vol. 1, pp. 201–241). Hillsdale, NJ: Erlbaum.

Newtson, D., Rindner, R. J., Miller, R., & LaCross (1978). Effects of availability of feature changes on behavior segmentation. *Journal of Experimental Social Psychology, 14,* 379–388.

Petty, R. E., & Cacioppo, J. T. (1986). The Elaboration Likelihood Model of persuasion. In L. Berkowitz (Ed.), *Advances in experimental social psychology* (Vol. 19, pp. 123–205). New York: Academic Press.

Ross, L. (1977). The intuitive psychologist and his shortcomings: Distortions in the attribution process. In L. Berkowitz (Ed.), *Advances in experimental social psychology* (Vol. 10, pp. 174–220). New York: Academic Press.

Siegel-Jacobs, K., & Yates, J. F. (1996). Effects of procedural and outcome accountability on judgment quality. *Organizational Behavior and Human Decision Processes, 65,* 1–17.

Simonson, I., & Nye, P. (1992). The effect of accountability on susceptibility to decision errors. *Organizational Behavior and Human Decision Processes, 51,* 416–446.

Smith, E. R., & Miller, F. D. (1979). Salience and the cognitive mediation of attribution. *Journal of Personality and Social Psychology, 37,* 2240–2252.

Storms, M. D. (1973). Videotape and the attribution process: Reversing actors' and observers' points of view. *Journal of Personality and Social Psychology, 27,* 165–175.

Taylor, S. E., & Fiske, S. T. (1975). Point of view and perceptions of causality. *Journal of Personality and Social Psychology, 32,* 439–445.

Taylor, S. E., & Fiske, S. T. (1978). Salience, attention, and attribution: Top of the head phenomena. In L. Berkowitz (Ed.), *Advances in experimental social psychology* (Vol. 11, pp. 249–288). New York: Academic Press.

Tetlock, P. E. (1985). Accountability: A social check on the fundamental attribution error. *Social Psychology Quarterly, 48,* 227–236.

Thompson, L. (1995). They saw a negotiation: Partisanship and involvement. *Journal of Personality and Social Psychology, 68,* 839–853.

Visher, C. A. (1987). Juror decision making: The importance of evidence. *Law and Human Behavior, 11,* 1–17.

Wells, G. L. (1980). Asymmetric attributions for compliance: Reward vs. punishment. *Journal of Experimental Social Psychology, 16,* 47–60.

Wilson, T. D., & Brekke, N. (1994). Mental contamination and mental correction: Unwanted influences on judgments and evaluations. *Psychological Bulletin, 116,* 117–142.

Zebrowitz, L. A. (1990). *Social perception.* Pacific Grove, CA: Brooks/Cole.

The Psychology of Entrapment

VANESSA A. EDKINS AND LAWRENCE S. WRIGHTSMAN

When people think of "entrapment" generally what comes to mind is an undercover police officer posing as a prostitute or a drug dealer in order to catch criminals. The fact of the matter is that claims of entrapment take on many forms, the above being some of them. The police sting operations that lead to the defense of entrapment can also be complicated and intricate schemes involving obscene amounts of money, or a bribe with the undertone of a threat. While the former types of operations can be beneficial in helping to stop so-called "victimless" crimes ("Entrapment: From Sorrells,"1993), the latter may be an example of law enforcement officials overstepping their boundaries.

TWO ENTRAPMENT CASES WITH DIFFERENT OUTCOMES

KEITH JACOBSON

In February, 1984, Keith Jacobson, a 56-year-old, unmarried Nebraska farmer, ordered two magazines through the mail from an adult bookstore. This seemingly innocent occurrence caught the attention of the United States government and eventually led to a criminal conviction of Jacobson and an appeal to the United States Supreme Court. Within three months after Jacobson had ordered his magazines, Congress, in May 1984, passed a Child

VANESSA A. EDKINS • Department of Psychology, University of Kansas, Lawrence, Kansas 66045 (E-mail: vedkins@ku.edu).   LAWRENCE S. WRIGHTSMAN • Department of Psychology, University of Kansas, Lawrence, Kansas 66045 (E-mail: wrights@ku.edu).

Protection Act, which made criminal the receipt of child pornography through the mail (specifically, the knowing receipt through the mail of a "visual depiction [that] involves the use of a minor engaging in sexually explicit conduct." The magazines (titled "Bare Boys I" and "Bare Boys II") that Jacobson ordered from a California bookstore contained depictions of nude preteen boys. The young men depicted in the magazines were not engaged in sexual activity, and at the time of his order, Jacobson broke no Nebraska or federal law (Nebraska had no such law until 1988). In fact, when questioned about the contents of the magazines, Jacobson reported that he had expected to receive photographs of young men 18 years or older, from what he thought was a "nudist type publication" with many of the photographs in a rural or outdoors setting. He claimed that he didn't see any sexual connotations in the photos.

However, because of his mail order, Jacobson became the object of an undercover operation by the federal postal authorities. In the very month that the Child Protection Act had been passed, postal inspectors found Jacobson's name on the mailing list of the bookstore that had mailed him the two magazines. Over the next two years, the government, through the use of five fictitious organizations and a bogus pen pal, aggressively provided a temptation for Jacobson to break the new law and order child pornography—he was sent nine mailings over a period of 26 months.

A Chronology of Contacts

January 1985: Jacobson receives a letter and a membership application from a fictitious organization, the American Hedonist Society. The goals of this organization supposedly included a belief in "the right to seek pleasure without restrictions being placed on us by outdated puritan morality" (*Jacobson v. United States*, 1992, p. 544). Jacobson enrolled in the organization and returned a sexual attitude questionnaire that asked him to rate on a scale of one to four his enjoyment of various sexual materials. He rated "preteen sex" as a two but indicated that he was opposed to pedophilia.

May 1986: Jacobson receives a solicitation from a fictitious research company, "Midlands Data Research," seeking a response from those who "believe in the joys of sex and a complete awareness of those lusty and youthful lads and lasses of the neophite [sic] age" (*Jacobson v. United States*, 1992, p. 544). Jacobson responded: "Please feel free to send me more information, I am interested in teenage sexuality. Please keep my name confidential" (p. 544).

Later in 1986: A letter was sent from yet another fictitious organization, "Heartland Institute for a New Tomorrow" (HINT), that enclosed another survey of sexual preferences, to which Jacobson replied.

A follow up letter from HINT portrayed itself as a lobbying organization that sought to eliminate any legal definition of the age of consent. The letter also provided Jacobson with a computer matching of pals who shared his interests. Jacobson did not initiate correspondence with any of them.

A letter from "Carl Long" expressed similar interests to those of Jacobson; he replied indicating his interest in "male-male items" and in a second letter, wrote "As far as my likes are concerned, I like good looking young guys (in their late teens or early 20s) doing their thing together" (p. 545). He made no reference to child pornography. After writing two letters Jacobson discontinues the correspondence.

March 1987: A second governmental agency, the Customs Service, gets involved, using the name of a fictitious Canadian company called "Produit Outaouais." Jacobson is sent a brochure advertising photographs of young boys engaging in sex. Jacobson places an order that was never filled.

About this time, the Postal Service again contacts Jacobson, this time as the "Far Eastern Trading Company Ltd." Its letter said: "[We] have devised a method of getting these to you without prying eyes of U. S. Customs seizing your mail . . . After consultations with American solicitors, we have been advised that once we have posted our material through your system, it cannot be opened for any inspection without authorization of a judge" (pp. 546–547). Jacobson responded, signing an affirmation that he was "not a law enforcement officer or agent of the U. S. Government acting in an undercover capacity for the purposes of entrapping Far Eastern Trading Company" (p. 547).

Upon Jacobson's request, this bogus company sent him a catalogue, from which he ordered a pornographic magazine titled "Boys Who Love Boys," that depicted young boys engaged in various sexual activities. Upon delivery, Jacobson was arrested on September 24, 1987. A search of his house found the "Bare Boys" magazines and the materials the government had sent him, but no other materials that had any relationship to child pornography.

At his trial, Jacobson claimed that he had been induced by the government and that, without its instigation, he would not have ordered any child pornography. His claim of entrapment led to an instruction to the jury to decide if, in fact, he did not have "any intent or disposition to commit the crime charged and was induced or persuaded by the law enforcement officers . . . to commit the crime" (p. 548, Footnote 1). The government had the burden of proving beyond a reasonable doubt that Jacobson was not entrapped. However, he was convicted, and a divided Court of Appeals for the Eighth Circuit, sitting *en banc*, upheld his conviction.

John Z. DeLorean

Twenty-five years ago, John Z. DeLorean was wellknown as the manufacturer of the sleek, gull-winged sports car that bore his name, but his

auto company had since become bankrupt and he was in desperate financial trouble. In July, 1984, he was arrested and went to trial for conspiracy to sell $24 million of Columbian cocaine. Television cameras had even
recorded him talking to undercover agents about the sale, in the presence
of 55 pounds of cocaine, and the government at the trial portrayed him
as a man predisposed to commit crimes because of his urgent need to save
his company from ruin. Although DeLorean claimed that he had been
entrapped (he reported he felt his life was in danger if he did not comply), experts expected him to be convicted. He was tried in federal court,
where the judge's instructions used a subjective definition of entrapment
(to be described in the next section) that most observers believe favors
the prosecution.

In contrast to Keith Jacobson, John DeLorean was found not guilty
(on all eight counts). Jurors, questioned after their verdict was announced,
gave several reasons for their decision to acquit DeLorean (Brill, 1989). Some
said the government had not proved its case or met, in the words of one
juror, its "hellacious burden of proof"; others said that the undercover investigation had sometimes slipped over the line into entrapment. "Without
the entrapment," said one man on the jury, "there would have been a hung
jury" (quoted by Lindsey, 1984, p. A1). One law review article (O'Neill,
1985) even concluded "the jury either misunderstood or misapplied [the
subjective] instruction" (p. 380).

It does seem that the jurors' concerns about the government's heavy-
handed actions were justified. For example, an FBI agent who had imper-
sonated a dishonest banker admitted to altering and "rewriting" some of
his investigative notes. Under cross-examination this same agent admitted
that no evidence supported his earlier claim that DeLorean had previously
been "involved in large-scale narcotics transactions" (quoted by Lindsey,
1984, p. B6). Another government agent, posing as a drug dealer, had back-
dated some forms. More important, the government's key witness, James
Timothy Hoffman, was quoted in court testimony as having promised government officials: "I am going to get John DeLorean for you guys." Prior
to the trial, Hoffman had demanded a tenth of any of DeLorean's assets
confiscated after his anticipated conviction.

DeLorean's guilt or innocence became largely irrelevant for the jurors,
and several legal experts have observed that the jury used a different definition of entrapment from the one given to them in the instructions from
the judge. The jury focused on the morality—or lack of same—of the government's actions. Harvard law professor Alan Dershowitz was quoted as
saying "There's not a court or judge in the country that would have acquitted DeLorean on the basis of the evidence. DeLorean's guilt or innocence
played no role in this. All the attention was focused on the government,
and he was presented as the victim" (quoted in Margolick, 1984, p. B6).

However, it is important to realize that "predisposition"—which is what DeLorean's jury was instructed to look at—can be an ambiguous category; does it refer to long-existing behaviors or more recent, urgent ones? Traditionally, evidence of predisposition consists of facts about the defendant's criminal record and views of his or her reputation and character. Kassin (1985) has concluded: "The case against DeLorean contained little along those lines. Instead, the jury was confronted with more transient, situation-specific facts concerning his state of financial need and, more directly, his overt behavior vis-à-vis the principals of the investigation. . . . Confronted with a causally ambiguous event in which the defendant capitulated under high levels of pressure, the jury quite rationally could not infer beyond a reasonable doubt that he was, on his own, *predisposed*" (pp. 12–13).

The two cases differ in significant ways, but the irony is striking. John DeLorean was acquitted despite the fact that he was apparently willing to participate in an illegal activity and furthermore, some would agree that he required little inducement to do it. In contrast, Keith Jacobson, who succumbed only after repeated incentives and showed no predisposition to otherwise act illegally, was convicted.

THE NATURE OF ENTRAPMENT AS A DEFENSE

As Slobogin (1998) notes, the greatest potential for entrapment happens when law-enforcement officials engage in undercover, or covert, activities. In their zeal to catch criminals, do the police go overboard and sometimes encourage criminal activity in order to stifle it? Should sting operations be based on the words of informants who, themselves, have criminal records? More basically, we might ask, as Katz (1987) does: "When a sting operation is used to bring to the surface a personal weakness that might never have surfaced otherwise, are we really punishing the criminal act or the criminal disposition?" (p. 4).

As Marx (1988) has observed, the use of deception as instigation to social control traces back to ancient times: "The Bible is filled with examples—Eve and the serpent, God testing Abraham and Job, and Judas informing on Jesus" (p. 17). "Sting" operations by the police have been around for more than 200 years. Francois Vidocq, head of an investigation unit within the Paris police force in the first two decades of the 1800s, initiated the efforts to have police agents "become directly, if surreptitiously, involved in the criminal world" (Marx, 1988, p. 18) by contriving crime opportunities, using informers, and having police impersonate criminals.

The decade of the 1980s brought the attention of the public, at least temporarily, to the use of entrapment as a criminal defense, as the "stings" on a group of Chicago judges ("Operation Greylord") and Washington Mayor Marion Barry became front-page news. These operations typically used paid informants and electronic surveillance. Were they too contrived and unjustifiably heavy-handed? Some defendants claimed so. Just like the defense of self-defense or the insanity defense, the defendant acknowledges committing the act but claims that he or she should be found "not guilty" because of the special circumstances surrounding the act. In the late 1970s—in what later came to be called "Abscam"—the FBI contrived opportunities to tempt United States senators, members of the House of Representatives, and municipal officials to accept bribes offered by the personal representatives of several fictitious Arabian sheiks—actually FBI agents and Melvin Weinberg, an experienced con man who had been convicted of mail fraud. The "sheiks" had "hundreds of millions of dollars" and were willing to provide undercover money for special favors, such as waving U. S. residence requirements, in order to establish businesses in the United States. The FBI claimed that it chose only those officials who were perceived to be receptive to bribes. A few of the officials who were approached refused (these included one representative, Edward Patton of New Jersey, and one senator, Larry Pressler of South Dakota), but every one of those sixteen who succumbed was found guilty and sentenced to prison. Harrison Williams, highly regarded before this as a courtly, aristocratic senator, spent three years in prison. Where entrapment had been offered as a defense, the jury rejected it.

But disparities in the legal system emerged when the convicted officials appealed. Different judges ruled in inconsistent ways, although most rejected the appeals. For example, the judge in the trial of several members of Congress, George Pratt, told the defendants that they "could simply have said 'no' to the offer" (quoted by Gershman, 1982, p. 1575). This judge refused to consider that any offer could be too compelling, saying, "no matter how much money is offered to a government official as a bribe or gratuity, he should be punished if he accepts" (quoted in Gershman, 1982, p. 1576). With a different judge, Congressman Richard Kelly fared better. (According to Thomas Puccio's account [1995], Kelly had been videotaped by the FBI stuffing scads of bills into his pockets.) Judge William Bryant of the District of Columbia set aside Kelly's conviction. Although recognizing the need for covert investigations to discover crimes, this judge was unwilling to allow the government to pursue that goal without restraints. He believed that the federal government had unleashed Abscam on Kelly without "the remotest suspicion" of prior, ongoing, or imminent criminal activity on his part. In fact, Judge Bryant labeled Abscam "governmental manufacture of crime" and said its testing should have ended when Congressman Kelly rejected the bribe offer the first time he was approached. He noted that, the "sheiks," in a return visit to Kelly, had dramatically spread $25,000 in $100 bills on the desk in front of him, and threatened him that if he didn't help them, they would make their investments in another congressional district (Katz, 1987).

Compared with these judicial reactions, the treatment of two Philadelphia municipal officials, Harry Jannotti and George Schwartz, was equally inconsistent but in a different way. After a jury found them guilty, Judge John Fullam set aside their convictions, expressing concerns like those of Judge Bryant. In this particular sting, the government agents had insisted to the Philadelphia officials that a hotel project would be dropped unless Jannotti and Schwartz accepted the sheik's gesture. The judge ruled that no factual evidence had been presented that showed the defendants were predisposed to accept bribes.

But the Court of Appeals for the Third Circuit reversed Judge Fullam's ruling and reinstated the jury's verdicts. This court ruled that the jury properly could have found that acceptance of money by the defendants, even if they did not originate the scheme, showed predisposition. Two of the circuit court judges strongly disagreed with the majority opinion and called the prosecutions "classic models of the type of entrapment that our society emphatically condemns."(as cited in Wrightsman, Nietzel, & Fortune, 1994, p. 190). They even compared the United States government to the Gestapo of Nazi Germany.

ONE PROBLEM: TWO DEFINITIONS OF ENTRAPMENT

Police sting operations are so commonplace that one can be sure errors are sometimes made. Is there a role for psychologists concerned with improving the operation of the criminal justice system? Psychologists have done a service to the public by highlighting the causes of mistaken identifications by eyewitnesses leading innocent people to be sent to prison, and thanks to the efforts of Gary Wells and his colleagues, the Department of Justice has produced a set of guidelines for law-enforcement officials to use in questioning crime eyewitnesses. More recently, the public has become aware of the effects of heavy-handed police interrogations on the inducement of confessions from innocent suspects, and because of the efforts of many of the contributors to this volume and others, the movement toward a universal requirement to videotape interrogations is building. But the public seems not to be concerned about the possible negative effects of police undercover operations; there is no "poster child" to dramatize the problem, not Keith Jacobson (whose conviction was overturned by the Supreme Court) and certainly not John DeLorean.

The defense of entrapment is worthy of psychological study for several reasons beyond the fact that police frequently engage in sting operations.

One is that currently two different legal definitions of entrapment are used in the various states and the federal government, and each places the emphasis on an entirely different aspect. Courts agree that at the very minimum, a causal link must exist between the solicitation and the crime, for the defense of entrapment to be accepted. But jurors are often faced with a legal definition that may be quite different from their own standards of justice and fairness, which may concentrate on the question of whether the government went "too far" in inducing crime. In fact, the first formal recognition of entrapment as a defense by the Supreme Court reflects this concern. The case of *Sorrells v. United States* (1932) was decided in the midst of the Prohibition Era. Katz describes the facts of the case as follows:

> One Sunday in July 1930 the defendant, Sorrells, who lived near a small town in North Carolina, received a visit from several of his friends. They brought with them a stranger named Martin, who introduced himself as a furniture dealer from Charlotte, just passing through town. When Sorrells discovered to his great pleasure that he and Martin shared a common ground—both having served in the 30th Division of the American Expeditionary Forces during World War I—the two became fast friends. Martin, Sorrells, and another friend of Sorrells's who had also served in the 30th Division then began to reminisce about their war experiences. After a little while, Martin asked Sorrells for some liquor. Sorrells apologized because he didn't have any. Some more time passed and the conversation was taking an increasingly nostalgic turn. Martin again asked Sorrells for some liquor. He explained that he was anxious to buy a half-gallon for a friend back home. Sorrells replied that he "did not fool with whiskey." As time went on Martin reiterated his request for liquor some six or seven times. Finally, Sorrells got up, excused himself for about twenty minutes, and returned with the requested half-gallon. Martin gratefully accepted and paid him five dollars. Alas, Martin turned out to be a prohibition agent posing as a tourist. Sorrells was arrested and prosecuted for the illegal sale of liquor. (Katz, 1987, p. 155)

The Supreme Court overturned Sorrells's conviction, concluding that the defendant's act "was instigated by the prohibition agent, that it was a creature of his purpose, that the defendant had no previous disposition to commit it but was an industrious law-abiding citizen, and that the agent lured the defendant, otherwise innocent, to its commission by repeated and persistent solicitation in which he succeeded by taking advantage of the sentiment aroused by reminiscences of their experiences as companions in arms in the World War" (*Sorrells v. United States,* 1932, pp. 440–441). But at the same time, this decision upheld the government's right to use undercover agents to enforce the law and the belief that the ready willingness of a suspect to commit a crime demonstrates his or her predisposition. The *Sorrells* decision contains a number of reasons why entrapment may be accepted as a defense; as governmental institutions began to formulate their laws, different ones chose particular aspects to use in their definition.

THE OBJECTIVE DEFINITION OF ENTRAPMENT

The minority of states uses the "objective test" to define entrapment. At present, 13 states use this definition (Marcus, 1989). It focuses entirely on the propriety of investigative methods, maintaining that entrapment occurs when the conduct of law enforcement officials is compelling enough to instigate a criminal act, even by an individual who is not otherwise ready and willing to commit it. Improper inducements include persistent harassment, appeals to sympathy, or offers of great material value (Park, 1976). The number of inducements to the suspect, as well as their attractiveness, is crucial. Within this framework the law offers that the determinative question may be the probable effect of a solicitation on the hypothetical "reasonable person." (That is, was the solicitation so overwhelming that it would have tempted other, non-predisposed citizens?) For example, let us say that a person legally purchased a ticket to the Super Bowl that cost $400. The Super Bowl is held in a state in which ticket scalping is illegal. The morning of the game the person is offered $10,000 for the ticket. Even though the person had fully intended to attend the game, he or she agrees to sell the ticket, and is immediately arrested by the undercover ticket buyer. Note that under the objective test, the person's predisposition is not an issue; if there is no indication of coercion from law-enforcement officials, then the claim of entrapment is rejected.

THE SUBJECTIVE DEFINITION OF ENTRAPMENT

In contrast, the "subjective test" is considered the majority view, because it is the law in most states and the federal government. Here the emphasis is on the defendant's state of mind rather on actions by law enforcement. If the defendant was behaviorally predisposed—that is, ready and willing—then the police are said merely to have afforded the opportunity to commit the offense. What procedure the authorities use is irrelevant. For example, in most large cities, a certain section (perhaps a particular city block) is known to be the place where prostitutes hang out. If a "John" responds to an enticement by an undercover police officer posing as a prostitute, his defense of entrapment is not likely to survive the government's argument that he was behaviorally predisposed by the very fact that he chose to come to that specific location.

Thus within this framework, the jury is responsible for evaluating the credibility of entrapment as a defense, and if the defendant was not predisposed the fact finders should conclude that entrapment was present, and the defendant should be found not guilty. In fact, in the federal courts (for example, the *Jacobson* trial), once the defense has raised the claim of entrapment, the government must disprove entrapment beyond a reasonable doubt.

A SECOND PROBLEM:
PUNISHMENT FOR ACTS OR FOR DISPOSITIONS?

A second psychologically intriguing aspect is that there is a fundamental incoherence in the entrapment doctrine that arises at the core of the defense. "Predisposition" is very difficult for jurors to assess, and "inducement" is never defined with respect to its limits. As Katz (1987) observes, the law punishes us for criminal acts, not for criminal dispositions. Entrapment loads the dice too heavily in the direction of punishing some of us for dispositions that may reside in many of us.

In regard to "predisposition," the prosecution often tries to demonstrate a prior criminal inclination on the defendant's part. This could include the defendant's bad reputation, past criminal conduct, or even rumored bad activities. In cases involving drug trafficking or prostitution, these procedures are often applicable, because such defendants often have criminal records. But politicians like Marion Barry and businessmen like John DeLorean usually do not. As noted earlier, Barry, former mayor of Washington, DC, was videotaped by the FBI using cocaine in a hotel room after being lured there by a female acquaintance.

But even when this procedure is applicable, it is still inconsistent with criminal law generally. Nowhere else does criminal law entitle a prosecutor to prove culpability (that is, show blame) for an act simply on the basis of the defendant's prior criminal acts. In the Federal Rules of Evidence, FRE 404 (b) states that prior crimes cannot be offered to prove the defendant was more likely to have committed the present crime. In fact, in contrast to usual restrictions, the jury is permitted to hear testimony about the defendant's character and background. Even worse, in the Abscam case involving the bribing of members of the U.S. Congress, the fact that the defendants accepted cash payments was found to constitute sufficient evidence that they had preexisting intentions to take a bribe. This is circular reasoning, with no independent demonstration of their predispositions. If a man shot another individual in self-defense would that make the shooter predisposed to murder? The suggestion is absurd.

In addition, Abscam probably stretched the concept of "inducement" to its psychological limits (Gershman, 1982). The "sheiks" met with officials as many as seven times before the bribe was accepted. Huge amounts were offered. Senator Harrison Williams was promised $170 million to finance his mining venture. A total of $150 million was offered Philadelphia city officials. Ordinarily, one would expect that the inducements tendered by the government should match, but not radically exceed, those that the target person had been exposed to in his or her previous criminal acts. When offers are so incredibly large, they prevent a fair assessment of the presence of predisposition. Similarly, inducements can be *too* persistent; in the case of Keith Jacobson, which introduced this paper, the United States Supreme Court (in *Jacobson v. United States*, 1992) overturned his conviction because of the heavy-handed efforts of the postal authorities and a lack of evidence supporting the claim that Jacobson was predisposed to commit the crime.

ANOTHER PROBLEM: JURORS' REACTION TO THE ENTRAPMENT DEFENSE

A third problem stems from juries' reactions to cases involving police undercover operations that lead to an arrest and then to a claim of entrapment. How do average citizens react to the defense of entrapment? First, they have difficulty understanding the judge's instructions about the definition of entrapment, especially when the objective definition is used (Borgida & Park, 1988). Second, if the subjective definition is used, and the defendant has a prior conviction, this admission heightens the likelihood of a guilty verdict (Borgida & Park, 1988). In general, laypersons react harshly to an entrapment claim. Jurors tend to reason, "He got caught, so he must be guilty," and they have a hard time believing that otherwise honest and intelligent people could be so easily induced into criminal behavior. But not always; the acquittal of John DeLorean is not an anomaly; one of the Chicago judges in the Operation Greylord sting was acquitted of bribery charges just ten days before DeLorean's verdict, and in 1983 the government failed to persuade a jury to convict United States District Judge Alcee Hastings of conspiracy to take a bribe from an undercover agent who posed as a criminal defendant.

RESEARCH ON ENTRAPMENT

As mentioned earlier, law-enforcement officials have used sting operations for several hundred years, and the frequency and breadth of undercover activities have made them commonplace. Recently, authorities have used the Internet to identify child molesters. In fact, in November of 2002 a man who had written two books on stupidity was arrested for apparently trying to arrange sex with a 15-year-old girl over the Internet (Associated Press, 2002). The "girl" turned out to be an undercover male detective, and the 61-year-old author of *The Story of Stupidity* and *Understanding Stupidity* was taken into custody at Pompano Beach, Florida.

Despite the huge number of undercover operations and the frequent use of entrapment as a defense, the phenomenon has been almost completely ignored by research psychologists; the number of published empirical studies can literally be counted on one hand. To our knowledge, only two studies have manipulated the main components of the two definitions (solicitation and predisposition) in a controlled experiment; one was a convention paper by Kassin (1985), the other an apparently unpublished Ph.D. dissertation by Lewis (1997). Our goal was to implement a program of research that partially rectified this virtual vacuum. First, we were struck by the controversial nature of the use of sting operations and sought to determine the structure of attitudes about undercover operations and the use of entrapment. Second, we sought to determine what influenced jurors' decisions when faced with a case in which the police claimed a criminal offense and the defendant claimed entrapment. Do attitudes about sting operations affect verdicts? Are the central aspects of the two definitions (predisposition in the case of the subjective definition, and police coercion in the case of the objective definition) influential in jury verdicts? Or, rather than paying attention to the judge's instructions, do jurors use their own "common sense" definitions of fairness when forming verdicts? We were also interested in whether jurors hold a higher standard for public officials who respond to sting operations, compared to private parties.

THE MEASUREMENT OF ATTITUDES

Our first goal was to determine the nature of respondents' attitudes toward undercover activities by law enforcement officials and the entrapment defense. Butler and Wrightsman (2002) constructed a 30-item Likert-type attitude scale (7-point) and administered it to 254 respondents from the introductory-psychology subject pool. To our knowledge, this is the first comprehensive attitude scale measuring reactions to entrapment.

The results of the factor analysis are presented in Table 1. Three factors emerged: Factor 1 reflects an explicit position supporting the police; Factor 2 reflects concerns for the due process of defendants, and Factor 3 is in the same direction as Factor 1, but its emphasis is on giving police unlimited power to catch criminals. Basically, it can be said that persons who score high on Factor 1 endorse the use of sting operations because their desire is to catch criminals, while persons who score high on Factor 2 are concerned about the pressures that may cause otherwise innocent persons to commit criminal acts.

The number of respondents in the factor analysis by Butler and Wrightsman (2000) was somewhat less than the recommended ratio of 10 respondents for each item. Therefore, DeGarmo (2003) administered the scale to a large sample of students in introductory psychology, permitting separate factor analyses of male and female respondents, with each sample having an N meeting the desired 10-to-1 ratio. She also did an analysis combining the male and female pools; the numbers of respondents were as follows: 317 males and 299 females, for a total of 616 respondents.

TABLE 1. Results of the Factor Analysis by Butler and Wrightsman

Factor 1: Ends Justify the Means	Mean = –5.96, SD = 6.92, α = 0.7575

14. Senators and members of Congress have sworn an oath to uphold the law, so that it is all right for the FBI to tempt them, in order to identify lawbreakers. 0.593

28. In order to detect the commission of certain crimes, such as taking kickbacks or computer theft, it is necessary for law enforcement officials to use under-cover tactics 0.544

8. Use of informants (who pose as friends but actually work for the police) is allowable if that is what it takes to catch lawbreakers. 0.506

12. If police suspect a person of a history of lawbreaking but can't catch him/her at it, it is all right to create an opportunity for the person to commit a crime where he/she can be caught. 0.503

10. Posing as a young girl on an Internet chat room is acceptable behavior for the FBI when they are trying to catch sexual predators. 0.470

20. When undercover law enforcement officers try to encourage a person to commit a crime, all he or she has to do is refuse, to say "no." 0.458

6. It is acceptable for women police officers to pose as prostitutes in order to catch "johns." 0.446

Factor 2: The Innocent Can Succumb	Mean = 0.83, SD = 5.9, α = 0.7636

17. Sometimes inducements to break the law are so overwhelming that honest people succumb to the temptation 0.775

9. Sometimes the conduct of the police is so compelling that is causes a person not otherwise inclined to break the law. 0.605

18. It is very hard to induce basically honest people into breaking the law. –0.578

23. The use of police inducements loads the dice too heavily in the direction of punishing some of us for dispositions that may reside in most of us. 0.494

19. The use of police officers disguised as prostitutes or drug dealers causes otherwise law-abiding persons to commit criminal acts. 0.464

25. When a sting operation is used to bring to the surface a personal weakness that might never have surfaced otherwise, we are punishing a person for succumbing to his or her temptations, not for committing a criminal act. 0.394

Factor 3: Unlimited Power	Mean = 0.92, SD = 4.03, α = 0.7608

30. Police should be allowed to do whatever is necessary to catch those who are breaking the law. 0.766

22. The crime rate is so high that we should give the police the power to catch criminals, whatever it takes. 0.753

24. Society wants police to catch criminals, but there are too many restrictions that prevent police from sometimes reaching this goal. 0.505

TABLE 2. DeGarmo's Factor 1

	Males	Females	Combined
1. Police should never tempt a person to commit a crime.	.604	.704	.606
3. If a person was lured by the police into committing a crime, he or she should be found not guilty at trial.	.624	.451	.526
4. It is acceptable for the police to coax persons to perform self-incriminating behaviors.	.493	.656	.579
11. It is morally wrong for the police to encourage law breaking in order to catch criminals.	.683	.697	.676
12. If police suspect a person has a history of lawbreaking, but cannot catch him in the act, it is all right to create an opportunity for the person to commit a crime, in order to apprehend that person.	—	.490	.471
13. If I were in Congress, I would vote for a law that makes it illegal for police to induce lawbreaking.	.738	.661	.671
14. Senators and members of Congress have sworn an oath to uphold the law, and because of this, it is all right for the FBI to tempt them, in order to identify lawbreakers.	—	.530	.503
19. The use of police officers disguised as prostitutes or drug dealers causes otherwise law-abiding persons to commit criminal acts.	.410	—	—
21. Police have enough to do in solving actual crimes without tempting people to commit new crimes.	.613	.502	.597
23. The use of police inducement loads the dice too heavily in the direction of punishing some of us for natural dispositions that reside in most people.	.482	—	—
25. When a sting operation is used to bring to the surface a personal weakness that might never have surfaced otherwise, we are punishing a person for succumbing to his or her temptations, not for committing a criminal act.	.548	—	—
27. Police should never offer bribes to government officials in order to test their honesty.	—	.504	.546
29. I would never vote in favor of a law that makes it legal for police to induce lawbreaking.	.734	.487	.628

Each of DeGarmo's three factor analyses identified two clear factors; however, the second factor was not consistent between males and females. For the male sample, 10 items loaded above .40 on Factor 1; for the female sample seven of these 10 loaded above .40. But for the second factor, the factors for the two genders were quite different. See Tables 2 and 3.

TABLE 3. DeGarmo's Factor 2

	Males	Females	Combined
3. If a person was lured by the police into committing a crime, he or she should be found not guilty at trial.	—	.425	—
4. It is acceptable for the police to coax persons to perform self-incriminating behaviors.	.449	—	—
5. If police try to induce a person to commit a crime once, and he or she refuses, they should leave this person alone in the future.	—	—	.416
9. Sometimes the conduct of the police is so compelling that it causes a person, not otherwise so inclined, to break the law.	—	.688	.616
12. If police suspect a person has a history of lawbreaking, but cannot catch him in the act, it is all right to create an opportunity for the person to commit a crime, in order to apprehend that person.	.441	—	—
16. Anyone who gets caught committing a crime, regardless of the instigation, should be found guilty.	.631	—	—
17. Sometimes inducements to break the law are so overwhelming that honest people succumb to the temptation.	—	.754	.775
18. It is very hard to induce basically honest people into breaking the law.	—	—	.473
19. The use of police officers disguised as prostitutes or drug dealers causes otherwise law-abiding persons to commit criminal acts.	—	.512	.630
22. The crime rate is so high that we should give the police the power to catch criminals, whatever it takes.	.838	—	—
23. The use of police inducements loads the dice too heavily in the direction of punishing some of us for natural dispositions that reside in most people.	—	.680	.648
24. Society wants police to catch criminals, but these are too many restrictions that prevent police from sometimes reaching this goal.	.527	—	—
25. When a sting operation is used to bring to the surface a personal weakness that might never have surfaced otherwise, we are punishing a person for succumbing to his or her temptations, not for committing a criminal act.	—	.639	.595
30. Police should be allowed to do whatever is necessary to catch those who are breaking the law.	.796	—	—

TABLE 4. A Proposed Two-Dimensional Scale
to Measure Attitudes toward Entrapment

Dimension 1: Rejection of Coercion

1. If police try to induce a person to commit a crime once, and he or she refuses, they should leave this person alone in the future.

2. Sometimes the conduct of the police is so compelling that it causes a person, not otherwise so inclined, to break the law.

3. Sometimes inducements to break the law are so overwhelming that honest people succumb to the temptation.

4. It is very hard to induce basically honest people into breaking the law.

5. The use of police officers disguised as prostitutes or drug dealers causes otherwise law-abiding persons to commit criminal acts.

6. The use of police inducement loads the dice too heavily in the direction of punishing some of use for natural dispositions that reside in most people.

7. When a sting operation is used to bring to the surface a personal weakness that might never have surfaced otherwise, we are punishing a person for succumbing to his or her temptations, not for committing a criminal act.

Dimension 2: Acceptance of Police Tactics

1. It is acceptable for the police to coax persons to perform self-incriminating behaviors.

2. Use of informants (who pose as friends but actually work for the police) is allowable if that is what it takes to catch lawbreakers.

3. Posing as a young girl on an Internet chatroom is acceptable behavior for the FBI, when they are trying to catch sexual predators.

4. If police suspect a person has a history of lawbreaking, but cannot catch him in the act, it is all right to create an opportunity for the person to commit a crime, in order to apprehend that person.

5. Senators and members of Congress have sworn an oath to uphold the law, and because of this, it is all right for the FBI to tempt them, in order to identify lawbreakers.

6. The crime rate is so high that we should give the police the power to catch criminals, whatever it takes.

7. Society wants police to catch criminals, but there are too many restrictions that prevent police form sometimes reaching this goal.

8. Police should be allowed to do whatever is necessary to catch those who are breaking the law.

The factor structure for the combined sample resembled the factor structure for the female sample more than it did for the male sample. For Factor 1, 10 items loaded above .40 on the combined sample—the identical 10 that loaded on the female sample. Only seven of these loaded above .40 on the male sample, and that sample had 3 other items loading above .40.

While specific differences exist among the samples, there is consistency in the emergence of two salient factors, one being an endorsement of police activities and the other being a concern for the rights of suspects. Based on the data from these samples, we have proposed a two-dimensional scale, detailed in Table 4.

DETERMINANTS OF VERDICTS

Our second goal was to determine what influenced the verdicts of mock jurors in trials where the defendant claimed entrapment as a defense. We posited the following as possible determinants:

1. *The type of judicial instructions: subjective definition of entrapment versus objective definition.* Borgida and Park (1988) tested the effects of these instructions by varying them to mock jurors, who then watched a videotape of a trial. The mock jurors deliberated, returned a verdict, and completed a questionnaire that measured their understanding of the instructions and evidence. Borgida and Park found that jurors' comprehension of the principal features of the objective definition was deficient. The admission of a prior conviction had a significant effect on verdicts for those given the subjective definition but not for those given the objective definition, suggesting that the subjective instructions encourage jurors to use prior convictions as evidence of guilt in the present trial.

2. *Effects of solicitation.* As illustrated in the Jacobson case, several real-world sting operations have included repeated contacts between law-enforcement officials and suspected law-breakers. Initial rebuffs may lead to increased inducements to commit a crime. Do repeated inducements influence jurors' assessments of guilt?

3. *Predisposition of the suspect.* Law-enforcement officials may often defend their actions by noting that the recipients had either a criminal record or had rumors about their willingness to break the law. Previous research has shown the influence of a prior record; what is the effect if police have suspicions about a possible law-breaker?

4. *Status of the recipient of the undercover operation: public official versus private citizen.* Some sting operations have been directed against public officials—Abscam, of course, Operation Greylord, and a massive operation against county purchasing agents in the state of New York. In contrast, typical sting operations,

using police officers acting as prostitutes or drug dealers, or more recently, as provocative teen-age girls on the Internet, are aimed at private citizens. Given that public officials swear an oath to uphold the law, jurors may apply a higher standard to them and be more willing to find them guilty under ambiguous conditions.

EDKINS' FIRST STUDY

Edkins (2003) completed two studies that examined the effects of these factors on verdicts. In the first of Edkins' studies, 160 respondents (introductory psychology students) were given some information about entrapment and then either an objective or subjective definition.

WORDING OF INSTRUCTIONS FOR THE OBJECTIVE DEFINITION?

The objective definition was worded as follows:

For all of the following cases, the defendant pleaded "not guilty" because he felt he was a victim of entrapment. This means that the defendant felt that he was compelled to commit the crime because of the police or FBI agents' activities. The jurors in these cases were given the following instructions: You may rule not guilty on the basis of entrapment if a consensus is reached that law enforcement employed methods of persuasion that any individual would find impossible to reject, regardless of their predisposition to commit an offense. In other words, if you find that the defendant's illegal activities were directly caused by questionably ethical law enforcement tactics, then he is not guilty.

Use these instructions when evaluating the following cases.

WORDING OF INSTRUCTIONS FOR THE SUBJECTIVE DEFINITION

In contrast, the instructions reflecting the subjective definition were as follows:

For all the following cases, the defendant pleaded "not guilty" because he felt he was a victim of entrapment. This means that the defendant believes himself to be an otherwise innocent person who was compelled to commit a crime by the actions of the police or other law-enforcement officials. In each case, the jurors were given the following instructions by the judge: You may rule not guilty on the basis of entrapment if a consensus is reached that the defendant would not have been *predisposed* to commit the offense if not for the opportunity provided by law enforcement. In other words, if you find the defendant would not otherwise have been prone to committing the offense he is charged with, if not for the inducement of law enforcement, then he is not guilty.

Use these instructions when evaluating cases.

THE SCENARIOS

Participants then read eight scenarios, each involving an attempt by law enforcement to induce a crime; these were modifications of 11 descriptions of undercover operations used by Kassin (1985) in an unpublished convention paper. Kassin's scenarios involved three different crimes, prostitution, narcotics, and bribery of a public official. Edkins (2003) chose to limit the crimes to either bribery or narcotics and to counterbalance these with actions by either a private citizen or a public official. Four of her scenarios thus involved public officials (a member of the U. S. House of Representatives, a Senator, a fire inspector, and an assistant district attorney); the others involved private citizens. The crime that was encouraged ranged from taking a bribe to the transport or purchase of narcotics (for a friend, in one scenario, and for oneself in another). Half of the scenarios described the targeted person as being chosen at random or free of previous crimes; the other half of the scenarios involved someone who had a prior conviction or was, according to supposition, an as-yet-unconvicted lawbreaker. As a third variation, half of the scenarios indicated that the suspected person complied upon first contact; in the other half, the targeted person initially refused to do what the police sought him to do, and only complied after the police approached him with inducements on several occasions. These scenarios were generally two paragraphs long and were presented to the respondents in random order. After reading each, participants responded to six questions about that particular case, dealing with entrapment, solicitation, predisposition, and their verdict.

The following scenario reflects a public official who was chosen at random (what in this study is called Low Predisposition) and who agreed to comply upon initial contact (Low Solicitation):

> Congressman Richard Kelley was one of the politicians chosen by a random sampling of high government officials during a recent FBI investigation of bribe taking. Congressman Kelley had not been previously implicated in any illegal matters.
>
> The agents initially approached the Congressman with an offer of $25,000 in return for some insubstantial matters dealing with the immigration office. The agent communicated to Congressmen Kelley that only a minor misplacing of documents would need to occur. Congressman Kelley, who had just gone through a difficult divorce, found that recently, his income was just barely covering living expenses after the alimony and child-support payments were deducted. He agreed to the bribe and was videotaped receiving a suitcase containing the $25,000 during a subsequent meeting. Congressman Kelley was immediately placed under arrest.

In contrast, the following scenario involves a private individual, high solicitation and high predisposition (in the sense that the suspect has had a narcotics addiction):

Roy Kern met Frank Shepard, an undercover police officer, at a rehab center where both were being treated for a long-term narcotics addiction. After several meetings between the two, Frank stated that he was not responding to the treatment. Frank then solicited Roy into helping him obtain some drugs. Roy, who had two previous drug-trafficking convictions, refused, saying that he did not want to spend the rest of his life in prison, citing the state's "three strikes" law. Frank dropped the subject.

As the two kept meeting at the rehab center, a friendship developed. Roy began inviting Frank to come along with him to different social events. During this time, Roy introduced Frank to his sister, Karen. Karen and Frank hit it off and began dating. The two began making plans to move in together.

After a couple of months, Frank began repeating his request for drugs saying things like, "If you were really my friend, you would help me out." Roy finally submitted. He still had contacts from his drug trafficking days so he started making calls. Roy soon acquired and sold the narcotics to Frank. Roy was then approached and placed under arrest.

To summarize, in Edkins' (2003) first study, half of the respondents received an objective definition of entrapment and half received a subjective definition. But all respondents were asked to react to each of the eight scenarios, in varying orders. Thus, the design was a 2x2x2x2, with one variable between subjects (Instructions) and three within subjects (Solicitation, Predisposition, and Public Official versus Private Citizen).

RESULTS OF EDKINS' FIRST STUDY

Edkins (2003) found each of three within-subjects independent variables to have significant effects. But the definition of entrapment had no significant effect. The results of these analyses are presented in Tables 5, 6, and 7. When the solicitation was extensive, only about one-third of the jurors (35%) were willing to find the defendant guilty, but when the solicitation was minimal, two-thirds (67%) did. Mock jurors hold public officials to a higher standard; when they commit a crime; 60% of the jurors judge them guilty, whereas only about 40% of respondents judge private citizens guilty under the same circumstances. Among the independent variables, predisposition of the suspect had the strongest effect: When people have a high predisposition to commit a crime and they *do* commit a crime, mock jurors are quite likely to judge them guilty—73% of mock jurors do. But when they have a low predisposition to commit a crime yet still do, respondents are much less likely to rule them guilty (29%).

It is worth noting that the independent variables had a cumulative effect, leading to huge differences in the percentages of mock jurors who assigned a guilty verdict to the defendant.

TABLE 5. Percentage of Mock Jurors Who Voted
Guilty for Low and High Solicitation

	Mean	Standard error
Low solicitation	67.3%	1.4%
High solicitation	35%	1.9%

$p < .0001$ $\eta^2 = 0.593$

TABLE 6. Percentage of Mock Jurors Who Voted
Guilty for Public and Private Citizens

	Mean	Standard error
Public citizen	60%	1.6%
Private citizen	42.3%	1.7%

$p < .0001$ $\eta^2 = 0.308$

TABLE 7. Percentage of Mock Jurors Who Voted
Guilty for Low and High Predisposition

	Mean	Standard error
Low predisposition	29.3%	1.9%
High predisposition	73%	1.4%

$p < .0001$ $\eta^2 = 0.725$

For example, under the subjective definition, a private individual who had a low predisposition and was heavily solicited to commit the crime was found not guilty by 96% of the jurors. In contrast, for the same type of person with the same instructions, but with low solicitation and a high predisposition, the percentages were reverse—96% voted guilty and only 4% not guilty.

Furthermore, high predisposition (versus low predisposition) increases likelihood of a guilty verdict for a private citizen (84%) more than for a public official (62%). (See Table 8.)

Most importantly, an interaction exists between solicitation and predisposition. (See Table 9.) When predisposition is high but solicitation is low, almost all respondents (94%) find the person guilty; there is no other explanation available. But when predisposition is high and solicitation is

TABLE 8. Effects of the Interaction between Predisposition
and Citizen on the Percentage of Guilty Verdicts

		Mean	Standard error
Public official	Low predisposition	22.7%	2.5%
	High predisposition	61.9%	1.9%
Private citizen	Low predisposition	35.9%	84.2%
	High predisposition	2.2%	2%

$p < .009$ $\eta^2 = .041$

TABLE 9. Effects of the Interaction between Solicitation and
Predisposition on the Percentage of Guilty Verdicts

		Mean	Standard error
Low solicitation	Low predisposition	40.6%	2.5%
	High predisposition	93.9%	1.4%
High solicitation	Low predisposition	18%	2.3%
	High predisposition	52.1%	2.5%

$p < .0001$ $\eta^2 = .115$

also high, only about half of the respondents (52%) find the defendant guilty—what we call "the DeLorean effect" because it replicates the apparent facts in that trial. Potentially, the respondents are more willing to dismiss a defendant's predisposition when law enforcement uses a potentially extreme level of force or enticement. This is an interesting finding since, according to social psychology's basic concept of the fundamental attribution error, individuals generally jump at the chance to use another individual's actions in order to infer disposition (Ross, 1977).

EDKINS' SECOND STUDY

Scenarios, as devices to manipulate variables such as level of solicitation or predisposition, have their limitations, because each may have unique qualities that contribute to mock jurors' verdicts more than the intended variables. Thus, for a second study, Edkins (2003) constructed six scenarios that were identical except that they manipulated the status of the defendant (public official versus private citizen) and the amount of solicitation or coercion (high, medium, or low). The amount of coercion was operationalized by the number of times the individual was approached (once, twice, or three times) regarding the illegal transaction. The design resulted in a 3 (amount of solicitation) x 2 (type of instructions) x 2 (type of citizen) matrix, with all factors between-subjects. The objective and subjective instructions were worded the same as in the first study.

Respondents were 170 undergraduate psychology students and, in contrast to the former study, they were asked to each evaluate only one case. As before, the respondent was given either an objective or subjective definition to read and to use to assess the case. Another addition to the second study was a manipulation check for the definition given to the respondent. In order to see if the respondent was in fact using the definition given, Likert scale questions were added. Each participant rated the amount of impact the behavior of law enforcement officials had on their verdict, and how much impact the defendant's own behavior had on their verdict.

The same trend was found for amount of solicitation as in the first study—as solicitation increased, so did verdicts of not guilty. Contrary to the previous study, no main effect was found for the citizen (public or private)—verdicts did not differentiate between the two groups.

One interesting finding was a main effect for type of instructions—something that was absent from the first study. In contrast to public opinion that the subjective definition favors the prosecution, the results showed that people given the subjective definition found the defendant guilty only about 27% of the time, compared to those given an objective definition who found the defendant guilty 46% of the time (See Table 10). What might account for part of this effect is the interaction found between the instructions and the amount of solicitation. When solicitation is high, both the objective and subjective definitions produced guilty verdicts between 20–30% of the time, but the difference is prominent with the low and moderate solicitation groups. Participants given the objective definition voted guilty about 60% of the time when solicitation was low or moderate. Those given the subjective definition voted guilty 36% of the time when solicitation was low, and only about 17% of the time when solicitation was moderate (see Table 11).

Why such a large difference? Supposedly, those given the subjective definition are supposed to focus on predisposition of the defendant and not the actions of law enforcement officials. Somewhat of an opposite effect was found. When given a subjective definition, individuals were significantly more likely to see the FBI as exerting more pressure on the defendant than those who were given an objective definition (see Table 12). Even more surprising was the finding that, with a public citizen, those given a subjective definition place more of an importance on the actions of law enforcement in determining their verdict than do those given an objective definition (see Table 13). Another possibility for the large difference is that individuals, in this study, were asked to focus on predisposition when applying the subjective definition but were given no history of the defendant; maybe that alone results in fewer guilty verdicts. If this were true,

TABLE 10. Percentage of Mock Jurors Who Voted
Guilty for Objective and Subjective Instructions

	Mean	Standard error
Objective	45.5%	5%
Subjective	27.1%	5%

$p < .004$ $\eta^2 = .042$

TABLE 11. Effect of the Interaction between Instructions
and Solicitation on the Percentage Guilty Verdicts

	Solicitation	Mean	Standard error
Objective	Low	55.2%	8.9%
	Moderate	60.7%	8.7%
	High	20.7%	8.5%
Subjective	Low	35.7%	8.7%
	Moderate	17.4%	8.5%
	High	28.1%	8.5%

$p < .014$ $\eta^2 = .052$

then we would not expect a relationship between the amount of pressure placed on the defendant and the judgment of the defendant's predisposition; yet a significant relationship exists where a low level of solicitation leads the respondents to assume that the defendant was more predisposed to commit the crime than when the solicitation was at a much higher level before the defendant succumbed to the temptation (see Table 14)—exactly what we would expect from attribution research (Ross, 1977). It seems that respondents had no trouble translating amount of solicitation into amount of predisposition. What may in fact be happening is a type of reactance—those told to ignore the tactics of law enforcement are more apt to focus, and place a significant amount of importance, on those tactics. Overzealous law enforcement tactics may cause the mock jurors to discount the evidence of the defendant's predisposition, and instead focus on the circumstances surrounding the crime.

WHAT REFORMS ARE NEEDED?

In summary, entrapment is a doctrine riddled with ambiguity and inconsistency. Psychologically, it is very difficult for jurors to operationalize.

TABLE 12. Effect of Type of Instructions on Amount
of Perceived Pressure on the Defendant

	Mean	Standard error
Objective	5.118%	.137
Subjective	5.706%	.135

1 = Very little pressure placed on defendant

7 = A lot of pressure placed on defendant

Sig, < .003 η^2 = .056

TABLE 13. Effect of Interaction between Instructions and Citizen
on Importance Placed on Actions of Law Enforcement

Instructions	Citizen	Mean	Standard error
Objective	Public	4.998	.212
	Private	5.330	.207
Subjective	Public	5.905	.205
	Private	5.190	.210

1 = FBI actions had little impact on verdict

7 = FBI actions had a large impact on verdict

$p < .013$ η^2 = .038

TABLE 14. Interaction between the Amount of
Solicitation and Perceived Predisposition

	Mean	Standard error
Low	3.982	.228
Moderate	3.000	.224
High	3.000	.222

1 = The defendant was not predisposed to commit the crime

7 = The defendant was definitely predisposed to commit the crime

$p < .002$ η^2 = .070

Even judges—even justices of the Supreme Court—disagree. The majority of the justices on the Court voted to overturn Keith Jacobson's conviction, concluding that it had not been proven that Jacobson possessed the requisite predisposition prior to the onslaught of attempts to get him to misbehave. But this decision reflected a bare 5-to-4 majority. Four justices

(O'Connor, Rehnquist, Kennedy, and Scalia) dissented, and it is instructive to quote from Justice O'Connor's dissent:

> Keith Jacobson was offered only two opportunities to buy child pornography through the mail. Both times, he ordered. Both times, he asked for opportunities to buy more. He needed no government agent to coax, threaten, or persuade him; no one played on his sympathies, friendship, or suggested that his committing the crime would further a greater good. In fact, no government agent even contacted him face to face. The government contends that from the enthusiasm with which Mr. Jacobson responded to the chance to commit a crime, a reasonable jury could permissibly infer beyond a reasonable doubt that he was predisposed to commit the crime. I agree. . . . Government agents admittedly did not offer Mr. Jacobson the chance to buy child pornography right away. Instead, they first sent questionnaires in order to make sure that he was generally interested in the subject matter. . . . .The Court, however, concludes that a reasonable jury could not have found Mr. Jacobson to be predisposed beyond a reasonable doubt on the basis of his responses to the government's catalogs, even though it admits that, by that time, he was predisposed to commit the crime. The government, the Court holds, failed to provide evidence that Mr. Jacobson's obvious predisposition at the time of the crime "was independent and not the product of the attention that the government had directed at petitioner." In so holding, I believe the Court fails to acknowledge the reasonableness of the jury's inference from the evidence, redefines "predisposition," and introduces a new requirement that government sting operations have a reasonable suspicion of illegal activity before contacting a suspect. . . . There is no dispute that the jury in this case was fully and accurately instructed on the law of entrapment, and nonetheless found Mr. Jacobson guilty. Because I believe there was sufficient evidence to uphold the jury's verdict, I respectfully dissent. (*Jacobson v. United States*, 1992, pp. 554, 555, 556, 561, citations deleted)

Lawyers, judges, and social scientists need to work together to clarify the definition of the entrapment defense. But we believe that reforms are needed before the trial phase. We offer the following as possible reforms.

JUST WHO SHOULD BE THE SUBJECT OF A STING OPERATION?

In tempting persons to commit crimes, law-enforcement officials insist that they only approach those for whom there is some indication of a past record or a predisposition to commit a crime. But there are no standards for justifying this claim, and some times the police rely on the word of convicted felons whose motives may be revenge, monetary gain, or relaxation of the penalties they are to receive. Why not require agents to have "reasonable suspicion" and convince a judge (i.e., require the issue of a warrant) before an undercover operation can be initiated? The results of several studies reported in this paper indicate that community sentiment is opposed to the police using heavy-handed manipulations against nominally innocent people. In a dissent concurring opinion in the case of *Sherman v. United States* (1958), Justice Felix Frankfurter wrote: "No matter what the defendant's past record, or the depths to which he has sunk in the estimation of society, certain police conduct to ensnare him into further crime is not to be tolerated by an advanced society" (p. 384).

SEEK TO CLARIFY THE DEFINITION OF ENTRAPMENT AND JURY INSTRUCTIONS

As noted earlier, empirical evidence also exists that jurors who receive the objective definition have more difficulty understanding the instructions than do jurors who are given the subjective definition (Borgida & Park, 1988). The concept of the hypothetically normally law-abiding person is difficult to understand. Jurors do not agree on what "normal" citizens will and will not do. Park (1976) described the normally law-abiding person as "one who may have a proclivity for the crime, but normally does not commit it" (p. 174). Some people are cynical about human nature; others are trusting and optimistic. Furthermore, some jurors confuse the normal law-abiding person with the average person; in fact, some judges, in their instructions, have even referred to the "average person."

Moirer, Borgida, and Park (1996) have suggested a modified objective definition and a broader instruction in entrapment-defense cases. It is:

First, what is entrapment? Under the law, a person cannot be found guilty if that person was entrapped into committing a crime. A person is entrapped when law enforcement agents use unfair methods to persuade the person to commit a crime.

Second, why is entrapment against the law? The idea behind the entrapment rule is that law-enforcement agents should be careful not to use unfair methods of persuasion. They will be more careful if they know what they do might cause a defendant to go free.

Third, what types of methods are unfair? Examples of unfair methods of persuading someone to commit a crime include threats, harassment, badgering, appealing to sympathy, and offering unusually large sums of money.

It is not against the law for a law-enforcement agent who is doing undercover work to ask a person to sell narcotics in order to gather evidence against that person. Just asking is not unfair, but law-enforcement agents must not go too far or push too hard.

When you decide whether the method used here was unfair, do not base your decision on whether the method would persuade you to commit the crime or whether it would persuade an average, ordinary person to commit the crime. Decide whether it would persuade someone who had a weakness for the crime but who normally would not commit the crime.

Does it matter whether the defendant was ready and willing to commit the crime? No, it does not. The question is whether the methods used were unfair, not whether the defendant was ready and willing. If you find that the law-enforcement agents used unfair methods, then you should find the defendant not guilty. This is true even if the defendant was ready and willing to commit the crime. (p. 1866)

Some will find this instruction unacceptable because they see it weighted in the direction of permitting law breakers to go free. But the researchers found that it improved the jurors' comprehension of key legal concepts and specific legal definitions.

INCLUDE A NULLIFICATION INSTRUCTION TO THE JURORS

The original reason that the United States established jury trials for a breadth of crimes was to permit ordinary citizens to render outcomes and prevent the government from overpowering the criminal justice system. When government agents go beyond the bounds, even when they elicit law-breaking activity, jurors should be permitted—even encouraged—to send a message to the government. One of the jurors in the DeLorean trial told the media afterward: "The way the government agents operated in this case was not appropriate, and I look forward to the future favorable impact of this [verdict] on the country" (Starr, 1984, p. 24). Prominent trial lawyer Melvin Belli echoed this sentiment: "I don't think there's any doubt that DeLorean was guilty as hell. The jury just resented the government coming in and putting up a case like this and doing all the lousy things they did. . . . If they can't read the message, I'll send them a pair of bifocals" (Mayfield, 1984, p. 3A). And Yale Kamisar of the University of Michigan Law School reaffirmed the view: "The case should teach the government a lesson: that it simply can't rely so heavily on people whose credibility is so low, whose truthfulness is so questionable" (Margolick, 1984, p. B6).

Jurors have the right to nullify the law, to find a defendant not guilty regardless of the weight of the evidence and the law, but judges are reluctant to inform them that they have this power; only three states have a jury nullification instruction available upon request.

DIMINISH THE USE OF THE SUBJECTIVE DEFINITION

The subjective definition of entrapment has been favored by the majority of the Supreme Court, but a minority has strenuously argued for the objective definition. As noted by several observers (e.g., Kassin, 1985), the two definitions of entrapment are based on different rationales for the purposes of the defense. The subjective definition reflects a goal of protecting the unwary, innocent individual. In contrast, the objective definition seeks to deter outrageous governmental conduct. In *Hampton v. United States* (1976), Justice Rehnquist claimed that the Court had ruled out the "possibility that the defense of entrapment could ever be based on governmental misconduct . . . where the predisposition of the defendant to commit the crime was established" (p. 488). But Rehnquist's opinion reflected the views of only three of the eight justices deciding this case; two others, Justices Blackmun and Powell, concurred in supporting the use of predisposition in most cases but were "unwilling to join the plurality in concluding that, no matter what the circumstances, neither due process principles nor our supervisory power could support a bar to conviction in any case where the Government is able to prove predisposition" (*Hampton v. United States*,1976, pp. 495). As Slobogin notes (1998), presumably the three dissenters agreed with this qualification.

Kassin and Wrightsman (1985) applied an attributional analysis to jurors' reactions to confessions evidence at trial. Such an analysis is applicable to conditions when entrapment is claimed as a defense, also, because the juror must choose between an explanation that emphasizes the pressures of the situation versus one that assumes a fundamental proclivity by the defendant.

But jurors are less likely to draw negative inferences about a defendant's predispositions to commit a crime when the immediate situation offers a sufficient (if not compelling) explanation for his or her actions. As Kassin (1985) expressed it, "Simply put, the more pressure the agents have to exert, the less certain we are that the defendant is so ready and willing a participant" (p. 9).

Kassin's (1985) unpublished study found that the single most important determinant of jurors' verdicts was "the pressure of the soliciting event, the focus of the objective model, and not the defendant's predisposition, as prescribed by the subjective test" (p. 8).

In court decisions there has been some movement toward a hybrid model in which the subjective definition of entrapment is supplemented by a due process defense. For example, even if a defendant is predisposed, he or she might be entitled to an acquittal on constitutional grounds if the police conduct were especially "outrageous" (for example, if police threatened physical force). The Supreme Court decisions in *United States v. Russell* (1973) and *Hampton v. United States* (1976) suggested this. In the first of these, Justice Rehnquist wrote, "we may some day be presented with a situation in which the conduct of law enforcement agents is so outrageous that due process principles would absolutely bar the government from invoking judicial processes to obtain a conviction" (pp. 431–432).

We believe that "outrageous conduct by law enforcement agents" will continue to increase unless the courts restrain the actions. One way is to adopt an objective definition that says in effect, "If you conclude that the defendant was unreasonably coerced, you should find the defendant not guilty." This could prevent results such as those in Edkins' second study (2003) from occurring—undue or excessive law enforcement tactics were viewed in a harsh light, especially when the jury is asked *not* to focus on them.

By no means are we suggesting an abandonment of the use of police sting operations. Many "victimless" crimes need to use such tactics in order to be successful. It is very difficult to halt the buying and selling of narcotics, as well as prostitution, without using sting operations. We are suggesting that if law enforcement officials feel the use of these operations are necessary in a certain situation, or regarding a certain individual, they should be required to provide sufficient evidence—akin to a warrant—before the targeting begins. Hopefully, this will help keep law enforcement behavior in check, and solicitation to a minimum.

Acknowledgments: The authors would like to thank Kelly Goodwin for her time and contributions.

REFERENCES

Associated Press. (2002, November 4). 'Stupid' author arrested in Internet sex case. *Lawrence Journal-World*, p. 4.

Borgida, E., & Park, R. (1988). The entrapment defense: Juror comprehension and decision making. *Law and Human Behavior, 12*, 19–40.

Brill, S. (1989). *Trial by jury.* New York: Simon & Schuster.

Butler, K. A., & Wrightsman, L. S. (2002, March). *Attitudes toward law enforcement and mock jurors' reactions to an entrapment defense.* Paper presented at the meetings of the American Psychology-Law Society, Austin, TX.

DeGarmo, E. L. (2003). *A factor analysis of attitudes toward entrapment.* Honors Thesis, Department of Psychology, University of Kansas, Lawrence, KS.

Edkins, V. A. (2003). *The defense of entrapment: The psychology behind juries' decisions.* Unpublished Masters Thesis, Department of Psychology, University of Kansas, Lawrence, KS.

Entrapment: From Sorrells to Jacobson–The development continues. (1993). *Ohio Northern University Law Review, 20*, Rev. 293.

Gershman, B. L. (1982). Abscam, the judiciary, and the ethics of entrapment. *Yale Law Journal, 91*, 1565–1591.

Hampton v. United States, 425 U. S. 484 (1976).

Jacobson v. United States, 503 U. S. 540 (1992).

Kassin, S. M. (1985, August). *Juries and the doctrine of entrapment.* Paper presented at the meetings of the American Psychological Association, Los Angeles, CA.

Kassin, S. M., & Wrightsman, L. S. (1985). Confession evidence. In S. M. Kassin & L. S. Wrightsman (Eds.), *The psychology of evidence and trial procedure* (pp. 67–94). Newbury Park, CA: Sage.

Katz, L. (1987). *Bad acts and guilty minds.* Chicago: University of Chicago Press.

Lewis, E. W. (1997). A social psychological investigation of legal entrapment. *Dissertation Abstracts International, Section B: The sciences and engineering, 58* (1-B), 458.

Lindsey, R. (1984, August 17). Jurors cite entrapment and failure to prove case. *New York Times*, pp. A1, B6.

Marcus, P. (1989). *The entrapment defense*. Charlottesville, VA: Michie.

Margolick, D. (1984, August 17). A case for DeLorean. *New York Times*, p. B6.

Marx, G. T. (1988). *Undercover: Police surveillance in America*. Berkeley: University of California Press.

Mayfield, M. (1984, August 17). Government stung by verdict. *USA Today*, p. 3A.

Morier, D., Borgida, E., & Park, R. C. (1996). Improving juror comprehension of judicial instructions on the entrapment defense. *Journal of Applied Social Psychology, 26*, 1838-1866.

O'Neill, K. H. (1985). Entrapment, DeLorean, and the undercover operation: A constitutional connection. *John Marshall Law Review, 18*, 365–405.

Park, R. C. (1976). The entrapment controversy. *Minnesota Law Review, 60*, 163–274.

Puccio, T. P. (1995). *In the name of the law: Confessions of a trial lawyer*. New York: Norton.

Ross, L. (1977). The intuitive psychologist and his shortcomings: Distortions in the attribution process. In L. Berkowitz (Ed.), *Advances in experimental social psychology* (Vol. 10, pp. 174–221). New York: Academic Press.

Sherman v. United States, 356 U. S. 369 (1958).

Slobogin, C. (1998). *Criminal procedure: Regulation of police investigation: Legal, historical, empirical and comparative materials* (2nd ed.). Charlottesville, VA: Lexis Legal Publishing.

Sorrells v. United States, 287 U. S. 435 (1932).

Starr, M. (1984, August 27). DeLorean: Not guilty. *Newsweek*, pp. 22, 24.

United States v. Russell, 411 U. S. 423 (1973).

Wrightsman, L.S., Nietzel, M., & Fortune, W.H. (1994). *Psychology and the legal system* (3rd ed.). Belmont, CA: Wadsworth.

Expert Psychological Testimony on the Psychology of Interrogations and Confessions

SOLOMON M. FULERO

As the research in the field of the psychology of interrogations and confessions begins to grow, as evidenced by the impressive work in this volume, it is to be expected that defense attorneys will increasingly look to forensic psychologists of both social psychology and clinical psychology backgrounds to provide expert testimony to triers of fact in cases in which a false confession is alleged to have been made. In that sense, we can expect that the case law will parallel the development of case law in the area of eyewitness identification (Leippe, 1995; Penrod, Fulero, & Cutler, 1995), and will be subject to the same tests (the *Frye* test and the *Daubert* test, discussed below), and will be subject to the same sorts of arguments both for and against admissibility. These cases have already begun to be reported; it is the intent of this chapter to look at the state of the law in this area as of the middle of 2003.

CRANE V. KENTUCKY (1986)

The jurisprudence of expert testimony on confessions would seem to begin with the case of *Crane v. Kentucky* (1986), decided by the United States

SOLOMON M. FULERO • Department of Psychology, Sinclair College, Dayton, Ohio 45402 (sol.fulero@sinclair.edu).

Supreme Court. The facts of the case, as set forth in the Supreme Court opinion, are not atypical of many confession cases. On August 7, 1981, a clerk at the Keg Liquor Store in Louisville, Kentucky, was shot to death, apparently during the course of a robbery. A complete absence of identifying physical evidence hampered the initial investigation of the crime. A week later, however, the police arrested Mr. Crane, then 16 years old, for his suspected participation in an unrelated service station holdup. According to police testimony at the suppression hearing, "just out of the clear blue sky," Crane began to confess to a host of local crimes, including shooting a police officer, robbing a hardware store, and robbing several individuals at a bowling alley. Their curiosity understandably aroused, the police transferred Crane to a juvenile detention center to continue the interrogation. After initially denying any involvement in the Keg Liquors shooting, he eventually confessed to that crime as well.

Subsequent to his indictment for murder, Crane moved to suppress the confession on the grounds that it had been impermissibly coerced in violation of the Fifth and Fourteenth Amendments to the Federal Constitution. At the ensuing hearing, he testified that he had been detained in a windowless room for a protracted period of time, that he had been surrounded by as many as six police officers during the interrogation, that he had repeatedly requested and been denied permission to telephone his mother, and that he had been badgered into making a false confession. Several police officers offered a different version of the relevant events. Concluding that there had been "no sweating or coercion of the defendant" and "no overreaching" by the police, the court denied the motion. It is worth noting that there was no videotape or audiotape of the confession or the process which led up to it.

The case proceeded to trial. In his opening statement, the prosecutor stressed that the Commonwealth's case rested almost entirely on Crane's confession and on the statement of his uncle, who had told the police that he was also present during the holdup and murder. In response, defense counsel outlined what would prove to be the principal avenue of defense advanced at trial—that, for a number of reasons, the story Crane had told the police should not be believed. The confession was rife with inconsistencies, counsel argued. For example, Crane had told the police that the crime was committed during daylight hours and that he had stolen a sum of money from the cash register. In fact, counsel told the jury, the evidence would show that the crime occurred at 10:40 PM and that no money at all was missing from the store. Beyond these inconsistencies, counsel suggested, "the very circumstances surrounding the giving of the [confession] are enough to cast doubt on its credibility." In particular, she continued, evidence bearing on the length of the interrogation and the manner in which it was conducted would show that the statement was unworthy of belief.

In response to defense counsel's opening statement, and before any evidence was presented to the jury, the prosecutor moved in limine to prevent the defense from introducing any testimony bearing on the circumstances under which the confession was obtained. Such testimony bore only on the "voluntariness" of the confession, the prosecutor urged, a "legal matter" that had already been resolved by the court in its earlier ruling. Defense counsel responded that she had no intention of relitigating the issue of voluntariness, but was seeking only to demonstrate that the circumstances of the confession "[cast] doubt on its validity and its credibility." Rejecting this reasoning, the court granted the prosecutor's motion. The court held that the defense could inquire into the inconsistencies contained in the confession, but would not be permitted to "develop in front of the jury" any evidence about the duration of the interrogation or the individuals who were in attendance.

After registering a continuing objection, Crane invoked a Kentucky procedure under which he was permitted to develop a record of the evidence he would have put before the jury were it not for the court's evidentiary ruling. That evidence included testimony from two police officers about the size and other physical characteristics of the interrogation room, the length of the interview, and various other details about the taking of the confession. The jury returned a verdict of guilty, and Crane was sentenced to 40 years in prison.

The sole issue in the ensuing appeal to the Kentucky Supreme Court was whether the exclusion of testimony about the circumstances of the confession violated Crane's rights under the Sixth and Fourteenth Amendments to the Federal Constitution. Over one dissent, the court rejected the claim and affirmed the conviction and sentence. The excluded testimony "related solely to voluntariness," the court reasoned. Although evidence bearing on the credibility of the confession would have been admissible, said the court, under established Kentucky procedure a trial court's pretrial voluntariness determination is conclusive and may not be relitigated at trial. Because the proposed testimony about the circumstances of Crane's confession pertained only to the voluntariness question, the court held, there was no error in keeping that testimony from the jury.

The United States Supreme Court reversed and remanded the case. Their reasoning was that the Kentucky Supreme Court had apparently assumed that evidence bearing on the voluntariness of a confession and evidence bearing on its credibility fall into conceptually distinct and mutually exclusive categories. Once a confession has been found voluntary, the Supreme Court of Kentucky believed, the evidence that supported that finding may not be presented to the jury for any other purpose. This analysis, said the Supreme Court, is premised on a misconception about the role of confessions in a criminal trial, and, under the circumstances of this case, contributed to an evidentiary ruling that deprived petitioner of his fundamental constitutional right to a fair opportunity to present a defense. The Court noted that "it is by now well established that '?certain interrogation techniques, either in isolation, or as applied to the unique characteristics of a particular suspect, are so offensive to a civilized system of justice that they must be condemned under the Due Process Clause of the Fourteenth Amendment.'?" To assure that the fruits of such techniques are never used to secure a conviction, the Court noted, "due process also requires 'that a jury [not] hear a confession unless and until the trial judge [or some other independent decisionmaker] has determined that it was freely and voluntarily given'" (*Jackson v. Denno*, 1964). And later in *Lego v. Twomey* (1972), the Court noted that nothing in the *Jackson* opinion "took from the jury any evidence relating to the accuracy or weight of confessions admitted into evidence. A defendant has been as free since *Jackson* as he was before to familiarize a jury with circumstances that attend the taking of his confession, including facts bearing upon its weight and voluntariness" (pp. 485–486).

The United States Supreme Court, then, expressly assumed that evidence about the manner in which a confession was secured will often be germane to the jury's assessment of its probative value. As they note, "the physical and psychological environment that yielded the confession can also be of substantial relevance to the ultimate factual issue of the defendant's guilt or innocence. Confessions, even those that have been found to be voluntary, are not conclusive of guilt. And, as with any other part of the prosecutor's case, a confession may be shown to be 'insufficiently corroborated or otherwise . . . unworthy of belief.'" And the Court noted that "indeed, stripped of the power to describe to the jury the circumstances that prompted his confession, the defendant is effectively disabled from answering the one question every rational juror needs answered: If the defendant is innocent, why did he previously admit his guilt? Accordingly, regardless of whether the defendant marshaled the same evidence earlier in support of an unsuccessful motion to suppress, and entirely independent of any question of voluntariness, a defendant's case may stand or fall on his ability to convince the jury that the manner in which the confession was obtained casts doubt on its credibility."

The question that remains after *Crane*, then, is not whether defendants may contest the accuracy or the weight to be given to a confession before the jury. Instead, the question is what sort of evidence may be presented. And that leaves the question of whether or not expert testimony is admissible. Just as with expert testimony on eyewitness identification, such a determination is subject to a threshold determination by the trial judge as to admissibility under Evidence Rule 702 (in federal court and in most state courts that have a version of this rule), and what in some states is their version of the so-called *Frye* rule (Inwinkelreid, 1992) or in other states and in federal courts is the *Daubert* rule (Penrod et al., 1995).

THE FRYE, RULE 702, AND DAUBERT STANDARDS

The classic but conservative Frye test (1923), which is still used in states such as New York to judge the admissibility of expert testimony, emphasizes that expert testimony must conform to a generally accepted explanatory theory (see Imwinkelried, 1996, for a critical discussion of the rule). By the mid-1970s, in response to criticism of the Frye rule, the new Federal Rules of Evidence (FRE) focused on other issues. Thus, Rule 702 states that expert testimony is admissible if the expert is qualified, the testimony assists the trier of fact, and the expert's testimony is sufficiently reliable. In 1993, the United States Supreme Court decided the Daubert case, which explicitly rejected Frye and complemented the FRE requirements by admonishing trial courts to consider research-related factors such as falsifiability of the theories, peer review and publication, known or potential error rate, and general acceptance (see Penrod et al., 1995; Faigman, 1995, 1999 for more on *Daubert* and admissibility of expert testimony generally). It will be these standards by which expert testimony on interrogations and confessions will be judged, depending on the jurisdiction.

CALIFORNIA V. PAGE

In 1991, the First District California Court of Appeals decided a case involving what appears to be the first use of expert testimony in a confession case. We discuss this case in detail, because it appears to be virtually a prototype for the types of issues that have come up repeatedly in subsequent cases involving expert testimony on interrogations and confessions.

On November 4, 1984, University of California at Berkeley (U.C. Berkeley) undergraduates Bradley Nelson Page, his girlfriend, Roberta "Bibi" Lee, and their friend, Robin Shaw, went jogging together in the Oakland hills. During the run, Bibi Lee became separated from the other two joggers and disappeared. Her disappearance and the ensuing search became a cause célèbre in the local media. A month after she disappeared, Ms. Lee's body was found near where she had been running with her friends. The next day, Page was questioned by the police for several hours. Page ultimately confessed that he had struck Bibi and left her unconscious in the woods. He also admitted he had gone back to the scene of the crime that night, where he had sex with Bibi's dead body, and buried her using a hubcap from his car. However, almost immediately, Page recanted his confession, claiming it was the product of police coercion and his own guilt and confusion.

The facts of the case are set forth in the opinion in detail, and again, they are instructive and illustrative. The morning after the discovery of the body, December 10, Page was asked to come to the Oakland Police Department for questioning. The case investigators, Sergeant Jerry Harris and his partner Sergeant Lacer, began questioning Page in a windowless interview room at 10:12 A.M. Initially, Page was advised of and waived his Miranda rights. The officers then questioned Page for approximately one hour, asking general questions. According to Sergeant Harris, this initial interview was not meant to be "probing." At the end of the initial interview, Harris left the interrogation room to get a tape recorder and to speak with another officer about setting up a polygraph examination for Page. He returned after about 20 minutes, and at 11:50 A.M. began taking the first of 4 taped statements from Page. Page specifically denied injuring Bibi.

After Page completed his first taped statement at 1:10 P.M., Sergeant Harris asked Page if he would submit to a polygraph examination. Page agreed, and Harris took him to the polygraph office and introduced Page to the polygraph examiner, Sergeant Furry. Furry administered an examination consisting of a pretest phase, the actual polygraph questioning, and a posttest interview. In the pretest phase, Furry explained to Page how the polygraph worked and told him he would have to be completely truthful in order to pass the test. During this phase, Page indicated he did not know where Bibi's body was found, and did not know what injuries she had received. Furry concluded that Page had tested deceptive for the entire test, and specifically told Page he believed he had "attempt[ed] deception" when asked if he had physically injured Bibi. Furry also told Harris and Lacer he believed Page had been deceptive during the examination. Page returned to the interrogation room at 3:15 P.M. and was left alone for about 25 minutes. When Harris returned to the room, Page had his head in his hands and was making a low moaning or wailing sound, and was saying, " 'I really loved her, but, I really loved her.' "

After Page composed himself, the officers continued their questioning. They repeatedly impressed on Page that they believed he had something to do with Bibi Lee's death. Harris said their suspicions were based on, among other things, the fact he had failed the polygraph test, as well as other behavioral issues such as having only searched "superficially" for Bibi when she was first lost. When faced with these accusations, Page said "'Well, if I did do something I must have blacked it out. I might have blacked it out.'" The officers again said they believed Page was lying, and that they didn't buy his "selective amnesia theory." Lacer suggested that Page close his eyes to try to remember what happened. Page did so and after a moment said " 'I remember hitting and kicking her, and wailing on her, or going off on her,' " but didn't remember when or where this occurred. This admission came at 4:10 P.M., or about six hours after Page had first come to the police station.

The officers repeatedly tried to get Page to give more details about the attack, but he continued to protest that he did not remember any details. The officers said they did not believe him, and told him Bibi's body had been discovered near the area where they had been jogging together. However, the officers did not tell Page precisely where the body was found or anything about its condition. About 4:30 P.M., Harris decided to try another tack by purposely lying to Page. He told Page they knew he was involved because they had found his fingerprints at the crime scene. This was untrue. Harris also suggested the crime might not be as serious as Page thought, that it might be something less than cold-blooded murder, such as an accidental killing or a killing arising from a quarrel. Page still maintained that he must have blacked out. The officers continued to "rehash" the reasons they thought Page was lying, but Page stuck to his story that he had blacked out his attack on Bibi. Shortly before 5 P.M., Harris decided to put additional pressure on Page by telling him a second lie. This time, Harris suggested they had a witness who saw Page's car south of the entrance to Roberts Park. Page responded that his car had not been down there, at least as far as he could recall, and that he must have blacked it out.

At 5 P.M. the officers decided to take a break to get something to eat. Lacer went to get food and left Harris alone in the interview room with Page. Harris and Page relaxed in their chairs, and Page began making casual conversation. Lacer returned at 5:30 P.M. and the officers continued their questioning. They went over their concerns about Page's story "again and again." About 10 or 15 minutes into the resumed interview, Harris told Page he believed he was lying. Harris said he believed Page had been involved in Bibi's death. Faced with this direct accusation, Page was silent for a moment. He then gave a statement implicating himself in her death, and also admitting having sexual intercourse with her dead body. The officers asked Page to repeat this story so they could take notes. He did so.

At 7:07 P.M. the officers began taking a second taped statement from Page. This time, Page essentially related the same story he had just told the officers. However, many of his responses seemed somewhat confused, tentative or vague. For example, when asked if he had sexual intercourse with Bibi he said "Yeah, I think so." He said he felt he pulled her clothing back on after having sex. Page said he "envision[ed] a slope, little bit of a slope . . . and put her up . . . the slope underneath the branches of the tree." Page said he didn't remember driving home or being home that night. Page completed his taped statement at 7:33 P.M. The officers told Page he would be arrested and held in custody for the murder of Bibi Lee. He then agreed to speak with a deputy district attorney.

Shortly after 9 P.M., Deputy District Attorney Aaron Payne and Inspector Kevin Leong arrived to question Page. This duo took a third taped statement from Page beginning at 9:09 P.M. After being advised of and waving his Miranda rights, Page immediately recanted his confession. He told the questioners that his confession had been a product of confusion, fear, and imagination. He again claimed that he never saw Bibi after he left Robin Shaw at Skyline Gate. The interview ended at 9:48 P.M. Payne told Harris Page had recanted his confession, and had claimed it was a product of his imagination.

Page was left alone in the interview room until 11:25 P.M. when he knocked on the door and told Harris and Lacer he wanted to talk. The officers spoke with Page until about 1 A.M. and then began the fourth and last taped statement. In a rambling statement, Page mentioned a number of factors which caused him to give a false confession: the officers said they found his fingerprints at the scene and were convinced he was involved in the killing; the polygraph scared him; he felt guilty for not having helped Bibi; the officers had said he would sit in jail and rot away from the inside if he could not remember. Because of all these factors, the officers convinced Page that he might have killed Bibi. Consequently, with the officers' assistance he "imagined" a scenario in which he could have killed her. After this final interview, Page was arrested and charged with the murder of Bibi Lee.

In his first trial, the jury acquitted Page of first and second degree murder, but could not reach a verdict on the charge of voluntary manslaughter. In the second trial, the jury convicted Page of voluntary manslaughter. On appeal, Page contended that the manslaughter conviction should be reversed because the trial court improperly restricted a defense expert's testimony on the psychological factors which allegedly caused Page to give a false confession.

As his final witness, Page had called Eliot Aronson, a professor of psychology at the University of California, Santa Cruz. Generally, Professor Aronson testified concerning factors which can lead a person to give an inaccurate statement in an interrogation setting. Aronson testified that a person may give inaccurate information when an authority figure lies to the person questioned, or puts that person under severe stress, or causes the person to feel guilty, or makes the person questioned feel he can't trust his own senses and memory. These factors may throw the person "off balance" and make him temporarily vulnerable to persuasion.

Aronson had listened to the tapes of the statements Page made to the police on December 10 and 11, but knew nothing else about the case. In listening to the tapes, Aronson identified certain characteristics of the interrogation that may have influenced the reliability of Page's confession. Generally, Aronson noted that when a trusted authority figure misleads or lies to another person, or puts that person under stress, or makes him feel guilty or doubt his own perceptions, it throws the other person off balance and makes him vulnerable to persuasion. Moreover, when a person is confronted with what seems like incontrovertible evidence that contradicts his own senses or memory, the person will struggle to make sense of the situation.

With respect to Page's interrogation, Aronson found a number of important factors at work. It was clear that Lacer and Harris were authority figures; Page seemed to believe they were being completely honest with him, and he seemed to be trying to please them. However, the officers lied to Page about the fingerprints and the eyewitness, and Page was struggling to make sense of this information. Aronson identified other factors in the taped statements affecting the reliability of the confession. First, Page seemed to feel guilty about having left Bibi in the park. According to the professor, Sergeant Lacer "made that guilt salient, in effect rubbed the defendant's nose in the guilt." Second, Page exhibited "a lot of stress and confusion" related to the ordeal of the previous five weeks. Third, the fact Lacer and Harris did not believe his story was, in itself, a very stressful event. Fourth, Page was alone in the interrogation with no support. And fifth, the police frightened Page when they told him he would spend the rest of his life in prison unless he "came up" with something. According to Aronson, "there is a lot of research in . . . the field of conformity/compliance/persuasion that shows that under these kinds of circumstances, people strive to make sense out of the discrepancies. They try to construct scenarios that link these disparate elements together. They're compliant. They tend to tell people what they think they want to hear, and they're susceptible. They tend to go along."

Aronson then discussed in detail the Asch (1956) experiments on conformity; he noted that one of the interesting things about this and similar studies is that the subjects are tentative in their selection of the line when they have been influenced by others. Aronson found similar tentativeness in Page's confession, and gave specific examples from the confession tape. During the hearing, Aronson reviewed several other classic social psychology experiments which he deemed relevant. One demonstrated how a feeling of guilt tends to "soften [people] up to conformity and compliance" (this was the work by Freedman, Wallington, & Bless, 1967); another showed "how an authority figure can persuade a person to espouse a position contrary to their own beliefs" (this was the work by Nel, Helmreich & Aronson, 1969), and another showed "how one's perception of one's ability to resist the influence of authority figures is grossly overinflated." He also discussed the Milgram obedience experiments in detail (Milgram, 1963). Aronson tied the Milgram experiment into the reliability of Page's confession by observing that "when we see or read about someone confessing . . . [to] things that most of us would find terribly obnoxious like having sexual intercourse with a dead body, we say to ourselves, 'My God, I would never confess to this if it weren't true.' . . . But in my opinion, that's exactly what people say when we present them with this Milgrim [sic] experiment. And yet we know that somewhere between 60 and 70 percent of the entire population would go all the way."

Defense counsel then attempted to ask Aronson if he had an opinion as to the reliability or accuracy of the statements made by Page. The trial court sustained the objection. As the appellate court noted, Aronson's proposed testimony fell into three general categories: (1) the general psychological factors which might lead to an unreliable confession, along with descriptions of the supporting experiments; (2) the particular evidence in Page's taped statements which indicated that those psychological factors were present in this case; and (3) the reliability of Page's confession, given the overall method of interrogation. It appears the court permitted testimony from the first category only, and excluded evidence from the other two categories. After he detailed his qualifications and experience, his testimony was limited to a discussion of the general factors (discussed above) which may influence a person to give a false confession, general examples of those factors, and an explanation of the relevant experiments.

Page's primary authority for his constitutional argument was, not surprisingly, *Crane v. Kentucky* (1986), discussed above. As the Page court noted in rejecting Page's argument, however, there are obvious and important differences between this case and Crane. Here, the trial court permitted Page and the prosecutor to thoroughly explore the physical and psychological environment in which the confession was obtained. Among other things, the jury learned that: Page was questioned by two police sergeants, both of whom were thoroughly cross-examined on the method of interrogation; the police lied to Page to extract his confession; the officers made him feel guilty; Page took and failed a polygraph exam; and Page had only recently learned of Bibi's death. The jury also knew Page's educational level and physical condition. With respect to the physical circumstances of the interrogation, the jury knew the size and layout of the interrogation room (through testimony and pictures), how long the interrogation sessions lasted, when Page ate, when he drank water, and used the restroom or the telephone. In short, the defense and prosecution painted a detailed picture of the physical and psychological circumstances of the interrogation. In addition, Page presented his own version of the interrogation itself which differed markedly from the version proffered by the prosecution and explained in detail how the "confession" came about. Finally, the court permitted Aronson to testify as to the psychological factors which could lead to a false confession. Although Aronson did not explicitly link those factors to Page's confession, the link was obvious, and was explicitly made by defense counsel in closing argument. In short, said the court, the restrictions on Aronson's testimony were a far cry from the "blanket exclusion" of evidence the Supreme Court faced in Crane. The court found no constitutional violation, nor did it find the judge's restrictions on the testimony to be an abuse of discretion.

THE SIGNIFICANCE OF *PAGE* FOR EXPERT TESTIMONY ON INTERROGATIONS AND CONFESSIONS

This case presages many of the arguments that have been made in similar cases that have arisen since then. As interrogations-and-confessions experts are increasingly being offered in court cases, these same issues recur. While of course there are the threshold issues under the tests of admissibility of general acceptance and scientific reliability and validity, the extent of the expert's testimony in such cases is also an issue.

This is true because, unlike the case of the expert on eyewitness reliability, who (like the judge, jury, and attorneys) was not at the scene and therefore does not have first-hand knowledge of the circumstances under which the eyewitness made the identification, the interrogations and confessions expert often gets a detailed look at the process leading up to the confession. It is clear from case law (e.g., *State of Ohio v. Buell*, 1986), as well as from logic, eyewitness experts are not permitted (nor should they) render opinions about a specific eyewitness' accuracy or inaccuracy. In eyewitness cases, it is up to the defense attorney to link the general scientific principles and factors discussed by the expert to the specific facts of the case and to argue the link to the jury. But similarly, in confession cases, experts should avoid the temptation to render opinions about the particular confession. Going beyond testimony on the general principles and the empirical work runs the risk of having the testimony objected to, not admitted, and creating a dangerous precedent for other judges to see—since it is by and large only the cases in which the expert testimony is limited or excluded entirely that reach appellate courts. In the next section, we will look at cases involving interrogations-and-confessions experts since *Page*.

RECENT CASE DECISIONS INVOLVING EXPERT TESTIMONY ON INTERROGATIONS AND CONFESSIONS

As just noted, because of the biased sample of cases that reach appellate courts, one must be careful in discussing case decisions in any area of expert testimony. However, other than *Page*, the seminal case thus far is *United States v. Hall* (1996), a federal Seventh Circuit case. Hall was charged with murdering a young girl. He initially denied involvement in the case, but after more than 17 hours of questioning, he made an admission. There were no notes, tape recordings, or video recordings of the session—only a statement written by an FBI agent and signed by Hall.

At the trial, Hall's defense was that he confessed to a crime he did not commit due to a personality disorder that made him susceptible to suggestion and pathologically eager to please. Dr. Richard Ofshe was tendered as an expert in the field of coercive police techniques and the phenomenon of false or coerced confessions. The trial court rejected Ofshe's testimony entirely, on the grounds that he would need to judge the credibility of testimony about what happened during the interrogation (thus invading the province of the jury), and that his testimony would add nothing to what the jury would know from common experience. Hall also proffered testimony from Dr. Traugott, a psychiatrist who had examined him. The district court allowed Dr. Traugott to testify about Hall's mental condition (e.g., his attention-seeking behavior and his high level of suggestibility) and to opine that one of the problems for someone interrogating Hall (including himself, as a professional) was that Hall could easily be led to give the type of response he believed the questioner was seeking. Hall's appeal also focused on other testimony that he wanted Dr. Traugott to offer, which the district court refused to allow. The proffer showed that Dr. Traugott would have testified about Hall's susceptibility to various interrogation techniques, the propriety of suggesting answers to Hall, and Hall's capability of confessing to a crime that he did not commit.

The appellate court reversed the exclusion of the testimony of both witnesses, stating that the trial court had overlooked the utility of valid social science evidence in confessions cases, and remanded the case for a hearing on admissibility using the *Daubert* standard. A subsequent hearing the next year resulted in most of Ofshe's testimony being admitted (*United States v. Hall*, 1997). Significantly, what was admitted was testimony about the existence of false confessions and the interrogation factors that may produce them. He was not allowed to testify about the specifics of Hall's confession, or whether the factors had produced a false confession in Hall's case.

A similar result occurred in *United States v. Shay*, 57 F.3d 126 (1st Cir. 1995). In that case, the federal First Circuit addressed a district court's decision to exclude expert testimony by Dr. Robert Phillips, a psychiatrist, on Munchausen's Disease, a mental disorder (known formally as "pseudologia fantastica") characterized as an extreme form of pathological lying. The defendant, Shay, Jr., had been accused of helping to build a bomb that had been placed under his father's car and that had detonated when police officers called by Shay, Sr. were attempting to dismantle it, killing one officer and wounding the other. Shay, Jr. wanted to argue to the jury that his statements after the fact, taking responsibility (in many ways, inaccurately) for the incident, were the result of his mental disorder. The district court excluded the testimony primarily because it believed that the jury could consider the reliability of Shay, Jr.'s statements without it.

The First Circuit reversed. The expert in Shay was prepared to testify that Shay, Jr. suffered from a mental disorder that caused him to make grandiose statements similar to those the government was trying to use against him. The court of appeals found that the jury was "plainly unqualified to determine without assistance the particular issue of whether Shay, Jr. may have made false statements against his own interests because he suffered from a mental disorder" (*United States v. Shay*, 1995, at 133–134). The expert, in short, would have given them a reason to reject the common sense evaluation of the facts that they would otherwise be entitled to use. The case was remanded for a hearing on admissibility under the *Daubert* standard. Other cases show that such testimony about the suggestibility or mental state of particular defendants is likely to be admissible (see *United States v. Corey*, 1980; *State v. Burns*, 1984).

State courts have also addressed the admissibility of false-confession expert testimony. In *Miller v. State* (2002), an Indiana Supreme Court case, the trial court had excluded Ofshe's testimony. In a proffer of what he would have testified about, Ofshe said that he would testify "one, about the general way in which police interrogation works which fits the description that [Detective] Converse gave about the tactics that he used; second, it will be about those things that can lead to someone giving a false confession; and third, it will be about how to take the undisputed record of the interrogation, the recorded part of it and analyze it, in terms of trying to figure out what is—what the indicia of a true or false confession might be—and thereby for the jurors to reach their decision about how much weight to give it. My role is only to point out what things ought to be considered" (*Miller v.* State, 2002, at pp. 771–772. He detailed specific things in the interrogation (the evidence ploy, the use of the word "accident," attempts to develop rapport, maximization/minimization, etc.) that he saw. Miller was convicted without Ofshe's testimony. The Indiana Supreme Court reversed, stating that the "general substance" of Ofshe's testimony would have assisted the jury regarding the psychology of interrogation, which was outside the common experience of jurors. But they also clearly stated that some of Ofshe's testimony would arguably encroach upon the legal prohibition of opinion testimony about the truth or falsity of the defendant's statements, and hinted that the trial judge, in the new trial, would have the ability to sustain individualized objections at trial. The court also noted that in a previous Indiana case, *Callis v. State* (1997), an appellate court had upheld a trial court ruling allowing Ofshe to testify about false confessions in general, but had sustained objections to questions asking about the interrogation process in Callis' case in specific. (It is worth noting that I too have testified in Indiana since these cases, in a fashion consistent with these rulings, in *State v. Spurlock*, Marion County Superior Court Case No. 49G010203MR084130, Judge Pratt, in March 2003.)

Other cases have begun to appear, using the reasoning of *Crane* to allow testimony from experts about the general phenomenon of false confessions, interrogation techniques that might increase false confessions, and about characteristics of suspects that might make them more likely to confess falsely. By and large, the cases still disallow testimony about the specifics of a given confession, though they do (and should) allow particularized testimony from clinical psychologists about the makeup of a defendant, without an opinion that the confession by that defendant was or was not false. Thus, *Holloman v. Kentucky* (2001) reversed a trial judge who had excluded expert testimony that a defendant' mental retardation had made him vulnerable to suggestion, manipulation and intimidation. *State v. Miller* (1997) reversed a Washington state trial judge for excluding expert testimony about "how and why someone could make a falsely incriminating statement." *Michigan v. Hamilton* (1987) reversed a trial judge for excluding a confessions expert. In *Pritchett v. Virginia* (2002), the Virginia Supreme Court held that a trial court judge had erred by excluding expert testimony about "two factors which characterize people who may be prone to false confessions." In *State v. Buechler* (1998), the Nebraska Supreme Court ruled that a psychologist should have been allowed to testify about a defendant's drug withdrawal and psychological disorders that might have resulted in a false confession. In *Baldwin v. State* (1997), a North Carolina trial court's exclusion of a confessions expert was reversed. In *People v. Lopez* (1997), a Colorado court reversed a trial court, stating that the proposed expert testimony by a psychologist related to "the psychological environment surrounding the interrogation" and had a bearing on the reliability of the confession. In Ohio, *State v. Stringham* (2003), the Ohio Supreme Court reversed a conviction for not allowing expert testimony on false confessions generally and about clinical aspects of false confessions. Interestingly, in that case, the expert (a psychiatrist) specifically stated that he would not opine about the truth or falsity of the confession, but was prepared to combine the general type of testimony about the social psychology of false confessions with specific testimony about his examination and testing of the defendant and the presence of certain traits, diagnoses, and characteristics. In *Lenormand v. State* (1998), a Texas appellate court ruled that testimony in general was admissible, but not about the specifics of the case or the defendant's guilt. In *Boyer v. Florida* (2002), a trial judge's exclusion of Dr. Ofshe was reversed by the appellate court. In *People v. Gilliam* (1996), an Illinois trial court's admission of expert testimony with limits was upheld; the judge had allowed expert testimony in general but not on the specifics of the confession in the case. In September 2003, I was permitted to testify in federal court in Ohio, after a *Daubert* hearing, in *United States v. Baldwin* (2003;

full cite is *United States v. Baldwin*, U.S. District Court, Western District of Ohio, Northern Division, Case No. 3:03CR720, Judge Katz).

On the other hand, some trial courts have, in the exercise of their discretion, refused to allow interrogation-and-confession expert testimony of any sort. In *State v. MacDonald* (1998), a Maine trial court's exclusion of testimony that adult children of alcoholics suffer from a syndrome that might explain why they would falsely confess was upheld under a *Daubert* analysis. In *State v. Monroe* (1998), a New Hampshire trial court's denial of funds to hire a confessions expert was upheld (though it did not say that the testimony was inadmissible). In *People v. Green* (1998), a New York trial court indicated that while expert testimony on false confessions might satisfy the *Daubert* standard, New York was a *Frye* state and that the testimony was not generally accepted yet. An Illinois appeals court held the same, in *People v. Rivera* (2001), as did a New Jersey court, in *State v. Free* (2002). Using the *Daubert* standard, two Florida cases, *Beltran v. State* (1997) and *Bullard v. State* (1995) upheld trial judges' exclusion of confessions experts. In Minnesota, *Bixler v. State* (1997) upheld the exclusion of a confessions expert, as did *State v. Ritt* (1999). Two Wyoming cases, *Madrid v. Wyoming* (1996) and *Kolb v. Wyoming* (1996), also upheld the exclusion of confessions experts by trial courts. United States Military Courts have also upheld the exclusion of confession expert testimony, in *United States v. Griffin* (1999). In *State v. Cobb* (2002), the Kansas Court of Appeals, reviewing the prosecution's cross-appeal, held an expert's testimony regarding false confessions violated the province of the jury. Similarly, in *State v. Davis* (2000), a Missouri court held that an expert's testimony regarding interrogation techniques violated the province of the jury, and that the issues were adequately addressed by cross-examination (see also *State v. Tellier*, 1987).

SUMMARY AND CONCLUSIONS

There is no doubt that these cases are the tip of the iceberg. As noted earlier, only those cases in which the expert is excluded or limited reach the appellate level; if the expert is admitted, there is no record created. (As of December 2003, I have now testified in state court cases in Indiana, New Hampshire, and New York, and in federal court in Ohio; none of these cases generated written opinions.) Interestingly, in the *Boyer* case, a footnote indicates that Ofshe stated that he had testified 134 times in criminal cases on confessions. Saul Kassin and Richard Leo, among others, have also testified numerous times, usually without generating a record. It is important in these cases that experts who are admitted to testify keep careful records of the case names, jurisdictions, case numbers, and judges, so that others who are proposed as experts can provide attorneys with this information to use as precedent in their motions to admit expert testimony.

The case law is also becoming clear on the parameters of expert testimony in such cases. Testimony about the phenomenon of false confessions, social psychological testimony about the police interrogation procedures that are commonly used, clinical psychological testimony about personality or clinical factors that might be linked to confessions, and even specific clinical testimony about a particular defendant, are likely to pass muster, while testimony that purports to determine if a particular confession is true or false is not. All of this expert testimony will be judged according to the *Daubert* or *Frye* standard, depending on the rule that is applied in the jurisdiction in which the case arises. It is clear to see that the trend favors admissibility under either standard. And as the scientific literature increases, so too does general acceptability, and scientific reliability and validity. In that sense, both the law and the science in this area will follow the "career path" of eyewitness identification research and expert testimony (Leippe, 1995; Penrod et al., 1995).

REFERENCES

Asch, S. E. (1956). Studies of independence and conformity: A minority of one against a unanimous majority. *Psychological Monographs, 70,* (whole No. 416).

Baldwin v. State, 482 S.E.2d 1 (N.C. 1997).

Beltran v. State, 700 S.2d 132 (Fla. 1997).

Bixler v. State, 582 N.W.2d 252 (Minn. 1997).

Boyer v. Florida, 2002 WL 925015, 27 Fla. L. Weekly D 1113 (Fla. 5th DCA 2002).

Bullard v. State, 650 S.2d 631 (Fla. 1995).

California v. Page, 2 Cal.App.4th 161 (1991).

Callis v. State, 684 N.E.2d 233 (Ind. 1997).

Crane v. Kentucky, 476 U.S. 683 (1986).

Faigman, D.L. (1995). The evidentiary status of social science under Daubert: Is it "scientific," "technical," or "other" knowledge? *Psychology, Public Policy, & Law, 1,* 960–979.

Faigman, D. (1999). *Legal alchemy: The use and misuse of science in the law.* New York: Freeman.

Freedman, J. L., Wallington, S., & Bless, E. (1967). Compliance without pressure: The effect of guilt. *Journal of Personality and Social Psychology, 7,* 117–124.

Holloman v. Kentucky, 37 S.W.3d 764 (Ky. 2001)

Inwinkelreid, E. (1992). Attempts to limit the scope of the Frye standard for the admission of scientific evidence: Confronting the real cost of the general acceptance test. *Behavioral Sciences and the Law, 10,* 441–454.

Jackson v. Denno, 378 U.S. 368 (1964).

Kolb v. Wyoming, 930 P.2d 1238 (Wyo. 1996).

Lego v. Twomey, 404 U.S. 477, 485–486 (1972),

Leippe, M. (1995). The case for expert testimony about eyewitness memory. *Psychology, Public Policy, and Law, 1,* 909–959.

Lenormand v. State, No. 09-97-150 CR, 1998 Tex.App. LEXIS 7612 (Dec. 9, 1998).

Madrid v. Wyoming, 910 P.2d 1340 (Wyo. 1996).

Michigan v. Hamilton, 163 Mich. App. 661 (Mich. 1987).

Milgram, S. (1963). *Obedience to authority*. New York: Harper & Row.

Miller v. State, 770 N.E.2d 763 (Ind. 2002).

Nel, E., Helmreich, R., & Aronson, E. (1969). Opinion change in the advocate as a function of the persuasability of his audience: A clarification of the meaning of dissonance. *Journal of Personality and Social Psychology, 1969, 12,* 117–124.

Penrod, S., Fulero, S., & Cutler, B. (1995). Eyewitness expert testimony before and after *Daubert:* The state of the law and the science. *Behavioral Sciences and the Law, 13,* 229–259.

People v. Gilliam, 670 N.E.2d 606 (Ill. 1996).

People v. Green, 250 A.D.2d 143 (N.Y. App. Div. 1998)

People v. Lopez, 946 P.2d 478 (Colo. 1997).

People v. Rivera, 777 N.E.2d 360 (Ill. App. Ct. 2001).

Pritchett v. Virginia, 263 Va. 182 (2002),

State v. Buechler, 572 N.W.2d 65 (Neb. 1998).

State v. Buell, 22 Ohio St. 3d. 124 (1986).

State v. Burns, 691 P.2d 297 (Ariz. 1984).

State v. Cobb, 43 P.2d 855 (Kan. Ct. App. 2002).

State v. Davis, 32 S.W.3d 603 (Mo. App. E.D. 2000).

State v. Free, 798 A.2d 83 (N.J. 2002).

State v. MacDonald, 718 A.2d 195 (Me. 1998).

State v. Miller, No. 15279-1-III, 1997 Wash.App. LEXIS 960 (1997).

State v. Monroe, 718 A.2d 878 (N.H. 1998).

State v. Ritt, 599 N.W.2d 802 (Minn. 1999).

State v. Stringham, 2003-Ohio-1100 (Mar. 7, 2003).

State v. Tellier, 526 A.2d 941 (Me. 1987).

United States v. Baldwin (2003), U.S. District Court, Western District of Ohio, Northern Division, Case No. 3:03CR720).

United States v. Corey, 625 F.2d 704 (5th Cir. 1980).

United States v. Griffin, 50 M.J. 278 (1999).

United States v. Hall, 93 F.3d 1337(7th Cir. 1996).

United States v. Hall, 974 F.Supp. 1198 (1997).

United States v. Shay, 57 F.3d 126 (1st Cir. 1995).

―――――12―――――

So What's a Concerned
Psychologist to Do?

*Translating the Research on Interrogations,
Confessions, and Entrapment into Policy*

ELIZABETH C. WIGGINS AND
SHANNON R. WHEATMAN

Psychologists studying the psychological issues inherent in police interrogation techniques have much to learn from the road traveled by psychologists who generated and helped integrate into policy the research on eyewitness evidence. As nearly all readers of this volume are likely to know, research on eyewitness evidence began in the mid-1970s and captured the intrigue of many legal research psychologists into the 1980s and 1990s. During this time, psychologists conducted numerous studies about the ability of people to accurately recall and report details about a witnessed event and to identify a witnessed perpetrator from a lineup. This research helped identify factors affecting eyewitness reliability over which the justice system has no control (so-called estimator variables such as length of exposure), as well as factors over which the justice system does have control (e.g., system variables such as lineup procedures) (Wells, 1978). The studies—many relying on sophisticated experimental methods and materials—were able to examine the effect of these factors on the accuracy of eyewitness memory and identification (Cutler & Penrod; Wells et al., 2000). Wells

ELIZABETH C. WIGGINS • Federal Judicial Center, Washington, D.C. 20002-8003 (bwiggins@fjc.gov).   SHANNON R. WHEATMAN • Federal Judicial Center, Washington, D.C. 20002-8003.

and his colleagues (2000) detailed the journey of psychologists in helping to translate this body of research on eyewitness identification into policy, and it is wisdom from that experience on which much of the current chapter is premised.

AFFECTING CHANGE THOUGH A
CONSENSUS-BASED "WHITE" PAPER

Perhaps the pivotal point for research on lineups was a 1998 scientific review paper commissioned by the American Psychology-Law Society (AP-LS), that is, Division 41 of the American Psychological Association. That paper was developed by a group of eyewitness researchers, circulated widely, and ultimately endorsed by the Society and published in its journal (Wells et al., 1998). Not only did the paper identify the critical psychological issues inherent in identification procedures and describe the extant related research, it also recommended how the research could be translated into identification procedures and practices.

There is a place for a similar paper with respect to the research on interrogations, confessions, and entrapment, although findings in this area are currently less numerous and robust. The advantage of such a paper would be establishing consensus-based recommendations for further study and recommendations for systemic changes. As in the eyewitness area, review papers outlining salient research questions and findings with respect to false confessions have been published, but, in the words of the author of perhaps the most recognized review:

> Legal scholars have long speculated that confession evidence is the most potent weapon for the prosecution, even more so than eyewitness testimony. Yet, despite hundreds of eyewitness studies conducted over the years, which have contributed a body of knowledge over which there is consensus among experts . . . the topic of confession evidence has largely been overlooked by the scientific community. As a result of this neglect, the current empirical foundation may be too meager to support recommendations for reform or qualify as a subject of "scientific knowledge" according to the criteria recently articulated by the U.S. Supreme Court (*Daubert v. Merrell Dow Pharmaceuticals, Inc.,* 1993). (Kassin, 1997, p. 231)

A call for additional research endorsed and delineated by leading experts on false confessions would encourage work to fill this void.

The paper (hereinafter, "the white paper") should define the critical psychological issues inherent in current police interrogation techniques and distinguish them from the secondary, subsidiary ones. Moreover, it should identify how the existing basic and applied research bears on those issues, what questions are left unanswered, and what studies are needed to fill the informational gaps. This analysis would naturally lead to recommendations to guide additional research, and some basic recommendations for conducting interrogations.

The chapters in this volume set the groundwork for such a paper. Below we set out some of the research questions that such a paper might address, with some short commentary.

1. *Can fact-finders, be they judges or juries, distinguish between a coerced confession and a voluntary confession and appropriately weight the confession in their judgments about the defendant?*

Since the 1980s, a program of research grounded in basic social psychological theory has focused on these questions. Its well planned and executed studies have yielded consistent results and highlight the importance of minimizing undue psychological pressure at the front end—that is, on the defendant during the interrogation process—rather than relying on the fact-finder to assess the influence of psychological pressure and appropriately discount any confession.

Basic person-perception research on correspondence bias suggests that distinguishing between coerced and voluntary confessions would be a difficult task for jurors and judges alike. *Correspondence bias* is a term coined for the "the tendency to see a person's behavior as caused by a stable personal disposition of the actor when it can just as easily be explained as a natural response to situational pressures" (Jones, 1990, p. 138). In other words, the correspondence bias is the tendency to assume that people's actions and words reflect their personality, their attitudes, or some other internal factor, rather than external or situational factors. According to this theory, when a defendant confesses, the fact-finder would tend to conclude the confession was voluntary and true, not that he or she confessed due to the circumstances of the interrogation. If the fact-finder perceives the interrogation process to be blatantly coercive, however, a corollary of correspondence bias theory suggests that the defendant's confession would be attributed to the pressures of the interrogation and the attributions to the defendant would be discounted. The flip side of the discounting principle is the augmentation principle. If the fact-finder perceives that the interrogation process should work against an involuntary, untrue confession, a defendant's confession would be more likely to be perceived as voluntary and true.

Saul Kassin and his colleagues have found support for these predictions (Wrightsman & Kassin, 1993; Kassin & McNall, 1991; Kassin & Wrightsman, 1980, 1981). If the interrogator directly threatened the suspect with punishment or implicitly threatened the suspect by maximizing the seriousness of the crime and the evidence against the suspect, their research participants were likely to judge the confession as involuntary and discount it in their verdicts. If, however, the interrogator promised the suspect leniency or other favorable treatment or minimized the implicit threat by, for example, undermining the seriousness of the crime or otherwise treating the defendant sympathetically, their research participants tended to judge the confession as involuntary. Participants nevertheless found the confession probative of the suspect's guilt.

Another study suggests that although people perceive confessions obtained under high pressure as involuntary, their judgments about a person's guilt are nevertheless influenced by the confession. Kassin and Sukel (1997) found that research participants were able to distinguish between high- and low-pressure interrogation techniques and reported that confessions obtained via high pressure were less voluntary. They also reported that their verdicts were less influenced by confessions obtained under the high pressure condition and by confessions that had been ruled inadmissible by judges. But, this self-perception was untrue—the presence of a confession, even if it was deemed obtained under high pressure and ruled inadmissible, increased the likelihood that participants judged the defendant guilty. For a more thorough review of this work, see Kassin (1997) and Lassiter and Geers (this volume).

2.   Are some people more prone to provide false confessions than others?

Several lines of basic social psychological research suggest that some people might be more susceptible to psychologically coercive interrogations, and by extension, more likely to provide a false confession. Two examples are the work on high versus low self-monitors, and the work on a high versus low need for personal control. Snyder (1979) has proposed and studied a personality characteristic, self-monitoring, that is defined by the degree of attention one gives to one's social surroundings. High self-monitors are highly responsive to the demands of any situation they find themselves in, are more likely to seek social approval, and are more likely to express a false attitude (Zanna & Olson, 1982). Other research has shown that people tend to differ in their desire for personal control and that people high in the desire for personal control may recognize and resent subtle attempts to influence them more than people with a low desire for personal control (Burger & Cooper, 1979).

More on point, the Gudjonsson Suggestibility Questionnaire was developed specifically to measure individual differences in the degree to which people are influenced by leading questions and the disapproval of others in the interrogation context, and such differences have been found among criminal suspects and in the general population. Moreover, a person's interrogative suggestibility, as measured by the scale, has been shown to vary along with situational factors such as sleep deprivation. (Gudjonsson, 1984, 1991, 2003, and more generally, Kassin, 1997). (Also, see the discussion below regarding the suggestibility of juveniles and persons with mental retardation.)

3. *What effect do commonly used interrogation techniques have on an inno-cent person's propensity to confess?*

The belief that interrogation techniques can lead an innocent person to confess to a crime is not new among legal psychologists. Indeed, one of Hugo Munsterberg's classic essays challenged the assumption that "it is inconceivable that an innocent man can confess to a crime of which he is wholly ignorant," and reported a case study of a young man wrongly exe-cuted based on a false confession obtained under stressful conditions (Mun-sterberg, 1908, p. 143).

More recently, legal researchers and scholars have focused on iden-tifying the factors within an interrogation session that may promote false confessions and believability of such confessions by interrogators. This work has focused primarily on the interrogation technique promoted by the commonly used manual, *Criminal Interrogations and Confessions,* by Inbau, Reid, Buckley, and Jayne (2001). It is described in various places in this vol-ume (e.g., Meissner & Kassin, Chapter 4).

The technique assumes interrogators can accurately assess whether a suspect is telling the truth, first in their assessment of whether a full inter-rogation should be undertaken, and, second, in the conduct of that inter-rogation. This assumption is not supported by the social psychological research on the detection of deception. This research has used two basic procedures for testing people's ability to detect deception. The more com-mon approach assesses people's ability to detect experimenter-produced lying and truth-telling, and the other assesses their ability to distinguish between known cases of lying and truth-telling. This research has shown that people's success at detecting lies is unimpressive—usually better than chance but not much more so (DePaulo & Freidman, 1998; Zuckerman, DePaulo, & Rosenthal, 1981). There is some evidence that training people to detect lying by giving them feedback on their accuracy can improve their performance to some degree (e.g., Zuckerman, Koestner, & Alton, 1984) and that people engaged in some professions that require them to be sen-sitive to deception, such as U.S. Secret Service agents, are sometimes slightly better than average in detecting deceit (e.g., Ekman & O'Sullivan, 1991). People are likely poor at detecting lying for several interrelated reasons. Several nonverbal signs do occur significantly more often in liars than in truth-tellers, but no single nonverbal cue *always* appears, some effective liars exhibit no nonverbal signs at all, and people's beliefs about what signs reflect lying are not accurate (DePaulo & Friedman, 1998; Zuckerman, DePaulo, & Rosenthal).

Meissner and Kassin (Chapter 4, this volume) raise the possibility that the training received by interrogators may exacerbate the difficulty of detect-ing deceit by encouraging interrogators to approach the task with the assumption that the suspect is guilty. This assumption, in turn, predisposes interrogators to attend to details that confirm the suspect's guilt, and, thus, they are more likely to believe both true and false confessions.

Basic social psychological theory and research underpin this proposition, and the recent study by Kassin, Goldstein, and Savitsky (2003) provides some empirical support for it. Social psychologists have shown that a person's predisposition toward a judgment can cause him or her to adopt a confirmatory test strategy—to look for evidence that supports or can be interpreted to support the predisposition, while disregarding evidence that disconfirms it (Lord, Ross, & Lepper, 1979; Nisbett & Ross, 1980).

The Reid technique also advocates a full range of psychologically based interrogation tactics, and researchers have begun to study their effects on the person being interrogated. For example, Kassin and Kiechel (1996) found in a laboratory study that presentation of false evidence can lead innocent people to confess to acts they did not commit and, sometimes, to internalize a belief in their guilt. Clearly more research like this, which is directly aimed at assessing the impact of specific interrogation tactics, would be useful. The white paper could delineate the recommended interrogation tactics, set out the psychological underpinnings of each, and describe what basic and applied research exists or needs to be conducted to assess the effects of the tactic.

Finally, basic psychology has much to offer by analogy in assessing the impact of the interrogation environment itself, including the physical design of the interrogation room and the psychological environment it creates. Social isolation may diminish self-awareness and a sense of control and promote de-individuation. When people are self-aware, they are more likely to attend to their emotional and cognitive states, carefully consider their behavioral options, and monitor their actions carefully. When individuals do not feel self-aware, they fail to monitor their actions, are likely to misconstrue the nature of the situation, be more reactive to the immediate situation and less responsive to the long-term consequences of their behavior, and may experience disturbances in concentration and judgment (Scheir & Carver, 1983; Carver & Scheir, 1981; Diener, 1979, 1980; Scheier, Carver, & Gibbons, 1979; Wicklund, 1980). Such situations may also render a person more susceptible to influence by an authority figure, in this case, the interrogator.

4. *Are there alternative interrogation techniques that could be used to maintain confessions by the guilty while minimizing pressures on the innocent? Do they produce the intended effects and any undesirable side-effects?*

Many of the chapters in this volume suggest ways interrogations might be conducted to minimize the occurrence of false confessions and provide some empirical support for the efficacy of some procedures. It is important for psychologists to consider and study whether these recommendations have unintended "side-effects," perhaps unduly minimizing the truthful information that can be obtained by investigators during an interrogation, or, alternatively, by perpetuating an inaccurate belief that psychologically coercive tactics were not used during the investigation.

For example, many reformers have recommended that all interrogations be videotaped, on the assumption that videotaping will act to deter police from using highly coercive interrogation strategies and provide an accurate, objective record of the interrogation for use during any suppression hearing or at trial. The research by Daniel Lassiter and his colleagues supports this recommendation, but suggests that it should be more fine-tuned. Their program of research, summarized in this volume, found that evaluations of videotaped confessions can be significantly altered by seemingly inconsequential changes in the camera perspective taken when the confessions are initially recorded. Videotaped confessions recorded with the camera focused on the suspect—compared to other camera points of view (e.g., focused equally on the suspect and interrogator) or to more traditional presentation formats (i.e., transcripts and audiotapes)—lead mock jurors to judge that the confessions were more voluntary and, most important, that the suspects were more likely to be guilty. The effect is extremely robust. Deliberations among mock jurors did not obviate it nor did warnings or judicial instructions about the possible biasing effect of camera angle. It was maintained when participants' attention was focused on the content of the confession and when their sense of accountability was heightened and in studies using simple stimulus materials as well as within the context of a full simulated trial. Students and non-student jury-eligible research participants and even judges experienced with confession evidence were found to be susceptible to the effect.

5. *How do interrogation techniques differentially affect children? What additional safeguards may be needed to safeguard the rights of these populations?*

The white paper should address the special problems that arise in the interrogation of juveniles, or, alternatively, a separate paper might be drafted. Redlich, Silverman, Chen, and Steiner (this volume) provide a succinct summary of the research directly addressing juveniles and interrogations:

- Juvenile detainees age 14 and younger are significantly less likely to comprehend their Miranda rights than are older teens and adults (Grisso, 1981).

- Based on survey research using hypothetical interrogation scenarios, it appears that juvenile detainees age 15 and younger are more likely to confess than are older teens and young adults (Grisso, in press).
- Based on a sole laboratory study, it appears that presentation of false evidence can lead innocent juveniles—just as it can lead innocent adults—to confess to acts they did not commit and, sometimes, to internalize a belief in their guilt. This effect is more pronounced for younger youths.
- Also, based on a sole experimental study, it appears that children who receive positive reinforcement are more likely to falsely claim knowledge about an event and to confess responsibility for it (Wood et al., 2000). Research in the context of child victims and witnesses, however, suggests that the relationship between positive reinforcement and making false confessions may be more complicated.

Redlich et al. (this volume) also note the relevance of the research on the accuracy of child victims and witnesses during forensic questioning and suggest that this research be extended to the interrogation process. More specifically, in the studies of child victims and witnesses, age has been shown to be negatively related to accuracy, completeness, and consistency, and positively related to suggestibility. Whether these effects hold for older adolescents, who are more likely to be subjected to police interrogation, is a topic for further study.

Drizin and Colgan (this volume) use case studies to describe the specialized problems that may arise in interrogations of juveniles and in the process help identify, along with Redlich et al. (this volume), where future research efforts should be focused. Specifically:

- Do multiple interview sessions result in juveniles incorporating information suggested by the police in their own narratives during later interviews?
- Are maximization techniques or minimization techniques more likely to elicit admissions of guilt from juveniles than adults?
- Are children more susceptible to selective reinforcement of their responses and to negative feedback than adults?
- Are juveniles more likely than adults to voluntarily make a false confession to protect a friend or family member?
- What is the optimal role of parents during the interrogation process?

The white paper could build on these chapters to provide a more extensive analysis of extant studies and propose where additional study, more targeted on the interrogation process, is needed.

6.   *How do interrogative techniques differentially affect persons with mental retardation? What additional safeguards may be needed to safeguard their rights?*

Chapter 7 in this volume quite nicely sets out what psychologists do and do not know about the vulnerability of suspects with mental retardation during interrogation and provides the basis for discussion of these issues and procedural reforms in the white paper. Most notably, substantial research indicates that persons with mental retardation have significant problems comprehending their Miranda rights and are more likely to confess compared to mentally typical persons. Moreover, persons with mental retardation are more prone to "interrogative suggestibility," as measured by the Gudjonsson Suggestibility Scale. That is, in comparison to mentally typical persons, they are more likely to respond to leading questions and shift their answers in the face of mild disapproval. It is suggested, but no empirical support is available, that persons with mental retardation are more susceptible to nonverbal coercive aspects of the interrogation situation, compared to mentally typical persons. Taken together, these findings suggest that persons with mental retardation may be more prone to provide false confessions, although there is no direct empirical evidence for this proposition.

AFFECTING CHANGE THROUGH THE INDIVIDUAL CASE

Psychologists can help put their research into practice by serving as an expert witness in a case involving a possible false confession, and more organizationally, by assisting in preparing an amicus brief to be filed in such a case. The white paper advocated above would be a useful tool in both of these endeavors.

EXPERT TESTIMONY

One way psychologists can bring research to the attention of the court in a specific case is to participate as an expert for one of the parties. With respect to false confessions, it would most likely be for the defense. Fulero (this volume) reports that the development of case law regarding the admissibility of such testimony is paralleling that of expert testimony on eyewitness identification. His report of the early cases suggest that some courts, but not all, are finding such testimony admissible under Federal Rule of Evidence 702 (or a state counterpart) and the standard set out by the Supreme Court under *Daubert*, or alternatively, under the *Frye* standard.

The white paper advocated above could help facilitate expert testimony on false confessions in two ways. First, it could identify the findings that are currently supported by research and provide an assessment of the depth and consistency of that research. This would help both experts and courts define the parameters of appropriate testimony.

Second, it could help preclude disagreement among psychologists about the appropriateness of testifying and the nature of the testimony. Many readers will recall the disagreements among psychologists over the appropriateness of eyewitness researchers testifying as experts. As reviewed by Williams, Loftus, and Deffenbacher (1992), the basis of the concerns over such testimony were multi-faceted and included, among others, the following arguments;

- Experimental psychologists cannot provide sufficiently precise information regarding eyewitness behavior that is not already part of the commonsense knowledge of jurors (McCloskey & Egeth, 1983).
- The research on eyewitness identification is not sufficiently developed and reliable, given the weight jurors will assign to the expert's testimony.
- On a related note, the extant research lacks mundane realism and cannot be generalized to real-world situations (Konecni & Ebbeson, 1986).
- Finally, there is no evidence that expert testimony improves the ability of the trier of fact to discriminate accurate from inaccurate testimony; instead, it just raises their level of skepticism (McCloskey & Egeth, 1983).

Some of the legal standards governing the admissibility of expert testimony have changed since these concerns were voiced. Nevertheless, they still raise legitimate issues that should be considered in the context of determining the appropriate contours of expert testimony on false confessions.

AMICUS BRIEFS

Filing an amicus curiae brief is another way psychologists can bring research on false confessions to the attention of the court in a specific case. An amicus brief is a brief filed with the court by someone who is not a party to the case.

The procedures by which the American Psychological Association (APA) determines whether to participate as amicus curiae in court proceedings was approved by the APA Board of Directors in 1996 and amended in 2003 (APA, 1996/2003). Under these procedures, all requests for APA amicus curiae participation are submitted to APA's Office of General Counsel, which then consults with the appropriate APA Directorates to determine whether the request should be further considered. If there is interest, the General Counsel's Office asks the Chair of the Ad Hoc Committee on Legal Issues (COLI) to appoint a panel to examine the request and make a recommendation to the Board of Directors about APA's involvement. If the Board approves participation as amicus curiae, the Office of General Counsel prepares the brief, in consultation with substantive experts and relevant Directorates, Divisions, and State/Provincial Associations.

The COLI panel is charged to consider many factors in determining whether APA should file an amicus brief. These factors include whether participation is consistent with the objectives and policies of APA; the significance of the case to psychology; whether APA can make a useful contribution to the case; whether there is sufficient research, data, and literature to present a strong position; the substantive views of relevant Divisions, State/Provincial Associations and others; how participation might be viewed by various APA constituencies; what the public results of the participation might be; and other appropriate issues.

COLI has translated this charge into a set of questions to guide their decision (Ad hoc Committee on Legal Issues, APA, 1983). Of most relevance here are the following questions about the involvement of psychologists in the case to date and the status of the research on the substantive issues at stake.

- At any time, have psychologists and/or APA been involved in the case?
- To aid in the just resolution of an issue in conflict, does APA have significant accurate, valid, and factual psychological information?
- If there is no accurate, valid, and factual psychological information available, is it possible for APA to generate this information?
- Is there a possibility that psychological research findings and concepts based thereon will be challenged?
- Are the facts of the case clear enough so that the research findings and/or concepts can be adequately defended?
- Can APA take a position that will reflect a consensus among its membership? If there is not a consensual position, can the opposing points of view be resolved? Is there consensual information that APA can provide in the case?

The white paper advocated above would help facilitate the participation of APA or other entity as an amicus curiae by clearly identifying findings on which the research community agreed. Often the time for preparing briefs is short; the request may come late in the legal process, and the process to determine whether participation by APA (or any other organization) is warranted is somewhat complicated, even at its best. If such a paper existed, the task would be the simpler one of applying its conclusions to the facts of the immediate case.

APA may turn down a request to participate as an amicus curiae for many reasons—some unrelated to the status of the research field and the merits of the case. For example, APA may determine not to participate in a case where the facts make it difficult to clearly apply and present the relevant psychology. In such instances, a division of APA may want to take on the role. The 2003 amendments to the APA procedures provide guidance in these situations. A division's request to participate as amicus curiae will be processed according to the procedures set out above and the Office of General Counsel will be responsible for reviewing and approving the brief.

AFFECTING CHANGE THROUGH EXECUTIVE BRANCH POLICY

The ultimate goal is for law enforcement agencies at the local, state, and national levels to use interrogation procedures that respect a suspect's fundamental rights, facilitate truthful reporting of information, and minimize false confessions and other misinformation. This is difficult to achieve, in part, because there are numerous different law enforcement agencies, operating under multiple lines of authority.

Much of the research on eyewitness identification was ultimately reflected in guidelines issued by the U.S. Department of Justice for collecting and preserving eyewitness evidence. The guidelines can be found in their entirety on the Department of Justice website at www.ojp.usdoj.gov/nij. As reported by Wells et al. (2000), several factors encouraged the federal justice system to develop these guidelines.

First, in 1996, the National Institute of Justice (NIJ) at the United States Department of Justice issued a report reviewing 28 cases in which post-conviction DNA testing exonerated a person who had been convicted of a serious crime. (This report is available online at www.NCJRS.org in the abstracts database.) In the majority of the cases, given the absence of DNA evidence at the trial, eyewitness testimony, which we now know was wrong, was the most compelling evidence at trial. After reviewing this report, Attorney General Janet Reno directed NIJ to address the shortcomings of the investigations leading up to the conviction of these 28 people. The result was the set of national guidelines for collecting eyewitness evidence, which were prepared by a working group of eyewitness researchers, prosecutors, defense attorneys, and law enforcement agents, under the direction of the National Institute of Justice.

There is similar documentation of cases in which post-conviction DNA testing exonerated defendants who had falsely confessed to the crime. The Innocence Project reports that the defendant had made a false confession in about 15% of the first 70 cases in which DNA evidence exonerated the defendant, and its website provides detailed descriptions of a number of cases involving false confessions where the actual perpetrator was eventually apprehended (www.innocenceproject.org). Other chapters in this volume report other such cases.

Wells et al. (2000) identified expert testimony of eyewitness researchers in individual cases as another factor that helped instigate the development of the national guidelines. Interestingly, however, they also attributed some of the friction in the Guidelines working group to the fact that researchers had participated as experts for the defense. Judges in individual cases cannot set up comprehensive systems to guide law enforcement practices. They can, however, encourage the law enforcement agencies to do so by allowing an expert to testify at trial about fallibility of evidence that has been obtained with questionable procedures or, more extremely, by suppressing it. The expert testimony on false confessions should work to the same effect.

There are many factors other than those described here that bear on the Department of Justice's decision to implement policy related to criminal investigations. For example, sometimes the administration's other priorities take precedence, and sometimes an issue is not mature enough for a national decision. The white paper could help remedy this latter impediment.

AFFECTING CHANGE THROUGH EDUCATION

An effective way for psychologists to affect interrogation practices is to participate in educational seminars for judges, prosecutors, and law enforcement agents. Although invitations for doing so may at first be hard to come by, such situations allow psychologists to explain their research outside the context of specific cases. The judges, prosecutors, and law enforcement agents can thus consider it from a policy, rather than case outcome, perspective. Under such circumstances, legal practitioners likely will be a more receptive audience.

Indeed, Wells et al. (2000) expressed surprise at the willingness of the law enforcement agents in the NIJ group to work toward the eyewitness identification guidelines, given that their practices were the ones at issue. However, it became clear that the law enforcement agents were motivated by the concern that identification of the wrong suspect not only leads to charges against an innocent person but also allows the true culprit to remain at large, and by the need for a set of identification procedures which would not leave them open to criticism. They were interested in what advice the researchers could lend. Judges, prosecutors, and law enforcement agents will likely be similarly interested in false confession research, particularly in policy-making and educational settings.

One caveat, however. It is not enough for educational programs to describe the negative psychological implications of current interrogation techniques. Indeed, doing so may close the lines of communication to investigators and prosecutors who have a job to do. To the extent possible given the current state of the research, educational programs should also suggest alternative practices that are more appropriate.

One way to precipitate invitations to participate in educational programs would be to include representative investigators, attorneys, and judges on the committee that drafts the white paper. Doing so would undoubtedly complicate the endeavor, but it would also help produce a product that might be perceived as more neutral and less defense-oriented and have a correspondingly greater impact. Professionals invested in writing the paper would be natural conduits of the information to their peer groups.

CONCLUSION

As we noted at the outset, a productive goal for psychologists studying false confessions would be to develop a consensus-based white paper, along the lines of that prepared and endorsed by AP-LS regarding eyewitness identification research. The chapters in this volume provide a good start for such a comprehensive review of the existing and desirable research concerning false confessions and recommendations for interrogation practices that might be drawn therefrom. The white paper would be a valuable resource for experts testifying about false confession research, organizations preparing amicus briefs, and researchers and others who participate in educational programs for legal practitioners. All these activities, in turn, would help instigate the incorporation of psychological research into policies and procedures governing interrogations.

ACKNOWLEDGMENTS: The views expressed in this chapter are those of the authors and not necessarily those of the Federal Judicial Center. We thank Gary Wells for the valuable discussion we had with him about the chapter and Steven Breckler for his review of it.

REFERENCES

Ad Hoc Committee on Legal Issues, American Psychological Association. (June, 1983). *Factors affecting APA involvement in litigation.* (Available from the Office of General Counsel, American Psychological Association, 750 First Street, NE, Washington, DC 20002-4242).

American Psychological Association. (December 1996, amended June 2003). *Procedures for submission of amicus curiae briefs.* (Available from the Office of General Counsel, American Psychological Association, 750 First Street, NE, Washington, DC 20002-4242).

Burger, J.M., & Cooper, H.M. (1979). The desirability of control. *Motivation and Emotion, 3,* 381–393.

Carver, C. S., & Scheir, M. F. (1981). *Attention and self-regulation: A control-theory approach to human behavior.* New York: Springer-Verlag.

Carver, C. S., & Scheir, M. F. (1983). Two sides of the self: One for you and one for me. In J. Suls & A. G. Greenwald (Eds.), *Psychological perspectives on the self* (Vol. 2, 123–157). Hillsdale, NJ: Erlbaum.

Connors, E., Lundregan, T., Miller, N., & McEwen, T. (1996). *Convicted by juries, exonerated by science: Case studies in the use of DNA evidence to establish innocence after trial.* Washington, D.C.: U.S. Department of Justice, National Institute of Justice.

Cutler, B. L., & Penrod, S. D. (1995). *Mistaken identification: The eyewitness, psychology, and the law.* New York: Cambridge University Press.

Daubert v. Merrell Dow Pharmaceuticals, Inc, 509 U.S. 579 (1993).

DePaulo, B. M., & Friedman, H. S. (1998). Nonverbal communication. In D. Gilbert, S. T. Fiske, & G. Lindzey (Eds.), *Handbook of social psychology* (4th ed., Vol. 2, pp. 3–40). New York: McGraw-Hill.

Diener, E. (1979). Deindividuation, self-awareness, and disinhibition. *Journal of Personality and Social Psychology, 37,* 1160–1171.

Diener, E. (1980). Deindividuation: The absence of self-awareness, and self regulation in group members. In D. Paulus (Ed.), *The psychology of group influence* (209–242). Hillsdale, N.J.: Erlbaum.

Ekman, P., & O'Sullivan, M. (1991). Who can catch a liar? *American Psychologist, 46,* 913–920.

Gudjonsson, G.H. (1984). A new scale of interrogative suggestibility. *Personality and individual differences, 5,* 303–314.

Gudjonsson, G.H. (1991). Suggestibility and compliance among alleged false confessors and resistors in criminal trials. *Medicine, Science, and the Law, 31,* 147–151.

Gudjonsson, G. H. (2003). *The psychology of interrogations and confessions: A handbook.* West Sussex, England: Wiley.

Grisso, T. (1981). *Juvenile's waiver of rights: Legal and psychological competence.* New York: Plenum.

Inbau, F. E., Reid, J. E., Buckley, J. P., & Jayne, B. C. (2001). *Criminal interrogations and confessions* (4th ed.). Gaithersberg, MD: Aspen.

Jones, E. E. (1990). *Interpersonal perception.* New York: Macmillan.

Kassin, S. M. (1997). The psychology of confession evidence. *American Psychologist, 52,* 221–233.

Kassin, S. M., Goldstein, C. J., & Savitsky, K. (2003). Behavioral confirmation in the interrogation room: On the dangers of presuming guilt. *Law and Human Behavior. 27,* 187–203.

Kassin, S. M., & Kiechel, K. L. (1996). The social psychology of false confessions: Compliance, internalization, and confabulation. *Psychological Science, 7,* 125–128.

Kassin, S. M., & McNall, K. (1991). Police interrogations and confessions: Communicating promises and threats by pragmatic implication. *Law and Human Behavior, 15,* 233–252.

Kassin, S. M., & Sukel, H. (1997). Coerced confession and the jury: An experimental test of the "harmless error" rule. *Law and Human Behavior, 21,* 27–46.

Kassin, S. M., & Wrightman, L. S. (1980). Prior confessions and mock juror verdicts. *Journal of Applied Social Psychology, 10,* 133–149.

Kassin, S. M., & Wrightman, L. S. (1981). Coerced confessions, judicial instruction, and mock juror verdicts. *Journal of Applied Social Psychology, 11,* 489–506.

Konecni, V.J., & Ebbson, E.B., (1986). Courtroom testimony by psychologists on eyewitness identification issues. *Law and Human Behavior, 10,* 117–126.

Lord, C. G., Ross, L., & Lepper, M. R. (1979). Biased assimilation and attitude polarization: The effects of prior theories on subsequently considered evidence. *Journal of Personality and Social Psychology, 37,* 2098–2109.

McCloskey, M. E , & Egeth, H. E. (1983). Eyewitness identification: What can a psychologist tell a jury? *American Psychologist, 38,* 550–563.

Munsterberg, H. (1908). *On the witness stand: Essays on psychology and crime.* New York: Doubleday.

Nisbett, R., & Ross, L. (1980). *Human inference: Strategies and shortcomings of social judgment.* Englewood Cliffs, N.J.: Prentice-Hall.

Scheier, M. F., Carver, C. S., & Gibbons, F. X. (1979). Self-directed attention, awareness of bodily states, and suggestibility. *Journal of Personality and Social Psychology, 37,* 1576–1588.

Snyder, M. (1979). Self-monitoring processes. In L. Berkowitz (Ed.), *Advances in experimental social psychology* (Vol. 12, pp. 85–128). New York: Academic Press.

Wells, G. L. (1978). Applied eyewitness-testimony research: System-variables and estimator variables. *Journal of Personality and Social Psychology, 36,* 1546–1557.

Wells, G. L., Small, M., Penrod, S. Malpass, R. S., Fulero, S. M., & Brimacombe, C.A.E. (1998). Eyewitness identification procedures: Recommendations for lineups and photospreads. *Law and Human Behavior, 22,* 603–647.

Wells, G. L., Malpass, R. S., Lindsay, R. C. L., Fisher, R. P., Turtle, J. W., & Fulero, S. M. (2000). From the lab to the police station: A successful application of eyewitness research. *American Psychologist, 55,* 581–598.

Wicklund, R. A. (1980). Group contact and self-focused attention. In P. B. Paulus (Ed.), *The psychology of group influence* (189–208). Hillsdale, NJ: Erlbaum.

Williams, K. D., Loftus, E. F., & Deffenbacher, K. A. (1992). Eyewitness evidence and testimony. In D.K. Kagehiro & W.S. Laufer (Eds.), *Handbook of psychology and law* (pp. 141–166). New York:Springer-Verlag.

Wood, J. M., Billings, J. Taylor, R. Corey, D. Burns, J., & Garven, S. (2000, June). *Guilty knowledge and false confessions regarding a staged theft: Effects of reinforcement on children's admissions.* Paper presented at the Annual Convention of the American Psychological Association, Miami, Florida.

Wrightsman, L. S., & Kassin, S. M. (1993). *Confessions in the courtroom.* Thousand Oaks, CA: Sage.

Zanna, M. P., & Olson, J. M. (1982). Individual differences in attitudinal relations. In M. Zanna, E.T. Higgins, & C.P. Herman (Eds.), *Consistency in social behavior: The Ontario Symposium* (Vol. 2, pp. 75–103). Hillsdale, NJ: Erlbaum.

Zuckerman, M., DePaulo, B. M., & Rosenthal, R. (1981). Verbal and nonverbal communication of deception. *Advances in Experimental Social Psychology, 14,* 1–59.

Zuckerman, M., Koestner, R., & Alton, A. O. (1984). Learning to detect deception. *Journal of Personality and Social Psychology, 46,* 519–528.

Index

Printed in the United States
32144LVS00003B/84

9 780306 484704